S0-GGO-081

U.S. troops prepare to jump from an Army UH-1D helicopter in Vietnam. The UH-1D was manufactured by Textron's Bell Helicopter Company of Fort Worth, Texas. The ship was used for a multitude of tasks, from medical evacuation to search and destroy missions. (Used by permission of Bell Helicopter.)

AIR WAR SOUTHEAST ASIA 1961-1973

An annotated bibliography and 16mm film guide

by

MYRON J. SMITH, Jr.

The Scarecrow Press, Inc.
Metuchen, N.J./London 1979

"Victory smiles upon those who anticipate the changes in the character of war, not upon those who wait to adapt themselves after they occur."--Giulio Douhet: Command of the Air, 1921.

Library of Congress Cataloging in Publication Data

Smith, Myron J
Air war Southeast Asia 1961-1973.

Includes index.
1. Vietnamese Conflict, 1961-1975--Aerial operations--Bibliography. 2. Vietnamese Conflict, 1961-1975--Aerial operations--Film catalogs.
I. Title.
Z3228.V5S63 [DS558.8] 016.959704'348 79-21046
ISBN 0-8108-1261-4

Manufactured in the United States of America

For my brother Fred,
the Smith family airman

TABLE OF CONTENTS

FOREWORD

Alfred F. Hurley (Colonel, USAF)*

Professor Smith deserves the thanks of scholars for identifying so many of the published materials in English on the 1961 to 1973 air war in Southeast Asia. By undertaking this work soon after the war ended, he has decreased the likelihood that more than a very few important contemporary materials have been overlooked.

This bibliography is largely a record of American air operations, a record that can be viewed in human, institutional, and technological terms. In spite of enormous political ambiguity, the work of the air and ground crews of the United States Air Force, Army, Navy, and Marine Corps was characterized by gallantry and professionalism. Institutionally, the air war experience caused the Air Force to take a wider view of air power than it had maintained before 1961. Technologically, American airmen found themselves in a multi-national struggle as they contended against a North Vietnamese air defense financed, equipped, and supervised by the Communist community. Moreover, the increasingly important role of American airmen and their equipment as substitutes for manpower gave them access to a technology that they had only speculated about before the war.

A full understanding of the air war demands more than a grasp of its operational dimension. National decision makers used excellent communications to keep a tight grip on their air instruments. In the case of the United States, Secretary of Defense

---

*Col. Hurley is head of the History Department of the United States Air Force Academy. The views expressed in this foreword are those of its author and should not be construed to be those of the Air Force Academy, the Department of the Air Force, or the Department of Defense.

Robert McNamara even involved himself in directing specific missions. Policy constraints may have been an unnoticed reason for the detailed supervision North Vietnamese ground controllers exercised over their pilots in combat. Unfortunately, the documented story of that American and North Vietnamese political control, to include analyses of their contemporary perceptions of the international climate and the bureaucratic responses of their military services and other government agencies to the war, probably will not appear during the lifetimes of most of us. Until that policy coverage is available, assessments of the role and effectiveness of air operations must be tentative.

We do know enough to venture a few generalizations about the air war. Because the Communist community did not equip the North Vietnamese for large-scale offensive air operations, the United States made extraordinary use of obsolescent and underpowered or weakly defended aircraft over South Vietnam and kept its carrier forces in offshore positions that would have been untenable in a general war. With air superiority assured, the American ground forces again fought with the freedom of action that they had enjoyed during the last years of World War II and throughout the Korean War.

The air superiority that came to American airmen by default over South Vietnam had to be fought for time and again over North Vietnam and parts of Laos. American preeminence in the air throughout the combat arena was a central factor in preventing the North Vietnamese from crushing the South in 1965, 1968, and 1972. Air superiority took on an ever larger meaning after 1968 while the withdrawal of United States ground forces went on and the Vietnamization of the war was tried.

The level of the American air effort in Southeast Asia was the highest in the history of air power, but not until 1972 would policy makers permit its serious application against the vital elements in the North Vietnamese military, industrial, and logistical structure. Before 1972, with their vital elements largely untouched, the North Vietnamese learned to cope with punishing yet often strategically pointless air attacks. Apparently, permission for the belated efforts of 1972 did not mean that the United States had decided to try to seek a resolution of the war in its favor, but rather, that Washington wanted more advantageous conditions for full withdrawal from the conflict. The American political context restricted the earlier air interdiction campaigns as well, so that the interdiction did not reduce as much as it might have the infiltration of personnel and equipment into South Vietnam.

We need to know a lot more about the internal history of North Vietnam and the lengths to which its Chinese and Russian patrons were prepared to go, before we can assert with any confidence what a better defined American bombing effort might have attained. In any case, through 1968, American policy makers seem to have been beset by a fear of a widening of the war, perhaps on the model of the Chinese intervention in Korea in 1950. After 1968, a consensus among the American people in favor of withdrawal from the war appears to have decisively affected their policy makers, who in turn limited what their airmen were allowed to do to hold off the disaster that was to overtake American policy and the nation of South Vietnam.

An assessment of that disaster and its causes may well include the point that United States decision making suffered from the lack of a balanced appreciation as to what air power could and could not do. It would seem that in the context of the limited war waged against underdeveloped North Vietnam, air power could forestall, but not end, the possibility of a Communist takeover of South Vietnam. The materials in this volume should help scholars to begin to test such an hypothesis and also, to develop a balanced appreciation of air power.

INTRODUCTION

In the years between 1961 and 1973, the United States, Australia, and South Vietnam committed almost every sort of rotary- and fixed-wing aircraft available to the prosecution of a Southeast Asian conflict of novel operational character. New techniques such as helicopter-gunship and airmobile assaults, defoliation, electronic warfare, and "smart bombs" were tried, while such "proven" air-war methods as "strategic" bombing, tactical airlift, close support for ground troops, search and rescue, and medical evacuation were employed and refined, often in unusual manner. Eventually, this undeclared fight became the most controversial and unsuccessful ever fought by those two English-speaking democracies. For South Vietnam, it ended in disaster and total defeat.

This, the twelfth military-oriented bibliography I have compiled for the Scarecrow Press, is the first to be prepared within a decade of the end of a given conflict. While much of the history of the Southeast Asian war is yet to be published, there are sound reasons for going ahead with this project now.

To prepare the 11 other bibliographies, it was necessary to seek sources often written many years earlier, sometimes in rather obscure publications. The compilation was sometimes extremely difficult. The reasons for tackling this topic within five years of the war's end are twofold. First, I want to provide a reference tool of immediate value to scholars and students of that conflict. Second, I hope to reduce some of the compilation nightmares awaiting future bibliographers by putting a preliminary handle on what has already become a large amount of war literature.

The emphasis in this compilation is primarily on the military aspects of our topic. Every effort has been made to avoid the political side of the subject. The literature on protests against the war and domestic political maneuvering is as extensive as--and maybe greater than--that concerned with actual operations or hardware. Draft resistance, organized opposition, demonstrations, peace initiatives, bombing pauses, tangential political goals, journalistic influence and other non-military aspects of the conflict are subjects worthy of separate bibliographic works. Those interested in these topics may find some information in the materials cited in this work, but such must be regarded as completely by the way. Those interested in the non-military side of the Indochina war might wish to begin with my fellow author, G. Louis Heath's Mutiny Does Not Happen Lightly (Scarecrow Press, 1976), or D. Hoerder's Protest, Direct Action, Repression (New York: K. G. Saur, 1977).

The criteria for inclusion in the bibliography are similar to those employed in my World War I in the Air (Scarecrow Press, 1977). The following types of English-language printed material are represented: books and monographs; scholarly papers; periodical, magazine, or journal articles; selected United States and translated foreign government documents; important general works; doctoral dissertations and masters' theses. Materials not noted include foreign-language works, fiction, children's works, newspaper articles (unless reprinted in periodicals or anthologies), book reviews, and poetry. Annotations of a non-critical nature are supplied to clarify contents or provide interesting extra data. Joint (jt.)-author, compiler, editor, and translator cross-references are to be found in the appropriate places in the text. A subject index keyed to the numbered entries may be found at the end of the book. The arrangement of entries is alphabetically word-by-word in the case of title entries; that is, "Air Power" precedes "Aircraft." The user looking, for example, for "Air Lift" should look also for "Airlift" some 40 entries later.

This work covers items published through December 1977; the few exceptions are important works published early in 1978. To keep abreast of the newest in Southeast Asian air war literature, readers should consult Section I, Bibliographic Sources.

Controversy has arisen over the accuracy and objectivity of some press reporting during the war. Readers should bear this in mind, especially when employing the more popular contemporary sources.

United States military aircraft stills may be obtained from sources given in Section V, Sources for Photographs; a special series of USAF Air University research studies, reports and theses is appended as Section III; and Section IV, the Guide to 16mm Films, lists and annotates the products of both private and government organizations. Borrowing information is provided.

For their advice, assistance, or encouragement in the compiling of this book, the following persons and libraries are gratefully acknowledged:

Douglas I. Pirus, American Aviation Historical Society, Garden Grove, Calif.

Col. Pearl Ward, commander, West Virginia Wing, Civil Air Patrol.

Robert B. Lane, director, Air University Library, Maxwell Air Force Base, Ala.

B. Franklin Cooling, assistant director, U.S. Army Military History Institute, Carlisle Barracks, Pa.

Laurence B. Epstein, chief, Historical Division, U.S. Army Troop Support and Aviation Material Readiness Command, St. Louis, Mo.

Dean C. Allard, head, Operational Archives Branch, U.S. Naval Historical Center, Washington, D.C.

Lieut. Col. Terry Hemeyer, chief, and Capt. Larry N. Baker, Pictorial/Broadcast Branch, Public Information Division, Office of Information, Department of the Air Force, Washington, D.C.

David Schoem, chief, Support Division, Office of Air Force History, Department of the Air Force, Washington, D.C.

Ray Merriam, Bennington, Vt.

Col. Wayne C. Anderson, Jr., commander, 1361st Audiovisual Squadron, AAVS (MAC), Arlington, Va.

Brig. Gen. E. H. Simmons, director, Marine Corps History and Museums, Washington, D.C.

Commander Rosario Rausa, U. S. N., Washington, D. C.

Col. William F. Strobridge, chief, Historical Services Division, Center of Military History, Department of the Army, Washington, D. C.

Robert A. Carlisle, Office of Information, Department of the Navy, Washington, D. C.

John J. Slonaker, chief, Historical Reference Section, U. S. Army Military History Institute, Carlisle Barracks, Pa.

Major John F. Shiner, History Department, U. S. Air Force Academy, Colorado Springs, Colo.

On the Salem College campus, special thanks are due to Dean Ronald O. Champagne, Prof. Gary McAllister, and the staff of the Benedum Learning Resources Center.

To Dr. Alfred F. Hurley, head of the History Department of the Air Force Academy: special thanks and appreciation for a fine foreword.

Finally tribute must be paid to the departed sons of the Mountain State. In proportion to the state's population, more West Virginia servicemen were lost in the Southeast Asian conflict than those of any other state in the Union.

Myron J. Smith, Jr.
Salem, West Virginia
June 6, 1978

PERIODICALS CITED

The articles which, in part, make up Section II were taken from the following list of periodicals. Complete details on particular journals, periodicals, or magazines may be found in: Union List of Serials in Libraries of the United States and Canada, 5 vols. (New York: H. W. Wilson Co., 1965); New Serial Titles, 1950-1960, 2 vols. (Washington: Library of Congress, 1961); New Serial Titles, 1961-1965, 3 vols. (New York: R. R. Bowker Co., 1967); New Serial Titles, 1966- (Washington: Library of Congress, 1967-); and Ulrich's International Periodicals Directory, 17th ed. (New York: R. R. Bowker Co., 1977).

The more common titles, e.g., Newsweek, Commonweal, are held by most public, school, and college libraries. For some of the more specialized works, e.g., US Army Aviation Digest, TAC Attack, users may have to visit one of the service academies, the Library of Congress, or a special military library such as the Air University Library, the Naval War College Library, or the library of the U.S. Army Military History Institute.

Aero Album

Aerospace Historian

Aerospace International

Aerospace Medicine

Aerospace Safety

Air Classics

Air Defense Management

Air Force and Space Digest

Air Force and Space Digest International

Air Force Civil Engineer

Air Force Magazine

Air Force Policy Letter for Commanders

Air Force Times

Air Pictorial

Air Progress

Air Reservist

Air University Review

Air Weather Service Observer

Airman

Airpower Historian

All Hands

America

American Aviation

American Aviation Historical Society Journal

American Forests

American Institute Planners Journal

American Legion Magazine

American Logistics Association Review

Approach

Armed Forces Journal International

Armed Forces Management

Armor

Army

Army Digest

Army Logistician

Army-Navy-Air Force Journal and Register

Army Quarterly

Asian Outlook

Asian Survey

Astronautics and Aeronautics

Atlantic Monthly

Australian Outlook

Aviation Week and Space Technology

Bulletin of the Atomic Scientists

Bulletin of the Concerned Asian Scholars

Business Week

Center Magazine

China Reconstructs (Peking)

Chinese Literature (Peking)

Christian Century

Combat Crew

Commanders Digest

Commentary

Commonweal

Congressional Quarterly Weekly Report

Contact

Current

Current History

Data

Defense Industries Bulletin

Department of State Bulletin

Eastern Horizon (Hong Kong)

Ebony

Electronic News

Electronic Warfare

Engineering News

Esquire

Far Eastern Economic Review

Field Artillery Journal

Fighter Weapons Newsletter

Flight

Flight International

Flying

Flying Review International

Forbes

Foreign Affairs

Foreign Policy

Fortune

Harper's Magazine

Hawk

Humanist

Illustrated London News

Infantry

Interavia

Interceptor

International Affairs (Moscow)
International Defense Review
Japan Quarterly
Journal of Contemporary History
Journal of the Armed Forces
Journal of the Royal Aeronautical Society
Journal of the Royal United Service Institution
Leatherneck
Liberation
Life Magazine
Lockheed Horizons
Look Magazine
MAC Flyer
Marine Corps Gazette
Metropolitan Life Statistical Bulletin
Military Affairs
Military Engineer
Military Journal
Military Review
Missiles and Rockets
NATO's Fifteen Nations
Nation
National Defense
National Defense Transportation Journal
National Geographic Magazine
National Guardsman
National Review
Natural History
Naval Aviation News
Naval War College Review
Navigator
Navy
New Leader
New Republic
New Society
New Statesman
New Times (Moscow)
New York Times Magazine
New Yorker
Newsweek
Officer
Orbis
Ordnance
Peking Review (Peking)
Popular Mechanics
Popular Science
Public Policy
Ramparts Magazine
Reader's Digest
Reporter
Round Table
Royal Air Forces Quarterly
Ryan Reporter
SEATO Record
Saturday Evening Post
Saturday Review
Scale Modeler
Science
Science News Letter
Scientific American Seapower
Senior Scholastic
Signal
Skyline
Soldiers
Southeast Asia
Soviet Military Review (Moscow)
Space/Aeronautics

Sperryscope

Strategic Review

TAC Attack

TIG Brief

Tactical Air Reconnaissance Digest

Tactical Airlift

Time Magazine

Today's Health

Transportation Proceedings

USAF Fighter Weapons Review

USAF Tactical Air Warfare Center Quarterly Report

U. S. Army Aviation Digest

U. S. Naval Institute Proceedings

U. S. News and World Report

United Aircraft Quarterly Bee Hive

Vietnamese Studies

Vital Speeches

Washington Monthly

World Today

I

BIBLIOGRAPHIC SOURCES

No book of this nature, with its inevitable omissions, can hope to include the efforts of everyone who has written or will write on the yet controversial topic of the war in Southeast Asia. To keep abreast of the newest aviation-related materials on the air war in the period 1961 to 1973, readers might keep in mind and make periodic searches of late issues of the following tools. Most of these were examined by the author in the preparation of this work and all are important.

1 America, History and Life: A Guide to Periodical Literature. Santa Barbara, Calif.: ABC-CLIO Press, 1964- , v. 1- . An important source for journal articles and abstracts, especially of non-English language materials.

2 American Historical Association. Writings on American History, 1962-1973. 4 vols. New York: Kraus for the AHA, 1975. Published through 1961 by the U.S. Government Printing Office, this now-commercial venture will be issued yearly. Includes a section for military history appropriate to our topic.

3 American Reference Books Annual. Littleton, Colo.: Libraries Unlimited, 1970- , v. 1- . Contains a section on military topics.

4 Biography Index: A Cumulative Index to Biographical Material in Books and Magazines. New York: H. W. Wilson Co., 1947- , v. 1- . Examine the index headings under "Aviation" and "Military."

5 Burt, Richard. Congressional Hearings on American Defense Policy, 1947-1971: A Bibliography. Lawrence: University Press of Kansas, 1974. Especially useful for the period 1961-1971.

6 Condit, D. M., et al. A Counterinsurgency Bibliography. Washington: U.S. Government Printing Office, 1963. Important, especially for the airmobile angle, for the early days of American involvement.

7 Council on Foreign Affairs. Foreign Affairs 50-Year Bibliography: New Evaluations of Significant Books in International Relations, 1920-1970. New York: R. R. Bowker, 1970. Of use for materials issued during the years 1961-1970.

8 Cumulative Bibliography of Asian Studies. 2 vols. Boston: G. K. Hall, 1969, 1972. An unannotated cumulation of the annual "Bibliography of Asian Studies" from the September issues of the Journal of Asian Studies. The periodical bibliographies for the years 1971-1973 and after will still need to be employed.

8a Cumulative Book Index [CBI]: A World List of Books in the English Language. New York: H. W. Wilson Co., 1933- . Monthly (except August); cumulated annually. Comprehensive.

9 Current Biography. New York: H. W. Wilson, 1940- , v. 1- . The 13 volumes issued between 1961 and 1973 offer a limited number of relevant biographies.

10 Dissertation Abstracts International. Ann Arbor, Mich., 1961- . Begun over 30 years ago as Dissertation Abstracts, this series is provided in two parts: Section A, Humanities and Social Sciences; and Section B, Physical Sciences and Technology.

11 Dornbush, Charles E. Unit Histories of the United States Air Forces. Hampton Bays, N.Y.: Hampton Books, 1968. Useful as a source for background data on many of the American air units which fought the war in Southeast Asia.

12 Essay and General Literature Index. New York: H. W. Wilson Co., 1934- , v. 1- . Readers will find the subject approach useful for entry into collected works; unfortunately, few compilations relative to the war have yet been analyzed.

13 Estep, Raymond. An Aerospace Bibliography. 3 vols. Maxwell Air Force Base, Ala.: Air University, 1962, 1965, 1967. Covers the period 1957 to 1966 with citations to many works of value.

14 Frank, Benis M. Marine Corps Oral History Collection Catalog. Washington: History and Museums Branch, Headquarters, U.S. Marine Corps, 1973. Includes all relative material up to the cut-off date; as more and more is made available, supplements or revised editions will undoubtedly be issued.

15 Freidel, Frank, ed. The Harvard Guide to American History, rev. ed. 2 vols. Cambridge, Mass.: Harvard University Press, 1974. Of great value to anyone investigating this field: includes helpful research, writing, and manuscript preparation information in the first volume.

16 Higham, Robin, ed. A Guide to the Sources of United States Military History. Hamden, Conn.: Archon Books, 1975. The most useful general compilation of its kind; readers should consult the Army, Navy, and Air sections.

17 Historical Abstracts: A Quarterly Covering the Worlds Periodical Literature, 1775-1945. Santa Barbara, Calif.: ABC-CLIO Press, 1955- , v. 1- . Companion to America, History and Life (q. v.), this series provides excellent coverage of non-English-language materials, in addition to those in English.

18 Holler, Frederick L., comp. The Information Sources of Political Science. 6 vols. Santa Barbara, Calif.: ABC-CLIO Press, 1975. See especially the "International Relations" section of Vol. 4.

19 Johnson, Donald C. A Guide to Reference Materials on Southeast Asia. New Haven, Conn.: Yale University Press, 1970. Provides some 2200 items arranged by subject field or form of publication.

20 Kuehl, Warren F., comp. Dissertations in History: An Index to Dissertations Completed in History Departments of United States and Canadian Universities, 1873-1972. 2 vols. Lexington: University Press of Kentucky, 1972. Includes citations to several studies of interest.

21 Leitenberg, Milton, and Richard D. Burns, eds. The Vietnam Conflict: Its Geographical Dimensions, Political Traumas, and Military Developments. (War-Peace Bibliography series.) Santa Barbara, Calif.: ABC-CLIO Press, 1973. The last-mentioned section is quite useful.

22 Mason, Elizabeth B., and Louis M. Starr. The Oral History Collection of Columbia University, 3d ed. New York: Microfilm Corp. of America, Inc., 1973. Several items of use to researchers are noted.

23 Master's Abstracts. Ann Arbor, Mich., 1962- , v. 1- . Several studies of interest are referenced.

24 Maston, John T. "An Interview." U.S. Naval Institute Proceedings, XCIX (July 1973), 42-47. A look at the Naval Institute Oral History Program by its director; provides some insight on what will become available relative to our topic.

25 Millett, Allan R., and B. Franklin Cooling, 3rd. Doctoral Dissertations in Military Affairs: A Bibliography. (Kansas State University Bibliography Series, no. 10.) Manhattan: Kansas State University, 1972. Updated annually in Military Affairs; provides the easiest entry into the world of relevant doctoral papers.

26 Moran, John B. Creating a Legend: A Descriptive Catalog of Writing about the U.S. Marine Corps. Chicago: Moran/Andrews, 1973. A labor of love by a former "leatherneck" which leaves unturned little appropriate material available prior to 1972; citations, unfortunately, are not altogether complete, making the tome somewhat difficult to use.

26a New York Times Index. New York: The Times, 1913- , v. 1- . Semi-monthly, with annual accumulations. See annotation, item 27.

27 Newspaper Index. Wooster, Ohio: Newspaper Indexing Center, Bell & Howell, 1972- , v. 1- . Monthly. Useful for daily coverage of the war's last year as provided by the Chicago Tribune, Washington Post, Los Angeles Times, and New Orleans Times-Picayune. Two other important newspaper indices are The New York Times Index and The Wall Street Journal Index (qq. v.).

By employing the Newspaper Index, New York Times Index, or Wall Street Journal Index, the reader can determine times of specific campaigns or events, thereby enabling him to employ any daily paper for details. Among the better newspapers for the purpose would be the Baltimore Sun, Chicago Daily-News, Chicago Tribune, Christian Science Monitor, Los Angeles Times, New Orleans Times-Picayune, Detroit Free Press, New York Herald-Tribune (ceased publication in 1967), New York Times, Wall Street Journal, Washington Post. Almost any daily newspaper of the reader's choice would provide some useful information.

28 R. R. Bowker Co. Forthcoming Books. New York, 1966- , v. 1- . Extremely useful for keeping up on what is being published. Users should also note this firm's two magazines, Library Journal and Publishers Weekly.

29 Rand Corporation. Selected Rand Abstracts. Santa Monica, Calif., 1963- . A number of these U.S. government-commissioned "think tank" studies on certain phases of the war, particularly the early years, are becoming available; most of the truly interesting works are, however, still being withheld.

30 Readers' Guide to Periodical Literature. New York: H. W. Wilson Co., 1904- , v. 1- . Volumes after 1961 are most important. Any of the Wilson indices mentioned here or others, such as the Social Science and Humanities Index (International Index) or Industrial Arts Index, are especially helpful.

31 Snoke, Elizabeth, comp. "Army Aviation Units." In United States Army Unit Histories, Special Bibliographic Series, no. 4 (Carlisle Barracks, Pa.: U.S. Army Military History Institute, 1978), p411-413.

32 Tregonning, Kenneth G. Southeast Asia: A Critical Bibliography. Tucson: University of Arizona Press, 1970. Includes some 2058 annotated entries arranged geographically.

33 United States. Air Force. Air University Library. Abstracts of Student Research Reports. Maxwell Air Force Base, Ala., 1949- , v. 1- . A number of these papers are quite useful. See Section IV of the present work.

34 _____. _____. _____. Air University Library Index to Military Periodicals. Maxwell Air Force Base, Ala., 1949- , v. 1- . Published quarterly with annual cumulations; the single most valuable source available on periodical literature relative to the subject.

35 _____. _____. Albert S. Simpson Historical Research Center. Oral History Collection. Maxwell Air Force Base, Ala., 1971- . Contains 700+ tapes and/or transcripts of conversations with USAF personnel; new acquisitions are made monthly.

36 _____. _____. _____, Archives Branch. A History of U.S. Military Aviation, Including Unit Histories, Monographs, Studies, and Supporting Documents and Private Collections of the USAF and Its Predecessors. Maxwell Air Force Base, Ala., 1907- . This citation is to the actual USAF collection, containing over 3 million pieces, many of importance to the subject.

37 _____. _____. _____. _____. Personal Collections in the USAF Archives. Maxwell Air Force Base, Ala., 1973. A guide to the previous citation.

38 _____. _____. Office of Air Force History. United States Air Force History: A Guide to Documentary Sources. Washington: U.S. Government Printing Office, 1973. Contains a Southeast Asia section.

39 _____. _____. _____. United States Air Force History: An Annotated Bibliography. Washington: U.S. Government Printing Office, 1971. Includes a useful section on Vietnam.

40 _____. _____. Office of Scientific Research. Prisoners-of-War and Political Hostages: A Select Bibliography. (Report A10-1.) Springfield, Va.: Monroe Corp., 1973. Useful for citations to POW's.

41 _____. Army. Peninsular Southeast Asia: A Bibliographic Survey. Washington: U.S. Government Printing Office, 1972. Important and quite extensive; 34 pages.

42 _____. _____. Combat Developments Command. Directory of Vietnam Combat Operational Data (VCOD). Alexandria,

Va.: Defense Documentation Center, 1973. Many important internal government studies on the subject are sent to the DDC--e.g., USAF Academy Technical Reports.

43 _____. _____. Military Academy. Library. Subject Catalog of the Military Art and Science Collection. 6 vols. Westport, Conn.: Greenwood, 1969. Includes references to books, articles, and papers in the West Point library relative to the subject through 1967.

44 _____. Commerce Department. National Technical Information Service. Government Reports: Announcements and Index. Washington, 1964- , v. 1- . Published biweekly; readers may obtain bibliographic access to all reports prepared by or for the U.S. government by employing the Subject Index, which is cumulated annually.

45 _____. Library of Congress. Library of Congress Catalog, Books: Subjects--a Cumulative List of Works Represented by Library of Congress Printed Cards. Washington: U.S. Government Printing Office, 1950- , v. 1- . Issued quarterly with annual cumulation; the best way to find material in the NUC relative to the subject. Consult the heading, "Vietnamese Conflict."

46 _____. _____. The National Union Catalog: Imprints. Washington: U.S. Government Printing Office, 1952- , v. 1- . The NUC is issued monthly by LC with quarterly and annual cumulations; every five years, the annual volumes are cumulated into sets and published by the New Jersey firm of Rowman and Littlefield. Difficult to employ without knowing author or corporate authors.

47 _____. Marine Corps. History and Museums Division. The Marines in Vietnam, 1954-1973: An Anthology and Annotated Bibliography. Washington: U.S. Government Printing Office, 1974. While relatively small, the bibliography is the most directly relevant to the subject yet to appear.

48 _____. Navy. Naval History Division. United States Naval History: A Bibliography, 6th ed. Washington: U.S. Government Printing Office, 1972. Contains a Southeast Asia section.

49 _____. Superintendent of Documents. Monthly Catalogue of United States Government Documents. Washington: U.S. Government Printing Office, 1961- . An important source for "official" works.

50 Wall Street Journal Index. New York: Dow Jones, 1959- . Monthly, with annual cumulations. See annotation, item 27.

51 Winch, Kenneth, comp. International Maps and Atlases in Print. New York: R. R. Bowker, 1974. As with Books in Print, this title lists appropriate maps and atlases.

51a Xerox University Microfilms, Inc. Comprehensive Dissertation Index. 37 vols. +. Ann Arbor, Mich., 1973- .

II

THE BIBLIOGRAPHY

52 "The A-37 Close-Support Attack Plane Gave a Superb Account of Itself in a Four-Month Vietnam Test Called 'Combat Dragon.'" Aerospace International, IV (March-April 1968), 48-49.

53 "A-37 Proves Effective in Vietnam Tests." Aviation Week and Space Technology, LXXXVIII (Feb. 19, 1968), 38-39+. The Cessna COIN aircraft vs. the Viet Cong.

54 "A. A. F. S. S. Battle Convertible." Flight International, LXXXVII (June 17, 1965), 962. A look at the Advanced Aerial Fire Support System.

55 "The AD Skyraider." Naval Aviation News (Jan. 1972), 20-21. A profile of one of the most useful close-air support planes of the SEA conflict, a propeller-driven fighter developed at the end of World War II and nicknamed the "SPAD."

56 Aarts, Harold. "Bombs for Little People." Far Eastern Economic Review, LXXVII (April 26, 1972), 23-24. A Dutch medical doctor's report on the effects of U.S. bombing raids on North Vietnam.

57 Abbott, Kenneth H. "Composite Aircraft Armor." Ordnance, LII (May-June 1968), 582-584. Protection for American fighting planes.

58 "Above and Beyond." Air Force Times, XXX (June 30, 1970), 13. The Medal of Honor exploits of Capt. James P. Fleming and Sgt. John Levitow.

59 Abrams, Arnold. "Professionalizing the War: The Airmen in Thailand." New Leader, LV (Oct. 2, 1972), 9-10. The "sanitary" use of high-level B-52 bombers.

60 "Accelerated Air Effort Mounted to Blunt North Vietnamese Offensive." Aviation Week and Space Technology, XCVII (Oct. 23, 1972), 18.

61 "An Account of Evasion and Survival in a Vietnamese Jungle."

U.S. Army Aviation Digest, XIV (Jan. 1968), 50-57. How a downed helicopter crew avoided capture.

62 "'Ace' Race on in Southeast Asia Skies." Air Force Times, XXXII (May 24, 1972), 8. U.S. fighters vs. North Vietnamese MI6's.

63 "Acting to Aid the Forgotten Men: The Attempt to Rescue U.S. POW's." Time, XCVI (Dec. 7, 1970), 15-18+. The unsuccessful raid on the North Vietnamese POW camp at Son Tay.

64 "Action at Dak To." Newsweek, LXX (Nov. 20, 1967), 79.

65 Adams, Nina, and Alfred W. McCoy, eds. Laos: War and Revolution. (A Publication of the Committee of Concerned Asian Scholars.) New York: Harper & Row, 1970. 482p. See especially Fred Branfman's essay, "Presidential War in Laos, 1964-1970," for information on the aerial conflict.

66 Addington, Larry H. "Antiaircraft Artillery Versus the Fighter Bomber: The Duel Over Vietnam." Army, XXIII (Dec. 1973), 18-20. A review of NVA success.

67 Adler, Bill, ed. Letters from Vietnam. New York: E. P. Dutton, 1967. 212p. A collection of epistles from members of the various U.S. armed forces, including air, describing the war around them and opinions on it.

68 Adwill, James. Helicopters in Action. New York: Meredith, 1969. 92p. A slim, but nicely illustrated examination.

69 "Aerial Combat Tactics." Interceptor, XIV (May 1972), 5-11. Interviews on air combat with majors Edward Woelfel and Larry Haight.

70 "Aerial Reconnaissance." Interavia, XIX (Feb. 1964), 180-210. An examination of the art just before it came into widespread American use in SEA.

71 Ahnstrom, D. Newell. The Complete Book of Helicopters, rev. ed. Cleveland: World Publishing Co., 1968. 175p. A well-illustrated directory with facts and figures, including U.S. combat helicopters in use in SEA to date of publication.

72 "Air Action in Vietnam: A Photographic Essay." Journal of the Armed Forces, CII (May 1, 1965), 16-17.

73 "Air Attacks on North Vietnam: A Pictorial." Air University Review, XVII (Jan.-Feb. 1966), 71-74.

74 "Air Attacks on North Vietnamese Oil Facilities, June 29, 1966."

In Richard P. Stebbins, ed., Documents on American Foreign Relations, 1966 (New York: Published for the Council on Foreign Relations by Harper & Row, 1967), p224-239. American statements justifying the action.

75 "Air Cargo Shows What It Can Do." Business Week, (July 16, 1966), 96-98. On the transport of American material to SEA by U.S. Air Force transport planes.

76 "Air Commandos: Preventive Medicine." Time, XCII (July 26, 1968), 37-38. These groups, wings, and squadrons, made up of various kinds of aircraft, were modeled on the Air Commando unit set up by Col. Philip Cochran in the CBI during World War II.

77 "Air Commandos Show Versatility: Two Years in Combat." Air Force Times, XXVIII (March 27, 1968), 20. A brief review of the work done in Vietnam by the U.S. Air Force 14th Air Commando Wing.

78 "An Air Force Almanac: The United States Air Force in Facts and Figures." Air Force Magazine, LX (May 1977), 132-145. Includes a number of "facts and figures" on our topic.

79 "Air Force and Army Agree on [Aviation] Roles and Missions." Aviation Week and Space Technology, LXXXIV (April 25, 1966), 26-27. The Army would be allowed to fly certain aircraft and helicopters in the Vietnam fighting.

80 Air Force and Space Digest, Editors of. "The Air Force Magazine Guide to Air Force Bases." Air Force and Space Digest, XLVIII (Sept. 1965), 196-207. Including those being established at the time in Vietnam.

81 "Air Force-Army Teamwork Hits Hard." Air Force Times, XXVI (August 3, 1966), 14. A look at "Operation Hawthorne."

82 "Air Force Attacks on the Rise in Laos." Air Force Times, XXX (April 29, 1970), 2. Operations designed to halt the advance of North Vietnamese supplies along the Ho Chi Minh trail.

83 Air Force Bases: A Directory of U.S. Air Force Installations, Both in the Continental United States and Overseas, 3d ed. Harrisburg, Pa.: Stackpole Books, 1965. 224p. Includes information on those then being established in South Vietnam.

84 "Air Force Civil Engineering Takes on Big Construction." Engineering News, CLXXVII (Oct. 27, 1966), 26-28. Building and improving air facilities in South Vietnam.

85 "Air Force Increases B-52 Capacity." Journal of the Armed Forces, CIII (Nov. 20, 1965), 1+. On the modification of their bomb bays to hold increased loads for delivery to Southeast Asian targets.

86 "Air Force, Naval Air Reservists Set Record in Support of Vietnam Troops." Officer, XLII (Feb. 1966), 27. Primarily in close air support missions.

87 "[Air Force of] Vietnam, Democratic Republic." Interavia, XXIII (May 1968), 641-642. Not a factor in the fighting south of the DMZ, the North Vietnamese Air Force (NVAF) nevertheless included many Russian and Chinese built MIG fighters and some Ilyushin Il-28 medium bombers.

88 "Air Force Organizes Anti-Guerrilla Units." Aviation Week and Space Technology, LXXVI (May 7, 1962), 32. The birth of the "Air Commandos," units equipped with non-jet aircraft for use over South Vietnam in accordance with the terms of the 1954 Geneva accords.

89 "Air Force Takes Over Caribous from Army." Air Force Times, XXVII (Jan. 18, 1967), 18. Redesignated C-7's, these transports were originally built in Canada by the famous firm of DeHavilland; the RAAF would also put a squadron of these light planes into action over South Vietnam.

90 "Air Lift Enhancing Vietnam Maintenance." Aviation Week and Space Technology, LXXXII (April 19, 1965), 91. The importance to the war effort of the Military Airlift Command's delivery of men and supplies by air.

91 "Air Mobile War." Army, XV (Feb. 1965), 49-53. On the use of helicopters for getting troops about in what became known as "vertical assaults."

92 "The Air Over Vietnam." Airman, VII (Feb. 1963), 24-25. A look at the operations of the USAF Air Commandos.

93 "Air Power Chokes Enemy Supply Flow." Air Force Times, XXIX (April 16, 1969), 14. In conjunction with "Operation Dewey Canyon."

94 "Air Power in the Land Battle: A U.S. Army Experiment." Interavia, XX (Feb. 1965), 155-157. More comment on troop use of helicopters.

95 "Air Power Over Indochina." Nation, CCXII (Feb. 22, 1971), 226.

96 "Air Power Provides Vietnam Leverage." Aviation Week and Space Technology, XCVII (Oct. 30, 1972), 7, 12-13. Keep-

ing the North Vietnamese at bay as American troops are withdrawn and "Vietnamization" proceeds.

97 "Air Power Proving Disruptive in SEA." Air Force Times, XXVIII (Sept. 6, 1967), 13.

98 "Air Raids Hit Red's Bases." Senior Scholastic, LXXXVI (Feb. 18, 1965), 30. Attacks on North Vietnamese MIG bases.

99 "Air Strikes Against VC Successful, [Air Force] Reports Show." Air Force Times, XXV (March 17, 1965), 10.

100 "Air Successes Hailed: Fewer Curbs, Better Weapons." Air Force Times, XXXII (June 21, 1972), 19. Continuing attacks on North Vietnam, Laos, and Cambodia communications targets.

101 "Air Support Liaison Officers Report on [Their] Work in Vietnam." Air Force Times, XXVI (April 6, 1966), 6. How Forward Air Controllers (FAC's) in light planes draw in close air support against Vietcong targets.

102 "Air Support Not Reduced in Speeded 'Nam Pullout." Air Force Times, XXXII (Dec. 1, 1971), 22.

103 "Air: The Essential Element in Vietnam." Air Force and Space Digest International, II (Aug. 1966), 32-39. Nine U.S. Air Force pilots recount personal involvement in the air war to the Air Force Association's 1966 national convention; see also "Nine Flying Roles in Vietnam," item 1811.

104 "The Air War." Nation, CCXIV (April 3, 1972), 421-422. A critical evaluation.

105 "Air War: A Turn for the Worse?" U.S. News and World Report, LXI (Aug. 29, 1966), 39. Political effects on the aerial operations, especially the potential danger of attacks on targets near the Chinese border.

106 "Air War Advances Detailed for Congress." Aviation Week and Space Technology, LXXXVII (Oct. 2, 1967), 24-25. The hearings are cited among the Congressional documents below.

107 "Air War Against the North: Tougher than Anyone Realizes." U.S. News and World Report, LXXIII (Aug. 21, 1972), 32. Increased losses due to antiaircraft artillery and SAM antiaircraft missiles.

108 "Air War Deadlier." Air Force Times, XXXIII (Sept. 13, 1972), 18.

109 "Air War: End of a Mig Sanctuary." U.S. News and World

Report, LXIII (Nov. 6, 1967), 12. U.S. strikes on the base at Phuc Yen.

110 "The Air War Grows." Newsweek, LXXIX (April 24, 1972), 32. Attacks on supply and communications targets and the response to the North Vietnamese Easter invasion.

111 "Air War Heats Up: Action Near the Chinese Border." Nation, CCII (May 16, 1966), 572. U.S. pilots were allowed to hit communications and supply targets within 35 miles of Red China.

112 "The Air War in Indochina: The Cornell Report." Congressional Record, CXVII (Nov. 18, 1971), E12412-E12414. A review of the Cornell University Air War Study Group's product cited below.

113 "The Air War in Vietnam." Air Force and Space Digest, XLIX (March 1966), 35-110. A series of articles on different phases of the topic, including an evaluation by Gen. Hunter Harris, Jr., commander-in-chief of U.S. Pacific Air Forces.

114 "The Air War in Vietnam" (photographs). Air Force and Space Digest, XLVIII (Oct. 1965), 50-51.

115 "Air War in Vietnam: Adding up the Scores." U.S. News and World Report, LXVII (Aug. 18, 1969), 26-27. A look at cost vs. damage, or how many $5 million jets were lost trying to knock out $500 bridges.

116 "Air War in Vietnam: Is It Worth the Price?" U.S. News and World Report, LXI (Aug. 8, 1966), 28-29. In lost planes and potential Chinese intervention.

117 "Air War in Vietnam: It Grows Bigger and Bigger." U.S. News and World Report, LXI (July 18, 1966), 8. Attacks on North Vietnamese oil facilities.

118 "Air War in Vietnam, the Statistical Side: A Special Report." Air Force and Space Digest, L (March 1967), 78-85. A review of activities in 1966.

119 "Air War: Less than a Success." Newsweek, LXVIII (Aug. 29, 1966), 21-22. Recounts recent activities and wonders why American bombers have not quashed North Vietnamese will to resist.

120 "Air War Resumes." Time, XCIX (Jan. 3, 1972), 34+. It never really ceased, especially over Laos.

121 Air War: The Third Indochina War. Washington: Indochina Resources Center, 1972. 50p. Prepared by a church-

related group of which Fred Branfman (see items 353-356) was director, this work is a resource guide of 17 sections listing key facts and useful quotations.

122 "Air Weapons Require Selective Employment." Journal of the Armed Forces, CII (July 17, 1965), 11. The problems of avoiding civilian casualties.

123 "Airborne Control of Vietnam Strikes." Flight International, XC (Aug. 11, 1966), 237-238. The work of the FAC's.

124 "Airborne Television in Vietnam." Naval Aviation News, (April 1967), 15. Supplied by U. S. Navy Aircraft.

125 "Aircraft." Army, XVIII (Nov. 1968), 165-166. As employed by the U. S. Army in Vietnam.

126 "Aircraft Fill the Sky Over [Cambodian] Border Area." Air Force Times, XXX (May 27, 1970), 15. During the sanctuary invasion of Cambodia by U. S. and South Vietnamese forces.

127 "Aircraft for Local Conflicts." Interavia, XVIII (Sept. 1963), 1397-1399. The Development of Counterinsurgency or COIN warplanes.

128 "Airlift Essential in Vietnam." Air Force Policy Letter for Commanders, no. 12 (Dec. 1965), 28. Both tactical and strategic.

129 "Airmobile Firepower." Army, XVIII (Jan. 1968), 55-58. Close support to soldiers by helicopter gunships.

130 Alexander, G. "[USAF] Air Rescue Service Pushes Modernization to Handle Expanded Search-Recovery Role." Aviation Week and Space Technology, LXXXI (Dec. 21, 1964), 40-43+. Demands placed on the service by the SEA conflict.

131 "All of Us Bear the Scars." U. S. News and World Report, LXXIV (April 16, 1973), 41. A look at the POW's and the implications of their return to America.

132 "All UH-1's to be Modified After Vietnam Reveals Weakness." Aviation Week and Space Technology, LXXI (June 8, 1964), 23. The need for additional guns and armor.

Allard, Dean C., jt. author see Hooper, Edwin B.

133 Allen, Ken. "The High Road to Rapid Recovery." Airman, XI (March 1967), 40-45. MAC use of C-141's for aeromedical evacuation flights from South Vietnam.

134 ______. "Red Horse: Symbol of Air Force Engineering Achieve-

ments." Airman, XIII (Dec. 1969), 25-29. The work of U.S. Air Force engineers in Southeast Asia.

135 Allen, Michael. "Sharing the Agony of Hanoi: An Air Raid Eyewitness Account." Christian Century, XC (Jan. 24, 1973), 91-94. Observations on the Christmas 1972 bombing attacks on North Vietnam which were designed to lead the North Vietnamese back to the peace table.

136 Allen, Robert J. "Navigating the AC-119G." Navigator, XVII (Fall 1969), 6-7. Plotting the way for a "Shadow" gunship.

137 Allgood, Frank E. "Progress and Prep Fires." Marine Corps Gazette, LI (Sept. 1967), 29-31. How to establish helicopter landing zones in Vietnam.

138 ______. "Where Do We Land?" Marine Corps Gazette, XLIX (Jan. 1965), 55+. On landing helicopters in combat areas of South Vietnam.

139 Allgood, Robert P. "Med-Evac: Vietnam Style." Marine Corps Gazette, LII (Aug. 1968), 33-36. The use of helicopters in speeding battlefield casualties to hospital.

140 "Alone at Last: B-52's Strike Mu Gai Pass." Newsweek, LXVII (April 25, 1966), 35-36. Stratofortress assaults on North Vietnamese and Viet Cong communications and supply.

141 Althoff, David L. "Helicopter Operations at Khe Sanh." Marine Corps Gazette, LIII (May 1969), 47-49. Reminiscences of combat during the great siege by the commander of Marine Medium Helicopter Squadron 262.

142 "Ambush at Con Thien." Newsweek, LXX (July 17, 1967), 45. North Vietnamese artillery attacks on this position led to a massive aerial retaliation, "Operation Neutralize."

143 American Helicopter Society. Tactical Uses of Vertifical Lift Aircraft, Advanced Papers. (2d Annual Technical Symposium.) 6 parts. Ft. Monroe, Va.: Headquarters, USCONARC, 1967. Papers sponsored by the U.S. Army and read at Ft. Monroe in November 1967.

144 "American Soldiers in Action: The 173rd Airborne Brigade in Zone D." Newsweek, LXVI (Nov. 22, 1965), 61-62. A report on this unit's airmobile operations.

145 "The American Way of Bombing." Harper's Magazine, CCXLIV (June 1972), 55-58. An excerpt from the report by the Cornell Air War Study Group which is cited below.

146 Americana Annual. New York: Americana Division, Grolier Corp., 1961-1973. These 12 volumes of the encyclopedia

yearbook contain coverage of the fighting in Vietnam, including air.

147 "America's War [in Cambodia] Ends, but Cambodia's Ordeal Goes On." U. S. News and World Report, LXXV (Aug. 27, 1973), 17-18. Examines the effects brought on by the end of U. S. air support.

148 "And the War Goes On." Newsweek, LXXXI (April 23, 1973), 37. American aerial operations over Laos and Cambodia.

149 Anderson, Orvil A. "Air Operations in Vietnam." Airpower Historian, XII (April 1965), 68. An editorial by a noted Army Air Force general of World War II.

150 Anderson, Tam. "Instant Reply over Banana Valley." Airman, XVIII (Jan. 1974), 20-25. Recounts how Capt. Richard S. Ritchie, flying a U. S. Air Force F-4E of the 555th Tactical Fighter Squadron, downed two North Vietnamese MIG-21's during one mission on July 8, 1972.

151 Anderton, David A. Martin B-57 Night Intruders and General Dynamics RB-57F. (Aircraft in Profile, no. 247.) Windsor, Eng.: Profile Publications, 1973, 25p. The former aircraft was a light night bomber while the latter was used for reconnaissance; both were Americanized versions of the English Electric Canberra light bomber.

152 _____. Strategic Air Command. New York: Scribner's, 1976, 316p. An examination of the deterrant force, including some comments on the use of strategic bombers and tankers over Southeast Asia.

153 _____, and John Batchelor. Jet Fighters and Bombers. London: Phoebus Publishing Co., 1976. 127p. This nicely-illustrated title, published in America simultaneously by the New York firm of Chartwell Books, gives excellent technical data on aircraft employed in SEA.

154 [Andrews, Hal, comp.] "U. S. Navy Airplanes, 1911-1969." In U. S. Navy Department, Naval History Division, Dictionary of American Naval Fighting Ships, vol. V (Washington: U. S. Government Printing Office, 1970), p526-628. With information on U. S. Navy carrier aircraft and helicopters employed over SEA; arranged by aircraft type.

155 Angeles, James. "Another Helicopter Concept." U. S. Army Aviation Digest, XVIII (April 1972), 24-27. Built, to some extent, on SEA experiences.

156 Annual Register of World Events: A Review of the Year. London: Longmans, Green. Begun in 1758, this annual provides some basic data: see the section, "Southeast Asia."

157 "Another Good Year for the Choppers." Data, XII (Aug. 1967), 11+. A review of helicopter usage in SEA during 1966-1967.

158 Anthis, Rollin H. "Airpower: The Paradox in Vietnam." Air Force and Space Digest, L (Aug. 1967), 34-38. Wonders why, with overwhelming air superiority, the U.S. could not bring the conflict to a speedy conclusion.

159 Appleton, D. O. "Denying the Guerrilla His Best Protection: Grumman's [OV-1] Mohawk." Data, XIII (Oct. 1968), 36. A look at the FAC and close air support aircraft.

160 Archer, Robert D. "Oldie but Goodie: The Canberra Jet Bomber." Scale Modler, IX (Dec. 1974), 56-62, 96. Details and capabilities of the English Electric light bomber used by the RAAF in Vietnam; photographs and illustrations of use to modelers.

161 ______. The Republic F-105 Thunderchief. Fallbrook, Calif.: Aero Publishers, 1969. 80p. A nicely-illustrated look at the workhorse of TAC over SEA.

162 Ardman, Harvey. "How Vietnam Tested U.S. Army Planning." American Legion Magazine, LXXXVIII (Feb. 1970), 8-13. Focuses on material and equipment, including helicopters, used in the guerrilla war.

163 "Area Cover in Southeast Asia with the RF-101." Tactical Air Reconnaissance Digest, II (Feb. 1968), 6-9. Examines the photo contribution of the reconnaissance version of the F-101 fighter.

164 Armed Forces Journal, Editors of. A Dictionary of American Military Anniversaries from 1775 to the Present. New York: Macmillan, 1974. Includes those of Southeast Asia.

165 "The Armed Helicopter Grows Up." Air Force and Space Digest, XLIX (June 1966), 49. Its use in South Vietnam.

166 Armstrong, Richard. "'It's Great to be Alive': The Daring Rescue of Mjr. Dafford W. Myers by Mjr. Bernard F. Fisher at Ashau." Saturday Evening Post, CCXXXIX (June 4, 1966), 21-26. Abridged in Reader's Digest, LXXXIX (Aug. 1966), 42-48, under the title, "Pilot Is Down." Air Force Major Fisher won the first congressional Medal of Honor for SEA when he landed his A-1E on the debris-strewn runway, picked up Myers, and took off in a hail of Communist fire.

167 Army, Editors of. "Air Mobility Symposium." Army, XIV (Dec. 1963), 64-71. On the mixing of helicopters with airborne troops.

168 "Army Aviation." Data, IX (Aug. 1964), 5-62. A special issue which includes a look at the subject vis-à-vis South Vietnam.

169 "Army Aviation Insignia." Army Digest, XXII (Sept. 1967), 30-31. Includes illustrations.

170 "Army Aviation Matures and Faces Adult Problems." Data, X (Aug. 1965), 7-9. A look at its application in SEA.

171 "Army Aviation Sets New Vietnam Record." Journal of the Armed Forces, CII (May 15, 1965), 2. Airmobility and the use of helicopters.

172 "Army Aviation's Mission to Vietnam." U.S. Army Aviation Digest, XII (Jan. 1966), 15-25. Vertical assault in the jungles and highlands.

173 "Army Cobras Blast Tanks Near An Loc." Aviation Week and Space Technology, XCVI (May 22, 1972), 14-15. AH-1G's vs. North Vietnamese armor during the Easter invasion.

174 "Army Helicopters: How Did We Ever Fight a War Without Them?" Data, XIII (Aug. 1968), 18-19+. Airmobility in the delivery of troops, supplies, and rescue.

175 "The Army Takes to the Air." Time, LXXXI (March 22, 1963), 17. On the development of the airmobility concept in SEA.

176 Army Times, Editors of. American Heroes of Asian Wars. New York: Dodd, Mead, 1968. 128p. Includes a few from the Southeast Asian conflict.

177 "The Army's Tank Aces." Armed Forces Journal, CIX (July 1972), 15-17. AH-1G Huey Cobras vs. North Vietnamese tanks at An Loc.

178 "Arrow of Death: The Twelve-Day Long Battle of the Khe-Sanh Valley." Time, LXXXIX (May 12, 1967), 24-25. Contains some information on U.S. close air support in the operation.

179 "As the U.S. Leaves Vietnam, A Bigger Role for Thailand." U.S. News and World Report, LXXIII (Aug. 21, 1972), 30-32. In providing bases for American warplanes.

180 "As the War Hits a Peak." U.S. News and World Report, LXXIV (Jan. 8, 1973), 17. Includes air.

181 Ashmore, Harry S., and William C. Gagga. Mission to Hanoi: A Chronicle of Double-Dealing in High Places. New York: Putnam, 1968. 369p. Two U.S. newsmen visit North Vietnam to discuss negotiations, find bombing a major issue, and fail in their mission.

182 "Assessing the Bombing." Time, XCII (Sept. 13, 1968), 29.

183 "Assessing the Laos Invasion." Newsweek, LXXVII (April 5, 1971), 25-6+. Some comment on heavy American helicopter losses.

184 "At Hanoi: The War's Flaming New Turn." Life, LXI (July 15, 1966), 20-25. Examines U.S. raids on North Vietnamese petroleum storage areas.

185 "At Last the Story Can Be Told." Time, CI (April 9, 1973), 19-20. American POW's in North Vietnamese prison camps.

186 "Attack Aircraft." Naval Aviation News, (Sept. 1969), 10-17. Includes a look at those employed over SEA.

187 "Attack at Dawn: The Defeat of North Vietnamese Regulars in Battle Near Tuy Hoa." Time, LXXXVIII (Jan. 1, 1966), 26+. Includes the air contribution.

188 "Attack on Da Nang." Newsweek, LXX (July 24, 1967), 43. Unsuccessful Vietcong raid on the big U.S. air installation.

189 "Aussie Strike Unit Arrives in Vietnam." Air Force Times, XXVII (May 3, 1967), 9. Royal Australian Air Force (RAAF) No. 2 Squadron equipped with English Electric Canberra light bombers.

190 Australian Outlook, Editors of. "A Special Issue on Vietnam." Australian Outlook, XXIII (April 1969), 7-80. With some limited attention to RAAF and Australian Army air involvement.

191 "The Average Fighter Pilot." Journal of the Armed Forces, CIII (May 5, 1966), 23. Including those in combat over SEA.

192 "Aviation Assault Troops in Vietnam." Naval Aviation News, (May 1965), 22-23. Marine Corps use of helicopters in vertical assault.

193 "Aviation Safety in Combat: An Appraisal of the Experiences of Army Aviation Unit Commanders in the Republic of Vietnam." U.S. Army Aviation Digest, XVIII (Feb. 1972), 36-45.

194 Aviation Week and Space Technology, Editors of. "Electronic Countermeasures [ECM] Symposium: A Special Report." Aviation Week and Space Technology, XCVI (Feb. 21, 1972), 33-40+. By this time, the use of ECM was fairly widespread by the air services in SEA.

195 ______. "Special Report on Electronic Warfare." Aviation

Week and Space Technology, XCIX (Jan. 27, 1975), 41-144. Contains some information on ECM not revealed in item 194.

196 ______. "Special Report on Vietnam: The New Interdiction Campaign." Aviation Week and Space Technology, XCVI (May 15, 1972), 9, 14-20. With emphasis on raids against the Ho Chi Minh trail.

197 "B-52 Pilot Who Said 'No!'" Newsweek, LXXXI (Jan. 22, 1973), 18. Major Michael Heck's refusal to participate in "Operation Linebacker II," the Christmas bombing of North Vietnam.

198 "B-52 Ranked Most Feared Vietnam Weapon." Aviation Week and Space Technology, LXXXVI (May 1, 1967), 55+. As the Viet Cong did not know when or where it would strike.

199 "B-52 Tail Gunners Credited with Two Migs." Aviation Week and Space Technology, XCVIII (Jan. 15, 1973), 18. On December 18 and 24, 1972, at least two MIG-21's unsuccessfully attempted to down Stratofortresses involved in "Linebacker II."

200 "B-52 Toll Laid to Lack of Earlier Strikes." Aviation Week and Space Technology, XCVIII (Jan. 1, 1973), 16-17. TAC fighter bombers did not have the chance to soften up SAM sites during the period before the opening of "Linebacker II" and thus North Vietnamese missiles claimed 15 Stratofortresses.

201 "B-52's and Live Ducks." Newsweek, LXVI (Oct. 18, 1965), 54. The first of the "Arc Light" operations in support of Allied ground forces.

202 "B-52's Drop 70,000 Tons on Cong Targets in Year." Air Force Times, XXVI (June 29, 1966), 4. A summary of "Arc Light" operations, June 1965-June 1966.

203 "B-52's Move to Thai Bases: From Guam to Thailand." Senior Scholastic, XC (April 7, 1967), 17-18. Cutting down the distance needed to be traveled during "Arc Light" strikes.

204 "B-52's: Raids' Effect on the War Course." Newsweek, LXVI (Oct. 25, 1965), 41. "Hitting gnats with sledgehammers."

205 "B-52's Top VC's Fear List." Air Force Times, XXVII (June 21, 1967), 14.

206 Babbs, Kenneth J. "A Special Gazette Report." Marine Corps Gazette, XLVII (July 1963), 5. A quick look at U.S. Marine Corps helicopter operations in Vietnam.

207 "Back of U.S. Decisions to Keep on Bombing in Cambodia."

U.S. News and World Report, LXXIV (April 16, 1973), 37-38. The dire need of Khmer soldiers for close air support.

208 "Back to Bombing." New Republic, CLXVI (Jan. 1, 1972), 9-10. Critical of such operations.

209 "Back to the Valley of Death: The Air Cavalry." Time, LXXXVII (April 8, 1966), 34-35. The 1st Air Cavalry in "The Iron Triangle."

210 Baggs, Andrew H. "Bombing, Bargaining, and Limited War: North Vietnam, 1965-1968." Unpublished Ph.D. dissertation, University of North Carolina at Chapel Hill, 1972. (University Microfilms no. 73-4798.) A look at operations and bombing pauses.

Baggs, William C., jt. author see Ashmore, Harry S.

211 Bailey, Tom. "The Cambodian Action: An Enemy Sanctuary Despoiled." Soldiers, XXVI (Sept. 1971), 34-42. A review of the 1970 airmobile invasion.

212 Baird, John R., and George E. Burnison. "Escort of Airmobile Formations." U.S. Army Aviation Digest, XI (May 1965), 2-4. Covering troop helicopters with helicopter gunships or COIN aircraft such as Skyraiders.

213 Baldwin, Hanson W. "Vietnam: A New Policy in the Making." Reporter, XXXIII (Aug. 12, 1965), 16-20. A review of strategy and operations, including air and airmobile.

214 Ballard, Jack S. "Military Civic Action." In Carl Berger, ed., The United States Air Force in Southeast Asia, 1961-1973 (Washington: U.S. Government Printing Office, 1977), p285-296. Medical and transport assistance.

215 ______. "The United States Air Force in Southeast Asia: The Development and Employment of Fixed-Wing Gunships, 1962-1971." Unpublished paper, Office of Air Force History, Washington, D.C. 1974. A detailed account of the coming of the AC-47, AC-119, and AC-130 gunships to the war in Indochina.

216 Barber, John M. "The Fire Team." U.S. Army Aviation Digest, XIV (Sept. 1968), 24-26. Helicopters over Dong Xoai.

217 Barker, A. J. Prisoners of War. New York: Universe Books, 1975. 249p. A general history with some attention paid to POW's of this conflict.

218 Barkley, James R. "Airborne Surveillance." U.S. Army Aviation Digest, XI (Dec. 1965), 26-30. The work of helicopters and FAC's.

219 Barksdale, William S. "Aerial Combat Photography." *Air University Review*, XVII (July-Aug. 1966), 60-69. The art, with examples from Vietnam.

220 Barnaby, Frank. "Environmental Warfare." *Bulletin of Atomic Scientists*, XXXII (May 1976), 36-43. A review of herbicides and their use in Vietnam in "Operation Ranch Hand."

221 _______. "Towards Environmental Warfare." *Current*, CLXXXII (April 1976), 55-59. A shorter version of the last entry.

222 Barrett, Peter J. "A Strange Kinda Bird." *U.S. Army Aviation Digest*, XVIII (May 1972), 2-3. Helicopters in battlefield support, e.g., the Huey Cobra.

223 Barrett, Thomas P. "Air Cavalry Employment." *U.S. Army Aviation Digest*, XVI (Jan. 1970), 45-46. Mostly in South Vietnam, with examples.

224 Barrymaine, Norman. "Memo from Haiphong, North Vietnam: Under American Bombs." *Look*, XXX (Nov. 29, 1966), 62. Reprinted in *Aviation Week and Space Technology*, LXXXV (Dec. 26, 1966), 47-48, under the title, "Bomb Damage in North Vietnam."

225 Bartecchi, Carl E. "The Airmobile Clinic." *U.S. Army Aviation Digest*, XII (Dec. 1966), 13-15. U.S. Army helicopter ambulances.

226 Bartlett, Merrill L. "The Intervention in Laos." *Marine Corps Gazette*, LVIII (Sept. 1974), 18-23. How the U.S. became involved; much on the air phase.

227 Bartos, Henry S. "The OV-10: The USAF's Battling Bronco." *Air Force Magazine*, LVI (April 1973), 36-40. The ideal heavily armed COIN aircraft introduced relatively late in the conflict.

228 "Bases Repulse Attacks." *Air Force Times*, XXVIII (March 6, 1968), 14. The Tet attacks on American airfields.

229 Bass, Arthur C. "Helicopter Warfare Opens a New Era." *Missiles and Rockets*, XVIII (March 28, 1966), 82-85. A review of airmobile warfare in Vietnam.

Batchelor, John, jt. author *see* Anderton, David

______, jt. author *see* Cooper, Bryan

230 Bateman, Kent C. "All Weather Cas: Fact or Fancy?" *Marine Corps Gazette*, LVI (June 1972), 41-43. Effectiveness of the A-6 Intruder.

231 "The Battle Goes On." Newsweek, LXXI (May 20, 1968), 31-33. The Tet offensive and the Allied response.

232 "A Battle in the Gulf of Bac Bo." Chinese Literature (Peking), no. 11, (1967), 54-71.

233 "The Battle of Dak To." Newsweek, XX (Nov. 27, 1967), 44. This fight in Kontum province was supported by 2000 tactical and B-52 strikes.

234 "Battle of the DMZ: The Reds' Worst Defeat." U.S. News and World Report, LXIII (Oct. 16, 1967), 8. North Vietnamese fire on American bases in that area was met by "Operation Neutralize," 3100 tactical and 820 B-52 sorties.

235 "Battle of the Dikes." Time, C (Aug. 8, 1972), 24-25. Claims and denials of U.S. bombing of North Vietnamese dikes.

236 Baxter, Cordon. 13/13, Vietnam: Search and Destroy. Cleveland: World Publishing Co., 1967. 120p. A pictorial, with some illustrations of close air support strikes.

237 Beach, Dwight E. "The Caribou in Southeast Asia." Army, XIII (Dec. 1962), 36-39. The DeHavilland aircraft's role as transport.

238 Bearden, Thomas E. "What Really Happened in the Air Defense of North Vietnam." Air Defense Management (April-June 1976), 8-15. A review of MIG and SAM use by the North Vietnamese and the resulting discomfort to American pilots.

239 Beaver, Richard C. "Instrument Flying in Vietnam." U.S. Army Aviation Digest, XV (Dec. 1969), 19-21. As employed by helicopters and COIN aircraft.

240 Beck, Dennis P. "Downed Pilot Tells of 51-Hour Ordeal." Air Force Times, XXX (Feb. 18, 1970), 13. The trials of Lt. Woodrow Bergeron, Jr., before his rescue.

241 Beecher, William. "Chemicals vs. the Viet Cong--'Right' or 'Wrong'?" National Guardsman, XX (Feb. 1966), 2-6. "Operation Ranch Hand" was always controversial, even during its application.

242 ______. "A Day with 'The Big Red One.'" National Guardsman, XXI (Feb. 1967), 2-7. A look at the August 13, 1966, "Operation El Dorado," as conducted by the U.S. 1st Division with air support.

243 ______. "U.S. Extends All-Weather Capability." U.S. Naval Institute Proceedings, XCIII (Nov. 1967), 151. A look at

the U.S. Air Force push-button bombing system as reported in the Aug. 2, 1967, issue of The New York Times.

244 "Behind the Furor over Bombs on the Red River Dikes." U.S. News and World Report, LXXIII (Aug. 14, 1972), 18-20.

245 Behr, Edward. "Saigon's Choppers, a Crash Waiting to Happen: The Problem of Maintenance." Newsweek, LXXVII (March 29, 1971), 35. Vietnamization and the Army of the Republic of Vietnam (ARVN) helicopter program.

246 Bell, Raymond E. "Close Air Support for the Small Unit Commander." Army, XIV (Jan. 1964), 46-49. Helicopters and COIN aircraft during the American advisory period.

247 "The Bell AH-1G Hueycobra." Interavia, XXII (Oct. 1967), 1560-1561. A look at the new U.S. Army helicopter gunship.

248 "The [Bell] AH-1G in Vietnam by Unit, January 1, 1973." American Aviation Historical Society Journal, XX (Fall 1975), 168-169. A listing.

249 "The Bell Hueycobra." Flight International, LXXXVIII (Sept. 30, 1965), 591. A report on its tests.

250 Bellamy, Mark L. "The Fine Art of Aerial Observation." U.S. Army Aviation Digest, XIII (May 1967), 32-33. Tips and comments on its application for Army fliers.

251 Bennett, Donald G. "Spot Report: Intelligence, Vietnam." Military Review, XLVI (Aug. 1966), 72-77. Does not neglect aerial reconnaissance.

252 Bennett, J. W. "The Canberra at War with No. 2 Squadron, RAAF." Air Pictorial, XXXIII (Feb. 1971), 62-63. Good photographs.

253 Bennett, Ralph K. "Air War Vietnam: The Tragic Paradox." Data, XII (Nov. 1967), 10-11. So much power and so few concrete results.

254 Bentley, John. "Phantom Foray: Air Defence and Interception by the 'Fighting Cocks.'" Flight International, XCVII (Jan. 8, 1970), 47-52. Reviews the work of the U.S. F-4's over Southeast Asia.

255 Bergaust, Erik. Aircraft Carriers in Action. New York: Putnam, 1968. 94p. A pictorial; much on those launching planes against North Vietnam.

256 Berger, Carl. "Air War in Cambodia." In Carl Berger, ed., The United States Air Force in Southeast Asia, 1961-1973,

Washington: U.S. Government Printing Office, 1977. p. 137-148. A review of events to August 15, 1973.

257 _____. "American POW's and Operation Homecoming." In Carl Berger, ed., The United States Air Force in Southeast Asia, 1961-1973 (Washington: U.S. Government Printing Office, 1977), p321-340. A review of the POW experience and the return of those men to America in the spring of 1973.

258 _____. "Medical Support." In Carl Berger, ed., The United States Air Force in Southeast Asia, 1961-1973 (Washington: U.S. Government Printing Office, 1977), p271-284. Although the most extensive review available, the subject is limited to its application by the U.S. Air Force.

259 _____. "Training and Manning the Combat Force." In Carl Berger, ed., The United States Air Force in Southeast Asia, 1961-1973 (Washington: U.S. Government Printing Office, 1977), p297-308. A review of training, both in the U.S. and Vietnam.

260 Berman, Jay M. "The Bush that Ran." Flying Review International, XXVI (Aug. 1970), 44-47. The use of helicopters in reconnaissance.

261 Bernstein, Donald I. "A Challenge: [an OV-1] Mohawk Infrared Mission." U.S. Army Aviation Digest, XIV (Oct. 1968), 18-23. A night reconnaissance mission.

262 Berrigan, Daniel. Night Flight to Hanoi: War Diary with Eleven Poems. New York: Macmillan, 1968, 140p. The journey of Father Berrigan and Howard Zinn to North Vietnam in February 1968 to effect the return of three captured U.S. pilots; treats in detail the perceived results of American bombing operations.

263 Berthelson, John. "'Magic Dragon': A 'Puff' Mission Near Da Nang." Newsweek, LXVIII (Oct. 31, 1966), 48. A noisy trip aboard a U.S. Air Force AC-47 gunship.

264 Besch, Edwin W. "The North Vietnamese Offensive: The Turning Point in 1972." National Defense, LX (March-April 1976), 371-373. A review of operations which gave a full indication of North Vietnamese strength on the ground.

265 Bethel, J. S. "Military Defoliation of Vietnam Forests." American Forests, LXXXI (Jan., Sept. 1975), 26-30+, 46-47.

266 "A Better Air-Ground Battle." Air Force Times, XXIII (March 9, 1963), 2. Operations during the American advisory period.

267 Beyer, Lawrence F. "The Fight to Live." U.S. Army Aviation Digest, XV (March 1969), 36-48. Search and rescue operations by Army helicopters in South Vietnam.

268 "Beyond the Worst Suspicions." Time, CI (April 9, 1973), 20+. North Vietnamese treatment of American POW's.

269 Bezreh, Anthony A. "Injuries Resulting from Hostile Action Against Army Aircrew Members in Flight over Vietnam." Aerospace Medicine, XLI (July 1970), 263-769. A technical medical discussion and a survey of the kinds of casualties most taken.

270 Bielinski, Henry E. "The F-4E: A Pilot's View." Air Force Magazine, LV (Nov. 1972), 34-39. Capabilities and characteristics of the Phantom.

271 "Bien Hoa." Air Force Times, XXVIII (April 10, 1968), 19. A brief look at the big American air installation.

272 "Big Bombers: How Useful in Vietnam?" U.S. News and World Report, LVIII (June 28, 1965), 8. Questions the use of B-52's against the Viet Cong.

273 "Bigger and Uglier: The Viet Cong Raid Against Da Nang and Other Operations." Time, LXXXII (July 9, 1965), 20-21. Recounts the guerrilla attack on the U.S. air base.

274 "Bigger Bombing: Where Will It Lead?" U.S. News and World Report, LXI (July 11, 1966), 31-33. American raids on the North Vietnamese fuel storage areas.

275 Binder, L. James. "Dean of the Dust-Offers." Army, XXI (Aug. 1971), 16-21. How Army helicopter pilot Warrant Officer Michael J. Novosel won the Congressional Medal of Honor for his rescue work.

276 "Binh Thuy." Air Force Times, XXVIII (March 27, 1968), 17. A brief look at the base.

277 "Binh Thuy Revisited." Air Force Times, XXIX (June 4, 1969), 14. Picks up where the last citation left off.

278 "'Bird Dog' Pilots Spy from the Sky and Call in Support Against the Viet Cong." Air Force Times, XXVI (Aug. 25, 1965), 9. A brief look at the job of the FAC's.

279 Birdsall, Steve. The A-1 Skyraider. Famous Aircraft Series. New York: Arco Books, 1970, 64p. A nicely illustrated examination of the prop-driven Skyraider, nicknamed "SPAD."

280 Bishop, Donald M. "Leadership, Followship, and Unit Spirit: Reflections on a Year in Vietnam." Air Force Magazine,

LX (Dec. 1977), 52-56. Due to the good chance of rescue, Air Force unit spirit remained high throughout most of the conflict.

281 "Bitter Bit: The Minh Thanh Battle." Newsweek, LXVIII (July 25, 1966), 31. The air supported U.S. 1st and ARVN 5th Divisions pushed on An Loc.

282 Blackwell, Brendan P. "HLH." U.S. Army Aviation Digest, XIX (Aug. 1973), 8-16. "Heavy Lift Helicopters," e.g., the Sikorsky CH-54 Tarhe.

283 Blair, Edison T. "The Air Commandos." Airman, VI (Sept. 1962), 18-23. Views the U.S. Air Force's 6th Fighter Squadron (Commando).

284 _____. "SAC's Role in Counterinsurgency." Airman, VI (Dec. 1962), 2-3. Written several years before the beginning of the "Arc Light" operations which pitted B-52's against the Vietcong.

285 Blair, Edward. "A Man Doing His Job." Airman, XIII (April 1969), 52-55. Capt. Merlyn H. Dethlefsen won the Congressional Medal of Honor for attacking SAM sites near Thai Nguyen, north of Hanoi, on March 10, 1967, after other F-105's in his flight were destroyed or forced away from the steel mill target.

286 _____. "Saga of a Fighting FAC." Airman, XIII (May 1969), 60-64. Capt. Hillard A. Wilbanks was posthumously awarded the Medal of Honor for drawing fire away from an ARVN Ranger battalion under attack near Dalat on February 24, 1967; the feat was performed with an M-16 rifle fired from an unarmed O-1 "Bird Dog."

287 Blair, Larry A. "Heliborne Engineer Operations." Military Engineer, LX (May-June 1968), 174-176. The use of helicopters in flying in supplies and engineers and in the actual engineering processes.

288 Blakely, Garth. "The F-100 Super Sabre." Aerospace Historian, XXIV (Sept. 1977), 149-152. A pictorial examining the role of an older fighter.

288a Blakey, Scott. Prisoner of War. The Survival of Commander Richard A. Stratton. Garden City, N.Y.: Doubleday, 1978. 397p. This Navy officer's life in a North Vietnamese POW environment from the time he was shot down until his release.

Blanchard, Wendell, jt. author see Dupuy, Trevor N.

289 Bland, Ruskin M. "Special Express." Air University Review, XVIII (July-Aug. 1967), 36-42. A look at U.S. Air Force transports and logistics, with reference to Vietnam.

290 Blaney, Daniel J. "Attack Helicopter Utilization." U.S. Army Aviation Digest, XVI (July 1970), 15-17. The kinds of missions carried out.

291 Blank, J. P. "Shot Down in North Vietnam: Captain Roger Locker's 23-Day Ordeal." Reader's Digest, CII (April 1973), 80-84. An interview recounting survival techniques.

292 Blank, Jonas L. "The Impact of Logistics on Strategy." Air University Review, XXIV (March-April 1973), 2-21. With a number of examples drawn from the SEA war.

293 Blanton, Eugene T. "Coin Weather Support." Air University Review, XV (June-July 1964), 66-72. The idea of changing weather patterns to assist in counterinsurgency warfare, an idea given some trial in SEA.

294 Blaylock, Monroe E. "Dearest Judy." Interceptor, X (Feb. 1968), 5-7. The rescue of an AC-47 crew from A-Shau in the spring of 1966.

295 Blewett, Donald A. "The Heliport at Qui Nhon, Vietnam." Military Engineer, LVIII (Sept.-Oct. 1966), 330-331. How it was built and some features thereof.

296 "Bloodiest Week: The Actions at Lai Khe and Tay Ninh." Newsweek, LXIX (April 3, 1967), 38+. The parachute drop of "Operation Junction City" in the "Iron Triangle" area of War Zone C.

297 "Bloody Dak To: Why It Was So Vital." U.S. News and World Report, LXIII (Dec. 4, 1967), 10+. With the support of 228 B-52 sorties, U.S. and ARVN troops beat off a determined attack on this Special Forces camp in November 1967.

298 "Bloody Trial: The North Vietnamese Try to Overrun the Marine Camp at Con Thien." Newsweek, LXIX (May 22, 1967), 46. Close air support also thwarted this enemy move.

299 "Blue Bombs on the Panhandle." Time, LXXXVIII (Sept. 2, 1966), 23. Air raids on North Vietnamese targets in that area.

300 "The Boeing B-52 Stratofortress." Air Progress, XXIV (Dec. 1968), 50-53. A look at the giant SAC bomber.

301 Boettcher, T. D. "Their Business Is Booming." Airman, XIII (Sept. 1969), 26-27. The instant landing-zone clearing operations known as "Commando Vault."

302 Bohannon, Richard L. "Aeromedical Evacuation." Air Force

Policy Letter for Commanders, no. 12 (Dec. 1965), 5. A summary of U. S. Air Force operations in this area.

303 ______. "The Most Tragic Face of War." Airman, X (July 1966), 24-28. An examination of aerial ambulances and medevac operations within Vietnam and between that country and America.

304 "Bomb Damage Assessment: A Pictorial." Naval Aviation News, (July 1968), 3-4. Pictures of damage to North Vietnamese targets done by U. S. Navy attack planes.

305 "Bomb Shortages?: An On-the-Scene Report." U. S. News and World Report, LX (May 2, 1966), 10. Such shortages did exist from time to time.

306 "Bombers Go North." Newsweek, LXXVI (Nov. 30, 1970), 14. More U. S. raids on North Vietnamese targets.

307 "Bombing Assessment." Naval Aviation News, (April 1968), 36. Success seen to that date.

308 "The 'Bombing Campaign' Against the Dikes: Setting the Record Straight." Seapower, XV (Sept. 1972), 4. An editorial which attempts to clear up the controversy.

309 "Bombing Controversy: Bombing North Vietnam." Time, LXXXIX (March 3, 1967), 21-22. Operations and domestic American politics.

310 "Bombing Coverup." Time, CII (July 30, 1973), 22. U. S. air operations over Cambodia.

311 "Bombing Fallout: Michael Heck's Refusal to Participate in Bombing Missions." Time, CI (Jan. 22, 1973), 21. A B-52 pilot's refusal to fly "Linebacker II" missions.

312 "Bombing for Peace." New Republic, CLXVI (May 20, 1972), 5-6. Sees American air operations as designed to force North Vietnam to make concessions at the peace table.

313 "Bombing, North and South." Commonweal, LXXXIII (Oct. 22, 1965), 77-78. Is not pleased with air operations over either South or North Vietnam.

314 "The Bombing Pause: Why It Is Not Total." Life, XLIV (April 12, 1968), 38-42. U. S. air operations against Communist lines of supply and close air support.

315 "Bombing Report." Journal of the Armed Forces, CIII (Feb. 19, 1966), 27. B-52 "Arc Light" operations in 1965.

316 "Bombing the North." New Republic, CLIV (April 23, 1966),

5-6. Increased air activity against Hanoi's communications lines.

317 "Bombing Toll: How North Vietnam Is Hurting." U.S. News and World Report, LXXIII (Sept. 4, 1972), 33-34. As a result of heavy U.S. air operations.

318 "The Bombing Toll in North Vietnam." U.S. News and World Report, LXIV (April 22, 1968), 61. Heavy damage is reported to have been inflicted.

319 "Bombings Disclosed." Senior Scholastic, LXXXVI (Feb. 4, 1965), 19. Combat over Laos.

320 "Bombs Away." Time, LXXXVI (Oct. 29, 1965), 32. B-52 "Arc Light" operations.

321 "Bombs Away: Growing U.S. Involvement [in Cambodia]." Newsweek, XXVI (Aug. 18, 1970), 39. Attacks on Communist targets.

322 "Bombs Fall Again." America, CXIV (Feb. 12, 1965), 219-220. Raids against North Vietnam.

323 "Bombs in Tonkin Gulf." Naval Aviation News, (Feb. 1967), 12. Flights from carriers on "Yankee Station."

324 "Bombsight and Hindsight at the OK Corral: The Use of the B-52 Stratofortress." Time, LXXXV (June 25, 1965), 37. The first "Arc Light" operation against the VC.

325 Bond, Gregg S. "Debut of 'Super Lou': Confessions of a Huey." U.S. Army Aviation Digest, XIII (April 1967), 16-19. A look at the Bell AH-1G Huey Cobra helicopter.

"The Bon Homme Richard Off Vietnam" see "The [USS] Bon Homme Richard ..."

326 Booda, L. "Air Force Expands Air Commando Forces." Aviation Week and Space Technology, LXXVIII (June 3, 1963), 48-49+. For COIN operations.

327 ______. "Army Attack Helicopter Plans Re-Oriented." Aviation Week and Space Technology, LXXVIII (May 6, 1963), 27. As a result of Vietnam experience.

328 ______. "McNamara Pushing USAF-Army Rivalry." Aviation Week and Space Technology, LXXVII (Jan. 14, 1963), 26-27. As to which will perform which air task.

329 ______. "USAF Pushes Vietnamese Pilot Training." Aviation Week and Space Technology, LXXVIII (April 20, 1964), 94-95. Early Vietnamization before that word was coined.

330 Booker, Stephen. "The Death of a Navy Pilot." Ebony, XXII (Jan. 1967), 25-28. A black U.S. Navy pilot drowned over North Vietnam.

331 "Boom-Boom Lon Nol." Newsweek, LXXVI (Nov. 9, 1970), 46. U.S. air operations over Cambodia.

332 Boone, James L. "Return of the ASCAT." USAF Tactical Air Warfare Center Quarterly Review, III (Nov. 1972), 9-13. A look at Anti-SAM Combat Assistance Teams.

333 Borman, Frank. "U.S. Prisoners-of-War in Southeast Asia." Department of State Bulletin, LXIII (Oct. 12, 1970), 405-408. The astronaut's remarks were made before a joint-session of Congress on September 22, 1970.

334 Boshoven, B. W. "TAC's Global Reach Helps Counter a Crisis." Air Force Magazine, LV (Aug. 1972), 36-40. U.S. Air Force Tactical Air Command aircraft dispatched to SEA to counter the 1972 North Vietnamese Easter invasion.

335 Bo-Thong-Tin, and Va-Thanh-Nien. Clearing the Undergrowth: What Are the Facts About Defoliation in South Vietnam? Saigon: Ministry of Information, Republic of Vietnam, 1964, 3p. A statement dismissing the ecological implications of "Operation Ranch Hand."

336 Bottomly, Heath. Prodigal Father: A Fighter Pilot Finds Peace in the Wake of His Destruction. Glendale, Calif.: Regal Books, 1975, 141p. Reminiscences of a pilot-turned-pastor with heavy emphasis on his turn towards God and away from the military.

337 Bowen, Bob. "Close Air Support." Leatherneck, L (May 1967), 22-25. As provided by U.S. Marine Corps aircraft in support of Marine operations in the I Corps area of South Vietnam.

338 Bowers, Peter M. Boeing Aircraft Since 1916. (Putnam Aeronautical Books.) London: Putnam, 1966, 444p. Includes much information on the B-52, then beginning "Arc Light" operations.

339 _____. Boeing B-52 A/H Stratofortress. (Aircraft in Profile, no. 245). Windsor, Eng.: Profile Publications, 1974, 12p. Technical and operational information.

_____, jt. author see Swanborough, F. Gordon

340 Bowers, Ray L. "Air Power in Vietnam." Unpublished paper, Eighth Military History Symposium, USAF Academy, 1978. Col. Bower's paper will be available in print when the U.S. Government Printing Office publishes the symposium's proceedings.

341 _____. "Air Transport in the Northern Provinces." Marine Corps Gazette, LX (June 1976), 39-49. U.S. Marine Corps C-130 operations in the I Corps area; contributions by the U.S. Army and Air Force are also noted as applicable.

342 _____. "Americans in the Vietnamese Air Force: The 'Dirty Thirty.'" Aerospace Historian, XIX (Sept. 1972), 125-131. The activities of 30 U.S. airmen assigned to serve with the VNAF C-47 squadrons in April 1962.

343 _____. "Tactical Airlift." In Carl Berger, ed., The United States Air Force in Southeast Asia, 1961-1973 (Washington: U.S. Government Printing Office, 1977), p169-186. A survey of U.S. Air Force tactical supply and delivery operations by such aircraft as the C-130 during the war years.

344 _____. "The USAF Airlift and Airmobility Idea in Vietnam." Air University Review, XXVI (Nov.-Dec. 1974), 2-18. An appraisal of the items covered in the survey above.

345 Boyd, Stuart R. "High Angle of Attack in the Swingwing." Aerospace Safety, XXVII (Aug. 1971), 1-4. Use of the FB-111 in Southeast Asia.

346 Bradbrook, Muriel C. The World's Helicopters. London: Bodley Head, 1972, 111p. Includes some American models used in Southeast Asia.

347 Bradford, Zeb B., Jr. "U.S. Tactics in Vietnam." Military Review, LII (Feb. 1972), 63-76. A general survey and analysis with mention of the airmobility concept of troop delivery.

348 Brady, James T. "Skyhawks." American Aviation Historical Society Journal, XV (Winter 1973), 217-221. A photographic review of the role of the A-4C.

Brady, Len, jt. author see Manning, Stephen O., 3rd

349 Brady, Patrick H. "'Dust-Off' Operations in Vietnam." Army Logistician, V (July-Aug. 1973), 18-23. Helicopter medevac and rescue missions.

350 _____. "Solo Missions." U.S. Army Aviation Digest, XII (July 1966), 2-6. Night intruder missions over Vietnam.

351 Brand, William F., Jr., et al. "Airmobile Firepower: Hallmark of the 1st Cavalry Division." U.S. Army Aviation Digest, XIII (March 1967), 18-23. A review of operations in Vietnam to date, with comments on the value of the unit's helicopters.

352 Brandstuder, Phillip V. "Updating the Air Cavalry Squadron."

Armor, LXXIX (March-April 1970), 41-43. Improvements based on experiences gained in SEA.

Brandt, Edward, jt. author see Denton, Jeremiah A., Jr.

353 Branfman, Fred. "America's Secret War." Progressive, XXXVI (June 1972), 29-33. The air war over Laos.

354 ______. "Laos: No Place to Hide." Bulletin of Concerned Asian Scholars, II (Fall 1970), 15-46. More on the air war.

355 ______. "The Wild Blue Yonder Over Laos." Washington Monthly, (July 1971), passim. Another look at U. S. air operations, based on interviews with refugees, TAC and FAC pilots, and U. S. officials.

356 ______, comp. Voices from the Plain of Jars: Life Under an Air War. New York: Harper & Row, 1972, 160p. With a provocative introduction by the compiler, the work presents translations of 16 statements collected about the American bombing in 1970-1971 from refugees in camps near Vientiane, Laos.

357 Braybrook, Roy M. "The MIG-19 'Farmer.'" Flying Review International, XIX (Feb. 1964), 22-25+.

358 ______. "The MIG-21 'Fishbed.'" Flying Review International, XIX (Nov. 1963), 20-22+.

359 ______. "The Perennial MIG-17." Flying Review International, XIX (Sept. 1964), 20-23. The material in this and the previous two citations provides technical and capability details on the three major kinds of interceptors met by American pilots over North Vietnam.

359a ______. "RAAF: Past, Present, and Future." Air Combat, VI (March 1978), 19-30, 98. Includes a few relative comments.

360 ______. "Under Combat Conditions." Flying Review International, XXII (Oct. 1966), 125+. Practical lessons of Vietnam fighter operations.

361 Brazzie, Tony. "'Patches' to Retire after Many Hits." Air Force Times, XXXI (Aug. 4, 1971), 18. Phasing out the C-123 "Provider" transport.

362 Breckner, William J. "Shootdown over Downtown." Interceptor, XVI (March 1974), 18-21. Combat over Hanoi.

363 Brighton, Peter. "The Ear in South Vietnam: Some Lessons in the Use of Air Power." Royal Air Forces Quarterly, VIII (Winter 1968), 289-293. A British view on the value of FAC's and close air support.

364 Brindley, Thomas. "A Legacy of Poison." Far Eastern Economic Review, LXXIX (March 5, 1973), 22-24. More on herbicides and "Operation Ranch Hand."

365 Brinkman, Dale. "Night FAC's Score Success in Delta." Air Force Times, XXX (Aug. 27, 1968), 14. Bringing fire down upon Vietcong positions in the Mekong Delta.

366 Brisbane, Glen E. "Combat Aircraft Revetments: A Review." Military Engineer, LXIV (March-April 1972), 92-94. Their purpose and construction.

367 Bristow, William D., Jr. "'On Fire and Going Down.'" U.S. Army Aviation Digest, XVII (May 1971), 32-34. The downing of an American helicopter; reprinted in Approach, XVII (Aug. 1971), 26-29.

368 Britannica Book of the Year. Chicago: Encyclopedia Britannica, Inc., 1961-1973. As with the Americana Annual (qv), this yearbook provides useful background coverage of the Southeast Asian conflict.

369 Brodie, Bernard. "The TET Offensive." In Noble Frankland and Christopher Dowling, eds. Decisive Battles of the 20th Century: Land, Sea, and Air. New York: David McKay, 1976, p. 320-334. A review of the grand 1968 Communist drive, its reception by Allied firepower, and the long-range effects.

370 ______. War and Politics. New York: Macmillan, 1974, 400p. To demonstrate the necessity for an approximate amalgam between strategy and politics, the author examines the impact (or lack thereof) of political objectives on the operational aspects of several conflicts, including the use of air power over North Vietnam.

371 Broughton, Jack. Thud Ridge. Philadelphia: Lippincott, 1969, 254p. "Thud" was the nickname bestowed by U.S. Air Force pilots on the F-105 Thunderchief; "Thud Ridge" was the name given the small chain of mountains in North Vietnam which led to the Hanoi area.

The author, a retired colonel, led a section of "Thuds" from the 355th Tactical Fighter Wing, based at Takhi, Thailand, against various targets near the North Vietnamese capital, personally flying 102 missions. Many of the combat sequences were written as he actually recorded them on his missions with a small portable tape recorder. While some of the terminology may be confusing, the book demonstrates the determination and professionalism of the American pilots as they struggled to achieve their objectives under severe political restrictions. The first and to date the best aerial reminiscences to come out of the Southeast Asian conflict.

372 Brown, David A. "The A-6A Fills Interdiction Mission in Vietnam." Aviation Week and Space Technology, LXXXIII (Dec. 27, 1965), 18-20. A look at the capabilities of this U.S. Navy attack aircraft, launched from carriers against Viet Cong and North Vietnamese targets.

373 ______. "The Armed Helicopter: A View on the Use of and Future of." U.S. Army Aviation Digest, XII (Oct. 1966), 14-16. An examination of its role, especially in Vietnam; the future appears to the author to be unlimited.

374 ______. "Hueycobra Offers High Maneuverability." Aviation Week and Space Technology, LXXXIV (June 13, 1966), 54-55+. A report on the trials of the AH-1G helicopter gunship.

375 ______. "U.S. Presses North Vietnamese Air War." Aviation Week and Space Technology, XCVII (July 3, 1972), 12-16. A recapitulation of events during the first six months of the year.

376 ______. "YAT-37D Shows Agility in Coin Role." Aviation Week and Space Technology, LXXXIII (July 12, 1965), 66-67+. Testing the Cessna A-37 counterinsurgency aircraft.

377 ______; Christopher F. Shores; and Kenneth Macksey. The Guinness History of Air Warfare. London: Guinness Superlatives, 1977, 247p. Contains a section on air warfare over Southeast Asia.

378 Brown, F. C. "Seal-Team Operations: Vietnam, 1966-1972." Military Journal, I (Sept.-Oct. 1977), 42-43. A brief review of operations, including co-ordination of the "frogmen" with U.S. Navy Seawolf helicopters.

379 Brown, George S. "The Airman in Charge in Southeast Asia: An Interview." Airman, XIII (Jan. 1969), 3-7. The general commanded the U.S. 7th Air Force, with headquarters at Tan Son Nhut airbase, from August 1, 1968, to August 31, 1970; herein, he provides thoughts on the operational aspects of the "in-" and "out-" country air war.

380 ______. "A Clearer Perspective." Air Force Policy Letter for Commanders, no. 6 (June 1971), 18-24. Remarks on the Vietnamese air war made before the Washington, D.C., Chapter of the American Ordnance Association on April 12, 1971.

381 Brown, Harold. "Air Force Posture Statement." Air Force Policy Letter for Commanders, no. 3 (March 1967), 2-19. The U.S. position as of February 2, 1967; the present Secretary of Defense was Secretary of the Air Force from October 1, 1966, to February 14, 1969.

382 ______. "The Air Force Role in Southeast Asia." Air Force Policy Letter for Commanders, no. 3 (March 1968), 25-34. Remarks made before the Michigan Aeronautics and Space Association on February 2, 1968.

383 ______. "Air Rescue in Vietnam--'That Others May Live.'" Air Force and Space Digest, L (March 1967), 86+. Reprinted from an address given before the Chamber of Commerce of San Antonio, Texas, on January 19, 1967.

384 ______. "The Air War in Vietnam and Transcript of the Question and Answer Period." Air Force Policy Letter for Commanders, no. 1 (Jan. 1967), 2-11. A talk before the December 8, 1966, meeting of the Aviation and Space Writers Association.

385 ______. "Close Air Support in Vietnam." Air Force Policy Letter for Commanders, no. 4 (April 1966), 15-18. Remarks made in a February 25, 1966, speech to the Executives' Club of Chicago.

386 ______. "The Importance of Tactical Aviation." Air Force Policy Letter for Commanders, no. 12 (Dec. 1965), 1-5.

387 ______. "A Modern Air Force." Vital Speeches, XXXII (April 1, 1966), 354-358. Another source for the Executives' Club of Chicago remarks noted in item 385.

388 ______. "The North Vietnamese Air War: Excerpts from the Comments of Air Force Secretary Harold Brown." Aviation Week and Space Technology, LXXXV (Dec. 12, 1966), 21. Taken from his December 8 meeting with the Aviation and Space Writers Association noted above.

389 ______. "Our Airmen in Vietnam: A Professional Team." Air Force and Space Digest, L (May 1967), 48-52. Their mission and spirit.

390 ______. "Progress of the Vietnamese Air Force." Air Force Policy Letter for Commanders, no. 7 (July 1968), 32. A brief but important statement made at a time when few Americans were thinking of the VNAF; the remarks were made before the Phoenix, Arizona, Chamber of Commerce on May 16, 1968.

391 ______. "Revolution in Airlift." Air Force Policy Letter for Commanders, no. 5 (May 1968), 18-24. These April 5, 1968, remarks to the Air Force Association Convention were reprinted in Air Force and Space Digest, LI (June 1968), 114-118.

392 ______, and John P. McDonnell. "Decisions Concerning the Air Campaign Against North Vietnam." Air Force Policy

Letter for Commanders, no. 11 (Nov. 1967), 15-17. Remarks at the Air Force Association Anniversary Dinner, September 12, 1967.

393 Brown, John L. "A Duty Day in Vietnam." U.S. Army Aviation Digest, XIV (March 1968), 12-13. Remembers an Army armed helicopter platoon's activities on one day in 1965.

394 Brown, Kevin V. "Helicopters in Vietnam." Popular Mechanics, CXXVII (Feb. 1967), 107-11+. Types and operations; written for the layman.

395 ______. "Sitting Ducks Who Call the Shots." Popular Mechanics, CXXIX (Jan. 1968), 89-92+. U.S. Air Force FAC's.

396 ______. "U.S. Warplanes in Vietnam." Popular Mechanics, CXXVI (Nov. 1966), 107-111+. Types and operations; written for the layman.

397 Browne, Malcolm W. The New Face of War. Indianapolis: Bobbs-Merrill, 1965, 284p. An AP correspondent's view of the early phases of the Vietnam war, with some information on aerial activities.

398 Brownfield, Orlon L. "The Legend of the Hercules." MAC Flyer, XXIV (Jan. 1977), 3-6. A look at the C-130 transport, including its Vietnam role.

399 Browning, Joseph. "'Bird Dogs' over the Jungle." National Guardsman, XXI (March 1967), 10-12. FAC's and the unarmed O-1 spotter plane.

400 ______. "Hide and Seek in the Delta." Army, XVI (June 1966), 26-28. "Bird Dogs" over the Mekong Delta area of South Vietnam.

401 ______. "Looking for Charlie." U.S. Army Aviation Digest, XXII (Oct. 1967), 43-46. More on the "bird dogs" and the elusive Viet Cong.

402 Brownlow, Cecil. "The AC-47 Broadens the Vietnam Attack Envelope." Aviation Week and Space Technology, LXXXVI (April 17, 1967), 54-55+. The addition of "Puff the Magic Dragon" gunships to the U.S. Air Force inventory.

403 ______. "Air Force U-10B's Play a Key Role in Psychological Warfare Tactics." Aviation Week and Space Technology, LXXXII (June 7, 1965). 69. Attempting to win "hearts and minds" by night broadcasts and leaflet dropping.

404 ______. "Air Force North Vietnam Effort Dependent on Thai Bases." Aviation Week and Space Technology, LXXXVI (April 3, 1967), 26-29. Base development and operations from same.

405 ______. "Air Losses Spark Phuc Yen Strike." Aviation Week and Space Technology, LXXXVII (Oct. 30, 1967), 16-17. Attacks on the North Vietnamese MIG base.

406 ______. "The Air War in Vietnam: The Army Employs the Sikorsky CH-37 to Save Downed Aircraft." Aviation Week and Space Technology, LXXXII (May 10, 1965), 108-109+. How downed helicopters and other aircraft were picked up and taken back for repair and restoration to active duty.

407 ______. "Airpower Gives the U. S. the Edge in Vietnam." Aviation Week and Space Technology, LXXXVI (Jan. 9, 1967), 16-21. On the value of overwhelming air superiority.

408 ______. "Army, Air Force Testing Air Support Roles." Aviation Week and Space Technology, LXXXI (Sept. 21, 1964), 77+. An examination of the capabilities and controversies surrounding each service's aims and punch.

409 ______. "Army Employs Sikorsky CH-37's to Save Downed Aircraft." Aviation Week and Space Technology, LXXXII (May 10, 1965), 108-109+. Recovery of shot down helicopters for repair and reassignment.

410 ______. "Army to Bolster Air Strength in Vietnam." Aviation Week and Space Technology, LXXXVI (March 20, 1967), 28-30+. The acquisition of more and different kinds of warbirds, including the AH-1G Huey Cobra gunship.

411 ______. "B-52s Prove Tactical Value During the Siege of Khe Sanh." Aviation Week and Space Technology, LXXXVIII (May 13, 1968), 26-30. As part of the "Operation Niagara," the joint American air effort designed to support the defenders of the Khe Sanh, SAC Stratofortresses flew 461 missions (2707 sorties) and dropped 75, 631 tons of bombs between January 14 and March 31, 1968.

412 ______. "Bombing Cut Spurs Resupply from [the] North." Aviation Week and Space Technology, LXXXVIII (May 6, 1968), 22-28. Throughout the war, this was the most serious cause for not calling the bombing halts or "pauses."

413 ______. "Burgeoning U. S. Use of Air Power Aimed at Forestalling a Ground War with the Chinese." Aviation Week and Space Technology, LXXXII (April 26, 1965), 26-31. Another idea seized upon by anti-war factions and used as a reason for halting the fighting--i. e., air attacks would bring Chinese intervention.

414 ______. "Combat Forces New Limited War Studies." Aviation Week and Space Technology, LXXXIV (March 28, 1966), 90-94. "The book" on counterinsurgency stood in need of rewriting in light of experiences gained in South Vietnam.

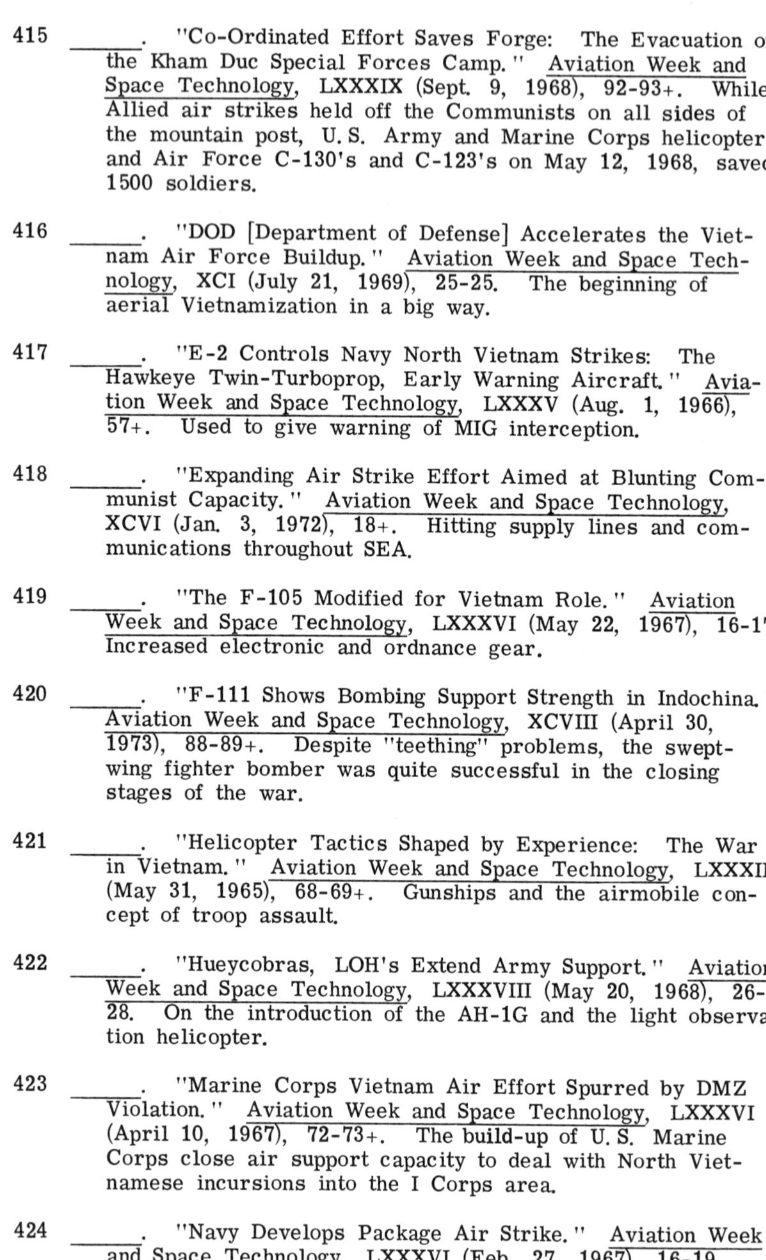

415 ______. "Co-Ordinated Effort Saves Forge: The Evacuation of the Kham Duc Special Forces Camp." Aviation Week and Space Technology, LXXXIX (Sept. 9, 1968), 92-93+. While Allied air strikes held off the Communists on all sides of the mountain post, U. S. Army and Marine Corps helicopters and Air Force C-130's and C-123's on May 12, 1968, saved 1500 soldiers.

416 ______. "DOD [Department of Defense] Accelerates the Vietnam Air Force Buildup." Aviation Week and Space Technology, XCI (July 21, 1969), 25-25. The beginning of aerial Vietnamization in a big way.

417 ______. "E-2 Controls Navy North Vietnam Strikes: The Hawkeye Twin-Turboprop, Early Warning Aircraft." Aviation Week and Space Technology, LXXXV (Aug. 1, 1966), 57+. Used to give warning of MIG interception.

418 ______. "Expanding Air Strike Effort Aimed at Blunting Communist Capacity." Aviation Week and Space Technology, XCVI (Jan. 3, 1972), 18+. Hitting supply lines and communications throughout SEA.

419 ______. "The F-105 Modified for Vietnam Role." Aviation Week and Space Technology, LXXXVI (May 22, 1967), 16-17. Increased electronic and ordnance gear.

420 ______. "F-111 Shows Bombing Support Strength in Indochina." Aviation Week and Space Technology, XCVIII (April 30, 1973), 88-89+. Despite "teething" problems, the swept-wing fighter bomber was quite successful in the closing stages of the war.

421 ______. "Helicopter Tactics Shaped by Experience: The War in Vietnam." Aviation Week and Space Technology, LXXXII (May 31, 1965), 68-69+. Gunships and the airmobile concept of troop assault.

422 ______. "Hueycobras, LOH's Extend Army Support." Aviation Week and Space Technology, LXXXVIII (May 20, 1968), 26-28. On the introduction of the AH-1G and the light observation helicopter.

423 ______. "Marine Corps Vietnam Air Effort Spurred by DMZ Violation." Aviation Week and Space Technology, LXXXVI (April 10, 1967), 72-73+. The build-up of U. S. Marine Corps close air support capacity to deal with North Vietnamese incursions into the I Corps area.

424 ______. "Navy Develops Package Air Strike." Aviation Week and Space Technology, LXXXVI (Feb. 27, 1967), 16-19. Fighters, bombers, and early warning aircraft.

425 ______. "Needs Outpace Strong Vietnam [Aerial] Reconnaissance

Gains." Aviation Week and Space Technology, LXXXVI (March 13, 1967), 19-22. On the need for more photo planes.

426 ______. "North Vietnam Air Loss Rate Slashed." Aviation Week and Space Technology, LXXXVII (Aug. 28, 1967), 26-27. After a number of fighter bombers were lost to MIG's.

427 ______. "North Vietnamese Intensify Combat Capabilities." Aviation Week and Space Technology, LXXXIX (July 8, 1968), 14-16. On the growing North Vietnamese Air Force MIG threat.

428 ______. "Oil Depot Bombings Mark New Vietnam Phase." Aviation Week and Space Technology, LXXXV (July 4, 1966), 20-23. On the destruction of targets previously "off-limits."

429 ______. "Pause Cuts Soaring Loss Rates." Aviation Week and Space Technology, LXXXIX (July 15, 1968), 14-16. While giving the North Vietnamese time to repair damage and prepare new antiaircraft installations.

430 ______. "Quick Strikes Follow Truce in Vietnam." Aviation Week and Space Technology, LXXXVIII (Jan. 1, 1968), 16. Hitting new targets after a bombing pause.

431 ______. "Reconnaissance Wings Face New Strain." Aviation Week and Space Technology, LXXXIX (Oct. 7, 1968), 95-97. On the need for more planes and better equipment.

432 ______. "SRAM Begins Operational Role with SAC B-52 Wing." Aviation Week and Space Technology, XCVII (Aug. 14, 1972), 15. The anti-missile capacity of the big Stratofortresses.

433 ______. "Six HH-43F's Handle the Bulk of Air Rescue." Aviation Week and Space Technology, LXXXII (May 3, 1965), 71+. U.S. Air Force rescue and recovery helicopters in Vietnam.

434 ______. "U.S. Improves Tactical Capability." Aviation Week and Space Technology, LXXXIX (Sept. 30, 1968), 89+.

435 ______. "U.S. Presses Independent Role for VNAF." Aviation Week and Space Technology, LXXXIX (Sept. 16, 1968), 128-129+. From 1965 on the VNAF was pretty much supressed under the weight of U.S. aerial combat "help."

436 ______. "U.S. Shifts Tactics over the North." Aviation Week and Space Technology, LXXXIX (July 22, 1968), 18-20. Attacking more sophisticated targets.

437 ______. "U.S. to Boost Viet Air Commitment." Aviation Week

and Space Technology, LXXXIV (Feb. 7, 1966), 22-24. More aerial escalation.

438 ______. "U.S. to Double [Air] Strength in South Vietnam." Aviation Week and Space Technology, LXXXII (Feb. 15, 1965), 11, 18-20. Aerial escalation.

439 ______. "U.S. to Keep Air Power in Southeast Asia." Aviation Week and Space Technology, XCVIII (Jan. 29, 1973), 22-23. At bases in Thailand.

440 ______. "USAF Accelerates Interdiction in the South." Aviation Week and Space Technology, LXXXIX (Aug. 12, 1968), 26-28. Employing the aircraft kept out of North Vietnam by the bombing pause.

441 ______. "USAF Boosts North Vietnamese ECM Jamming." Aviation Week and Space Technology, LXXXVI (Feb. 6, 1967), 22-25. Electronic countermeasures.

442 ______. "USAF Effectiveness: Loss Rate Improving." Aviation Week and Space Technology, LXXXVI (Feb. 13, 1967), 28-32.

443 ______. "USAF Presses Advanced Airlift Concepts." Aviation Week and Space Technology, LXXXIX (July 29, 1968), 72-73+. The continued development of tactical airlift capability.

444 ______. "USAF Stresses High-Speed Rescue Need." Aviation Week and Space Technology, LXXXVIII (June 17, 1968), 56-58. The need for better helicopters in the recovery role.

445 ______. "USAF to Rectify Problem of Oversupply." Aviation Week and Space Technology, LXXXIX (Oct. 14, 1968), 79-80+. Examines the logistical situation.

446/7 ______. "USAF to Strengthen F-105 Survivability." Aviation Week and Space Technology, LXXXIX (Sept. 23, 1968), 78-79+. New tactics and electronics.

448 ______. "USAF Wins Right to Use Jets in Vietnam." Aviation Week and Space Technology, LXXXII (March 8, 1965), 18. Resolution of the Army-Air Force air controversy.

449 ______. "VNAF Effectiveness Keyed to Leadership." Aviation Week and Space Technology, LXXXII (May 10, 1965), 30-32. Thoughts on the South Vietnamese air force before it seemed to be placed on a backburner by massive American aerial assistance.

450 ______. "VNAF Seeks the Means to Train Its Own Pilots." Aviation Week and Space Technology, LXXXII (June 7, 1965), 62-63. Most training provided by the U.S.

451 _____. "Vietnam Action Dramatizes SAM Deficiencies." Aviation Week and Space Technology, LXXXV (July 11, 1966), 26-29. Points out the possibilities for pilots to escape being downed by surface-to-air missiles.

452 _____. "Vietnam Air Force Gains in Professionalism." Aviation Week and Space Technology, XCVII (Aug. 7, 1972), 16-18. Aerial Vietnamization.

453 _____. "Vietnam-Generated Advances Reach [that] Theater: Testing Sensors and Electronic-Countermeasures Hardware." Aviation Week and Space Technology, LXXXVI (May 22, 1967), 68-69+.

454 _____. "Vietnam Ground Effort Keyed to Airlift Bases." Aviation Week and Space Technology, LXXXVI (May 8, 1967), 87+. A look at tactical airlift.

455 _____. "Vietnam Operations Spur New A-6 Interest." Aviation Week and Space Technology, LXXXVI (April 24, 1967), 67+. The U.S. Navy all-weather attack plane.

456 _____. "The Vietnam Target Envelope May Expand: USAF Tactical Commanders Press to Hit MIG Bases, Factories, and other Military Support Facilities." Aviation Week and Space Technology, LXXXVI (March 27, 1967), 16-21. And so by phases it came to pass.

457 _____. "The War in Vietnam." Aviation Week and Space Technology, LXXXII (May 3-June 7, 1965), 18-21, 30-32, 32-34, 48-50, 29-30, 62-63. Reviews of the aerial aspects.

458 Bruggink, Gerald. "Ditching the Huey." U.S. Army Aviation Digest, XIII (May 1967), 36-46. How to put down a damaged UH-1 without crashing; many Vietnam examples.

459 "The Brushfire Burns Hot: Vietnam." Air Force and Space Digest, L (Sept. 1967), 121-126+. A look at the conflict with emphasis on the aerial phase.

460 "The Brutal Battle of Con Thien." U.S. News and World Report, LXIII (Oct. 9, 1967), 40-41. With some comment on aerial support therein.

Buchanan, W. L., jt. author see Rider, J. W.

461 Bueschel, Richard M. Communist Chinese Air Power. New York: Praeger, 1968. 238p. North Vietnam receive some aerial support and base help from this quarter.

462 "Bui Tin and Phan Thai: The Two U.S. Dry-Season Counter-offensives in 1965-1966 and 1966-1967." Vietnamese Studies, no. 16 (1968), 32-63. With some information on the air-mobile aspects.

463 Bulban, E. J. "Armed Helicopters Escort U. S. Troop Cargo Aircraft in the Vietnam Guerrilla War." Aviation Week and Space Technology, LXXVII (Dec. 24, 1962), 38-41. How Hueys aided the Caribous.

464 ______. "Navy Using Armed Helicopters in Vietnam." Aviation Week and Space Technology, LXXXVIII (May 20, 1968), 69+. Seawolves.

465 Burbage, Paul, et al. "The Battle for the Skies over North Vietnam, 1964-1972." In A. J. C. Lavalle, ed., USAF Southeast Asia Monograph Series, Vol. I (Washington: U.S. Government Printing Office, 1976), p97-193. Undocumented, but a valuable examination of bombing raids and dogfights.

466 Burchett, Wilfred G. Vietnam Will Win! New York: Monthly Review Press, 1969. 215p. An Australian journalist presents the Communist versions of the battles of Bau Bang and Khe Sanh.

467 Burck, Charles G. "What the U. S. Is Leaving Behind in Vietnam." Fortune, LXXXIV (Oct. 1971), 82-87. The VNAF for one thing.

468 Burleigh, Robert H. "The ARVN Cavalryman: 'Ky Binh.'" Armor, LXXVII (Sept.-Oct. 1968), 44-47. A look at ARVN airmobile activities.

469 Burnett, Leo. "The Chinook Story." U. S. Army Aviation Digest, VIII (Aug. 1972), 8-14. A review of CH-47 helicopter operations, including those in South Vietnam.

Burnison, George E., jt. author see Baird, John R.

Burroughs, Larry, jt. author see Flaherty, Thomas

470 Burroughs, Leonard H. "Chinook Deployability." U. S. Army Aviation Digest, XI (April 1965), 12-15. Uses for the big CH-47A in Southeast Asia.

471 Burton, Paul. "The 'Red Ball Express' Sprouts Wings." United Aircraft Quarterly Bee Hive, XLI (Spring 1966), 2-7. A look at aerial logistics and evacuation of casualties in, to, and from South Vietnam.

472 "The Busiest Bombing Month." Time, XC (September 8, 1967), 19-20. Increased air raids North and South of the DMZ.

473 Butera, J. L. "Rescue Concepts: Before and After." Aerospace Historian, XXI (March 1974), 8-11. An examination of aerospace search and recovery procedures.

474 Butterworth, W. E. The Flying Army: The Modern Air Arm of the U. S. Army. Garden City, N. Y.: Doubleday, 1974.

A look at the many kinds of helicopters and light planes employed, with some comments on their use in Southeast Asia.

475 Buttinger, Joseph. Vietnam: A Dragon Embattled. 2 vols. New York: Praeger, 1967. An historical survey with some material relative to the air war to be found in the second volume.

476 Butz, J. S., Jr. "Air Power in Vietnam: The High Price of Restraint." Air Force and Space Digest, XLIX (Nov. 1966), 40-44. Operations and the bombing pauses and target limitations.

477 ______. "Close Air Support in Vietnam." Air Force and Space Digest, LXIX (April 1966), 34-36. During the December 1965 U. S. Marine Corps and ARVN counterattack south of Da Nang known as "Operation Harvest Moon."

478 ______. "F-105's in Vietnam: New Lustre for a Tarnished Image." Air Force and Space Digest, LXIX (Oct. 1966), 37-43. Condemned as unsuitable for certain operations, the Thunderchief quickly became the premier Air Force fighter bomber.

479 ______. "Forward Air Controllers in Vietnam: They Call the Shots." Air Force and Space Digest, XLIX (May 1966), 60-66. This look at the FAC's was reprinted in Air Force and Space Digest International, II (July 1966), 22-27.

480 ______. "How the USAF Is Putting Computers to Work." Air Force and Space Digest, LIII (Feb. 1970), 44-47. Target selection and assistance.

481 ______. "Intratheater Airlift in Vietnam: A Question of Quantity and Control." Air Force and Space Digest, XLIX (July 1966), 36-40. Sees some problems in tactical airlift.

482 ______. "Our Pilots Call Hanoi 'Dodge City.'" Air Force and Space Digest, XLIX (Dec. 1966), 28-33. Air defenses and combat with North Vietnamese MIG's.

483 ______. "The Realities of the American [Air] Effort in Vietnam." Air Force and Space Digest, XLIX (Sept. 1966), 62-68. How effective?

484 ______. "Tactical Air Power in 1965: The Trial by Fire." Air Force and Space Digest, XLIX (March 1966), 35-38+. This examination was reprinted in Air Force and Space Digest International, II (Aug. 1966), 12-14+.

485 ______. "Taking the Night Away from the Viet Cong." Air Force and Space Digest, XLIX (June 1966), 40-51. Flares and the introduction of the AC-47 gunship.

486 ______. "The Test of Fighter Aircraft." Air Force and Space Digest, XLVIII (Feb. 1965), 26-31. Under combat conditions in Vietnam.

487 ______. "Those Bombings in North Vietnam." Air Force and Space Digest, XLIX (March 1966), 42-46+. An analysis reprinted in Air Force and Space Digest International, II (Aug. 1966), 22-24+.

488 Byerley, B. E. "Towards Improved Direct Fire Support." U. S. Army Aviation Digest, XIV (April 1968), 20-24. Helicopter gunship support of ground troops.

489 Byerley, Sam J. "A Concept for Directing Combat Air Operations." Air University Review, XXI (March-April 1970), 10-19. The Tactical Air Control system as employed in Vietnam.

490 CBS News. Face the Nation: The Collected Transcripts from the CBS Radio and Television Broadcasts, 1954-1976. 19 vols. Metuchen, N. J.: Scarecrow Press, 1970-1977.

491 "C-47 Becomes Attack Aircraft." Air Force Times, XXVI (Dec. 8, 1965), 4. On its conversion into the AC-47 gunship.

492 "The [CH-47] Chinook in Vietnam." Transportation Proceedings, II (Jan. 1968), 11-13+. U. S. Army use of the giant helicopter.

493 "CH-37 Recovers Downed UH-1B While Under Fire in South Vietnam." Aviation Week and Space Technology, LXXXII (Feb. 1, 1965), 78-81. How one Army helicopter pilot saved another.

494 "C-141, F-5 Tested in Combat Roles." Air Force Times, XXVI (Feb. 23, 1966), M10. A cargo plane and a fighter flown over Vietnam.

495 "C-130 Hercules: Lockheed's Aerial Workhorse." Aerospace Historian, XXIV (Sept. 1977), 158-162. A pictorial.

496 "C-123K Slated for Vietnam." Air Force Times, XXVII (April 26, 1967), 19. Sending a tactical airlift cargo plane.

497 "C-123's Defoliate Jungle Stronghold of the Viet Cong: Illustrations." Aviation Week and Space Technology, LXXXVI (May 8, 1967), 82-85. "Operation Ranch Hand."

498 "C-123's Put to the Test in Siege of Khe Sanh." Air Force Times, XXVIII (June 12, 1968), 15. Delivering supplies to the surrounded Marines.

499 Cagle, Malcolm W. "The 'Hanoi Hilton' Heroes." Navy, XIV

(June 1971), 13-16. A discussion on U.S. Navy prisoners-of-war.

500 ______. The Naval Aviation Guide, 2d ed. Annapolis, Md.: United States Naval Institute, 1969. 401p.

501 ______. ______, 3d ed. Annapolis, Md.: United States Naval Institute, 1976. 476p. Useful for background information on Navy flying.

502 ______. "Task Force 77 in Action Off Vietnam." In Frank Uhlig, Jr., ed. The Naval Review, 1972. Annapolis, Md.: United States Naval Institute, 1972. p. 66-109. The most useful summary of U.S. Navy carrier operations available to the date of this compilation.

503 Caiden, Martin. The Long Arm of America: The Story of the Mighty [C-130] Hercules Air Assault Transport and Our Revolutionary Global Strike Forces. New York: E. P. Dutton, 1963. 369p. Valuable background information written at the time of the American advisory role in South Vietnam.

504 "Calculated Deception: The Administration's Reasons for Heavy Bombings in the North." Nation, CCXIV (Jan. 17, 1972), 66-67. Providing cover for U.S. troop withdrawals.

505 "Cam Rahn Bay." Air Force Times, XXVIII (March 13, 1968), 18-19. Provides a look at the large U.S. air facility there.

506 "Cambodia: Bombs Then and Now." National Review, XXV (April 17, 1973), 881. "Open" vs. "secret" bombing.

507 "Cambodia: Caught in a Crossfire." Newsweek, LXXV (May 4, 1970), 22-25. The Allied invasion.

508 "Cambodia Doubles Work: Getting Planes to Targets." Air Force Times, XXX (May 20, 1970), 15. Aerial problems of the Allied incursion.

509 "Cambodia: Growing Debacle." Nation, CCXII (Feb. 1, 1972), 130-131. Communist successes and U.S. air operations.

510 "Cambodia Operation Assessed." Air Force Times, XXX (May 13, 1970), 1+. The capture or destruction of Communist sanctuaries.

511 "Cambodia: The Perils of Moving In." Life, LXVIII (May 8, 1970), 36-39. Some thoughts on air operations included.

512 "Cambodia: To Bomb or Not to Bomb." Newsweek, LXXXI (May 21, 1973), 37. The "secret" American air support of non-Communist positions.

513 "Cambodia: Will It Fall if Air Strikes End?" U. S. News and World Report, LXXIV (May 28, 1973), 82. The central question surrounding the "secret" bombings.

514 "Cambodian Coverup." New Republic, CLXVIII (May 19, 1973), 9-10. U. S. air operations in support of the Lon Nol government.

515 "Cameras Record Air Force and Navy Strikes on North Vietnamese Oil Areas." Aviation Week and Space Technology, LXXXV (July 18, 1966), 80-81. Pictures of the results.

516 Cameron, James. Here Is Your Enemy. New York: Holt, 1966. 144p. A British journalist remembers his December 1965 visit to North Vietnam and describes, among other things, the reactions to and defenses against American bombers. The countryside was deserted by day, but was becoming a graveyard for U. S. warplanes.

Camp, R. O., jt. author see Davis, Raymond

517 Campbell, Bruce B. "A New Look for Army Aviation." U. S. Army Aviation Digest, XV (Aug. 1969), 32-35. Helicopter gunships and troop carriers.

518 Campbell, Herbert G. "The Protective Aircraft Shelter." Air Force Civil Engineer, X (May 1969), 2-5. Its purpose and construction.

519 Campbell, Raymond P., Jr. "Helicopter Gunnery Training in Vietnam." U. S. Army Aviation Digest, XIII (May 1967), 4-5. Practice runs before actual combat.

520 "Can Choppers be Vietnamized?" Newsweek, LXXVII (March 15, 1971), 41. Questions whether the South Vietnamese can take over the mechanical maintenance requirements of the whirlybirds.

521 Candlin, A. H. S. "The Spring Offensive in Vietnam." Army Quarterly, CII (July 1972), 411-418. A look at the North Vietnamese Easter invasion.

522 "The Cap Chao Bombings." Naval Aviation News, (January 1967), 25. By warbirds from the U. S. carrier Coral Sea.

523 "[Capt. Charles B.] De Bellevue Bags [his] Fifth MIG." Air Force Times, XXXIII (Sept. 27, 1972), 15. In combat on September 9, 1972.

524 "[Capt. Jeff] Feinstein's Fifth MIG Gives the Air Force Three Aces." Air Force Times, XXXIII (Nov. 1, 1972), 51.

525 Cardosi, Richard. "When the Sergeant Says--Listen!" Navi-

gator, XXI (June 1974), 11-12. U. S. Air Force search and rescue operations in Southeast Asia.

526 Carey, Gordon T. "Air Mission Commander (and a Little Luck)." U. S. Army Aviation Digest, XIII (Aug. 1967), 28-30. Each airmobile operation had such a commander and this piece tells us what his duties and responsibilities were.

527 Cargo, Marcello, Jr. "The Mission: Air Evacuation in Southeast Asia." Air Force Times, XXXI (Dec. 16, 1970), 22. Taking out the wounded.

528 "Caribous Perform Massive Airlift: C-7A's Excel in Landing on Primitive Airstrips." Air Force Times, XXVII (June 14, 1967), 18. The most memorable feature of this DeHavilland Canada transport was its ability to get in and out of tight fields.

529 Carll, Frederick J. "'They Wouldn't Believe Me: I Flew More than 800 Hours OH-13S Time on Armed Reconnaissance Missions.'" U. S. Army Aviation Digest, XIV (Feb. 1968), 14-19. How the author performed this feat in a "Sioux" over South Vietnam.

530 Carmen, Jonathan. "The OV-10: A Versatile Battlefield Aircraft." Army, XVI (Nov. 1966), 16+. The Bronco was employed by both the Army and Air Force in the closing stages of the war.

531 Carmichael, Robert B. "Operation New Life." Infantry, LVII (Jan.-Feb. 1967), 43-47. The November 21, 1965, helicopter assault by the U. S. 173rd Airborne Brigade on a dirt airstrip 40 miles east of Bien Hoa was well supported by Air Force C-130 transports in the days which followed.

532 Carr, Richard E. "So You're Going to Guam." Navigator, XVII (Spring-Summer 1970), 32-33. B-52's in "Arc Light" operations.

533 Carr, William K. "The Faceless POW." Naval War College Review, XXX (Fall 1977), 88-96. A vicarious study of the Vietnam situation with comment by U. S. Air Force Col. Jon A. Reynolds, a former prisoner-of-war.

534 "Carriers Launch Strikes Against North Vietnam." Aviation Week and Space Technology, LXXXVI (Feb. 27, 1967), 50-53. A photographic summary.

535 Carrigan, Larry E. "It May Be a Long Walk." TAC Attack, XVII (Aug. 1977), 4-8. The difficulties of being shot down and problems to be expected if search and rescue aircraft are delayed.

536 Carroll, John S. "Report." Atlantic Monthly, CCXXII (Oct. 1968), 4+. A review of the battle of Khe Sanh.

537 Carson, Donald. "Flying the 'Thud.'" Air Force Magazine, LVII (April 1974), 18-23. A pilot's report on the F-105 Thunderchief.

538 ______. "Vampires, Take It Down." Airman, XVII (May 1973), 42-47. The reliance of U.S. Air Force fighter pilots on the electronically equipped EB-66's and the "Wild Weasel" F-100's and F-105's to warn them of radar emissions from North Vietnamese "Fan Song" equipment which signalled that they were being tracked or that a SAM firing was iminent. A look at the electronic counter-measures war in the North.

539 Carter, Walter. "Air Power Confronted." Hawk, XXVI (1964), 12-20. Close air support over South Vietnam.

540 "Case History: A Trainer at War." Air Force Times, XXVIII (Jan. 31, 1968), A37. South Vietnamese use of the T-28.

541 Casey, William B. "The AC-119: The USAF's 'Flying Battleship.'" Air Force and Space Digest, LIII (Feb. 1970), 48-50. The transport's conversion to a gunship.

542 Castan, Stephen. "The Navy War in Vietnam: An Assault from the USS Coral Sea." Look, XXIX (Nov. 30, 1965), 28-31. Nicely illustrated look at a routine air mission from a carrier on "Yankee Station."

543 "Casualties in the Vietnam War from January 1, 1961-January 13, 1968." Air Force Times, XXVIII (Jan. 31, 1968), 6. A table.

544 Catton, Jack J. "The Air Force Today and Tomorrow." Air Force Policy Letter for Commanders, no. 8 (Aug. 1967), 16-22. Reprint of the general's June 22, 1967, address to the National Space Club with comments on the Vietnam air war.

545 ______. "Electronic Warfare in the Air Force." Air Force Policy Letter for Commanders, no. 11 (Nov. 1967), 26-29.

546 ______. "Military Airlift in Southeast Asia." Air Force Magazine, LV (Oct. 1972), 47-49. An interview with the U.S. Air Force general on the topic.

547 "Cavalry Charge to Khe Sanh by Road and Chopper." Life, LXIV (April 19, 1968), 82-84. Relieving the siege.

548 "Cease-Fire Sparks Major USAF Airlift." Aviation Week and Space Technology, XCVIII (Feb. 5, 1973), 28-29. Removing U.S. forces from South Vietnam.

549 "Celebration of Men Redeemed." Time, CI (Feb. 19, 1973), 12-18. "Operation Homecoming," the return of U.S. POW's to America.

550 "Center Co-ordinates Tactical Air Power." Air Force Times, XXX (June 24, 1970), 16. The Direct Air Support Center at Pleiku air base.

551 "The Cessna A-37." Air Progress, XXIII (Dec. 1967), 36-37+. A COIN aircraft employed in Vietnam.

552 "Cessna's YAT-37D Is Tailored to the COIN Role." American Aviation, XXIX (Nov. 1965), 149-152. Details on the A-37 counterinsurgency aircraft.

553 Chaffe, John H. "POW Treatment: Principles vs. Propaganda." U.S. Naval Institute Proceedings, XCVII (July 1971), 14-17. Addressing the question of POW survival in North Vietnam.

554 Chaliand, Gerard. "The Bombing of Dai Lai." Liberation, XII (Dec.-Jan. 1967/68), 67-69. Critical of an American assault.

555 Chamberlain, Edwin W., Jr. "The Assault at Ap Bac." Army, XVIII (Aug. 1968), 50-57. The January 2, 1963, defeat of the heliborne ARVN 7th Division despite air support and U.S. advisors.

556 Champion, Jasper K. "Medevac: Chinook Style." U.S. Army Aviation Digest, XIV (June 1968), 10-13. Casualty removal by CH-47.

557 "Chances of the Game: Unintended Targets." Newsweek, LXVIII (Sept. 5, 1966), 29. The problem of mistaken identities and bomb spillage.

558 Chandler, Frank R. "The Unsung Canberras." Airman, XI (Dec. 1967), 12-15. Activities of RAAF No. 2 Squadron.

559 "Change of Weather: Operation Rolling Thunder." Time, XC (Dec. 29, 1967), 23. "Rolling Thunder" was the overall code-name applied to the U.S. Air Force tactical fighter bomber assaults on North Vietnam.

560 Chapelle, Dicky. "Helicopter War in South Vietnam." National Geographic, CXXII (Nov. 1962), 723-754. The famous woman correspondent's account is well illustrated by photographs and constitutes one of the best available reports on the helicopter role during the American advisory period.

561 Chapman, Andrew J. "The Employment of Tactical Air Power in COIN Operations." Air University Review, XV (March-

April 1964), 55-61. A theory for close air support in counterinsurgency fighting.

562 Chapman, Roy M. "Tactical Airlift Management in Vietnam." Signal, XXIV (Aug. 1970), 35-37. Communications aspects.

563 Chapman, William C. "The Air War in Southeast Asia." U.S. Naval Institute Proceedings, XCVIII (July 1972), 100-101. A brief review.

564 "Charges Dropped Against [Major General John] Lavelle" Air Force Times, XXXIII (Nov. 8, 1972), 3. The general was relieved and brought up on charges for authorizing air strikes beyond his power or responsibility; the incident was a major scandal for the Air Force.

565 Charlton, Richard G. "Vietnam Report." Ordnance, LI (Jan.-Feb. 1967), 376-381. A look at technological aspects of the war, especially as they affect American firepower capability.

566 "Charting the Aircraft Losses." Journal of the Armed Forces, CV (June 15, 1968), 4-5+. How losses were incurred.

567 Cheatham, Thomas P., Jr. "Tactical Air Power: An Intimate Blend of Men and Machines." Air Force and Space Digest International, I (Dec. 1965), 17-18. An examination of the U.S. TAC.

568 Cherne, Milton P. "Game Old Dame." U.S. Army Aviation Digest, XI (Jan. 1965), 19. The CH-1 helicopter.

569 ______. "A Page in History." U.S. Army Aviation Digest, IX (May 1963), 16-18. On the first U.S. Army helicopter unit in Vietnam.

570 Chesley, Larry. Seven Years in Hanoi: A POW Tells His Story. Salt Lake City, Utah: Bookcraft, 1973. 158p. Reminiscences of a U.S. airman downed over North Vietnam in 1966.

571 "Chinooks Permit Rapid Deployment of Artillery Units." Aviation Week and Space Technology, LXXXV (July 25, 1966), 90-91. How Army CH-47's transported guns about South Vietnam.

572 Chin-Pa. "Defeating the U.S. Flying Bandits." China Reconstructs (Peking), XV (Feb. 1966), 32-35. A Chinese Communist view of the air war over Vietnam.

573 Chodes, John J. The Myth of America's Military Power. New York: Brandon House, 1973. 224p. Includes an impressive attack on the idea of air power as employed over Southeast Asia.

574 "The Choice of COIN's." Flying Review International, XX (June 1965), 31+. An examination of various trial counter-insurgency aircraft.

575 "Chopper Pilot Wins Medal of Honor." Air Force Times, XXVIII (May 29, 1968), 5. Capt. Gerald O. Young of the air/rescue service.

576 "Choppers Carry Out Counterinsurgency." Air Force Times, XXVII (Jan. 18, 1967), 19. The role of the helicopter in Vietnam.

577 Christaldi, S. J. "'Crown': The Air Rescue Command Post." Air Force Times, XXVIII (May 29, 1968), 14. Sending help upon call.

578 Christy, Douglas. "The Magpies Always Score." Airman, XIV (June 1970), 44-45. The Canberras of RAAF No. 2 Squadron.

579 "Chronology: A Generation of Conflict." Time, C (Nov. 6, 1972), 28-29. Includes a few Vietnam "air dates."

580 "Chronology of Key Seventh Fleet Actions." Navy, IX (Aug. 1966) 60-61. A look at U.S. Naval actions off Vietnam, including air, from the 1964 Gulf of Tonkin incident through May 29, 1966.

581 "Chu Lai." Naval Aviation News, (Sept. 1965), 10-12. Its use as an air base.

582 "Civilians Weren't the Target, but ...: U.S. Air Raids in North Vietnam." U.S. News and World Report, LXIX (Jan. 9, 1967), 17-18. Hitting civilian targets.

583 Clapp, Archie J. "Shu-Fly Diary." U.S. Naval Institute Proceedings, LXXXIX (Oct. 1963), 42-53. U.S. Marine Corps helicopter operations in South Vietnam during the advisory period.

584 Clapp, Frederick L. "A New Kind of War." U.S. Army Aviation Digest, XI (July 1965), 12-19. The use of helicopters in South Vietnam.

585 ______. "Test of a Tactic." Army, XVI (April 1966), 57-60. Airmobile operations of the 1st Air Cavalry Division in South Vietnam.

586 Clark, Kenneth B. "Sledgehammers and Flyswatters: The Air War in Vietnam." Hawk, XXVIII (1966), 20-30. A review of the use of B-52's and FAC's.

587 Clark, L. G. "Seizing the Initiative in Counter-Guerrilla

Operations." Military Review, LXIII (Dec. 1963), 87-96. An Australian Army officer tells how aircraft, helicopters, paratroops, and paradrops could be effectively used against insurgents in South Vietnam.

588 Clarke, P. C. "The Battle that Saved Saigon: An Loc." Reader's Digest, CII (March 1973), 151-156. With comments on Huey Cobra attacks on North Vietnamese tanks.

589 Clelland, Donald. "Air Interdiction: Its Changing Conditions." Air Force and Space Digest, LII (June 1969), 52-56. North Vietnamese air defenses vs. U. S. electronic counter-measures and night operations.

590 Clifford, Clark M. "A Vietnam Reappraisal." Foreign Affairs, XLVII (July 1969), 601-622. Wholly political, but important as Clifford had an overwhelming impact on the formation of President Johnson's last bombing decisions.

591 Clifton, Thomas. "Alice-in-Wonderland East." Newsweek, LXXXII (Aug. 13, 1973), 29-30. Cambodia and the end of American air operations there.

592 Coburn, Judith. "Cambodia: War at the End of the Tunnel." Ramparts, XII (July 1973), 40-44. Very critical of American air operations there.

593 Coburn, R. F. "Carriers Feel the Pinch of War Airlift Needs." Aviation Week and Space Technology, LXXXVIII (Feb. 26, 1968), 30. Naval logistics.

Cochran, James A., jt. author see Miller, Roger J.

594 "Code Names." Naval Aviation News, (Feb. 1968), 12. How they were applied to various operations.

595 Cohen, R. J. "Helicopters: Panacea or Pipe Dream?" Army Quarterly, CIII (July 1973), 429-439. The 1972 George Knight Clowes Memorial Prize Essay examines the whirlybird role in future operations based on those conducted in Southeast Asia in the past.

596 Coker, George T. "POW." U. S. Naval Institute Proceedings, C (Oct. 1974), 41-46. Reminiscences of a U. S. Navy pilot downed and held in North Vietnam.

597 Colby, Carroll B. Jets of the World: New Fighters, Bombers, and Transports, rev. ed. New York: Coward-McCann, 1966. 48p. An illustrated guidebook; includes many jets in use over Southeast Asia.

598 Cole, David K. "Against All Odds." Airman, XV (May 1971), 24-29. How A1C Joel E. Talley earned the Air Force Cross for a daring rescue mission.

599 ______. "Agony of an Airlifter." Airman, XVII (Jan. 1973), 44-47. How T/S Charlie Shaub won the Air Force Cross for his daring during a Vietnam tactical airlift mission.

600 ______. "Another Monday Morning." Airman, XVI (Sept. 1972), 44-47. Looks at crew chiefs at U-Tapeo air base, Thailand.

601 ______. "The Connies of College Eye." Airman, XVII (March 1973), 4-7. The EC-121 electronic counter-measures task force in Southeast Asia.

602 ______. "Matron of the Lumbering Loads." Airman, XVI (April 1972), 43-44. The C-124 cargo plane.

603 ______. "Sierra Hotel." Airman, XVI (Nov. 1972), 2-5. A look at aces Capts. Steve Ritchie and Charles DeBellevue.

604 ______. "Time of the Tigers." Airman, XVI (Oct. 1972), 6-10. KC-135 Stratotanker refueling missions over Southeast Asia.

605 ______. "A Time to Teach, a Time to Learn." Airman, XVI (Aug. 1972), 2-7. U.S. Air Force advisors to the VNAF.

606 ______. "War Paint on a Hornet Bird." Airman, XV (Sept. 1971), 3-8. Looks at the new A-7D Corsair II.

607 Cole, J. L. "An Old Airplane in a New War." Aerospace Historian, XVIII (June 1971), 71-74. The C-47 in Vietnam.

608 Colebrook, Joan. "Prisoners-of-War." Commentary, LVII (Jan. 1974), 30-37. Looks at their treatment and release.

609 Coleman, J. D. "Saturation Patrolling." Army, XVII (Dec. 1967), 54-57. The airborne aspects of "Operation Henry Clay," July 3-27, 1966.

610 ______, ed. 1st Air Cavalry Division, Memories of the First Team, Vietnam, August 1965-December 1969. Tokyo: Dai Nippon, 1970. 296p.

611 Collier, Basil. A History of Air Power. New York: Macmillan, 1974. 358p. Includes a little information on the SEA air war.

612 Collier's Encyclopedia Yearbook. New York: Crowell-Collier-Macmillan, 1961-1973. Like the Americana and Britannica yearbooks, these also look at the Southeast Asia war in annual fashion.

Collinge, G. B., jt. author see Underwood, John W.

613 Collins, David C. "Doctrine Development for the Employment

of Tactical Air Forces." Air University Review, XIX (Nov.-Dec. 1967), 44-49. Theories of warfare based on experiences, some gained in Southeast Asia.

614 Collins, George J. "Marine Corps Aviation Today." In Frank Uhlig, Jr., ed. The Naval Review, 1965 (Annapolis, Md.: United States Naval Institute, 1965), p200-221. Includes some information on U.S. Marine Corps planes in Vietnam.

Collins, James L., jt. author see Larsen, Stanley R.

615 Collins, P. E. "Anti-Tank Helicopters." Journal of the Royal United Service Institution, CXIX (June 1974), 45-48. Mentions the Huey Cobras vs. North Vietnamese tanks at An Loc in 1972.

616 "Colonel [William A. James, 3rd] Awarded Medal of Honor." Air Force Times, XXXI (Aug. 19, 1970), 5. For his heroic actions while flying an A-1H Skyraider against enemy positions northwest of Dong Hoi, North Vietnam, in support of a rescue mission on September 1, 1968.

617 "Combat Art." Naval Aviation News, (Feb. 1968), 14-15. Shows a couple of scenes of Naval aviation on "Yankee Station."

618 "Combat Cruise of the USS Kearsarge." Naval Aviation News, (July 1967), 20. An American carrier off Vietnam.

619 "Combat Photographs Click Solidly--And Here's How They Do It." Air Force Times, XXIX (May 21, 1969), 16-17. A look at reconnaissance cameras and those attached to aircraft guns.

620 "Combat Pilots Haven't Time to Worry About Ground Fire." Air Force Times, XXVI (Nov. 24, 1965), 15. Too busy just delivering their ordnance.

621 "Commandos the First Air Force Unit to Get Navy Plane." Air Force Times, XXIV (Jan. 8, 1964), 25. The A-1E Skyraider.

622 Committee of Concerned Asian Scholars. The Indochina Story: A Fully Documented Account (New York: Praeger, 1971), 347p. The analysis is designed to show how U.S. policy and warfare methods, including air, continue to legacy of foreign exploitation begun by the French.

623 "Complete Air Support Given [Operation] Paul Revere." Air Force Times, XXVII (Sept. 28, 1966), 22. Close air support given the ARVN-1st Air Cavalry airmobile ground operation in the summer of 1966.

624 Compton, Keith K. "A Job to Do." Combat Crew, XIX (July 1968), 2-3. Flying B-52's in "Arc Light" operations.

625 "Con Thien: The Hellish Place of Angels." Life, LXIII (Oct. 13, 1967), 42-43. North Vietnamese attacks on the place were beaten off, to a large extent through the use of American air power.

626 "The Concept of COIN." Flying Review International, XXI (Oct. 1965), 89+. The need for a heavily-armed slow-flying counterinsurgency aircraft.

627 Congressional Quarterly, Inc. Congress and the Nation, 1945-1972. 3 vols. Washington, 1965-1973. See especially the section "Foreign Policy" for information relative to the subject.

628 Connolly, T. F. "The Attack Aircraft Carrier Shows New Potency in Vietnam." Navy, X (Feb. 1967), 12-16+. The idea of having floating airfields close to trouble spots.

629 Constantio, George E. "Have Confidence in HSS." Marine Corps Gazette, LIII (Sept. 1969), 47-48. Helicopter Support Sections in U.S. Marine Corps logistics.

"The Constellation Off Vietnam" see "The [USS] Constellation ..."

630 "The Construction of the Air Base at Cam Ranh Bay." Air Force Policy Letter for Commanders, no. 11 (Nov. 1966), 31. Designed to inform airmen of its official existence.

631 Cook, John C., Jr. "The Attack Helicopter." U.S. Naval Institute Proceedings, XCVIII (Oct. 1972), 97-100. A look at the only such U.S. Navy unit in Vietnam from 1967-1972, Helicopter Attack (Light) Squadron 3 or HA(L)-3.

632 Cook, W. J. "First Mission: Capt. M. W. Burr's Crash and Survival." Newsweek, LXVI (Nov. 8, 1965), 44. Designed to show the difficulties airmen encountered.

633 Cooling, B. Franklin, 3d. "A History of U.S. Army Aviation." Aerospace Historian, XXI (June 1974), 102-109. Up to and through the Vietnam experience.

634 Cooper, Bryan, and John Batchelor. Fighter: A History of Fighter Aircraft (New York: Scribner's, 1974), 153p. Cooper takes credit for the text and Batchelor, the drawings and color illustrations.

635 Cooper, Chester L. The Lost Crusade: America in Vietnam (New York: Dodd, Mead, 1970), 559p. A valuable examination of U.S. policy-making and operations; includes an extensive bibliography.

636 "Co-operation: Vietnam Byword." Air Force Times, XXV (March 24, 1965), 5. Between the air arms of all of the U. S. and Vietnamese services.

637 "'Copter 'Ambulances' Improve Survival Rate." Journal of the Armed Forces, CIII (Dec. 11, 1965), 12. Helicopter medevac operations in South Vietnam.

638 "'Copter Loss in Combat Passes 175." Air Force Times, XXVI (Aug. 10, 1966), M12. There would be hundreds more in the next six years.

639 "'Copter Success Is Temporary, Air Force Officials Feel." Air Force Times, XXVI (Dec. 15, 1965), 19. The U. S. Air Force view of U. S. Army helicopter activities in Vietnam when the two services were still fighting over which would play which aerial role.

Cornell University Air War Study Group see Littauer, Raphael, ed.

640 Correll, John T. "MIG Sweep." Airman, XIX (April 1975), 34-37. A U. S. Air Force F-4 Phantom strike north of Hanoi in January 1967.

641 ______. "No Other Way." Airman, XIX (March 1975), 42-47. How U. S. Air Force OV-10 pilot Capt. Steven L. Bennett won the Medal of Honor for attacks on a North Vietnamese unit near Quang Tri City on June 29, 1972; his plane badly shot up and his observer's parachute shredded, Bennett ditched in the Gulf of Tonkin where the observer escaped but he did not.

642 "The Corsair [II's] Are Coming." Flying Review International, XXIII (Jan. 1968), 7-10. A look at the A-7 attack aircraft.

643 Corum, Delbert, et al. "The Tale of Two Bridges." In A. J. C. Lavelle, ed., USAF Southeast Asia Monograph Series (Washington: U. S. Government Printing Office, 1976), p1-96. Monograph #1; an undocumented look at the war-long U. S. Air Force assault(s) on the Paul Doumer and Thanh Hoa spans.

644 "Cost and Results in the Air War." U. S. News and World Report, LXI (Dec. 19, 1966), 55. Losses vs. gains.

645 "Cost Goes up Again: The Bombing of the Thai Nguyen Iron and Steel Complex." Time, LXXXIX (March 17, 1967), 30. U. S. Navy and Air Force jets disrupted but did not halt production during two days of strikes, March 10-11, 1967.

646 Cote, Jean, and Donald Grantham. "The Skyraider Bows Out and the Corsair II Enters Combat." U. S. Naval Institute

Proceedings, XCIV (July 1968), 79-95. A recapitulation of the Skyraider's accomplishments with a look to the Corsair's promise as a replacement.

647 Coughlin, William J. "Report from Vietnam." Missiles and Rockets, XVIII (March 28, 1966), 44-48+. A review of the air war to date of publication.

648 "Countdown in Cambodia." Newsweek, LXXXII (July 16, 1973), 34-35. To the end of American aerial involvement.

649 "Counterinsurgency (COIN) Aircraft." Interavia, XIX (Aug. 1964), 1119-1123. Examines the concept.

650 Cousins, Norman. "Of Bombs and Bruises: The Context in which Asians View the Bombing." Saturday Review of Literature, XLIX (Feb. 19, 1966), 34. Suggests the unhappiness of those on the receiving end of American bombs.

651 Cowan, Sidney C. "Ride a Slick Ship." U.S. Army Aviation Digest, XII (June 1966), 23-25. Helicopters and the U.S. 1st Cavalry Division in the 1965 Battle of the Ia Drang Valley.

652 Cowley, John. "Australian Military Operations in Vietnam." Journal of the Royal United Service Institution, CXIII (Nov. 1968), 58-59. A quick review.

653 Coyne, James P. "Rescue from the Gulf of Tonkin." Air Force and Space Digest, XLIX (July 1966), 41-45. How a U.S. Air Force pilot, forced to ditch, was promptly picked up.

654 Crabb, Merle L. "The Low Altitude SAM Threat." Marine Corps Gazette, LV (Feb. 1971), 48-49. Briefly sets forth the problem which, when coupled with antiaircraft artillery fire, was quite serious.

655 Crane, John. "100-Bullet-a-Second Machine Gun." Popular Science, CXC (April 1967), 86-87. The GE Mini-gun as employed aboard the AC-47 gunship.

656 "Craters Within Craters." Time LXXXVIII (Sept. 23, 1966), 31. Suggests this result after the fury of American bombing raids on North Vietnam subsides.

657 Creek, Raymond S. "Installation Security Is a No Front War." Armor, LXXVII (Sept.-Oct. 1968), 12-14. The problem of guarding airfields and other bases.

658 Croft, Alfred J. "Dateline: Vietnam." Marine Corps Gazette, XLVII (Oct. 1963), 18. Briefly chronicles an ARVN-U.S. Marine Corps heliborne assault in Quang Ngai Province.

659 Cross, Richard T. "The Loh-Fac Tactical Fighter Team." U. S. Army Aviation Digest, XVI (Nov. 1970), 24-26. Mixing Huey Cobras and Broncos and close air support aircraft over South Vietnam.

660 Crouch, Bud. "Roll Back the Curtain of the Night." Air Force and Space Digest, LIV (Jan. 1971), 36-38. On the use of night interdiction aircraft.

661 "'Crown' Goes to the Rescue." Air Force Times, XXVII (Feb. 15, 1967), 19. The HC-130 airborne command post in rescue operations.

662 Currier, Donald R. "Vietnam: The Right Place and the Right Time." Air University Review, XVII (July-Aug. 1966), 70-74. An early view of the political and military implications for the U. S. in the battle against nasty Communism.

663 "Curtain of Fire: North Vietnam." Time LXXXVII (April 29, 1966), 34. North Vietnamese defenses.

664 Curtin, R. H. "The Air Force Engineers' Problems in Southeast Asia." Air University Review, XVIII (Nov-Dec. 1966), 76-84. One of the few pieces on the problems in constructing air bases.

665 Cushman, Robert E. "The Vertical Assault: Its Present and Future." In Frank Uhlig, Jr. The Naval Review, 1964 (Annapolis, Md.: United States Naval Institute, 1964), p160-173. A U. S. Marine Corps examination of a concept then just coming into vogue in South Vietnam.

666 "DOD [Department of Defense] Admits Higher Air Losses." Aviation Week and Space Technology, (Feb. 20, 1967), 16. At a time when the situation was seen to be bright.

667 Dalby, Marion C. "Combat Hotline." Marine Corps Gazette, LIII (April 1969), 27-30. A look at helicopters in support of the 3d Marine Division's Task Force Delta's operations in 1968.

668 _____. "Operations in Vietnam." Journal of the Royal United Service Institution, CXI (Feb. 1966), 4-13. A study of U. S. Marine Corps ground and air operations during 1965; readers should also note Gen. Simmons' work (items 2233-2237).

669 _____. "Task Force Hotel's Inland Beachheads." Marine Corps Gazette, LIII (Jan. 1969), 35-38. The 1968 operations of the 3d Marine Division in Quang Tri Province whereby the leathernecks adopted amphibious techniques to helicopter operations.

670 Daley, Jerome R. "The AH-1G [Hueycobra] versus Enemy

Tanks at An Loc." Armor, LXXXI (July-Aug. 1972), 42-43. Reprinting of an address given before the U. S. Armor Association at Ft. Knox, Kentucky, on May 19, 1972.

671 Daly, Richard W. "By Hook or by Crook." Military Engineer, LXI (July-Aug. 1969), 257-265. Supply activities of the U. S. Army CH-47 Chinook helicopter in Vietnam.

672 Damron, Jerry. "Come Along on a B-52 Strike." Air Force Times, XXVII (June 21, 1967), 14. Gives some idea of what the "Arc Light" operations were like from the viewpoint of a Stratofortress crew.

673 "Da Nang." Air Force Times, XXVIII (May 8, 1968), 18. A look at the U. S. air installation there.

674 "Da Nang Security Boosted Against Viet Cong Raids." Aviation Week and Space Technology, LXXXII (March 1, 1965), 60-61. Following a serious enemy attack on the base.

675 Danby, Peter A., ed. United States Air Force Serials, 1946-1969 (Liverpool, Eng.: Merseyside Society of Aviation Enthusiasts, 1969), 71p. Examines the serial numbers of U. S. Air Force warbirds through the years, including those of our era.

676 ______. United States Navy Serials, 1941-1976, 3d ed. (Merseyside, Eng.: Merseyside Society of Aviation Enthusiasts, 1976), 100p. Does the same for the U. S. Navy as for the Air Force in the last entry.

677 "The Dangerous Air War Becomes Deadly." U. S. News and World Report, LXIII (Sept. 18, 1967), 41. More targets and more losses.

678 Darcourt, Pierre. "Buildings in Hanoi Crumble, Haiphong Is Ruined: An Interview." U. S. News and World Report, LXVII (Dec. 22, 1969), 39-40. A Frenchman's recollections of the results of American bombings in North Vietnam in the fall of 1969.

679 "Daring [Air] Raids in Vietnam: The Purpose of Nixon's Move." U. S. News and World Report, LXIX (Dec. 7, 1970), 22-23. Son Tay POW raid.

680 "Darkness Dies Screaming." Airman, XVI (Oct. 1972), 35-37. U. S. supply interdiction missions over the Ho Chi Minh trail.

681 Daum, John P. "Observation Techniques." U. S. Army Aviation Digest, XV (Jan. 1969), 24-25. Tips for Army pilots.

682 David, Heather M. "Operation Rescue." (New York: Pinnacle

Books, 1971), 191p. The unsuccessful U. S. Army heliborne assault on the Son Tay POW camp in North Vietnam.

683 Davis, Clive E. The Book of Air Force Airplanes and Helicopters (New York: Dodd, Mead, 1967), 112p. An illustrated look at many used in Southeast Asia.

684 Davis, Dale. "Airborne Guns and Rockets." Ordnance, LVII (March-April 1973), 388-391. Types and uses.

685 Davis, Gordon M. "'Dewey Canyon': An All Weather Classic." Marine Corps Gazette, LIII (July 1969), 32-40. Examines a major U. S. Marine Corps air ground operation in the I Corps area.

686 Davis, Howard A. "Air Support to Army Units in Vietnam." Air Force Policy Letter for Commanders, no. 2 (Feb. 1966), 18-22. Text of a speech before the American Ordnance Association meeting at Philadelphia, January 13, 1966, on the 1st Air Cavalry Division.

687 Davis, Lou. "Shifting Tactics of Army Aviation." Flying, LXVIII (March 1961), 22-23+. The new emphasis on helicopters.

688 Davis, Raymond G. "Combined Operations with ARVN." Marine Corps Gazette, LIII (Oct. 1969), 18-29. With remarks on aerial support and airmobile aspects.

689 ______, and R. O. Camp. "Marines in Assault by Helicopter." Marine Corps Gazette, LII (Sept. 1968), 22-28. A review of U. S. Marine Corps airmobile operations in Vietnam to date.

690 Davison, Michael. "Freedom from the Tyranny of Terrain." Army, XV (Nov. 1965), 72-73+. As provided by the use of helicopters in Vietnam.

691 Day, George E. "Escape in Vietnam." Air Force Magazine, LIX (Sept. 1976), 84-86+. How the Medal of Honor winning airman escaped from his POW camp, only to be recaptured.

692 Day, William R. "Devarty Night Party." U. S. Army Aviation Digest, XIII (Nov. 1967), 22-25+. Night helicopter operations.

693 "Daylight at Midnight." Airman, XI (Feb. 1967), 28-31. U. S. Air Force flare-dropping aircraft and AC-47 gunships.

694 "Deadly Defense: The Air Defense System at Kep." Newsweek, LXVIII (Oct. 17, 1966), 40-41. A look at North Vietnamese ability to resist American air power through the use of antiaircraft and SAM's.

695 "Dear Senator: Letters from U. S. Fliers [with] Views about the Bombing in Indochina." New York Times Magazine, (June 18, 1973), 64. Comments adverse to air operations over Cambodia and Laos.

696 Deare, C. L., Jr. "Air??? Lift in Vietnam: The PACAF's 315th Air Division." Air Force and Space Digest, XLIX (Nov. 1966), 45-50. Examines the commands work and operations.

697 "Death Among the Rubber Trees: The Battle of Loc Ninh." Time, XC (Nov. 10, 1967), 36+. Includes information on close air support of this Communist attack on a ARVN-U. S. Army position in the III Corps area that month.

698 "Death by Starlight: U. S. Night Operations in Vietnam Carried Out by Teams of Helicopters." Time, XC (July 21, 1967), 38. Hitting Vietcong positions; compare with William R. Day's piece, item 692.

699 "Death in the Hills: Khe Sanh." Newsweek, LXIX (May 15, 1967), 42. Another look at the progress of the famous siege.

700 "Death of a MIG-21." Airman, XI (May 1967), 38-39. As reported by Col. Daniel "Chappie" James of the U. S. Air Force 8th Tactical Fighter Wing.

701 Deatrick, Eugene P., Jr. "The Role of Fighter-Type Aircraft in Limited War." Air Force Policy Letter for Commanders, no. 11, (Nov. 1967), 18-21. Close air support operations.

702 DeBerry, Drue L. "Vietnamese Air Force Technical Training, 1970-1971." Air University Review, XXIV (Jan. -Feb. 1973), 43-51. Details on the technical end of VNAF Vietnamization.

703 DeBorchgrave, Arnaud. "Cambodia: A Reporter's Diary." Newsweek, XV (June 15, 1970), 88-89. A look at the incursion, including close air support and airmobile aspects.

704 DeClairmont, Ralph G. "Bac Giang by Flak Light." Air Force Magazine, LIV (March 1971), 49-53. A night reconnaissance mission over an important North Vietnamese town.

705 Deen, Sisco. "How [Capt.] Steve Ritchie Got His Fifth MIG." Air Force Magazine, LV (Oct. 1972), 28-29. Details of an air-to-air combat.

706 DeGroote, Albert J. "Profile." Airman, XII (Feb. 1968), 28-31. A look at the U. S. Air Force 90th Tactical Fighter Squadron.

707 "The DeHavilland AC-1 Caribou." Aviation Week and Space Technology, LXXXIII (Jan. 23, 1961), 59-69. An extensive look at the U. S. Army transport noted for its ability to get into and out of tight airfield situations.

708 Deitchman, S. J. "The Implications of Modern Technological Developments for Tactical Air Tactics and Doctrine." Air University Review, XXIX (Nov.-Dec. 1977), 23-45. An important study with citations to the Southeast Asian air war.

709 Deken, George T. "Adaptable 'Birds' for Counterinsurgency." Tactical Air Warfare Center Quarterly Report, II (Sept. 1970), 12-21. A look at such aircraft as the OV-10 Bronco.

710 Delear, Frank J. Helicopters and Airplanes of the U. S. Army. (New York: Dodd, Mead, 1977), 96p. A nicely illustrated look at individual warbirds.

711 Delvey, Francis K. "Use All Fire Support Effectively." U. S. Army Aviation Digest, XIV (Nov. 1968), 24-29. Draws on Vietnam experience to suggest improvements.

712 "Demilitarizing the Zone: 'Operation Hickory.'" Time, LXXXIX (May 26, 1967), 24-25. U. S. Marine Corps operations near the DMZ.

713 Denno, Bryce F. "The Fate of American POW's in Vietnam." Air Force and Space Digest, LI (Feb. 1968), 40-45. One of the earliest reports on the topic.

714 ______. "The Viet Cong Defeat at Phuoc Chau." Marine Corps Gazette, XLIX (March 1965), 34-39. With comments concerning American air and ground aid in the November 2, 1962, encounter.

715 Denton, Jeremiah A., Jr., and Edward Brandt. When Hell Was in Session (New York: Reader's Digest Press, 1976), 246p. A close look at the American POW experience.

716 Derrick, Thales A. "The 'Fighting Crusaders' Log 2,000 Hours of Combat." Air Force Times, XXVI (Sept. 29, 1965), 15. The U. S. Air Force 481st Tactical Fighter Squadron.

717 DeSandro, John. "Skyraider Squadron." Air Force Times, XXVII (Nov. 2, 1966), 26. The 1st Air Commando Squadron.

718 "Design for the Air Force Medal of Honor." Air Force and Space Digest, XLVI (Dec. 1963), 27. A look at the new medal.

719 "Destroying the Haven: 'Operation Junction City.'" Time,

LXXXIX (March 3, 1967), 30. A report on the ground and airmobile aspects of the big ARVN-U. S. Army operation in War Zone C.

720 "The Destruction of Indochina." Humanist, XXXI (Jan.-Feb. 1971), 14-17. Concerns the dropping of herbicides; based on a study done by the Stanford University Biology Study Group.

721 "Developed for Vietnam." Interavia, XXII (March 1967), 287-288. New aircraft and operations.

722 "Developments in U. S. Military Reconnaissance." Interavia, XXVII (April 1972), 373-375. Examines many aspects born of the Vietnam War.

723 DeVoss, Daniel. "Air War: To See Is to Destroy." Time, XCIX (April 17, 1972), 39-40. A look at close air support and the war on Communist supply lines.

724 Dewey, Arthur E. "Thrust Into the Vitals of Zone D." Army, XIV (Feb. 1964), 46-49. How Engineers and the Army Aviation team constructed an airfield at Rang Rang, South Vietnam.

725 ______. "We Support." U. S. Army Aviation Digest, IX (May 1963), 12-15. The U. S. Army 1st Aviation Company in South Vietnam.

726 Dexter, George E. "Search and Destroy in Vietnam." Infantry, LVI (July-Aug. 1966), 36-42. How it was done; includes air and airmobile aspects.

727 Diamond, Stewart. "Interservice Effort Pays Off." Air Force Times, XXVI (Dec. 8, 1965), 16. Close air support.

728 Dickerman, Sherwood. "A Taste of What's to Come in the Ugly Delta War: The Song Than-Deckhouse V Operation." Reporter, XXXVI (Feb. 23, 1967), 37-39. Examines as well the air and airmobile aspects of these riverine operations in the area south of Saigon.

729 Dibble, John, Jr. "Airmobility Searches for Answers to Limited Warfare Puzzles." Data, IX (Dec. 1964), 13-15. The use of helicopters in troop movements in South Vietnam.

730 Dilger, Robert G. "One Hole to Two?" USAF Fighter Weapons Review, (Spring 1975), 13-22. Damage to fighters employed over Southeast Asia.

731 Dille, John. "Good 'Copters, but Bum Tactics: U. S. Helicopter Tactics in South Vietnam." Life, LVIII (April 16, 1965), 34D. A brief look at reasons for losses.

732 "Diminishing Heartland: Bombing Along the Red River." Time, LXXXIX (June 2, 1967), 23. U. S. Air Force and Navy air attacks on targets in that area.

733 "Dinh Tuong: Hell in a Small Place." Time, C (Sept. 11, 1972), 24. Examines the late summer 1972 fighting in that area, including air and airmobile aspects.

734 "Diplomacy by Terror: What the Bombing Did." Newsweek, LXXXI (Jan. 8, 1973), 10-12. The military and political effects of B-52 raids in "Operation Linebacker II."

735 Disosway, Gabriel P. "A Chat with TAC's Boss." Airman, X (April 1966), 12-15. An interview with the TAC chief about operations in Vietnam.

736 ______. "TAC: The Air Force Counterinsurgency Punch." Data, X (Dec. 1965), 29-32. The role of this U. S. Air Force command in Southeast Asia.

737 Disosway, W. C., Jr. "Tactical Airpower." Ordnance, XLVIII (July-Aug. 1963), 45-49. A look at its potential power in COIN operations.

738 Dittmer, Karl K. "Hunt with a 'Bird Dog.'" Aerospace Safety, XXII (June 1966), 14-15. FAC work with the O-1 observer plane.

739 "Division From the North: 'Operation Hastings.'" Time, LXXXVIII (July 29, 1966), 21. With comment on the air aspects of this I Corps operation.

740 Dobbs, Erwin. "And the Beep Goes On." USAF Tactical Air Warfare Center Review, IV (Spring 1973), 4-13. Air-dropped sensor technology in Southeast Asia.

741 Dodd, Daniel. "Navy Gunship Helicopters in the Mekong." U. S. Naval Institute Proceedings, XCIV (May 1968), 91-104. An excellent pictorial concerning operations in connection with riverine forces in the Delta area south of Saigon.

742 Doglione, John A., et al. "Airpower and the 1972 Spring Invasion." In A. J. C. Lavalle, ed., USAF Southeast Asia Monograph Series (Washington: U. S. Government Printing Office, 1976), vol. II, p1-113. Monograph # 3. An undocumented but careful study of the effects of American warplanes on the Communist Easter offensive.

743 "Doing Is Not Accomplishing: U. S. Bombing." America, CXXVIII (May 19, 1973), 455-456. U. S. air operations over Cambodia.

744 Dommen, Arthur. "Laos: The Year of the Ho Chi Minh

Trail." Asian Survey, XII (Feb. 1972), 138-147. American aerial efforts to cut off Communist troop movements and supplies in that area.

745 Donaldson, Charles W. "The Cavalry-Air Cavalry Team." Armor, LXXVIII (Sept.-Oct. 1969), 23-25. Combined helicopter and tank operations in South Vietnam.

746 Do-Ngoc-Nhan. "Initiative in the Vietnamese War." Military Review, LII (Aug. 1972), 77-86. South Vietnamese operations, including airmobile.

747 Donlon, Robert H. C., as told to Warren Rogers. Outpost of Freedom (New York: McGraw-Hill, 1965), 206p. U.S. Army Special Forces Capt. Donlon won the Congressional Medal of Honor for the defense of Camp Na Nam Dong, on the Vietnam/Laos border, in July 1964; his story contains some thoughts on helicopters and close air support and dismisses the American use of herbicides as so much "Commie" propaganda.

748 Donnelly, John. "Death Valley: A Battle in the Que Son Valley." Newsweek, LXXI (Jan. 29, 1968), 32-33. Examines ground and air operations in that region at the year's turn.

749 Donovan, James A. The A-1 [Skyraider] Aircraft in Southeast Asia. [Air War College Professional Study.] Maxwell Air Force Base, Ala.: Air University, 1970, 19p. A brief history of "SPAD" operations during our period.

750 ______. Militarism, USA (New York: Scribner's, 1970), 265p. Includes some information on the allotment of U.S. air sorties over North Vietnam per week.

751 Doty, Roland W., Jr., and Doris A. Krudner. "Control of Strike and Defense Forces." In Carl Berger, ed. The United States Air Force in Southeast Asia, 1961-1973 (Washington: U.S. Government Printing Office, 1977), p223-234. Examines radar and air controller systems.

752 "The Douglas A-4 Skyhawks." Naval Aviation News, (March 1968), 6-13. A close look at the U.S. Navy attack aircraft often flown over Southeast Asia from carriers on "Yankee Station."

753 "The Douglas AD-1 Skyraider." Naval Aviation News (April 1962), Sept. 1967, July 1968), 14-15, 10-11, 18-27. A U.S. Navy view of the prop-driven close air support aircraft employed on many occasions over South Vietnam.

754/5 "The Douglas B-66 Destroyer." Air Progress, XXIV (Oct. 1968), 46-48. The U.S. Air Force tactical bomber often employed to lead squadrons of fighter bombers into North Vietnam.

756 Dowd, John. "The Truest Sport: Jousting with Sam and Charlie." Esquire, LXXXIV (Oct. 1975), 156-159+. U.S. fighters and flighter bombers vs. North Vietnamese surface-to-air missiles and MIG's.

757 Drago, Alfred. "The High Price of Air Control." Marine Corps Gazette, XLVIII (March 1964), 30-31. Outlines and details the duties and problems of Marine aerial observers and FAC's.

758 "Dragonships Create Success Story: 20,000 Combat Missions." Air Force Times, XXIX (Dec. 25, 1968), 15. Hails the AC-47 gunship.

759 Drake, Francis V. "Let's Fight to Win in Vietnam: A Proposal to Bomb Military Targets in North Vietnam." Reader's Digest, XC (May 1967), 67-72. The author was a noted bombing advocate who had suggested intensive air action as early as World War II.

760 Drake, Katherine. "Our Flying Nightingales in Vietnam." Reader's Digest, XCI (Dec. 1967), 73-79. Women in the air forces, especially nurses.

761 Dramesi, John A. Code of Honor. New York: W. W. Norton, 1975. 271p. A former POW tells his story.

762 "Drawing the Noose?: The Battle of Khe Sanh." Newsweek, LXXI (Feb. 5, 1968), 39-40. Looks at the siege and U.S. attempts to resupply the Marines by air.

763 Drendel, Lou. The A-7 Corsair II in Action. Warren, Mich.: Squadron/Signal Publications, 1976. 50p. A well illustrated account with much on the plane's role over Southeast Asia.

764 _____. The A-6 Intruder in Action. Warren, Mich.: Squadron/Signal Publications, 1975. 50p. An illustrated account on the U.S. Navy attack warbird with much on the plane's role over Southeast Asia.

765 _____. The Air War in Vietnam. New York: Arco, 1969. 95p. A well-illustrated pro-air examination of the various U.S. air services to early 1968.

765a _____. Aircraft of the Vietnam War: A Pictorial Review. New York: Arco, 1971. 64p. Planes of all American services with notes on each.

766 _____. "... and Kill MIGs." Warren, Mich.: Squadron/Signal Publications, 1974. 63p. U.S. Air Force/Navy aerial combat over North Vietnam; highly illustrated. Includes a brief section on North Vietnamese MIG's.

767 _____. F-4 Phantom II in Action. Warren, Mich.: Squadron/Signal Publications, 1976. 50p. An illustrated look at the U.S. Air Force/Navy fighter, with much on its role over Southeast Asia.

768 _____. F-105 Thunderchief in Action. Warren, Mich.: Squadron/Signal Publications, 1974. 49p. An illustrated view of the U.S. Air Force fighter bomber with combat details limited exclusively to Southeast Asia.

769 _____. Gunslingers in Action. Warren, Mich.: Squadron/Signal Publications, 1974. 49p. An illustrated account of U.S. Army helicopters over Southeast Asia, especially such armed versions as the Huey Cobra.

770 _____. Phantom II: A Pictorial History of the McDonnell-Douglas Phantom II. Warren, Mich.: Squadron/Signal Publications, 1977. 62p. An expanded version of item 767.

771 _____. TAC: A Pictorial History of the USAF Tactical Air Forces, 1970-1977. Warren, Mich.: Squadron/Signal Publications, 1978. 64p. The opening section is useful for SEA interest.

772 Drenkowski, Dana. "The Tragedy of 'Operation Linebacker II.'" Journal of the Armed Forces, CXIV (July 1977), 24-27. Concludes that many U.S. POW's were killed in the Christmas 1972 B-52 bombings. For the U.S. Air Force response to this excerpt from a September 1976 issue of Soldier of Fortune magazine, see Journal of the Armed Forces, August 1977, p24-25 and Capt. H. E. Rutledge's article in item 2095.

773 Drew, Allan N. "Forward Air Control: Why? How? When? Where?" USAF Tactical Air Warfare Center Review, IV (Spring 1973), 18-21. With examples drawn from the Southeast Asian experience.

774 Duckworth, Walter L., Jr. "Dawn Reconnaissance." U.S. Army Aviation Digest, XV (April 1969), 32-35. Looking for a North Vietnamese Army battalion in South Vietnam.

775 Duehring, Craig W. "A Christmas Story." TAC Attack, XVI (Dec. 1976), 18-19. Air action over the Plain of Jars, December 1970.

776 "Duels in the Sun." Time, LXXXVII (May 6, 1966), 28. Aerial combat over North Vietnam.

777 Duncan, David D. "Inside the Cone of Fire: Con Thien." Life, LXIII (Oct. 27, 1967), 28D-42C. The noted photographer's pictures and account of air and ground operations.

778 _____. "Khe Sanh." Life, LXIV (Feb. 23, 1968), 20-28C. Pictures and impressions of the famous siege.

779 _____. War Without Heroes. New York: Harper & Row, 1970. 252p. A compilation of the noted photographer's Vietnam photographs, including air, with commentary.

780 Duncan, Donald. The New Legions. New York: Random House, 1967. 275p. A former Green Beret discusses his service in and views of the war in South Vietnam, including helicopter raids, with a scathing attack on the horrors caused by U.S. bombing attacks on villages. For a fictional pro-war early view of Special Forces and helicopters, see Robin Moore's The Green Berets (New York: Crown, 1965).

781 Duncan, Scott. "The Combat History of the F-105." Aerospace Historian, XXII (Sept. 1975), 121-128. The Thunderchief over Southeast Asia.

782 _____. "Rolling Thunder." Airman, XVIII (Oct. 1974), 24-28. A look at F-105 crews flying from Korat and Takhli, Thailand, on raids over North Vietnam in 1965-1968.

783 Dunn, Carroll H. Base Development in South Vietnam, 1965-1970. (Vietnam Studies series.) Washington: U.S. Army, Center of Military History, 1972. 164p. Army engineers in work on airfields and heliports.

784 DuPre, Flint. "Above and Beyond." Air Force and Space Digest, LI (March 1968), 42-44. The Medal of Honor to Major Merlyn H. Dethlefsen and posthumously to Capt. Hillard A. Wilbanks; includes a look at their feats.

785 _____. "Rescue at a Place Called Kham Duc." Air Force and Space Digest, LII (March 1969), 98-100. How Lt. Col. Joe M. Jackson won the Medal of Honor for a daring rescue of three men at a Special Forces camp with his C-123 on May 12, 1968.

786 Dupuy, R. Ernest, and Trevor N. Dupuy. The Encyclopedia of Military History, rev. ed. New York: Harper & Row, 1976. 1,488p. Provides useful coverage to the subject and its military background.

787 Dupuy, Trevor N., and Wendell Blanchard. The Almanac of World Military Power, 2d ed. New York: R. R. Bowker, 1972. 373p. First published in 1970, readers should consult the nations involved in the Southeast Asian fighting.

788 Durrenberger, William J. "New Teeth for Choppers in

Vietnam." Journal of the Armed Forces, CII (Aug. 28, 1965), 2+. Increasing the armament of the UH-1B.

789 Dvorin, Eugene P., ed. The Senate's War Powers: Debate on Cambodia from the Congressional Record. Chicago: Markham, 1971. 244pp. With particular emphasis on the incursion and bombing operations.

790 Dye, Harold A. "Close Fire Support." Military Review, XLVII (Sept. 1967), 36-43. Its value to infantry; includes close air support.

791 "ECM Stymies North Vietnamese Sam's." Aviation Week and Space Technology, XCVI (April 24, 1972), 14-15. Electronic counter-measures cause them to miss American aircraft.

792 "Each Mission Is Special." Airman, XI (Sept. 1967), 24-25. Differences in COIN aircraft fire support calls.

793 Eade, George J. "Air Power: Instrument of National Policy." Air Force Policy Letter for Commanders, no. 5 (May 1973), 24-31. Its use to further political goals, e.g., Cambodia and Laos.

794 ______. "Reflections on Air Power in the Vietnam War." Air University Review, XXV (Nov.-Dec. 1973), 2-9. A valuable summary.

795 ______. "The USAF Prepares for Future Contingencies: The Lessons of Vietnam." Air Force Magazine, LVI (June 1973), 34-40. A less-scholarly version of item 794.

796 "Eagle Flight: Bell UH-1B's Carry Vietnamese Troops to Attack Positions in the Mekong Delta." Aviation Week and Space Technology, LXXXII (Feb. 22, 1965), 50-51. ARVN vertical assaults on Vietcong hideouts south of Saigon.

797 "'Eagle Thrust': The Huge Airlift Sets a Mark for SEA." Air Force Times, XXVIII (Jan. 3, 1968), 14. Bringing men and equipment to South Vietnam.

798 Eaker, Ira C. "About Bombing North Vietnam." Air Force Times, XXXIII (Feb. 7, 1973), 13. Thoughts on "Operation Linebacker II." One of America's most famous airmen, Gen. Eaker commanded both the 8th Air Force and the Mediterranean Allied Air Forces during World War II. His AFT commentaries served the same purpose during the SEA war as did Adm. William V. Pratt's for Newsweek during the Second World War.

799 ______. "Actions in the North Deserve Support." Air Force

Times, XXXI (Dec. 16, 1970), 13. Aerial bombing and its domestic opposition.

800 ______. "The Bombing of the North Is Vital." Air Force Times, XXVII (Aug. 9, 1967), 13. To destroy North Vietnamese will and ability to fight.

801 ______. "Costs of the Vietnam War." Air Force Times, XXXIII (April 11, 1973), 13. In men, planes, treasure, and prestiege.

802 ______. "Curtailed Bombing Helps the North Strengthen Its Position." Air Force Times, XXVIII (June 5, 1968), 13. Argues that pauses allow time for rebuilding and building better antiaircraft defenses.

803 ______. "The F-111 in Southeast Asia." Air Force Times, XXXIII (May 2, 1973), 13. Its problems and successes.

804 ______. "'Jolly Green Giants' Earn Their Praise." Air Force Times, XXVIII (Jan. 24, 1968), 13. U.S. Air Force helicopter rescue operations.

805 ______. "Khe Sanh Outlived Its Need." Air Force Times, XXVIII (July 31, 1968), 13. On abandoning that base after the famous siege.

806 ______. "Limited War." Air Force Times, XXVIII (Nov. 29, 1967), 13. The strategy of such operations.

807 ______. "The Lost Vietnam War." Air Force Times, XXXIV (Sept. 5, 1973), 11. Thoughts on the closing of the conflict.

808 ______. "On Arming South Vietnam." Air Force Times, XXIX (Oct. 23, 1968), 2. Providing arms and training to the VNAF.

809 ______. "Reports from Vietnam Indicate Low Morale." Air Force Times, XXVIII (July 24, 1968), 13. The reports were true in many cases.

810 ______. "The Secret Bombing of Cambodia." Air Force Times, XXXIV (Aug. 22, 1973), 13. How it came to pass and how it ended.

811 ______. "South Vietnamese Fighters." Air Force Times, XXVIII (May 15, 1968), 13. A look at Vietnamese fighter pilots.

812 ______. "Tactics Changing in the Vietnam War." Air Force Times, XXX (June 17, 1970), 13. Increased use of electronic counter-measures.

813 _____. "Vietnam Approach Questioned." Air Force Times, XXVII (Feb. 1, 1967), 11. Dissent to the bombing campaign.

814 _____. "Where Did We Go Wrong?" Air Force Times, XXXV (May 7, 1975), 11-12. Thoughts on American failure in Southeast Asia.

815 _____. "Why the North Vietnamese Attack Failed." Air Force Times, XXXII (July 12, 1972), 13. Air power and the Easter invasion.

816 Eaton, Loren D. "Armed Chinooks." U.S. Army Aviation Digest, XII (July 1966), 26-29. This look at the use of CH-47A use was reprinted in Aerospace International, III (May 1967), 24-26.

817 Edney, Benney E. "The Air Cavalry Rides High." Armor, LXXVII (March-April 1968), 37-39. The use of helicopters by the 1st AirCav in South Vietnam.

817a Edwards, Charles H., Jr., ed. History of the 114th Assault Helicopter Company, 1 January-31 December 1967. Taipei, Taiwan: China Color Printers, 1968. 85p. Unit history of one Army whirlybird unit in South Vietnam.

818 Edwards, Edmund B. "Air Operations in Vietnam, II." Journal of the Royal United Service Institution, CXII (Feb. 1967), 26-31. For Part I, see P. W. Helmore, item 1156.

819 "Effects of the Bombing." Time, XCIX (June 26, 1972), 31. On North Vietnam.

820 "Efficient Thunder: The Bombing of Hanoi's Outskirts." Time, XCIX (May 12, 1967), 25. Fighter bomber attacks on airfields and industrial sites.

821 "Electronic Warfare Gains Key Vietnam Role." Aviation Week and Space Technology, LXXXVIII (Jan. 1, 1968), 48-49. Its use by air forces of the Allies, mostly American.

822 "Electronics Warfare." Naval Aviation News, (August 1971), 14. As employed by the U.S. Navy over Southeast Asia.

823 Eley, D. L. "The Role and Arming of Helicopters." Royal Air Force Quarterly, VII (Summer 1967), 100-107. As witnessed in South Vietnam.

824 Eliot, Bert. "A-37's Fly Last Sorties." Air Force Times, XXX (July 22, 1970), 16. Many of these Cessna COIN aircraft were turned over to the North Vietnamese Air Force.

825 Eliot, George F. "Vietnam: How the Ground War Is Fought." American Legion Magazine, LXXXII (May 1967), 14-18. With the aid of helicopters and close air support.

826 Elkins, Frank C. The Heart of a Man, ed. by Marilyn R. Elkins. New York: W. W. Norton, 1973. 139p. Diary of a U.S. Navy pilot stationed with Task Force 77 off Vietnam and downed on a bombing raid over North Vietnam in 1966.

827 Elling, Robert F. "Automation Improves Airlift." Tactical Airlift, I (April 1971), 12-13. Especially in Southeast Asia.

828 Elliott, J. M. "The Minigun's the Answer." Marine Corps Gazette, XLIX (April 1965), 55. A quick look at the rapid-fire aircraft cannon.

829 Elliott, James C. The Modern Army and Air National Guard. Princeton, N.J.: Van Nostrand, 1965. 178p. U.S. Air National Guardsmen flew many missions over Southeast Asia.

830 ______. "'Time Out' for a Bit of War." National Guardsman, XX (July 1966), 22-24. Tennessee air guardsmen haul cargo to South Vietnam.

831 Ellison, Robert. "The Agony of Khe Sanh." Newsweek, LXXI (March 18, 1969), 29-36. A newsman's look at the siege, including air aspects, with photographs.

832 Ellsberg, Daniel. "The Quagmire Myth and the Stalemate Machine." Public Policy, XIX (1971), 217-274. The author, who leaked the Pentagon Papers, suggests that U.S. leaders chose to escalate the war out of ideological commitments and fear of the short-term domestic repercussions of defeat. Useful background study for an understanding of American strategy.

833 Elsdon, Ronald C. "The B-52G: Mastering the Magnificent Monster--A Pilot's Report." Air Force Magazine, LVII (Nov. 1974), 46-51. The bomber's conversion from a high-level bomber.

834 "Emergency Duty: From Vietnam Comes a Story of Army Aviation Flexibility." U.S. Army Aviation Digest, XI (Oct. 1965), 21.

835 Emerson, Gloria. "Arms and the Woman: Career Officers of the 1st Air Cavalry Division." Harper's Magazine, CCXLVI (April 1973), 34+. See also the discussion on p99-100 of the Harper's June 1973 issue.

836 _____. Winners and Losers: Battles, Retreats, Gains, Losses and Ruins from a Long War. New York: Harcourt, 1978. 448p. Reminiscences by a New York Times correspondent.

837 "Emotional Exuberant: Welcome Home." Time, CI (Feb. 26, 1973), 13-17. "Operation Homecoming" and the return to America of the POW's.

838 "The End of Round Four." Newsweek, LXXIII (May 5, 1969), 58. In the air war caused by a pause.

839 "Enemy Transportation Suffers Heavy Losses." Air Force Times, XXVIII (Sept. 13, 1967), 18. Caused by American air action.

840 Engle, Eloise K. "An Aggressive 'Gooney Bird' and the Man Behind It." Data, XIV (Jan. 1969), 20-21. The AC-47 gunship.

841 _____. Medic: America's Medical Soldiers, Sailors, and Airmen in Peace and War. New York: John Day, 1967. 255p. Based on personal interviews.

842 Enthoven, Alain C., and K. Wayne Smith. How Much Is Enough?: Shaping the Defense Program, 1961-1969. New York: Harper & Row, 1971. 364p. Includes much information relative to our topic; suggests at one point that 65 per cent of all bombs dropped on targets in South Vietnam were dumped on suspected as opposed to known "enemy" positions.

843 Epstein, Charles S. "Supersonic Delivery of Conventional Weapons: Fact or Fancy?" Air University Review, XXIV (Sept.-Oct. 1973), 55-65. With some look back to Southeast Asia.

844 Erbe, Robert F. "'Sixteen Tons--And What Do I Get?'" Aerospace Safety, XXIV (Dec. 1968), 6-9. Airlift operations.

845 Erickson, David. "VF-96's Finest." American Aviation Historical Society Journal, XIX (Winter 1974), 246-249. How U.S. Navy Lt. Randy Cunningham downed North Vietnamese ace Toon over Hai Duong on May 10, 1972.

846 "Escalation in the Air, Ordeal on the Ground." Time, XCIX (April 24, 1972), 26-28. Aerial response to and events of the Easter invasion.

847 Evans, David L., 3d. "Lessons from Counter-Insurgency Operations." Air University Review, XV (March-April

1964), 48-54. Learned in South Vietnam during the American advisory period.

848 Everett, Robert P. "Alone, Unarmed, and Occasionally Afraid." *Airman*, XII (May 1968), 18-19. Aerial reconnaissance and FAC work over South Vietnam.

849 ______. "The Big Ugly Fat Fellow." *Airman*, XIII (March 1969), 4-7. The U.S. Air Force HH-53 rescue helicopter.

850 ______. "Combat Weathermen." *Airman*, XIV (January 1970), 13-15. U.S. Air Force weather forecasters for Southeast Asia.

851 ______. "Destroy Doumer Bridge." *Airman*, XII (March 1968), 26-29. The U.S. Air Force fighter-bomber attacks on the objective made on August 11, 1967.

852 ______. "Guardians of the Glidepaths." *Airman*, XIII (Feb. 1969), 46-47. U.S. Air Force air traffic controllers in the Vietnam conflict.

853 ______. "Just a 'Shadow' of Its Former Self." *Airman*, XIV (Feb. 1970), 11-14. The AC-119 gunship.

854 ______. "New Day for the VNAF." *Airman*, XIII (Dec. 1969), 4-7. Vietnamization of the South Vietnamese air force.

855 ______. "Pedro's Peril: A Rescue Attempt that Failed, Yet Succeeded." *Airman*, XIV (Jan. 1970), 18-20.

856 ______. "Rapid Area Maintenance." *Airman*, XIV (March 1970), 51-52. Aircraft servicing and repair in South Vietnam.

857 ______. "Rescue at Do Khe." *Airman*, XII (Feb. 1968), 38-43. A look at the events of July 2-3, 1967.

858 ______. "Sandys of the 602nd." *Airman*, XII (Feb. 1968), 10-13. A look at the 602nd Fighter Squadron (Commando).

859 ______. "Sweat and No Sweat." *Airman*, XIII (Nov. 1969), 56-61. Assembly and loading of bombs aboard B-52's in Thailand.

860 ______. "The Tactical Air Control Party." *Airman*, XII (Nov. 1968), 56-60. Airmen, who served with troops on the ground, radioed for help.

861 ______. "The 'Thud' Is No Dud." *Airman*, XII (May 1968), 4-8. A look at F-105 Thunderchief activities in Southeast Asia.

862 ______. "The Vietnam Airlift Is a Human Thing." Airman, XII (Oct. 1968), 4-9. Bringing to and taking from South Vietnam the men and materiel of war.

863 ______. "Wing Commander Mobile." Airman, XIV (Feb. 1970), 52-54. The work of Col. R. R. Melton, 12th Tactical Fighter Wing, Cam Ranh Bay air base.

864 "Evolution of the Air War in Vietnam." Air Classics, II (Aug.-Sept. 1965), 4-12. An illustrated operational review.

865 Evrard, James A. "Planning an Airmobile Assault." Army, XVIII (June 1968), 60-64. Considerations for a heliborne operation in South Vietnam.

866 Ewing, Lee. "Southeast Asia Effort Goes On: U.S. Role Explained to the House." Air Force Times, XXXIII (May 30, 1973), 1+. American air operations over Laos and Cambodia.

867 "The Extension of the Vietnamese War into North Vietnam Has Significant Overtones." Ordnance, XLIX (May-June 1965), 602-603. Suggests that the war is not a simple COIN conflict.

868 "Eyes in the Sky: Air Photographs of the 460th Tactical Reconnaissance Wing." Time, LXXXVIII (July 29, 1966), 20. Operations and uses of data gathered.

869 "FAC's Deed Wins Medal of Honor." Air Force Times, XXVIII (Feb. 7, 1968), 11. Capt. Hillard A. Wilbanks.

870 "FAC's Help Beat Off Attack on Dong Ha." Air Force Times, XXVII (May 17, 1967), 18. Examines the role of "bird dogs" in the fight.

871 "FAC's in Cambodia Get 'Head Beagle.'" Air Force Times, XXX (June 17, 1970), 16. U.S. Air Force OV-10's vs. the Khmer Rouge.

872 "F-5's in Vietnam." Flight International, LXXXIX (March 10, 1966), 408. Combat evaluation of the Northrop Freedom Fighter.

873 "F-4's Rip Truck Convoy in a Raid Near Quang Tri." Air Force Times, XXXII (June 14, 1972), 47. Success claimed.

874 "F-100 Used in North for Controller Flights." Air Force Times, XXVIII (Dec. 20, 1967), 23. Guiding F-105's in attacks over North Vietnam.

875 "The [F-105] Thunderchief: Vietnam's Versatile Heavyweight." Flying Review International, XXII (July 1967), 699-702. A look at the U.S. Air Force-Republic fighter bomber.

876 "The Face of Victory: Van Tuong." Time, LXXXVI (Aug. 27, 1965), 18-19. Air and ground combat between the U.S. Marine Corps and the 2d Vietcong Regiment in the lowlands of Quang Ngai province, South Vietnam.

877 "Facts in a Propaganda War Over U.S. Bombing: Civilian Casualties." U.S. News and World Report, LXII (Jan. 9, 1967), 6+. Civilians in Vietnam did suffer, but not intentionally.

878 Facts on File. New York: Facts on File, Inc., 1961-1973. Similar to Kessing's Contemporary Archives (q.v.) with shorter reports; cumulated annually into the News Directory. Includes reports on the SEA air war subject.

879 Fahey, James C., ed. The Ships and Aircraft of the United States Fleet, 8th ed. Annapolis, Md.: United States Naval Institute, 1965. 64p. Later editions have been published by the same firm; useful for U.S. Navy-Marine Corps aircraft of the Vietnam era.

880 Fair, Stanley. "No Place to Hide." Army, XIV (Sept. 1963), 54-55. The use of herbicides in South Vietnam.

881 Fairbanks, H. G. "Setback in Vietnam: The Defeat at Ap Bac." Commonweal, LXXVII (March 1, 1963), 593-595.

882 Fairweather, Robert S., Jr. "Helicopter Slingloads in Flight." U.S. Army Aviation Digest, XV (March 1969), 16-21. A technical discussion.

883 ______. "The Mixed Fleet in the Air Assault." Army, XX (Jan. 1970), 26-31. Helicopters, COIN aircraft, and close air support with examples from Southeast Asia.

884 ______. "Tomorrow's Gunships: No Free Lancing." Army, XXIII (March 1973), 13-19. With a look towards the helicopters of the Vietnam era, the author discusses new craft purpose built as gunships.

885 Fall, Bernard B. "Air Raids, Leftover Puzzles: North Vietnam's Reaction to Raids on Petroleum Storage Areas." New Republic CLV (July 16, 1966), 7-8. A look at U.S. action and North Vietnamese reaction to raids made in June 1966.

886 ______. Last Reflections on a War. Garden City, N.Y.: Doubleday, 1967. 288p. Contains some thought on the possible results of air activities.

887 _____. "The Theory and Practice of Insurgency and Counter-insurgency." Naval War College Review, XVII (April 1965), 20-38. A lecture, based on long Southeast Asian observation, given at the Naval War College on December 10, 1964.

888 _____. The Two Vietnams: A Political and Military Analysis. New York: Praeger, 1963. 493p. An important piece prepared during the American advisory period and based on years of observation.

889 _____. Vietnam Withness, 1953-1966. New York: Praeger, 1966. 363p. Includes much on aerial activities as they relate to strategy and operations.

890 "Fall of a Fortress: A Shau." Time, LXXXVII (March 18, 1966), 32-33. Includes a look at air power in the fight, especially the gallant rescue operations.

891 Famiglietti, Gene. "The Air War Escalates, MIG Airstrips Hit." Air Force Times, XXVII (May 10, 1967), 6. U.S. attacks on North Vietnamese Air Force bases in the Hanoi area.

892 _____. "Army Helicopters Are Here to Stay." Data, XIV (Aug. 1969), 14-16. Based on their work in South Vietnam.

893 _____. "USAF Pinch Hits for the Army and Strikes Out." Data, XIV (May 1969), 14-15.

894 Farrell, Gail F. "Effort for Peace." Combat Crew, XXIII (April 1973), 4-11. B-52 raids on North Vietnam in "Operation Linebacker II."

895 "Fatal Error: Allied Ships Attacked by U.S. Planes." Time, XCII (Aug. 9, 1968), 31. A case of mistaken identity off the Vietnamese coast.

896 "A Feeling for Freedom: Airman Twice Shot Down Over North Vietnam and Twice Rescued." Time, LXXXVIII (July 29, 1966), 13.

897 Ferguson, Gilbert W. "Guns at Da Nang." Marine Corps Gazette, L (Feb. 1966), 27-31. A Viet Cong raid on the big American air installation.

898 _____. "Vietnam: A Report on the War." In: J. L. Moulton, ed. Brassey's Annual: The Armed Forces Yearbook. New York: Praeger, 1967. p. 10-22. An overall review with some attention to air activities.

899 Ferguson, James. "Tactics and Technology: The Unlimited War on Limited War." Air University Review, XIX (Nov.-

Dec. 1967), 8-18. The rush to develop new weapons and equipment.

900 Fernandez, Richard R. "Air War in Indochina: Some Responses." Christian Century, LXXXVIII (Dec. 1, 1971), 1404-1405. Critical of the American effort.

901 "Fierce War on the Ground." Time, XCIX (May 1, 1972), 16-19. Allied response, including air, to the Communist Easter invasion.

902 "Fighter Flares Pierce Darkness: Operation Night Owl." Air Force Times, XXV (May 26, 1965), 4.

903 "Fighters Reduced in Southeast Asia." Air Force Times, XXXI (Dec. 2, 1970), 19. American pullback in the Vietnamese fighting.

904 "Fighters Strike North Vietnamese Oil Complex: Photos." Aviation Week and Space Technology, XCVI (May 29, 1972), 14-15. An episode from "Operation Linebacker I," launched in response to the North Vietnamese Easter invasion of South Vietnam.

905 "The Fighting First in Vietnam." Data, XII (Aug. 1967), 22-24. The U.S. Army's 1st Aviation Brigade.

906 "Fighting General with a Unique Role: Creighton Abrams and the Air-Naval War." U.S. News and World Report, LXXII (April 24, 1972), 18. The general's control over air activities is of interest here.

907 Fink, D. E. "McNamara Faces Vietnam Aircraft Probe." Aviation Week and Space Technology, LXXX (May 18, 1964), 31-32.

908 "Fire from the Skies: American Air Power in the Vietnamese Conflict." Flying Review International, XXII (March 1967), 405-407+. A review.

909 Firkens, Peter. The Australians in Nine Wars: Waikato to Long Tan. New York: McGraw-Hill, 1973. 448p. Ends with Vietnam; useful to the subject.

910 "The 1st Air Cavalry Division." Military Review, XLV (Sept. 1965), 98-101. A look at the force then arriving in Vietnam.

911 "The First SR-71 High Altitude Reconnaissance Photos Ever Made Public." Armed Forces Journal International, CXIII (July 1976), 20-23. A series of views of the Son Tay POW prison camp raid of November 1970.

912 "The First Team: The U.S. 1st Cavalry (Airmobile) Division." Time, LXXXVI (Sept. 24, 1965), 33-34. The unit's deployment in South Vietnam.

913 Fishel, Wesley R., comp. Vietnam: Anatomy of a Conflict. Itasca, Illinois: F. E. Peacock, 1968. 879p. Political and military background and operations.

914 Fisher, R. Grove. "The Awkward Angel of the Vietnamese Airlift." Air Force Times, XXX (Sept. 3, 1969), 15. The C-7 Caribou transport.

Fitzgerald, Oscar P., jt. author see Hooper, Edwin B.

915 "Five Big Battles in Vietnam." U.S. News and World Report, LXXIII (Dec. 18, 1972), 28-29. Combats growing out of the Easter invasion.

916 Flaherty, Thomas, and Larry Burrows. "Air War." Life, LXI (Sept. 9, 1966), 44-57. One of the best photographic efforts to come out of our topic's end of the conflict; the photos were taken by Burrows.

917 "Flare-Dropping Missions Protect Base from the VC." Air Force Times, XXVII (Jan. 10, 1968), 15. Guarding Tan Son Nhut airdrome.

918 "Flare Ships Put to Increased Use." Air Force Times, XXVII (March 15, 1967), 20. As above in guard duty and also to illuminate enemy positions.

919 "Fliers in Vietnam Say: 'It's a No Half-Win War.'" U.S. News and World Report, LXI (Dec. 26, 1966), 24-26. Interviews with American pilots.

920 "Flies Army Helos." Naval Aviation News, (Jan. 1967), 26. U.S. Navy helicopter squadron HC-1 in South Vietnam.

921 Flint, Roy K. "Campaigning with the Infantry in Vietnam." Air Force and Space Digest, LIII (Aug. 1970), 47-51. With information on the air and airmobile aspects of the subject.

922 Flohr, Rex. "Helicopter Tactical Employment." U.S. Army Digest, X (Dec. 1964), 28-31. For use in areas like South Vietnam.

923 Flood, Charles B. The War of the Innocents. New York: McGraw-Hill, 1970. 480p. Observes the U.S. Air Force 31st Tactical Fighter Wing and looks at the roles and problems of airmen in Southeast Asia.

924 Flying, Editors of. "Army Aviation: A Special Report."

Flying, LXX (May 1962), 22-61. With some information on operations in South Vietnam and a look at the types of helicopters and aircraft the Army was or would be using there.

925 "Flying Cranes." U.S. Army Aviation Digest, XII (July 1966), 30-31. Profiles the Sikorsky CH-54A Skycrane.

926 "The 'Flying Horsemen' Arrive in Vietnam." Journal of the Armed Forces, CI (Sept. 18, 1965), 13. The 1st Air Cavalry.

927 Flynn, John. "US Bombers Are Blasted in Vietnam: Bien Hoa Airbase." Life, LVII (Nov. 13, 1964), 50-51. Looks at the results of a costly Vietcong attack.

928 "For Conspicuous Gallantry." Airman, XII (May 1968), 7. Major Merlyn H. Dethlefsen's Congressional Medal of Honor.

929 Forte, David L. "Night Artillery Adjustment." U.S. Army Aviation Digest, XIII (Nov. 1967), 29-31. By night flying U.S. Army aircraft and helicopters.

930 "The 14th Air Commando Gets Hueys." Air Force Times, XXVII (March 15, 1967), 20.

931 "The 42nd Attack Squadron, US Navy." United Aircraft Quarterly Bee Hive, XL (Spring 1965), 2-7. Equipped with A-6's.

932 "The 463rd TAW [Tactical Airlift Wing] Plays Vital Role at Khe Sanh." Tactical Airlift, I (July 1971), 7. Supplying the Marines in 1968.

933 "Forward Air Controller: Airborne Eyes of the Infantry, Artillery, and Air Force, the FAC Gets There First, Goes in Close, and Doesn't Always Come Out on Top." Air Classics, VII (Sept. 1971), 57-61+. Examines the role of the FAC in close air support.

934 "Forward Air Controller: The Vietnam L-19." Air Classics, VII (Sept. 1971), 56-61. An aircraft and operational analysis of the 0-1 "Birddog."

935 Foxley-Norris, C. N. "Air Power: Some Lessons from Recent Experiences in the East." Hawk, XXVII (1965), 12-16. A British Air Vice Marshal's views of American operations.

936 Francis, John, Jr. "The F-111: A Pilot's View." Air Force Magazine, LIV (April 1971), 30-39. A valuable look into the flying of the swept-wing fighter bomber.

937 Frederick, Cynthia. "Cambodia: Operation Total Victory No. 43." Bulletin of the Concerned Asian Scholars, II (April-July 1970), 3-19. The Allied incursion of 1970 is viewed critically.

938 Freed, Darryl W. Psychological Warfare: A Case of Credibility. (Air Command and Staff College Research Study.) Maxwell Air Force Base, Ala.: Air University, 1971. 41p. On its use by the U.S. Air Force and other services during the conflict.

939 Freel, William F. "Laos: Secret War and Crucial Test." Navy, XIII (April 1970), 26-31. Political and air aspects examined in light of information then available.

940 Freeman, Edgar. "The Douglas A-4 Skyhawk." Air Classics, VIII (April 1972), 26-35. Profiles the U.S. Navy attack plane with comments on its use over Southeast Asia.

941 Freeman, Roger A. "Another Look at the United States Air Force." Air Pictorial, XXVIII (Dec. 1966), 436-440. In combat over the Vietnams.

942 ______. "US Air Force Claims in Vietnam: July 10, 1965-January 31, 1968." Air Pictorial, XXX (March 1968), 96. A table of claimed combat victories over North Vietnam.

943 ______. "USAF Unit Code Letters." Air Pictorial, XXXII (Feb., Aug. 1970), 62-64, 276-277. Those markings on aircraft which identify squadron or wing; many from the Southeast Asian fighting.

944 Fricker, John. "Air Armament 1968: A State of the Art Review." Flying Review International, XXIII (March 1968), 133-135+. Including the armament on U.S. planes and helicopters in use over Southeast Asia.

945 ______. "Helicopters in War." Flying Review International, XIX (Feb. 1964), 13-17. Based on the U.S. experience in South Vietnam.

946 ______. "On the Other Side of Coin." Flight International, LXXXVIII (Aug. 19, 1965), 299-300. On the development of counterinsurgency aircraft.

947 ______. "Realms of the Coin." Flying Review International, XX (Jan. 1965), 11-15. Examines the COIN aircraft concept and the bird's potential uses; some information relative to our topic.

948 Frisbee, John L. "Air Drop at An Loc." Air Force Magazine, LV (Nov. 1972), 40-42. Resupplying Allied defenders there during the Easter invasion.

949 _____. "The Air War in Vietnam." Air Force Magazine, LV (Sept. 1972), 48-56. A progress report.

950 _____. "The B-52: The Phoenix that Never Was." Air Force Magazine, LVI (Feb. 1973), 4. Linebacker II.

951 _____. "How the A-7D Rewrote the Book in Southeast Asia." Air Force Magazine, LVI (Aug. 1973), 30-36. The success of Corsair II missions against Communist supply lines.

952 _____. "Igloo White." Air Force Magazine, LIV (June 1971), 48-53. Electronic air warfare over Southeast Asia.

953 _____. "Mission: Troops in Contact--The Air War in Southeast Asia." Air Force Magazine, LV (Oct. 1972), 35-38. The Cessna A-37 COIN aircraft in action.

954 _____. "Not with a Whimper, but a Bang." Air Force Magazine, LVI (March 1973), 5-6. "Ending" the Vietnam War with "Operation Linebacker II."

955 _____. "The Panorama Unfolds." Air Force and Space Digest, LIII (Sept. 1970), 48-57. Indochina aerial operations, Vietnam, Laos, Cambodia.

956 _____. "Surviving in Hanoi's Prisons." Air Force Magazine, LVI (June 1973), 28-33. Interviews with Cols. Robbie Risner and George Day as to their POW experiences.

957 _____. "The USAF's Changing Role in Vietnam." Air Force Magazine, LIV (Sept. 1971), 40-45. The emphasis on Vietnamization.

958 _____. "The VNAF Meets the Test." Air Force Magazine, LV (June 1972), 50-53. Its ability to pick up the combat load being left by the U.S. Air Force.

959 Frith, L. H., 2d. "Wild Weasel." Navigator, VIII (Spring 1970), 27-28. Electronic counter-measures missions in North Vietnam air space.

960 "From First to Last: The Role of the Helicopter in Vietnam." Newsweek, LXXVIII (Dec. 27, 1971), 26. A review.

961 Fudge, Eugene. "The Fundamentals of Armed Helicopter Flying." U.S. Army Aviation Digest, XIV (Dec. 1968), 6-7. A summary of the art.

962 "The Full Panoply of Air Power Made Khe Sanh an Allied Victory." Contact, XXII (July-Aug. 1968), 7-8. A review of aerial operations in support of the Marines there.

963 Fulton, William B. Riverine Operations, 1966-1969. (Vietnam

Studies series.) Washington: U.S. Army, Center of Military History, 1973. 210p. Joint U.S. Army-Navy operations with attention to aircraft and helicopter participation.

964 "Fury at Ia Drang: Now the Regulars--U.S. 1st Air Cavalry Activities." Newsweek, LXVI (Nov. 29, 1965), 21-23. A look at the division's first successful operation in South Vietnam.

965 Futrell, R. Frank. "Air Operations in South Vietnam, 1962-1964." In Carl Berger, ed., The United States Air Force in Southeast Asia, 1961-1973 (Washington: U.S. Government Printing Office, 1977), p.15-36. An examination of the U.S. advisory period.

966 "GE's 'Gatling Guns': 'Old Timers' Get into the Fight." Air Force Times, XXVI (Dec. 15, 1965), M10. Multi-barrel "Miniguns" aboard U.S. Air Force AC-47 gunships.

967 Gablehouse, Charles. Helicopters and Autogiros: A Chronicle of Rotating-Wing Aircraft. Philadelphia: Lippincott, 1967. 254p. Pays some attention to military helicopters of the Vietnam War.

968 Gaetze, Frank C. "Routine Mission." U.S. Army Aviation Digest, XV (Dec. 1969), 10-12. Gunship escort of a truck convoy in South Vietnam.

969 Gaither, Ralph. With God in a POW Camp. Nashville, Tenn.: Broadman, 1973. 152p. A review of one pilot's POW experience in North Vietnam.

970 Gallagher, Barrett. "USS Guam." U.S. Naval Institute Proceedings, XCII (Feb. 1966), 84-100. A pictorial concerning the U.S. Navy helicopter Amphibious Assault Ship LPH-9.

971 "Gallery of U.S. Air Weapons." Air Force and Space Digest, XLIV-LVI (1961-1973), passim. Regular features of the September issues, 1961-1969, and of the May issues, 1970-1973. Includes brief rundowns on attack planes, bombers, fighters, transports, helicopters, and training aircraft.

972 Galloway, G. E. A Historical Study of United States Army Engineer Operations in the Republic of Vietnam, January 1965-November 1967. Ft. Leavenworth, Kansas: U.S. Army Command and General Staff College, 1968. Includes references to airfield and heliport construction and development.

973 Gallucci, Robert L. Neither Peace nor Honor: The Politics of American Military Policy in Vietnam. Baltimore, Md.: The Johns Hopkins University Press, 1975. 187p. With commentary on air and airmobile operations.

974 Gallup, John F. "Camouflage and Dispersion of Chinooks." U.S. Army Aviation Digest, XI (Nov. 1965), 19-21. How to maintain the safety of CH-47A's in South Vietnam.

975 Galvin, John R. Air Assault: The Development of Airmobile Warfare. New York: Hawthorn Books, 1969. 365p. Part III deals with American airmobile operations in Vietnam.

976 _____. "The Relief of Khe Sanh." Military Review, L (Jan. 1970), 88-94. Air, ground, and airmobile aspects.

977 _____. "Three Innovations: Prime Tactical Lessons of the Vietnam War." Army, XXII (March 1972), 16-24. All having to do with the airmobile-FAC concepts.

978 "Gamest Bastards of All: The Medical Evacuation Teams." Time, LXXXVI (July 2, 1965), 25. Helicopter medevac in South Vietnam.

979 Gann, Harry. The Douglas A-4 Skyhawk. (Aircraft in Profile, no. 102.) Windsor, Eng.: Profile Publications, 1967. 12p. Details on an attack aircraft employed by both the U.S. Navy and Marine Corps in the Vietnam conflict.

980 _____. The Douglas Skyraider. (Aircraft in Profile, no. 60.) Windsor, Eng.: Profile Publications, 1971. 12p. Technical and operational details on the famous propeller-driven "SPAD."

981 Garland, Albert N., ed. Combat Notes from Vietnam. Ft. Benning, Ga.: Infantry Magazine Press, 1968. 96p. Personal narratives of small unit U.S. Army actions, almost all involving helicopters in support or transport roles.

982 _____. Infantry in Vietnam. Ft. Benning, Ga.: Infantry Magazine Press, 1967. 409p. Accounts of small unit actions with information on helicopter and fixed-wing aircraft support.

983 Garlett, Harold F. "Running the Roads." Tactical Air Reconnaissance Digest, III (Aug. 1969), 12-15. Aerial reconnaissance over South Vietnamese highways.

Garr, Robin, 3d, jt. author see Nelson, David C.

984 Garrett, Stephen A. "The Lessons of Vietnam." Center Magazine, IV (July-Aug. 1971), 10-20. With some attention to the air war subject.

985 _____. "Vietnam: How Nixon Plans to Win the War." Ramparts Magazine, IX (Feb. 1971), 26-31. Bombing.

986 Gates, Edward. "F-111's Return to Southeast Asia, Air Force Presence Decreased." Air Force Times, XXXIII (Oct. 11, 1972), 6. Vietnamization and the return of the controversial fighter bomber to combat.

987 _____. "Huge Air Raids Strike at North." Air Force Times, XXXIII (Jan. 3, 1973), 1. B-52's in "Operation Linebacker II."

988 Gayler, Noel M. "Strike Warfare: The Target-Oriented Approach." Air Force and Space Digest International, I (Dec. 1965), 26+. Bombing raids on Communist objectives in Vietnam.

989 Geary, John C. "The Chinook, Advanced Battlefield Mobility." U.S. Army Aviation Digest, VIII (Aug. 1962), 3-8. On the troop carrying capacity of the CH-47A.

990 Geddes, J. Philip. "SRAM Enters the USAF Inventory." Interavia, XXVII (June 1972), 614-615. The Short Range Attack Missile was employed against North Vietnamese air defenses.

991 _____. "SRAM: The U.S. Air Force's New Defense Suppression Missile." International Defense Review, V (June 1972), 258-260.

992 George, James A. "'All for One!'" Airman, XIII (Feb. 1969), 50-53. How Capt. Donald D. Stevens won the Air Force Cross for a daring rescue mission.

993 _____. "The Best Base in Vietnam?" Airman, XI (Nov. 1967), 11-13. Cam Ranh Bay airdrome.

994 _____. "He Had to Help." Airman, XII (Dec. 1968), 52-55. Major Robert E. Turner bombs a vital North Vietnamese supply target on January 6, 1967.

995 _____. "Last Man into the Sling." Airman, XII (Nov. 1968), 52-54. The helicopter rescue exploits of Capt. Donald B. Price.

996 _____. "The Making of an Air Commando." Airman, X (Dec. 1966), 10-14. A look at the U.S. 1st Air Commando Wing.

997 _____. "The Provider." Airman, VII (March 1963), 46-47. The C-123 transport in South Vietnam.

998 _____. "The Shortest Line." Airman, XII (Oct. 1968), 52-55. A February 6, 1967 mission earns Sgt. Duane D. Hackney the Air Force Cross.

999 ______. "To Build an Air Base." Airman, XI (Aug. 1967), 4-7. The Tuy Hoa facility in South Vietnam.

1000 George, Jonathan D. "Mohawk." Infantry, LIX (March-April 1969), 37-39. FAC's and the OV-1 observation plane.

1001 Gerassi, John. North Vietnam: A Documentary. Indianapolis: Bobbs-Merrill, 1969. 200p. More than half of this book consists of documents issued by various branches of the Hanoi government on the effects of the American bombing campaign.

1002 ______. "Report from North Vietnam." New Republic, CLVI (March 4, 1967), 13-15. On the effects of American bombing.

1003 Gettleman, Marvin, et al., eds. Conflict in Indochina: A Reader on the Widening War in Laos and Cambodia. New York: Random House, 1970. 464p. Provides much background material; the concluding chapters are devoted to the areas of SEA outside Vietnam.

1004 Gibson, J. McKinley. "An Air Line of Communications for Armor." Military Review, LIV (April 1974), 25-31. Tank-air communication and co-operation.

1005 Gillem, Alvan C., 2d. "SAC in Southeast Asia." Air Force Policy Letter for Commanders, no. 7 (July 1968), 9-13. Remarks made to the April 4, 1968, Air Force Association meeting on B-52 "Arc Light" operations.

1006 Gillespie, Frank W., Jr. "Limited Asset Airmobile Operations." Infantry, LXI (May-June 1971), 12-15. The Cambodian incursion is an example.

1007 Gillette, Robert. "Smart Bombs: Air Warfare Undergoes a Reluctant Revolution." Science, CLXXVI (June 9, 1972), 1108-1109. The use of television-guided bombs over North Vietnam.

1008 Gillette, Samuel G. "Airmobile Operations in Vietnam." Armor, LXXV (Sept.-Oct. 1966), 10-14. A review of the 1st Cav's first year.

1009 Gilster, Herman L. "Air Interdiction in a Protracted War: An Economic Evaluation." Air University Review, XXVIII (May-June 1977), 2-18. A well documented look at the subject as it relates to the Indochina conflict.

1010 ______. "The Commando Hunt V Interdiction Campaign." Air University Review, XXIX (Jan.-Feb. 1978), 21-37. Following up the above study, this report looks at the air campaign in southern Laos from October 1970 to June 1971.

1011 Ginsburgh, Robert N. "The Air Force in Southeast Asia: A Team Effort." Air Force Policy Letter for Commanders, no. 11 (Nov. 1973), 10-17. A review of the subject as given in a July 6, 1973, talk to the Air Force ROTC Field Training Encampment Dining-in.

1012 _____. "Strategy and Air Power: The Lessons of Southeast Asia." Strategic Review, I (Summer 1973), 18-24. What could and could not be accomplished with aircraft.

1013 _____. "The Tides of War." Air Force and Space Digest, LI (Feb. 1968), 46-51. The aerial campaign to that date.

1014 Girling, J. L. S. "Crisis and Conflict in Cambodia." Orbis, XIV (Summer 1970), 349-365. A review with some comments on aerial aspects.

1015 Gleason, Robert L. "Psychological Operations and Air Power: Its Hits and Misses." Air University Review, XXII (March-April 1971), 34-46. Mostly misses over Southeast Asia.

1016 Glines, Carroll V. "The Most Meritorious Flight of the Year." Airman, IX (May 1965), 40-43. How a U.S. C-47 crew rescued six wounded Vietnamese soldiers from Loc Ninh on July 23, 1963.

1017 _____. "Tribute to the 'Goon.'" Airman, X (March 1966), 18-21. The Douglas C-47 in South Vietnam.

1018 Goliszewski, Czeslaw. Tactical and Operational Problems of Air War in Vietnam. TT 66-30136. Washington: Joint Publications Research Service, 1966. Reprinted and translated from the December 18-19, 1965, issues of Zolnierz Wolnosei.

1019 Gonzalez, Arturo F., Jr. "Defoliation: A Controversial U.S. Mission in Vietnam." Data, XIII (Oct. 1968), 12-15. Remains controversial to this day!

1020 _____. "Get Me Air: FAC's in South Vietnam." Data, XIII (May 1968), 34-35. Forward Air Controllers and their O-1's over South Vietnam.

1021 _____. "Tan Son Nhut: The World's Craziest Airport." Data, XIII (June 1968), 40-42. A look at the big American air facility in South Vietnam.

1022 Goodson, Wayne. "No Green Grunts." Airman, XVII (Nov. 1973), 28-30. The bomb-loading work of the U.S. Air Force 307th Munitions Maintenance Squadron at U-Tapao airdrome, Thailand.

1023 Goodstadt, Leo. "The Crunch Comes to Hanoi." Far Eastern Economic Review, LXXVI (May 13, 1972), 9-10. U.S. attacks on rail facilities and the mining of North Vietnamese harbors.

1024 Goolrich, Chester. "Reconn Sense." U.S. Army Aviation Digest, XIII (July 1967), 36-51. Tips on the art and how not to get shot down in the observation process.

1025 "Gooney Becomes Gunship." Air Force Times, XXVI (Feb. 9, 1966), 15. Conversions of C-47's into AC-47 gunships.

1026 Gorton, William A. "Close Air Support: An Employment Concept." Air University Review, XXI (March-April 1970), 101-108. Recommendations on how to choose the appropriate aircraft to respond to a given need; examples from Southeast Asia.

1027 Gough, Jamie. "Airpower and Counterinsurgency." Airman, VI (Aug. 1962), 2-7. With illustrations from the war in South Vietnam.

1028 Goulding, Philip G. "United States Policy on Bombing and Targeting in North Vietnam." Air Force Policy Letter for Commanders, No. 2 (Feb. 1967), 15-19. Text of a December 30, 1966, letter from the author to U.S. Rep. Ogden R. Reid.

1029 Graff, Henry F. The Tuesday Cabinet: Deliberation and Decision on Peace and War Under Lyndon B. Johnson. Englewood Cliffs, N.J.: Prentice-Hall, 1970. 200p. Contains some thoughts on the Southeast Asian air war, including Defense Secretary McNamara's estimate of a cost expenditure of $30,000 per B-52 sortie.

1030 Graham, Gordon M. "Fighter Forces and Operations." Air Force Policy Letter for Commanders, no. 2 (Feb. 1969), 10-16. A January 19, 1969, talk before the American Institute of Aeronautics and Astronautics.

1031 Graham, T. P. "LOH: Its Role in Ground Operations." Marine Corps Gazette, LIV (Oct. 1970), 25-28. The Light Observation Helicopter.

1032 Grant, Z. B. "What Are We Doing in Thailand?" New Republic, CLX (May 24, 1969), 19-21. Air bases.

1033 Grant, Zalin. Survivors. New York: W. W. Norton, 1975. 345p. Reminiscences of and details on the POW experience.

Grantham, Donald, jt. author see Cote, Jean

1034 Graves, Larry D. "Combined Arms Are Effective." Armor, LXXIX (May-June 1970), 19-21. On the operational use of tanks and helicopters.

1035 Graves, William S. "Hanoi Tonight." U.S. Naval Institute Proceedings, XCV (July 1969), 136-139. A lone U.S. Navy A-6 Intruder from a carrier in Tonkin Gulf mounts a raid on October 30, 1967.

1036 Gray, Paul L. "How Computer Technology Is Streamlining Frag Preparation." Air Force and Space Technology, LII (Jan. 1969), 48-53. The right bombs daily for U.S. Air Force strike orders.

1037 Grayson, Eugene H. "Compromise! Compromise! Compromise!" U.S. Army Aviation Digest, XVIII (May 1972), 16-17. Communications security during tactical operations.

1038 Grayson, Stan. "Tiger Surprise." Army Digest, XXVI (Jan. 1971), 8-9. A-37 operations in South Vietnam.

1039 "The Great Bomb Flap: Claims that Hanoi Was Bombed." Time, LXXXVIII (Dec. 23, 1966), 23-24. "Facts" and "rumors."

1040 Green, Felix. Vietnam! Vietnam!: In Photographs and Text. Palo Alto, Calif.: Fulton Publishing Co., 1966. 175p. With some attention to air and airmobile operations.

1041 Green, William, comp. The Observer's Book of Aircraft. 12 vols. New York: Warne, 1961-1973. An annual look at new world aircraft developments, including many U.S. warbirds and helicopters used or tried in Southeast Asia.

1042 _____. The World Guide to Combat Planes. 2d ed. 2 vols. Garden City, N.Y.: Doubleday, 1967. Includes models employed in Vietnam.

1043 _____. The World's Fighting Planes. 4th, rev. ed. Garden City, N.Y.: Doubleday, 1965. 216p. Includes models employed in Vietnam.

1044 _____, and G. J. Pollinger, comps. The Aircraft of the World, 3d ed. Garden City, N.Y.: Doubleday, 1965. 360p. Includes models employed in Vietnam.

1045 _____, and F. Gordon Swanborough, comps. The Observer's Basic Military Aircraft Directory. New York: Warne, 1974.

1046 Greenbacker, John E. "The Lesson of Vietnam." U.S. Naval Institute Proceedings, XCIX (July 1973), 18-25. USNIP Prize Essay.

1047 Greene, Jerry. "Airpower's Buildup in Vietnam." Air Force and Space Digest, XLVIII (June 1965), 33-43. A review and report.

1048 ______. "New Air Warfare Lessons Evolve from Flight in Vietnam." Aviation Week and Space Technology, LXXVII (Aug. 1962), 68-76. The role of U.S. and VNAF aircraft in the guerrilla war during the American advisory period.

1049 ______. "U.S. Airpower in Vietnam: A Scalpel Rather than a Broadsword." Air Force and Space Digest, XLVIII (May 1965), 33-36. On hitting politically-selected targets.

1050 Greene, Richard L. "Observations of a Scout." U.S. Army Aviation Digest, XV (March 1969), 32-35. Army reconnaissance missions over South Vietnam.

1051 Greene, Wallace M., Jr. "The Bombing Pause: Formula for Failure." Air Force Magazine, LIX (April 1976), 36-39. The effect of that political process on the air campaign against North Vietnam.

1052 ______. "The Marines in Vietnam." Ordnance, LII (July-Aug. 1967), 38-42. Including aviation units.

1053 Greenhalgh, William H., Jr. "'A-OK': Airpower Over Khe Sanh." Aerospace Historian, XIX (March 1972), 2-9. Aiding the besieged Marines in 1968.

1054 ______. "Tactical Reconnaissance." In Carl Berger, ed., The United States Air Force in Southeast Asia, 1961-1973 (Washington: U.S. Government Printing Office, 1977), p.211-222. A well-illustrated review of U.S. Air Force operations in this regard.

1055 Greenwood, Gordon, and Norman Harper, eds. Australia in World Affairs, Vol. III: 1961-1965. Vancouver: University of British Columbia Press, 1968. 510p.

1056 ______. Australia in World Affairs, Vol. IV: 1966-1970. Vancouver: University of British Columbia Press, 1974. 499p. During the years covered by these two volumes, Australian troops and aircraft became heavily involved in the Vietnam war; this work represents a record and analysis of this situation--and others--from the Australian viewpoint.

1057 Greer, William A., Jr. "Reconnaissance by Helicopter-Mounted Searchlights." Armor, LXXV (Sept.-Oct. 1966), 48-49. The role of the helicopter in night observation.

1058 Gregory, Gene. "Tale of the Trail: The Ho Chi Minh

Trail." National Review, XXIII (June 29, 1971), 701-702+. A U.S. aerial interdiction attention.

1059 Grey, James W. "Route Security--By Air." Infantry, LIII (Jan.-Feb. 1963), 20-21. Covering truck convoys with armed helicopters or COIN aircraft.

1060 Griffin, William P. "Army Aviation in Support of Counter-Guerrilla Operations." U.S. Army Aviation Digest, VIII (Sept. 1962), 9-14. Theory with some practical notes from South Vietnam.

1061 Griffith, Albert A. "Put Them All Together." Infantry, LX (July-Aug. 1970), 6-11. Air-ground operations in South Vietnam and Cambodia.

1062 Griminger, Charles O. "The Armed Helicopter Story." U.S. Army Aviation Digest, XVII (July-Dec. 1971), 14-17, 14-19, 10-13, 18-25, 17-24, 22-24. A history with major emphasis on operational use in Southeast Asia.

1063 Grinter, Lawrence E. "How They Lost: Doctrines, Strategies, and Outcomes of the Vietnam War." Asian Survey, (Dec. 1975), 1111-1132. A review with some mention of air/airmobile aspects.

1064 Groth, Richard. Fifty Famous Fighter Aircraft. New York: Arco, 1968. 96p. Arranged by year and includes several for our topic, e.g., F-4 Phantom, F-105 Thunderchief, MIG-21.

1065 "The Grumman A-6 Intruder." Air Progress, XXIV (May 1968), 22-25.

1066 _____. Naval Aviation News, (June 1967, April, June 1968, Oct. 1971), 6-11, 7, 69, 20-21.

1067 _____. United Aircraft Quarterly Bee Hive, XLI (Spring 1965), 2-7.

1068 Guelzo, Carl M. "The Air-Ground Problem." Infantry, LV (Jan.-Feb. 1965), 20-25. Difficulties in close air support.

1069 Guerrieri, Vincent R. "We Keep Them Flying." U.S. Army Aviation Digest, XIV (June 1968), 22-25. The U.S. Army 34th General Support Group (AM & S).

1070 Guimond, Gary A. "Clean Sweep of the Enemy." Airman, XIV (July 1970), 32-36. How Capt. Garth A. Wright won the Air Force Cross.

1071 _____. "'Hot Flare! Hot Flare!'" Airman, XIV (June 1970), 26-31. How A1C John L. Levitow flung himself on top of an enemy shell which had entered his AC-47 while on patrol on February 24, 1969 and was able to throw it out the cargo door just before it exploded; for saving his ship and fellow crewmen, Levitow received the Congressional Medal of Honor from President Nixon on May 14, 1970.

1072 ______. "Mission Accomplished." Airman, XV (Sept. 1971), 17-18. Activities of the U.S. Air Force 31st and 355th Tactical Fighter Wings over Southeast Asia.

1073 "Gunship Success Spurs Advanced Models." Aviation Week and Space Technology, LXXXVII (Aug. 14, 1967), 27. Improvements to the AC-47 Dragonship.

1074 "Gunships Pushed to Interdict Routes into South Vietnam." Aviation Week and Space Technology, LXXXVIII (April 1, 1968), 25. More on the activities of the AC-47.

1075 Gunston, William T. "Bill." Attack Aircraft of the West. New York: Scribner's, 1975. 271p. Examines many which were involved in the Southeast Asian fighting, including the FB-111, A-4, A-7, A-6, etc.

1076 ______. Bombers of the West. New York: Scribner's, 1973. 283p. Includes such Southeast Asian participants as the B-52 and Canberra.

1077 ______. "Coin Aircraft." Flight, LXXXIII (April 18, 1963), 567. Including some employed by the U.S. in South Vietnam, e.g., the AD-1 or "SPAD."

1078 ______. The Encyclopedia of the World's Combat Aircraft: A Technical Directory of Major Warplanes from World War I to the Present Day. New York: Chartwell Books, 1976. 229p. Nicely illustrated with brief technical details; includes all Allied and North Vietnamese aircraft employed in the Vietnam War.

1079 ______. F-4 Phantom. New York: Scribner's, 1977. 112p. A technical and operational history of the famous McDonnell-Douglas fighter.

1080 ______. Helicopters at War. London and New York: Hamlyn, 1977. 127p. Primary emphasis on Vietnam; illustrations by John Batchelor.

1081 ______. "Military Aircraft." Flight International, LXXXVI (Aug. 20, 1964), 280-295. A brief survey with scale drawings; includes many warbirds in use or shortly to be in use over Southeast Asia.

1082 ______. "New Developments in Aircraft and Missiles." In

J. L. Moulton, ed., Brassey's Annual (New York: Praeger, 1965), p156-168. Includes those in use over Vietnam.

1083 _____. Night Fighters: A Development and Combat History. New York: Scribner's, 1976. 192p. Much on American aircraft in use over Southeast Asia.

1084 Gurney, Gene. A Pictorial History of the United States Army in War and Peace, from Colonial Times to Vietnam. New York: Crown, 1966. 815p. Ends with airmobile operations in Vietnam in 1965.

1085 Gwathmey, Lomax. "Artillery Raid." Army Digest, XXII (July 1967), 22-23. Operations of the 10/66 airmobile 105mm howitzer battery.

1086 "HH-3C Crews Rescue Downed Fighter Pilots." Aviation Week and Space Technology, LXXXIV (April 25, 1966), 92-93. U.S. Air Force aerospace search and recovery efforts.

1087 Haas, Donald A. "Phan Rang Air Base." Military Engineer, LVIII (Nov.-Dec. 1966), 431-433. Its construction and development.

Hackworth, David H., jt. author see Marshall, Samuel L. A.

1088 Haggerty, James J., and Warren R. Smith. The U.S. Air Forces: A Pictorial History in Art. New York: Books, Inc., 1966. 261p. Ends with combat scenes of Vietnam.

1089 Haid, Donald J. "How to Shoot a Duck." Military Review, XLV (Sept. 1965), 3-12. Armed helicopters.

1090 Hai-Thu. North Vietnam Against the U.S. Air Force. Hanoi: Foreign Languages Publishing House, 1967. 93p. Boasts the success of North Vietnamese antiaircraft defenses.

1091 Halberstam, David. The Best and the Brightest. New York: Random House, 1973. 688p. One of the most famous books to come out of the conflict, this reporter's study shows the decision-making process that took America into the Vietnamese War and kept her there; some comments on the air campaign (military and political) and air leaders from the Pentagon to the field.

1092 _____. The Making of a Quagmire. New York: Random House, 1965. 352p. A New York Times correspondent examines Vietnam in 1962-1963, providing a description of the military system and scoring American military advisors, including air and helicopter.

1093 ______. "The Programming of Robert McNamara." Harper's Magazine, CCXLII (Feb. 1971), 37-40+. The Defense Secretary and the air war.

1094 Haldeman, Steve. "Jungle Medevac." Army Digest, XXIV (Aug. 1969), 44-45. The Air-Ambulance Platoon, 15th Medical Battalion, U.S. 1st Air Cavalry Division.

1095 Halloran, Barney. "Red Hot Mission." Soldiers, XXVII (Jan. 1973), 17-19. Helicopter air rescue over South Vietnam.

1096 Hamilton, James A. "Flying Safety and Flying Combat." Aerospace Safety, XXIII (Sept. 1967), 18-19. The relationship of one to the other over Southeast Asia.

1097 Hamilton, Maynard G. "Base Operation and Maintenance in Southeast Asia." Air Force Civil Engineer, IX (May 1968), 14-15. A survey.

1098 Hamlin, Ross E. "Side-Firing Weapons Systems: A New Application of an Old Concept." Air University Review, XXI (Jan.-Feb. 1970), 76-88. An examination of miniguns aboard the AC-47, AC-119, and AC-130 gunships.

1099 Hammer, Richard. One Morning in the War. New York: Coward-McCann, 1970. 207p. While primarily a look at the Song My massacre, the work contends that the American military, including air, brought much impersonal warfare into the lives of common Vietnamese villagers thereby frustrating U.S. political goals.

1100 Hammond, J. W., Jr. "Combat Journal." Marine Corps Gazette, LII (July-Aug. 1968), 20-29, 46-51. A look at air-ground operations in the I Corps area.

1101 Hampe, D. E. "Tactics and the Helicopter." Military Review, XLVI (March 1966), 60-63. Airmobile aspects.

1102 "Hanoi Attacks and Blasts a Dream." Newsweek, LXXIX (April 10, 1972), 41-42. The Easter invasion and the shattering of American hopes for an easy exit from the war in Vietnamization.

1103 "Hanoi's High Risk Drive for Victory." Time, XCIX (May 15, 1972), 24-29. The Easter invasion.

1104 "Hanoi's Strategy: Hit Them Everywhere." Newsweek, LXXIX (May 8, 1972), 53-54. More on the Easter invasion.

1105 Hardaway, Benjamin F. "Searchlight for Helicopters." U.S. Army Aviation Digest, XII (Jan. 1966), 26-27. Employing armed helicopters at night.

Harper, Norman, jt. editor see Greenwood, Gordon

1106 Harrigan, Anthony. A Guide to the War in Viet Nam. (Best Books on Unconventional Warfare and Counterinsurgency series.) Boulder, Colorado: Panther Publications, 1966. 134p. A look at operations and tactics, including helicopter.

1107 _____. "New Air-Sea Warfare in Vietnam." Officer, XLII (Nov. 1966), 8-9. The role of carriers and their aircraft.

1108 _____. "Vietnam Seen Proving a Need for a Genuine Maritime Strategy." Navy, IX (Sept. 1966), 6-9. More on the use of aircraft carriers.

1109 Harrington, Charles F. "'Nite Owl' Operations." Tactical Air Warfare Center Quarterly Report, II (Dec. 1970), 4-11. F-4's of the U.S. Air Force 497th Tactical Fighter Squadron flying from Ubon airdrome in Thailand.

1110 Harris, Hap. "Combat Partners for Peace." Airman, X (June 1966), 32-35. The U.S. and Vietnamese air forces.

1111 _____. "Operation Quick Service." Airman, XII (Feb. 1968), 18-21. U.S. Air Force tactical airlift operations in South Vietnam.

1112 _____. "Prop Pushers of Bien Hoa." Airman, X (Jan. 1966), 34-37. U.S. Air Force Skyraiders.

1113 _____. "Welcome Big Brother, O-2." Airman, XI (Oct. 1967), 24-25. A new aircraft for FAC operations.

1114 Harris, Hunter, Jr. "Air Power Staves Off the Viet Cong at Plei Me, 19-28 October." Air Force Policy Letter for Commanders, no. 12 (Dec. 1965), 24-27. A report on air operations and messages to Air Force Secretary Brown, October 29-30, 1965.

1115 _____. "PACAF: Grown Task in a Critical Area." Air Force and Space Digest, XLIX (March 1966), 53-54+. PACAF's commander reports on his command's role in Southeast Asia.

1116 Harrison, Donald F. "Developments in Air Mobility in the U.S. Army." U.S. Army Aviation Digest, XV (June 1969), 20-24. Helicopters in the transport of troops and supplies.

1117 "Harrowing War in the Air." Time, XCIX (May 1, 1972), 14-16. A report on combat over Indochina.

1118 Hart, John W. "Master of the Century." Airman, XII (July 1968), 30-31. Thoughts of an F-100 Supersabre pilot in combat over SEA.

1119 Harvey, Frank. "The Air War in Vietnam." Flying, LXXIX (Nov. 1966), 38-95. A review, analysis, and report to that date.

1120 ______. Air War--Vietnam. New York: Bantam Books, 1967. 185p. On the scene reports by a veteran aviation writer as adapted and expanded from the previous entry.

1121 ______. "Time of Eagles." Flying, CI (Sept. 1977), 276-280. A brief review of the Southeast Asian air war.

1122 Harvey, Thomas H., Jr. "Air Cavalry in Battle: A New Concept in Action." Armor, LXXVII (May-June 1968), 5-10. The work of the heliborne 1st Air Cavalry in South Vietnam.

1123 ______. "COD--Cargo on Demand." U.S. Army Aviation Digest, X (Nov. 1964), 6-10. Resupply missions by Caribous to Army Special Forces personnel in the Vietnam mountains.

1124 Haseltine, William. "Automated Air War." New Republic, CLXV (Oct. 16, 1971), 15-17. The impersonal air interdiction campaign.

1125 Haugland, Verne. "Airborne Ordnance." Ordnance, LI (March-April 1967), 478-482. Close air support.

1126 ______. "Assault by Air." Ordnance, XLIX (Sept.-Oct. 1964), 169-173. Vertical assault by troops from helicopters.

1127 ______. "Navy Wings for Vietnam." Ordnance, LII (March-April 1968), 471-474. U.S. Navy air operations over North Vietnam.

1128 ______. "Wings over Vietnam." Ordnance, LI (May-June 1967), 591-595. A review of the air war.

1129 Hawkes, Robert. "The Air Force Throws Out the Book in Vietnam Operations." American Aviation, XXVII (April 1964), 16-18+. New tactics, including FAC's, over Southeast Asia.

1130 ______. "Air Reconnaissance Is Vital in Vietnam." American

Aviation, XXVIII (July 1964), 23-27. The use of aircraft and helicopters for visual and photo observation.

1131 _____. "How Good Is the Armed Helicopter?" American Aviation, XXVIII (June 1964), 14-16+ Answer: very good.

1132 Hawley, Earle, ed. The Face of War: Vietnam, the Full Photographic Report. North Hollywood, Calif.: Milton Luros, 1965. 83p. Some scenes of aircraft and helicopters.

1133 Hay, John H., Jr. "Air Force Cited for 'Junction City' Support." Air Force Policy Letter for Commanders, no. 5 (May 1967), 31.

1134 _____. Tactical and Materiel Innovations. (Vietnam Studies series.) Washington: U.S. Army, Center of Military History, 1974. 197p. A valuable study with much on airmobile aspects.

1135 Hayden, Tom. "Prospects of the Vietnam Offensive." Ramparts Magazine, XI (Aug. 1972), 21-25. Would the Easter invasion force the U.S. out faster, despite the success of counterattacks, especially from the air?

1136 Hays, R. J. "The A-6A Intruder in Vietnam." U.S. Naval Institute Proceedings, XCIII (Jan. 1967), 120-123. The U.S. Navy attack plane vs. North Vietnamese targets.

1137 Head, Richard G. "The Air Force A-7 Decision: The Politics of Close Air Support." Aerospace Historian, XXII (Winter 1974), 219-224. How the Corsair II was chosen to play its U.S. Air Force role over Southeast Asia.

1138 Heaton, Leonard D. "Medical Support of the Soldier: A Team Effort in Saving Lives." Army, XIX (Oct. 1969), 85-88. With much on medevac helicopter operations.

1139 Heavner, Robert O. "Interdiction--A Dying Mission?" Air University Review, XXII (Jan.-Feb. 1971), 56-59. Cost in losses vs. results over Southeast Asia.

1140 Heilbrunn, Otto. "Counterinsurgency Targets: A Question of Priorities." Army Quarterly, XCIII (Jan. 1967), 202-205. A German officer's view printed in a British professional journal based on World War II and Vietnam tactical air strikes.

1141 _____. "Tactical Intelligence in Vietnam." Military Review, XLVIII (Oct. 1968), 85-87. An analysis, including air.

1142 Heimback, William W., Jr. "'I'm Below Bingo! Get Me a Tank.'" Air Force and Space Digest, LIII (Dec. 1970),

44-46. Armed helicopters and close air support strikes on North Vietnamese armor during the war.

1143 Heinl, Robert D., Jr. "A Measure of the Combatants at Da Nang." Navy, IX (Jan. 1966), 23-26. Marine ground and air forces in I Corps.

1144 "Helicopter Heroism." Naval Aviation News, (July 1971), 4. Air-sea rescue.

1145 "The Helicopter in Land Battle." Journal of the Armed Forces, CIX (Jan. 1972), 24-25. Airmobile and gunship aspects.

1146 "A Helicopter Raid in Vietnam." New York Times Magazine, (July 29, 1962), 8-9. Made in support of South Vietnamese soldiers.

1147 "Helicopter Survey." Flying Review International, XIX (Feb. 1964), 13+. Includes those in use in Vietnam or under development.

1148 "The Helicopter War Runs Into Trouble." Time, LXXXI (Jan. 11, 1963), 29-30. Losses to antiaircraft fire over South Vietnam.

1149 "Helicopter War: The Laotian Campaign." Newsweek, LXXVII (March 15, 1971), 39-40. A report on the many losses suffered.

1150 "Helicopter War: Vietnam War." Forbes, CXV (May 1, 1975), 15-16. A review.

1151 "Helicopters." Lockheed Horizons, I (Spring 1965), 58-80. A look at the use of whirlybirds in South Vietnam.

1152 "Helicopters Boost Battlefield Mobility." Interavia, XVIII (Sept. 1963), 1314-1317. Their use as troop carriers in vertical assault.

1153 "Helicopters for Combat." Flying Review International, XXII (Nov. 1966), 171-176, 181-187. A review of types employed in South Vietnam.

1154 "Helicopters for Military Mobility." Interavia, XVIII (Sept. 1963), 1314+. Seven special articles, including the one cited above.

1155 Hellman, Harold. Helicopters and Other VTOLS. Garden City, N.Y.: Doubleday, 1970. 140p. Illustrated; includes many in use over Southeast Asia.

1156 Helmore, P. W. "Air Operations in Vietnam, I." Journal

of the Royal United Service Institution, CXII (Feb. 1967), 26-31. For Part II, see Edmund Edwards, item 818.

1157 Henderson, D. K. "Annual American Helicopter Society Forum Is Told that Vietnam Is Building the Statute of the Helicopter." American Aviation, XXX (June 1966), 89-90. Praise from Defense Department officials.

1158 ______. "The Wild Blue Yonder Is Taking on a Khaki Hue." American Aviation, (Sept. 1964), 16-18+. Army helicopters in Vietnam.

1159 Henderson, F. D. "Cleared In--Wet!" Air Force and Space Digest, LI (Aug. 1968), 38-41. A close air support mission.

1160 Hendricks, J. D. "Vietnam Straining MAC Fleet, Facilities." Aviation Week and Space Technology, LXXXVIII (March 18, 1968), 114-120. The problems of the U.S. Military Airlift Command in meeting the personnel and supply needs of American forces.

1161 Henington, H. M. "Report on Air Force Reconnaissance Operations." Data, XI (April 1966), 51-52. Operations over Southeast Asia.

1162 Henri, Jean. "The Mood of Hanoi: Lonely and Alert." Time, XCIX (May 15, 1972), 35. An on-the-scene report with comment on the air campaign.

1163 Henry, John B., 2d. "February 1968." Foreign Policy, IV (Fall 1971), 3-33. The Tet offensive.

1164 "Herbicidal Warfare." Scientific American, CCXXX (April 1974), 49-50. A review of "Operation Ranch Hand" in South Vietnam.

1165 "Here's a Rundown on U.S. Planes in Use in Vietnam: Most Are Conventional." Air Force Times, XXV (April 19, 1964), 4.

1166 Herman, Edward S. Atrocities in Vietnam: Myths and Realities. Boston: Pilgrim Press, 1970. 104p. Has much to say relative to the air war subject, including figures (p57) showing that the U.S. dropped 3,751,131 tons of munitions in the years 1967-1969.

1167 "Hero Lost: American Plane Losses." Time, LXXXVII (Aug. 19, 1966), 27. U.S. losses to antiaircraft fire over North and South Vietnam.

1168 Herr, Michael. "Conclusion at Khe Sanh." Esquire, LXXII

(Oct. 1969), 113-123+ The air-ground relief on the besieged Marines in 1968.

1169 ______. Dispatches. New York: Knopf, 1977. 260p. A well-written collection of articles based on the author's 1967-1968 assignment to Vietnam for Esquire; includes the articles on Khe Sanh cited here.

1170 ______. "Khe Sanh." Esquire, LXXII (Sept. 1969), 118-123+. The great siege of 1968 with comments on air support and supply.

1171 Hersh, Seymour M. "How We Ran the Secret Air War in Laos." New York Times Magazine, (Oct. 29, 1972), 18-19+. A political-military-covert operations review.

1172 Heslop, J. M., and D. R. Van Orden. From the Shadow of Death: Stories of POW's. Salt Lake City, Utah: Deseret, 1973. 350p. Based on interviews with men returned in "Operation Homecoming."

1173 Hess, Carl L. "Chinooks IFR (CAV) Style." U.S. Army Aviation Digest, XV (July 1969), 10-14. CH-47 instrument missions in the 1968 A Shau Valley campaign known as "Operation Delaware."

1174 Hessler, William H. "Southeast Asia in Ferment." In Frank Uhlig, Jr., ed., The Naval Review, 1964 (Annapolis, Md.: United States Naval Institute, 1964), p98-123. A political-military-air review.

1175 Hessman, James. "The Airborne: Obsolete?" Journal of the Armed Forces, CVI (Nov. 9, 1968), 12-13. Suggests not and points to operations in Vietnam, especially "Junction City."

1176 Hewitt, A. G. "Navigation Techniques in Southeast Asia." Navigator, XV (Fall 1967), 17-18. Getting planes to their targets.

1177 Heyman, Hans, Jr. Civil Aviation and U.S. Foreign Aid: Purposes, Pitfalls, and Problems for U.S. Policy. R-424-RC. Santa Monica, Calif.: RAND Corp., 1964. Some comment on operations in Laos.

1178 Heymont, Irving. "Faster Response in Air-Ground Coordination." Army, XIII (July 1963), 35-36. The need for quicker close air response.

1179 Hickman, Gerry. "Freedom Fighters Tested in Combat." Air Force Times, XXVI (March 23, 1966), 14. The Northrop F-5 over South Vietnam.

1180 Hickox, Robert F. "A Report from the Helicopter War." United Aircraft Quarterly Bee Hive, XLII (Spring 1967), 8-14. U.S. Army airmobile and helicopter gunship operations over South Vietnam.

1181 Hiestand, Harry H. "Military Intelligence and Enemy Air Defenses." U.S. Army Aviation Digest, XX (Sept. 1974), 2-3. With some comment on how it was in Southeast Asia.

1182 Hiett, Robert L. "Search and Save." Air Force and Space Digest, LIII (Dec. 1970), 40-43. U.S. Air Force search and recovery operations over Southeast Asia.

1183 Higham, Robin. Air Power: A Concise History. New York: St. Martin's Press, 1972. 282p. For the SEA war, see especially Part Six, Chapter Four.

1184 ________, and Abigail T. Siddall, eds. Flying Combat Aircraft of the USAAF-USAF. 2 vols. Ames: Iowa State University Press, 1975, 1978. Includes information on planes participating in the Southeast Asian conflict; good illustrations.

1185 "Highlights of '67 in the War Zone." Air Force Times, XXVIII (Jan. 17, 1968), 15. A review.

1186 "Highlights of the War in Vietnam Since July 7, 1964." Air Force and Space Digest, XLVII (Oct. 1964), 23. A run-down with air activity centered around the U.S. response to the Tonkin Gulf incidents.

1187 Hilbert, Marquis D., and Everett Murray. "The Use of Army Aviation in Counterinsurgency Operations." U.S. Army Aviation Digest, VIII (Oct. 1962), 3-9. Much of the theory discussed herein would be tried over South Vietnam in the next few years.

1188 Hill, Adrian. "Air War over Vietnam." Journal of the Royal United Service Institution, CXXI (Jan. 1977), 27-31. A review and analysis.

1189 Hill, Edward Y. "Real Pros." National Guardsman, XXII (Sept. 1968), 2-9. A report on Air Guard flyers in the Vietnam War.

1190 Hill, James C. "The Corsair II: As I See It." U.S. Naval Institute Proceedings, XCIV (Nov. 1968), 38-42. Its uses and acquisition by and for the U.S. Navy.

1191 Hilton, Richard D. "What Every Ground Commander Should Know About Guided Bombs." Army, XXIII (June 1973), 28-33. Including "Smart" bombs.

1192 Hines, O. J. "Tactical Air Reconnaissance." Infantry, LX (Jan.-Feb. 1970), 50-53. Its value to ground soldiers.

1193 Hirsch, Phil, ed. Vietnam Combat. New York: Pyramid Books, 1967. 173p. Accounts of small unit actions, many involving helicopters.

1194 Hirsch, Thomas M. "Diary of a Phantom." Airman, XII (April 1968), 48. Thoughts of an F-4 pilot on Vietnam flying.

1195 "History Book Battle: The Red Defeat at Khe Sanh." U.S. News and World Report, LXIV (May 6, 1964), 43-44. How it was accomplished, with mention of air support.

1196 "Hitting North Again." Time, XCVI (Nov. 30, 1970), 10. Renewed U.S. air activity over North Vietnam.

1197 Ho-Yen-sheng. "The POW Rescue Attempt and the Vietnam War." Asian Outlook, VI (Jan. 1971), 42-44. The unsuccessful Son Tay prison camp raid.

1198 Hoag, Robert J. "It's as Different as Night and Day." USAF Fighter Weapons Review, (Winter 1972), 14-17. U.S. Air Force night fighter operations.

1199 Hoang-Xuan-Binh. "Military Events in 1971." Vietnamese Studies, I (1972), 23-56. A review from the South Vietnamese viewpoint.

1200 Hobson, Kenneth B. "Logistics Is the Lifeline." Air University Review, XVIII (July-Aug. 1967), 2-9. Especially as noted in South Vietnam.

1201 ______. "USAF Weapons at 'Go' Halfway Around the World." Sperryscope, XVII (Winter 1965), 6-10. The Air Force Logistic Command's accomplishments in support of the Vietnamese war effort.

1202 Hodgman, James A. "Market Time in the Gulf of Thailand." In Frank Uhlig, Jr., ed., The Naval Review, 1968 (Annapolis, Md.: United States Naval Institute, 1968), p36-67. The successful U.S. Navy sea-air effort to prevent Communist infiltration of the Gulf of Thailand.

1203 Hoeffding, Bernard. Bombing North Vietnam: An Appraisal of Economic and Political Effects. (RM-5213-1-ISA.) Santa Monica, Calif.: RAND Corp., 1966. 35p. An important "think tank" piece which concludes that the effects would not be decisive to ending the conflict.

1204 Hoge, Thomas A. "The Cambodian Story." American Legion

Magazine, XC (May 1971), 8-12+. A review of the incursion, with some mention of air aspects.

1205 Holder, William G. The Boeing B-52 Stratofortress. Fallbrook, Calif.: Aero Publishers, 1975. 104p. A developmental and operational history.

1206 Holloway, Bruce K. "Our Aerial Armament." Ordnance, LII (March-April 1968), 460-462. Guns, bombs, and rockets carried aboard American warplanes, many over Southeast Asia.

1207 Holmquist, C. O. "Developments and Problems in Carrier-Based Attack Aircraft." In Frank Uhlig, Jr., ed., The Naval Review, 1969 (Annapolis, Md.: United States Naval Institute, 1969), p194-213.

1208 ______. "Developments and Problems in Carrier-Based Fighter Aircraft." In Frank Uhlig, Jr., ed., The Naval Review, 1970 (Annapolis, Md.: United States Naval Institute, 1970), p224-253. Both works are histories with attention paid to aircraft of the SEA conflict.

1209 Holsinger, Michael J. "Air Mission: Psychological Warfare." Airpower Historian, XII (April 1965), 48. Activities over South Vietnam in the early days of U.S. involvement.

1210 ______. "Talking Planes in Vietnam." Air Force Times, XXV (March 10, 1965), 5. The U.S. Air Force in psychological warfare missions.

1211 Holton, William J. "The TAC Role in Special Operations." Air University Review, XXVIII (Nov.-Dec. 1976), 54-68. With some examples from our topic.

1212 "Home at Last: With a Portfolio." Newsweek, LXXXI (Feb. 26, 1973), 16-20. This look at "Operation Homecoming" was abridged in Reader's Digest, CII (May 1973), 94-99, under the title, "Home at Last: The POW's Return."

1213 Homer, Frank. "Navy [Air] Tactical Weapons Are Paying Off in Vietnam." Navy, VIII (Oct. 1965), 23-25. U.S. Navy air strikes against Vietcong and North Vietnamese targets.

1214 Hooper, Edwin B. Mobility, Support, Endurance: A Story of Naval Operational Logistics in the Vietnam War, 1965-1968. Washington: U.S. Government Printing Office, 1972. 278p. A look at the supply end of the conflict, including air, from a naval viewpoint by the former 7th Fleet logistics chief who later served as Director of the Naval Historical Center.

1215 ______; Dean C. Allard; and Oscar P. Fitzgerald. Setting the Stage to 1959. Vol. I of The United States Navy and the Vietnam Conflict. Washington: U.S. Government Printing Office, 1976. 419p. Although this work covers material prior to the scope of this bibliography, it is entered here so that users will be aware of the U.S. Navy's official history, now in progress.

1216 Hooper, John L. "Eyewitness to Valor." U.S. Army Aviation Digest, XV (Aug. 1969), 2-4. How SP4 Gary G. Wetzel won the Congressional Medal of Honor for a daring feat under fire.

1217 Hoopes, Townsend. "Former Under Secretary Speaks Out on Vietnam." Journal of the Armed Forces, CVII (Sept. 20, 1969), 20-21. An interview with a one-time Air Force official; comments similar to those expressed in the following item.

1218 ______. The Limits of Intervention: An Inside Account of How the Johnson Policy of Escalation in the Vietnam War Was Reversed. New York: McKay, 1969. 245p. The Air Force Under Secretary, 1967-1969, concentrates on the political end of the air war with an emphasis on the role of Clark Clifford.

1219 Hopkins, Charles K. "Linebacker II: A Firsthand View." Aerospace Historian, XXIII (Sept. 1976), 128-135. An examination of the Christmas 1972 bombings of North Vietnam.

1220 Hopkins, J. C. "Aerial Refueling." In Carl Berger, ed., The United States Air Force in Southeast Asia, 1961-1973 (Washington: U.S. Government Printing Office, 1977), p201-210. With emphasis on the role of PACAF KC-135's.

1221 Hopkins, Philip B., Jr. "Interdiction at Night in Adverse Weather." USAF Tactical Air Warfare Center Quarterly Review, III (Jan. 1972), 4-9+. With examples from the air war on the Ho Chi Minh Trail.

1222 Hornstein, Edward H. "Chopper Delivery." Infantry, LIV (Sept.-Oct. 1964), 22-23. Helicopter delivery of an Army mortar team into action in South Vietnam.

1223 Horowitz, Leo. "2.75-Inch Rocket Provides Tank Kills." U.S. Army Aviation Digest, XIX (June 1973), 14-15. When fired from the AH-1G Huey Cobra.

1224 Horowitz, Robert S. "Secret Hearings Held on Vietnam Air Support." Air Force Times, XXVI (Oct. 6, 1965), 3. The hearings are cited in item 2557.

1225 "HO's Blasted Bridges." Time, LXXXV (May 7, 1965), 34-35. An early part of the U.S. air war on North Vietnam.

1226 Hoskinson, Charles E. "You Too Can Adjust Artillery." U.S. Army Aviation Digest, XV (Sept. 1969), 2-6. Army aviation artillery spotting in South Vietnam.

1227 Hotz, Robert. "B-52's Over Hanoi." Aviation Week and Space Technology, XCVIII (Feb. 12, 1973), 7. A quick analysis of "Operation Linebacker II."

1228 ______. "Burning Fuse." Aviation Week and Space Technology, LXXXI (July 27, 1964), 11. The Vietnam air war during the American advisory period.

1229 ______. "Escalating War." Aviation Week and Space Technology, LXXXI (July 20, 1964), 11. An editorial on the increased U.S. participation, including air, in the Vietnam conflict.

1230 ______. "The Interdiction Role." Aviation Week and Space Technology, XCVII (Nov. 13, 1972), 9. On U.S. air efforts to cut off the flow of Communist supplies.

1231 ______. "Laurels for 1967." Aviation Week and Space Technology, LXXXVII (Dec. 25, 1967), 11. The 1967 air contribution to the Vietnam conflict.

1232 ______. "Military Reversal." Aviation Week and Space Technology, XCVII (Oct. 30, 1972), 7. Thoughts on Vietnamization and the growing "insurgent" power, throughout Southeast Asia.

1233 ______. "Missile Myths Exploding." Aviation Week and Space Technology, LXXXIV (Jan. 24, 1966), 21. Thoughts on North Vietnamese SAM's.

1234 ______. "More Effective Air Power." Aviation Week and Space Technology, LXXXV (July 11, 1966), 21. American raids on North Vietnamese oil facilities.

1235 ______. "New Lessons from Vietnam." Aviation Week and Space Technology, XCVI (May 22, 1972), 7. Uses of electronic counter-measures.

1236 ______. "Rearguard in the Air." Aviation Week and Space Technology, XCVI (Jan. 10, 1972), 9. The role of U.S. and North Vietnamese Air Force planes during the American withdrawal.

1237 ______. "Spreading the Big Lie: The Report of U.S. Bomb Damage of the [North Vietnamese] Dike System." Aviation

Week and Space Technology, XCVII (Aug. 7, 1972), 9. Contends little damage was done.

1238 "House Probes." Air Force Times, XXXII (May 31, 1972), 8. How 7th Air Force CG John D. Lavelle was recalled in April 1972 for authorizing certain "protective reaction" strikes beyond those permitted by the "rules of engagement." The probe is cited in item 2560.

1239 Houseman, C. A. "Detect, Locate, and Jam Is the Mission of ECM Aircraft." Marine Corps Gazette, LII (May 1968), 10-11. A brief look at such operations over Vietnam.

1240 "How Accidents Happen: Air Force Drops Napalm on the U.S. Lines." Time, LXXXVIII (Sept. 2, 1966), 23. Such errors have occurred in every war in which airplanes have played a role.

1241 "How an Airfield in the North Got Clobbered." Air Force Times, XXVIII (Nov. 15, 1967), 22. U.S. raids on Phuc Yen Mig base in North Vietnam.

1242 "How Army Aviation Proved Itself--In Combat." Armed Forces Management, XXI (Feb. 1966), 51-52. The role of helicopters and light planes in Vietnam.

1243 "How It Happened: Two U.S. Thunderchiefs Shot Down by North Vietnamese MIG's." Time, LXXXV (April 16, 1965), 24. Communist interception tactics.

1244 "How North Vietnam's Army and People Beat the U.S. Air Marauders." Peking Review, XI (March 15, 1968), 25-28. Valor and Chinese help.

1245 "How Smart Bombs Are Squeezing North Vietnam." U.S. News and World Report, LXXII (June 5, 1972), 22-24. U.S. employment of television-guided bombs against communications targets.

1246 "How the Battle of Khe Sanh Was Won." Time, XCI (April 19, 1968), 30-32. Much on the air role in the victory.

1247 Howard, John D. "An Loc: A Study in U.S. Power." Army, XXV (Sept. 1975), 18-24. For example and during the period April 6-28, 1972, "enemy" positions were hit by B-52's, close air support strikes, and Huey Cobra gunships.

1248 ______. "They Were 'Good Ol' Boys'!: An Infantryman Remembers An Loc and the Air Force." Air University Review, XXVI (Jan.-Feb. 1975), 26-39. An expanded and more scholarly version of the above citation.

1249 Howard, William. "Carrier Strike Force: Joint Action in Vietnam." All Hands, no. 580 (May 1965), 2-5. Task Force 77 air strikes on February 7-9, 1965.

1250 _____. "Vietnam Log." All Hands, no. 582 (July 1965), 6-9. A chronology, July 1964-1965, including naval air activities over North and South Vietnam.

1251 Howson, Peter. "The Royal Australian Air Force in Action." Royal Air Forces Quarterly, V (Autumn-Winter 1965), 207-209, 315-317. Examines the early role of the RAAF over Vietnam.

1252 Howton, Harry G. "Airlift Keeps Outposts Alive." Air Force Times, XXVI (Feb. 2, 1966), 14-15. U.S. Air Force tactical airlift missions to remote Special Forces camps in South Vietnam.

1253 Hubbell, John G. "Brave Men in Frail Planes: Forward Air Controllers." Reader's Digest, LXXXVIII (April 1966), 76-80. Examines FAC operations and exploits.

1254 _____. "Jumping Angels of the USAF." Reader's Digest, LXXXI (Nov. 1962), 157-158+. The air rescue service.

1255 _____, et al. POW: A Definitive History of the American Prisoner-of-War Experience in Vietnam, 1964-1973. New York: Reader's Digest Press, 1977. 633p. Based on records and interviews, this work is the most useful currently available on the topic.

1256 "Huey Cobra." U.S. Army Aviation Digest, XII (May 1966), 13-15. A review of the Bell AH-1G gunship.

1257 "Huey Cobra Attacks Viet Cong Targets: Photographs." Aviation Week and Space Technology, LXXXVIII (May 20, 1968), 64-67. A valuable visual presentation.

1258 "Huey Cobra: Forerunner of the AAFSS Armed Helicopter." Interavia, XXI (Feb. 1966), 170-171. Features of the gunship.

1259 "Huey Cobra Joins Army Action in Vietnam." Aviation Week and Space Technology, LXXXVII (Oct. 16, 1967), 30-31. The introduction of the AH-1G helicopter gunship into battle.

1260 "Huey Cobra Praised for Vietnam Action." Aviation Week and Space Technology, LXXXVIII (Jan. 15, 1968), 33. For its effectiveness as a gunship.

1261 "Huey Cobras Escort CH-54's in Vietnam." Aviation Week

and Space Technology, LXXXVII (Dec. 11, 1967), 28-29. Gunship aid to troop-carriers in case of antiaircraft or landing zone fire.

1262 Hughes, Wayne P., Jr. "Vietnam: Winnable War?" U.S. Naval Institute Proceedings, CIII (July 1967), 60-65. Contends that the operation could have been handled successfully, but for political bungling.

1263 Huglin, Henry C. "Our Gains from Success in Vietnam." Air University Review, XX (Jan.-Feb. 1969), 71-78. New weapons and experiences.

1264 Hull, Donald R. "The Way of the Future: Low Level." U.S. Army Aviation Digest, XVIII (Oct. 1972), 2-3. New helicopter tactics.

1265 Humphries, James F. "Spectre in the Night Sky." Airman, XVII (July 1973), 2-6. The AC-130 gunship in Vietnam.

1266 "Hurburt's Air Commandos Proud of the Veteran C-47." Air Force Times, XXV (Feb. 24, 1965), E8. The old Douglas transport's Vietnam role.

1267 "Hurting: How North Vietnam Is Retaliating Against U.S. Raids." Newsweek, LXVIII (July 18, 1966), 28. Propaganda and stepped up activities in South Vietnam.

1268 Husband, Dave. "Supporting Sea Operations." Air Weather Service Observer, XVIII (Sept. 1971), 4-5. Especially search and rescue activities.

1269 Huu-Mai. "Wings." Eastern Horizon (Hong Kong), V (Dec. 1966), 54-64. A look at American air activities in Vietnam.

1270 Hymoff, Edward. The 1st Air Cavalry Division: Vietnam. New York: M. W. Lads Publishing Company, 1967. 153p. A review of its activities from September 1965 through 1966.

1271 ______. "The First Marine Aircraft Wing: Vietnam. New York: M. W. Lads Co., 1969. 124p. A review of activities in the I Corps area; useful illustrations.

1272 ______. The 1st Marine Division: Vietnam. New York: M. W. Lads Publishing Co., 1967. 130p. A review of its 1965-1966 activities with some attention to vertical assault.

1273 "'I Thought I'd Better Shoot': Dogfights." Time, LXXXVIII (Sept. 30, 1966), 29. U.S. fighters vs. North Vietnamese MIG's.

1274 Ilg, Paul. "Shot Down in North Vietnam: A Pilot Tells His Story of Pursuit and Rescue." Life, LIX (Aug. 6, 1965), 24-25. Personal recollections of a commonly hairy problem of the air war.

1275 The Illustrated Encyclopedia of 20th Century Weapons and Warfare. 20 vols. Terre Haute, Ind.: Columbia House, 1975-1978. An excellent set first published in Britain with much information on the weapons, aircraft, and helicopters of the SEA conflict.

1276 "Improvement in the Air." Time, XCIII (April 11, 1969), 39. The North Vietnamese Air Force.

1277 "In the Air, On the Ground." Newsweek, LXV (Jan. 25, 1965), 39-40. An early report from Vietnam.

1278 In the Name of America: The Conduct of the War in Vietnam by the Armed Forces of the United States as Shown by Published Reports, Compared with the Laws of War Binding on the United States Government and Its Citizens. New York: Clergy & Laymen Concerned About Vietnam, 1969. 421p. Excerpts from reports preceded in arrangement by quotations of war laws from various conventions; the U.S. armed services, including air, are shown to have broken almost every established standard. A decidedly negative view of the war.

1279 "Inching Toward an End to a Long and Costly War." Congressional Quarterly Weekly Report, XXXI (Jan. 20, 1973), 86-90. A chronology of American participation, 1950-1973.

1280 "Indochina's Electronic War: 'The Death Harvesters' by Michael Mallory [and] 'The Blind Bombers' by T. D. Allman." Far Eastern Economic Review, LXXV (Jan. 29, 1972), 16-20. Two views of electronic counter-measures warfare over Southeast Asia.

1281 Infantry Magazine, Editors of. A Distant Challenge: The U.S. Infantryman in Vietnam, 1967-1970. Birmingham, Ala.: Birmingham Publishing Co., 1971. Much on airmobile aspects.

1282 Information Please Almanac. New York: Simon & Schuster, 1961-1973. See especially "The Vietnam Story," a special section in the 1967 annual volume.

1283 Inouye, Harvey H. "B-52 Most Feared Allied Weapon." Air Force Times, XXIX (June 18, 1969), 14. High flying and unannounced.

1284 "Inside North Vietnam's Prisons: How Americans Coped."

U.S. News and World Report, LXXIV (March 26, 1973), 58-61. Interviews with survivors.

1285 Institute for Strategic Studies. Strategic Survey. London, 1967-1973. An annual providing a description and analysis of issues in conflict around the world including Southeast Asia.

1286 "Interdiction: All Conditions--Grumman's Flexible Intruder." Flying Review International, XXIII (July 1968), 367-369. A look at the U.S. Navy A-6A.

1287 International Conference on Vietnam. Act of the International Conference on Viet-Nam Between the United States of America and Other Governments, Signed at Paris, March 2, 1973. (Treaties and Other International Acts series.) Washington: U.S. Government Printing Office, 1973. 37p. Text of the Paris accords which finally took America out of the Vietnam war.

1288 "Interpretation: Ecological Effects of the Vietnam War." American Institute Planners Journal, XXXVIII (Sept. 1972), 297-307. The effects of chemical and herbicidal warfare.

1289 "Into a New Blue Yonder: Objective, Red Sanctuary." Life, LVII (Feb. 26, 1965), 28-33. An illustrated look at American air raids on North Vietnam.

1290 "Into Exile: Air Strikes Against Two MIG Bases." Time, XC (Nov. 3, 1967), 24. Attacks designed to ground North Vietnamese interceptors which had been having fair success against U.S. fighter bombers.

1291 "Into the Barrel: Missions from Thai Bases." Time, XC (Oct. 13, 1967), 34-35. B-52 and fighter bomber.

1292 "Into the Buffer Zone: Bombing Within Twelve Miles of China." Time, XC (Aug. 25, 1967), 14-15. A calculated political risk.

1293 "Into the Valley of Death." Air Classics, VIII (Sept. 1972), 18-23. How U.S. Air Force Major Bernard F. Fisher won the Congressional Medal of Honor.

1294 "Intruder Strike." Naval Aviation News, (June 1967), 9. Flown by U.S. Navy A-6's from USS Enterprise.

1295 "Iron Triangle: 'Operation Cedar Falls.'" Newsweek, LXIX (Jan. 23, 1967), 38-39. How U.S. and South Vietnamese troops, with air and airmobile support, sealed off the "Triangle" and systematically swept the woods, bunkers, and caves north of Saigon; when the Vietcong returned, a second assault was necessary a few weeks later.

1296 Irvin, Matthew W. "A Ground Pounder Rides with the FAC." Airman, XII (July 1968), 10-11. A report on Forward Air Control operations.

1297 Irving, Frederick F. "The Battle of Hue." Military Review, XLIX (Jan. 1969), 56-63. With some mention of U.S. and South Vietnamese air strikes on the "enemy" defenders of the town taken during the 1968 Tet Offensive.

1298 Jackson, B. R. The Douglas Skyraider. Fallbrook, Calif.: Aero Publishers, 1969. 144p. Covers the operations of the A-1 through June 1966.

1299 ______. "MIG Killers Four." American Aviation Historical Society Journal, XII (Spring 1967), 52-53. How four Skyraiders combined to down a Communist jet on June 20, 1965.

1300 Jackson, Robert. The Dragonflies: The Story of Helicopters and Autogiros. London: Barker, 1971. 204p. With some attention paid to U.S. craft in the Vietnam war.

1301 ______. "F-100 Ripple Bombing." Fighter Weapons Newsletter, I (March 1968), 1-6. Supersabre attacks on North Vietnamese targets.

1302 Jackson, Wilfred A. "'Stay Clear of Hue!'" U.S. Army Aviation Digest, XVI (April 1970), 12-14. How WO Frederick E. Ferguson won a Congressional Medal of Honor for a rescue mission near that city on January 30, 1968.

1303 Jacobi, L. H. "Tough Tests for the Ten-A." Skyline, XXIV (Dec. 1966), 12-17. The North American OV-10 in combat over South Vietnam.

1304 Jaggers, Joseph N., Jr. "The Huey Cobra." Army Digest, XXII (April 1967), 6-9. The AH-1G enters the Vietnam fighting.

1305 James, Charles D. "Combat Intelligence for Aviation." U.S. Army Aviation Digest, XVI (Jan. 1970), 15-18. Its value to heliborne and gunship operations.

1306 "Jets Rushed to Vietnam in Build-Up." Air Force Times, XXV (Aug. 19, 1964), 2. The beginning of U.S. fighter-bomber involvement.

1307 Johansen, H. O. "The F-5: Our Bantam Supersonic Jet."

Popular Science, LXXXVIII (March 1966), 77-81. A profile of the Northrop Freedomfighter which would be tested in Vietnam combat.

1308 Johnson, C. B. "Dogfighting with MIG's: An Interview with Edwin A. Greathouse." Aviation Week and Space Technology, LXXXIII (July 26, 1965), 11. American combat with North Vietnamese interceptors.

1309 Johnson, Darel S. "The Gallant 'Bird Dog'--Oops--0-1." Army, XVII (Jan. 1967), 49-52. FAC and observation work over South Vietnam.

1310 Johnson, Harold R. "Pacific Air Forces Communications." Signal, XXIV (Oct. 1969), 11-14. Keeping in touch.

1311 ______. "Pacific Air Forces Data Communications." Signal, XXV (Nov. 1970), 6-12.

Johnson, J. L., jt. author see McDaniel, Eugene B.

1312 Johnson, Keith B. A Neglected Weapon: Psychological Warfare. Air War College Professional Study. Maxwell Air Force Base, Ala.: Air University, 1971. 15p. Laments that the U.S. Air Force failed to make greater efforts.

1313 Johnson, Lyndon B. Public Papers of the Presidents: Lyndon B. Johnson, 1963-1969. 9 vols. Washington: U.S. Government Printing Office, 1965-1970. Includes all of LBJ's public statements, while in office, relative to the subject.

1314 ______. The Vantage Point: Perspectives on the Presidency, 1961-1969. New York: Holt, 1971. 636p. Includes reminiscences of the political and military ends of the Vietnamese air war.

1315 Johnson, Raymond W. Postmark: Mekong Delta. Westwood, N.J.: Revell, 1968. 96p. Thoughts on the ground-air-sea battle for that rich area south of Saigon.

1316 Johnson, Rich. "On a Clear Day You Can See Forever, but...." USAF Tactical Air Warfare Center Review, III (April 1972), 20-28. The effects of clouds on tactical air warfare.

1317 Johnson, Roy L. "Two Years After the Gulf of Tonkin." Navy, IX (Aug. 1966), 8-14. A review of U.S. Navy involvement in the Vietnam War to date, including naval air.

1318 Johnson, William G. "Helicopter COC: Forward Helicopter Combat Operations Centers Are Enhancing the Air and

Ground Efforts in Vietnam." Marine Corps Gazette, LI (July 1967), 25-28. The command ship concept.

1319 Johnson, William W. "A Unique Aviation Safety Inspection Team Travels Vietnam." U.S. Army Aviation Digest, XVIII (Feb. 1972), 26-27. Checking to make sure that Allied helicopters are in safe, flyable condition.

1320 Johnston, Donald P. "Time to Punch Out." U.S. Army Aviation Digest, XXIII (March 1977), 32-33. A review of the accomplishments of the OV-1 Mohawk.

1321 Johnston, Robert L. "Combat Evaluation of the A-37." Ordnance, LII (March-April 1968), 424+. Testing the COIN aircraft over South Vietnam.

1322 ______. "The Invader Returns." Air University Review, XV (Nov.-Dec. 1963), 9-22. The World War II Douglas A-26 light bomber as a COIN aircraft over South Vietnam.

1323 Johnstone, L. Craig. "Ecocide and the Geneva Protocol." Foreign Affairs, XLIX (July 1971), 711-720. The spraying of herbicides over South Vietnam.

1324 Jones, David R. "Combat Trap--Von Clausewitz Revisited." Air University Review, XXI (March-April 1970), 68-73. How Task Force "Combat Trap" devised a quick way to clear a helicopter landing zone in the South Vietnamese jungle.

1325 Jones, Lloyd S. U.S. Bombers. Fallbrook, Calif.: Aero Publishers, 1974. 256p. Illustrated with details on such aircraft as were employed over Southeast Asia and in earlier wars.

1326 ______. U.S. Fighters. Fallbrook, Calif.: Aero Publishers, 1975. 352p. Illustrated with details on such aircraft as were employed over Southeast Asia and in earlier wars.

1327 ______. U.S. Navy Fighters, 1922-1980's. Fallbrook, Calif.: Aero Publishers, 1977. 352p. Illustrated with details on such aircraft as were employed over Southeast Asia and in earlier wars.

1328 Jones, Lowell W., and Don A. Lindbo. "Tactical Airlift." Air University Review, XVIII (Sept.-Oct. 1967), 6-19. A look at the process as employed over Southeast Asia and elsewhere.

1329 Jones, Melvin. "Cambodian Blitz." Armor, LXXX (Jan.-Feb. 1971), 21-24. The 1970 incursion, including air and helicopter aspects.

1330 Jones, Raymond G. "The 12th Aviation Group." U.S. Army Aviation Digest, XII (Oct. 1966), 5-7. Its Vietnam role.

1331 Jones, T. S. C. "The Attack Helicopter in Close Support." Royal Air Forces Quarterly, XIII (Summer 1973), 123-127. With examples from the American use in Southeast Asia.

1332 Jordan, Curtis. "Air Power in Vietnam." Air Forces Times, XXVI (Oct. 13, 1965), 12. Its growing role in the conflict.

1333 ______. "Uncovering Charlie: Spray Destroys Hiding Places of the Viet Cong." Air Force Times, XXVI (May 11, 1966), 14. The use of herbicides in "Project Ranch Hand."

1334 Jury, Mark. The Vietnam Photobook. New York: Grossman House, 1971. 160p. Pictures of the war, including aerial aspects.

1335 Just, Ward. "General Lavelle's Private War." New Statesman, LXXXIV (Sept. 22, 1972), 376. How the general exceeded his orders and was relieved.

1336 "'Just Say It Was the Comancheros.'" Newsweek, LXXXVII (March 15, 1971), 39-44. A review of the helicopter war over Southeast Asia.

1337 Kambrod, Matthew R. "The Blast Barons." U.S. Army Aviation Digest, XIV (Oct. 1968), 32-33. The 269th Combat Aviation Battalion in Vietnam.

1338 ______. "Smoke: A Tactical Concept." U.S. Army Aviation Digest, XV (Oct. 1969), 6-9. As employed in Vietnam by the 269th Combat Aviation Battalion.

1339 Kaplan, Burton H. "Combat Night Flying." U.S. Army Aviation Digest, XIII (Nov. 1967), 14-15. U.S. Army helicopter operations between dusk and dawn.

1340 Kaplan, H. R. "The Coast Guard Played a Vital Role in the Vietnam War." Navy, XIII (Nov. 1970), 31-34. With attention to its air-sea rescue service.

1341 Karges, Donald K. "By Order of the President." Tactical Air Reconnaissance Digest, II (Nov. 1968), 12-16. How the 20th Tactical Reconnaissance Squadron (PACAF) won a Presidential Unit Citation.

1342 Karnow, Stanley. "Mr. Nixon's Return Engagement in Cambodia: Back to Bombing." New Republic, CLXVII (April 28, 1973), 15-17. Comments on the "secret" bombing of Communist targets.

1343 Karpman, Laurence I. "Fuel Fallacies: Cobra Style." U.S. Army Aviation Digest, XIX (Feb. 1973), 8-9. Endurance of the AH-1G gunship helicopter.

1344 Karstetter, William B. "Air Rescue." In Carl Berger, ed., The United States Air Force in Southeast Asia, 1961-1973 (Washington: U.S. Government Printing Office, 1977), p235-244. Well illustrated with details on overall planning and individual exploits.

1345 Karten, Dave. "Air Force Logistic Support in Southeast Asia." American Logistics Association Review, LIII (July-Aug. 1973), 29+. Strategic and tactical airlift support throughout the Vietnam War.

1346 Kashiwahara, Ken. "Combat Controllers: First In, Last Out." Airman, XII (Nov. 1968), 5-9. Communications and close air support in South Vietnam.

1347 _____. "Lifeline to Khe Sanh." Airman, XII (July 1968), 4-8. Aerial resupply of the besieged Marines.

1348 Kasler, James H. "The Hanoi Pol Strike." Air University Review, XXVI (Nov.-Dec. 1974), 19-28. A detailed look at the 1966 strikes on North Vietnamese oil facilities.

1349 Kasulka, Duane A. "Identification Letters: U.S. Navy and Marine Corps Air Units." American Aviation Historical Society Journal, XVI (Winter 1971), 294-302. Including many from the Southeast Asian war.

1350 _____. "USN and USMC Units and Their Identification Codes." American Aviation Historical Society Journal, XXI (Summer, Fall 1976), 129-143, 185-198. Including many from the Southeast Asian conflict.

1351 Kaus, Jay. "'69 Proved Tactical Air Power." Air Force Times, XXX (Jan. 21, 1970), 4. A brief look at TAC over Vietnam in 1969.

1352 Keehn, Richard C. "Night Hunter Operations." U.S. Army Aviation Digest, XV (May 1969), 16-20. COIN aircraft and armed helicopters vs. Communist infiltration.

1353 "Keep 'em Flying." New Republic, CLXIX (July 21, 1973), 10-11. Comments on the "secret" bombing of Cambodia.

1354 "Keep on Top of Close Air Support." Journal of the Armed Forces, CIII (Feb. 12, 1966), 11+. Its role in Vietnam.

1355 Kellar, Robert S. "The Heliborne Command Post." U.S. Army Aviation Digest, XV (Jan. 1969), 14-21. With examples of its use over South Vietnam.

1356 ______. "Tactical Air Mobility Is the Answer." U.S. Army Aviation Digest, XV (July 1969), 2-8. Helicopters in troop movements.

1357 Kelly, C. Brian. "Two Wars for the Air Force in Southeast Asia." Data, XIII (March 1968), 22-27. Close air support in the South and "strategic" bombing in the North.

1357a Kelly, Daniel W., Jr. "Downing a MIG." Air Combat, VI (Jan. 1978), 32-34. How U.S. Navy fighter pilot M. H. Isaacks downed a North Vietnamese MIG on July 21, 1967.

1358 Kelly, Emmett. "Into the A Shau." Infantry, LIX (March-April 1969), 45-48. Allied "Operation Delaware" in April 1968.

1359 Kelly, Francis J. U.S. Army Special Forces, 1961-1971. (Vietnam Studies series.) Washington: U.S. Army, Center of Military History, 1973. 227p. Includes a look at the Green Berets' use of helicopters and tactical airlift and close air support.

1360 Kelly, George P. "Guardian Angels." U.S. Army Aviation Digest, XVIII (Aug. 1972), 2-6. Air traffic controllers in Vietnam.

1361 Kelly, Richard. "Until the Eagle Soars." Airman, XV (May 1971), 32-35. Vietnamization and U.S. Air Force help to the VNAF.

1362 Kennedy, Jerry W. "Luck of the Irish." Airman, XVIII (April 1974), 8-11. Recounts a Southeast Asian rescue mission.

1363 Kennedy, John F. Public Papers of the Presidents: John F. Kennedy, 1961-1963. 3 vols. Washington: U.S. Government Printing Office, 1963-1964. Includes all of JFK's public statements while in office relative to the subject. The literature on this President and Vietnam continues to grow; readers might wish to start with Arthur M. Schlesinger, Jr., A Thousand Days: John F. Kennedy in the White House (Boston: Houghton, Mifflin, 1965), Theodore C. Sorensen, Kennedy (New York: Harper & Row, 1965), L. J. Paper, The Promise and the Performance; The Leadership of John F. Kennedy (New York: Crown, 1975), Roger Hilsman, To Move a Nation: The Politics of Foreign Policy in the Kennedy Administration (Garden City, N.Y.: Doubleday, 1967), and Joan I. Newcomb, John F. Kennedy: An Annotated Bibliography (Metuchen, N.J.: Scarecrow Press, 1977).

1364 Kennedy, William A. "The Chopper Comes of Age." Airman,

X (Aug. 1966), 8-11. Use of the helicopter by the U.S. Air Force in South Vietnam.

1365 Kent, John L. "The Helicopter War." Ordnance, LII (Sept.-Oct. 1967), 160-163. A review of the airmobile war in South Vietnam.

1366 Kent, Richard S. "Close Air Support." Infantry, LIX (May-June 1967), 15-17. Strikes in aid of ground troops in South Vietnam.

1367 Kerby, Robert L. "Air Force Transport Operations in Southeast Asia, 1960-1963." Aerospace Historian, XXII (March 1975), 6-13. An important study of the American advisory period.

1368 ______. "American Military Airlift During the Laotian Civil War, 1958-1963." Aerospace Historian, XXIV (March 1977), 1-10. Like the previous citation, this represents the best analysis and review of the topic currently available.

1369 Kernins, Allan K. "Inflight Refuel." Marine Corps Gazette, LVI (July 1972), 44. A brief look at VMGR-152's Da Nang-based KC-130 Hercules operations in South Vietnam.

1370 Kerr, Wendell. "To Save a Guard Pilot, the Army Helps the Air Force." Air Reservist, XXI (June 1969), 4-5. How an Army chopper saved a downed Air Guard flyer.

1371 Kerrigan, Evans E. American Badges and Insignia. New York: Viking Press, 1967. 286p. Includes those worn, displayed, or earned in Southeast Asia.

1372 ______. American War Medals and Decorations. New York: Viking Press, 1964. 149p. Like the above title, this too is illustrated.

1373 ______, ed. The Medal of Honor in Vietnam. Noroton Heights, Conn.: Medallic Publishing Co., 1971. 108p. Presents photographs of the recipients along with their official citations.

1374 Kessing's Contemporary Archives. London: Kessing's Publications, Ltd., 1931- . Begun in 1931, this weekly looseleaf service consists of reports, arranged by country, and based on data selected, translated, condensed, or summarized from newspapers, official publications, periodicals, and news agencies. Much on the SEA conflict.

1375 Kestner, David G. "The Changing Role of the AFRCE in Vietnam." Air Force Civil Engineer, XI (May 1970), 8-9+. The Air Force Regional Civil Engineers.

1376 Kettering, A. J. "Evolution of the Heavy Lift." Marine Corps Gazette, LVII (May 1973), 20-24. The capacity of U.S. Marine Corps helicopters.

1377 Key, John H. "More CAS for Your Dollar." Marine Corps Gazette, LVIII (April 1974), 39-40. The Seacobra, U.S. Marine Corps version of the Bell AH-1G Huey Cobra.

1378 "Key Victory for Marines, but Was the Battle Necessary?: The Three Hills Overlooking the U.S. Base at Khe Sanh." U.S. News and World Report, LXII (May 15, 1968), 8+. An analysis of the great siege.

1379 "Khe Sanh: Airmen Have Close Calls at Besieged Base." Air Force Times, XXVIII (April 3, 1968), 14. The difficulties of U.S. Air Force airlift operations.

1380 "Khe Sanh Draws U.S. Air Forces." Aviation Week and Space Technology, LXXXVIII (Feb. 19, 1968), 16-17. Close air support missions, B-52 strikes, helicopter work, and air resupply operations.

1381 "Khe Sanh Operation Ends with a Big [Air] Lift." Air Force Times, XXXI (May 5, 1971), 18.

1382 "Khe Sanh: 6,000 Marines Dug in for Battle." Life, LXIV (Feb. 9, 1968), 26-29. Illustrated.

1383 "Khe Sanh: Symbol No More." Time, XCII (July 5, 1968), 32-33. The siege and subsequent abandonment of the base.

1384 "Khe Sanh: Tension, Heavy Casualties, Tightening Ring." U.S. News and World Report, LXIV (March 11, 1968), 30-31. Ground and air operations during the siege.

1385 "Khe Sanh Tested Air Force Ingenuity." Air Force Times, XXVIII (May 8, 1968), 21. Airlift operations.

1386 "Khe Sanh: The Siege Is Broken." U.S. News and World Report, LXIV (April 15, 1968), 16. Relief of the defenders.

1387 "Khe Sanh: U.S. Girds for Red Blow." U.S. News and World Report, LXIV (Feb. 26, 1968), 29-30. Preparing for the siege.

1388 Kilbourne, Jimmy W. "Combat Controller to Fighter Pilot." Airman, XIII (Jan. 1969), 34-36. A profile of Capt. John O. Teague in South Vietnam.

1389 ______. "A Cross for York." Airman, XIII (Aug. 1969),

50-54. How Major Glen P. York won the Air Force Cross for a daring rescue of a downed pilot only 30 miles from Hanoi.

1390 _____. "Only One Returned." Airman, XIII (March 1969), 12-16. Gerald O. Young's November 8, 1967, exploit which won for him the Congressional Medal of Honor.

1391 _____. "Open Season at Duc Lap." Airman, XVII (March 1973), 20-22. U.S. Air Force airlift operations.

1392 _____. "'Sandy One, You're on Fire.'" Airman, XIV (Sept. 1970), 42-47. How Col. William A. Jones won the Congressional Medal of Honor.

1393 _____. "A Superb Display of Guts." Airman, XIII (Oct. 1969), 58-62. By U.S. Air Force Col. James R. Brickel on a reconnaissance mission.

1394 _____. "Three Miracles in One Day." Airman, XIII (May 1969), 20-23. U.S. Air Force rescue operations.

1395 King, Frank. "Airport Control Towers for War." Military Engineer, LX (March-April 1968), 114-115. Their construction in South Vietnam.

1396 King, Herbert T. "Naval Logistic Support, Qui Nhon to Phu Quoc." In Frank Uhlig, Jr., ed., The Naval Review, 1969 (Annapolis, Md.: United States Naval Institute, 1969), p84-111. Including support of U.S. Marine Corps air.

1397 King, Horace F. The World's Fighters. Chicago: Follett Publishing Co., 1973. 127p. An illustrated account, including several which saw action in Southeast Asia.

Kinkaid, Francis G., jt. author see Winkler, John L.

1398 Kinnard, Harry W. O. "Airmobility Expands the Scope of 1st Cavalry Division (Airmobile) Missions." Data, XI (Dec. 1966), 19-21. The author was leader of that heliborne-force from its organization through early activities in South Vietnam.

1399 _____. "Army Air Mobility." Data, XIV (Oct. 1969), 26-28. Heliborne-troop delivery.

1400 _____. "Battlefield Mobility of the New U.S. 1st Air Cavalry Division." NATO's Fifteen Nations, XI (April-May 1966), 38-41. A report on the unit for America's allies.

1401 _____. "1st Cav's Exploits in Vietnam Lauded by Former

Commanding General." Data, XI (Aug. 1966), 37-40. A review of Ia Drang Valley operation in late 1965.

1402 ______. "Report from Vietnam by the Commanding General of the 1st Cavalry Division (Airmobile)." Data, X (Dec. 1965), 19-21. Fighting the Ia Drang Valley campaign.

1403 ______. "A Victory in the Ia Drang: The Triumph of a Concept." Army, XVII (Sept. 1967), 71-91. A review of 1st Air Cavalry Division exploits in the Ia Drang Valley from October 19 to November 26, 1965.

1404 Kinney, William A. "The Jet Set." Airman, XIII (May 1966), 43-46. U.S. Air Force aces of the Vietnam conflict.

1405 ______. "Symbols that Soar the Skies." Airman, XII (May 1968), 28-31. U.S. Air Force aircraft insignia.

1406 ______. "TACAIR Vietnam." Airman, XII (July 1968), 40-43. U.S. Air Force tactical air operations over Vietnam.

1407 Kipp, Robert M. "Counterinsurgency from 30,000 Feet: The B-52 in Vietnam." Air University Review, XIX (Jan.-Feb. 1968), 10-18. A look at Stratofortress "Arc Light" operations over South Vietnam.

1408 ______. "The Search for B-52 Effectiveness in the Vietnam War." Aerospace Commentary, (Winter 1970), passim.

1409 Kirk, Donald. Wider War: The Struggle for Cambodia, Thailand, and Laos. New York: Praeger, 1971. 305p. With information on aerial operations and bases.

1410 Kirk, William L. "Gradualism" in the Air War over North Vietnam. Air War College Professional Study. Maxwell Air Force Base, Ala.: Air University, 1970. 26p. Politics and bombing strategy.

1411 Klare, Michael T. War Without End: American Planning for the Next Vietnams. New York: Knopf, 1972. 448p. Includes discussion of the new technology as employed in Vietnam, especially the U.S. Air Force airlift capacity.

1412 Knight, Emmett F. "Aircraft Recovery in Vietnam." U.S. Army Aviation Digest, XV (March 1969), 30-31. On the salvage of downed Army helicopters for repair and reassignment.

1413 Knightly, Philip. The First Casualty, from the Crimea to Vietnam: The War Correspondent as Hero, Propagandist, and Myth Maker. New York: Harcourt, 1975. 465p. The final two chapters are relative to our topic.

1414 Knoebl, Kuno. Victor Charlie: The Face of War in Vietnam, translated by Abe Farbstein. New York: Praeger, 1967. 304p. A European journalist's view which equates U.S. air and other war-making power in Vietnam as "mechanized mass murder."

1415 Knopf, Robert P. "The AC-47." Airman, XI (June 1967), 44-46. An illustrated look at the famous gunship, "Puff, the Magic Dragon."

1416 Koch, Christopher. "The Enemy: 20,000 Missions Later." Newsweek, LXVI (Oct. 11, 1965), 44-48. A report on the first year or so of the American bombing campaign against North Vietnam.

1417 Kolchum, E. H. "Improved North Vietnamese Air Capacity Cited." Aviation Week and Space Technology, LXXXVII (Dec. 4, 1967), 32. A brief report on "enemy" MIG's and their interception abilities.

1418 Kolko, Gabriel. "Nixon's Firepower: Substitute for Manpower." Nation, CCXIV (May 8, 1972), 585-588. On the use of air power during the American withdrawal phase.

1419 Kosier, Ed. "A Vietnam Veteran Joins the Air Force." Airman, X (Dec. 1966), 8-9. Transfer of the Army's Caribou transports to the Air Force and their redesignations as C-7A's.

1420 Kovit, B. "Limited-War Logistics." Space/Aeronautics, XLV (April 1966), 110-119. Roles of the large fleet of air transports and helicopters in air drops and resupply in Vietnam.

1421 Kraft, Joseph. "Letter from Hanoi." New Yorker, XLVIII (Aug. 12, 1972), 58+. With comments on the American air campaign.

1422 Krepon, Michael. "Weapons Potential Inhumane: The Case of Cluster Bombs." Foreign Affairs, LII (April 1974), 595-611. With some thoughts on their use in Southeast Asia.

1423 Krisman, Michael J. "The 'Can Do' Helicopter." Army Digest, XXI (July 1966), 12-16. The UH-1F Iroquois.

1424 Kriss, R. P. "Bombing: A Dangerous Way to Deliver a Message." Saturday Review, LV (May 6, 1972), 34. Comments on the Indochina air war and peace prospects.

1425 Kritt, Robert R. "B-52 'ARC Light' Operations." In Carl Berger, ed., The United States Air Force in Southeast

Asia, 1961-1973 (Washington: U.S. Government Printing Office, 1977), p149-168. An illustrated look at Stratofortress missions over South Vietnam.

1426 Krivinyi, Mikolaus, et al., eds. World Military Aviation: Aircraft, Air Forces, and Weaponry, translated by Elke C. Weal. New York: Arco Publishers, 1973. 224p. Including much which was employed over SEA.

Krudner, Doris A., jt. author see Doty, Roland W., Jr.

1427 "L-19 Team in Vietnam Aids in Tactical Air Operations." Air Force Times, XXIII (Nov. 24, 1962), 6. Spotters.

1428 Lacoste, Yves. "Bombing the Dikes: A Geographer's On-the-Site Analysis." Nation, CCXV (Oct. 9, 1972), 298-301. Contends some damage was done.

1429 Ladd, Jonathan F. "White Swan." Military Review, XLIV (June 1964), 13-25. An aerial operation in which a tactical command post was moved from Ba Lam to Cau Long.

1430 LaFond, C. D. "Air Force Turning Attention to Better Tactical Support." Missiles and Rockets, XVIII (March 28, 1966), 105-108. Close air support in South Vietnam.

1431 LaFrance, George A. "EW: A New Impetus." Navigator, XVI (Spring 1969), 12-13. Electronic warfare in the Vietnam conflict.

1432 Laird, Melvin R. "Shift from Ground to Air Power in SEA Is Stressed." Commander's Digest, IX (Jan. 30, 1971), 3-4. Text of the Defense Secretary's remarks on the air strategy during the American withdrawal period.

1433 Lambermont, Paul M., and Anthony Pirie. Helicopters and Autogiros of the World, rev. ed. Cranbury, N.J.: A. S. Barnes, 1970. 446p. Includes many of the former employed over SEA.

1434 Lambert, Mark. "The Bell AH-1G Huey Cobra." Flight International, XCII (July 27, 1967), 154-166. An analysis of the new gunship helicopter.

1435 ______. "Through the Paces." U.S. Army Aviation Digest, X (Jan. 1964), 8-11. The U.S. Army's OV-1 Mohawk.

1436 Lamm, John F. "Gang Tackling the VC." U.S. Army Aviation Digest, XV (Oct. 1969), 2-5. Air reconnaissance aspects of the U.S. 9th Division's operations "Jitterbug" and "Seal." See also the Malone citation, item 1608.

1437 Landau, David. "The Diplomacy of Terror: Behind the Decision to Bomb the Dikes." Ramparts Magazine, XI (Oct. 1972), 21-25, 52-56. Politics and operations.

1438 Lange, Monte. "1968: Airpower Played a Vital Role." Air Force Times, XXIX (Jan. 29, 1969), 16. A summary of U.S. Air Force Vietnam operations for 1968.

1439 Lansdale, Edward G. In the Midst of Wars: An American's Mission to Southeast Asia. New York: Harper & Row, 1972. 386p. By 1961, U.S. Air Force Brig. Gen. Lansdale had long been leading and training the South Vietnamese in covert operations.

1440 "Laos Invasion: The U.S. Gamble." U.S. News and World Report, LXX (Feb. 22, 1971), 15-18. Political, air, and airmobile aspects.

1441 Larsen, Stanley R., and John L. Collins, Jr. Allied Participation in Vietnam. (Vietnam Studies series.) Washington: U.S. Army, Center of Military History, 1975. 189p. Especially useful for Australian participation.

1442 Larson, Gerald D. "How a Fighter Pilot Sees the Air War in Vietnam." Air Force and Space Digest, L (July 1967), 45-49. An F-4 pilot's account of missions, men, and equipment as recalled for a May 18, 1967, address to the Aviation and Space Writers Convention.

1443 Lasch, Christopher. "Unthinkable Target: Why the Bombing Has to Stop." Nation, CCI (April 16, 1965), 74-75+. Fear of involving Red China.

1444 "Lasers Help Fight the War." Air Force Times, XXIX (June 25, 1969), 34. On boresights for the aligning of aircraft weapons.

1445 "Last Bombing Show: Marine Air Group Twelve." Time, CI (Feb. 5, 1973), 15. The unit's Southeast Asian activities.

1446 "Last Fighter Unit Leaves Vietnam: VNAF Gets 8th SOS Jets." Air Force Times, XXXIII (Oct. 25, 1972), 47. The U.S. Air Force pull-out.

1447 Laurence, Robert deT. "From Out of Nowhere." Airman, VI (Dec. 1962), 24-25. An aerial counterattack in South Vietnam during the American advisory period; reprinted in Marine Corps Gazette, XLVII (March 1963), 16.

1448 ______. "USAF Aids South Vietnam." Airman, VI (Aug. 1962), 38-44. With planes and advisors.

1449 "The Lavelle Case." Commonweal, XCVI (July 14, 1972),

371-372. On the relief of the general for exceeding his orders.

1450 "The Lavelle Case." Time, C (Sept. 15, 1972), 20.

1451 "Lavelle's Back Flips." Newsweek, LXXX (Oct. 2, 1972), 45.

1452 "Lavelle's Crime." New Republic, CLXVII (Oct. 7, 1972), 10.

1453 "Lavelle's Private War: Unauthorized Bombing Raids." Time, XCIX (June 26, 1972), 14.

1454 Lawson, Ted E. "'Blind Bat' Hunts Enemy at Night." Air Force Times, XXVII (July 19, 1967), 14. Night interdiction.

1455 Leavitt, William. "The U.S. Air Force's Technological Response to Vietnam." Air Force and Space Digest, XLIX (March 1966), 84-85+. A look at arms, planes, and equipment; reprinted in Air Force and Space Digest International, II (June 1966), 33-34.

1456 Leckie, Robert. The Wars of America. 2 vols. New York: Harper & Row, 1968. Vol. II ends with Vietnam.

1457 Lederer, William J. Our Own Worst Enemy. New York: W. W. Norton, 1967. 287p. The coauthor of The Ugly American suggests that America was fighting several kinds of wars in Vietnam, including a large-scale bombing campaign, and losing them all; after much muckraking, suggestions for changes in the military/political approach are suggested.

1458 Lee, Irvin H. "Canberra Over Vietnam." Airman, XII (April 1968), 19. The exploits of RAAF No. 2 Squadron.

1459 ______. "Controlling the Lifeline." Airman, XII (April 1968), 16-17. A look at the Airlift Control Center at Tan Son Nhut air base.

1460 ______. "Crown Bird Over Vietnam." Airman, XI (October 1967), 12-13. C-130 Hercules transport activities.

1461 Leftwich, William G., Jr. "Decision at Duc Co." Marine Corps Gazette, LI (Feb. 1967), 35-38. Air-ground combat of August 8-11, 1965.

1462 Lehnert, Richard A. "The Ghost Rider in the Sky." Air Force Magazine, LVI (Sept. 1973), 118-122. Employment of the AC-130 gunship over Southeast Asia.

1463 Le-Hong-Linh. Ap Bac: Major Victories of the South Vietnamese Patriotic Forces in 1963 and 1964. Hanoi:

Foreign Languages Publishing House, 1965. 138p. A North Vietnamese view of the Vietcong victories, won despite the use by the Allies of aircraft.

1464 Leider, Robert, and Seymour Samuels, 3rd. "Airdrop--Emergency Room of Supply." Army Logistician, VI (Jan.-Feb. 1974), 24-27. With examples drawn from the SEA war.

1465 Leifner, Michael. "The Anguish of Cambodia." Foreign Affairs, LX (Oct. 1973), 270-279. A review of diplomatic and military, including air, events since the 1970 incursion.

1466 _____. "Peace and War in Cambodia." Southeast Asia, I (Winter-Spring 1971), 59-73. A review of events between March 1970 and May 1971.

1467 LeMay, Curtis E. "Civic Action by the Air Force." Vital Speeches, XXX (Dec. 15, 1963), 150-152. An October 19, 1963 speech on U.S. Air Force activities in South Vietnam.

1468 _____. "Counterinsurgency and the Challenge Imposed." Airman, VI (July 1962), 2-9. Views of the U.S. Air Force Chief-of-Staff.

1469 _____. "General LeMay Tells How to Win the War in Vietnam." U.S. News and World Report, LXI (Oct. 10, 1966), 36-37+. On bombing the "enemy" into the "stone age."

1470 _____. "The USAF: Power for Peace." National Geographic Magazine, CXXVIII (Sept. 1965), 291-297. With a few comments on Vietnam.

1471 _____, with MacKinley Kantor. Mission with LeMay. Garden City, N.Y.: Doubleday, 1965. 581p. The general's memoirs end with thoughts on Vietnam.

1472 Lenderman, Robert. "Airmobile Tactics and Techniques." U.S. Army Aviation Digest, XI (Jan. 1965), 2-6. Most of which would be tried out by the 1st Air Cavalry Division.

1473 Leonberger, L. B. "Topping the Tanks in Thailand." Airman, XI (Aug. 1967), 15-17. Aviation spirits delivery to U-Tapao air base.

1474 Lessels, Robert J., Jr. "Shadow: AC-119 Gunships in Southeast Asia." Air Force Magazine, LIV (Nov. 1971), 38-40. A review of their activities.

1475 Lessons from the Vietnam War: Report of a Seminar Held at the Royal United Service Institution on 12 February

1969. London: Royal United Service Institution, 1969. A summary of topics discussed, including air.

1476 "Lessons the U.S. Has Learned in the Helicopter War." U.S. News and World Report, LXIX (Nov. 23, 1970), 49-50. Airmobile tactics and operations.

1477 Letzer, George J. "Corsair II De-Tails." American Aviation Historical Society Journal, XVII (Winter 1972), 244-254. A detailed examination of the A-7 attack plane.

1478 ______. "Phantom II De-Tails." American Aviation Historical Society Journal, XII (Summer 1967), 114-119; XV (Spring 1970), 49-55. A detailed look at the McDonnell-Douglas F-4.

1479 Leventhal, Albert R. War. New York: Playboy Press, 1973. 252p. A photographic survey of warfare since 1850 with the final section devoted to Vietnam, including air.

1480 Levy, Milton L. "Naval Air Reservists' Airlift to Vietnam." U.S. Naval Institute Proceedings, XCIV (Jan. 1968), 127-129. An account of the mission.

1481 Lewallen, John. Ecology of Devastation: Indochina. Baltimore, Md.: Penguin Books, 1971. 179p. On the effects of herbicides and such chemical warfare weapons as napalm.

1482 Lewis, Jim. "Air Power in the Pacific." All Hands, no. 555 (April 1963), 22-24.

1483 Lewis, Russ. "Togetherness." U.S. Army Aviation Digest, XII (March 1966), 28-29. The joint work of Army and Air Force en route air controllers in South Vietnam.

1484 Liefer, Richard P. "Air Operations in Cambodia Summed Up." Air Force Times, XXX (July 29, 1970), 16. A review.

1485 Lien, Maurice L. "The Plight of the Prisoners We Have Not Forgotten." Air Force and Space Digest, LIII (June 1970), 32-37. POW's in North Vietnamese camps.

1486 Liggett, William R. "FB-111 Pilot Report." Air Force Magazine, LVI (Feb. 1973), 30-37. Flying the swept-wing fighter bomber.

1487 "Light Observation Helicopters for the U.S. Army." Interavia, XX (Dec. 1965), 1930-1933. LOH's for deployment to Vietnam.

1488 Lightfoot, R. B. "The Heavy Assault Transport Helicopter." Journal of the Royal Aeronautical Society, LXX (Oct. 1966), 914-922. Development and deployment of the U.S. Marine Corps Sikorsky CH-53A.

1489 Ligon, Lynn M. "Business Is Booming in 'Commando Vault.'" Air Force Times, XXX (June 3, 1970), 16. A U.S. Air Force airlift operation.

Lindbo, Don A., jt. author see Jones, Lowell W.

1490 Lindstrand, Nelson L., Jr. "A Deadlier Sting for Our Airmobile Forces." Army Information Digest, XX (Sept. 1965), 11-15. New helicopter armament.

1491 Littauer, Raphael, and Norman Uphoff, eds. The Air War in Indochina, rev. ed. (Cornell University Program on Peace Studies, Air War Study Group.) Boston: Beacon Press, 1972. 289p. The Air War Study Group herein provides for public consumption a useful collection and analysis of information on the operations of American fixed-wing (non-helicopter) aircraft in Southeast Asia through the end of 1971; the first edition was privately printed for distribution to the press and Congressmen.

This important study, the most detailed multi-service approach to date, came from the perception of war opponents that the U.S. ground withdrawal from Vietnam was being accompanied by a stable or growing air commitment. Additionally, the compilers found the use of air power to be an extension of the "capital intensive" warfare preferred by the U.S. in order to utilize its greater technological capacity to save the lives of soldiers. A thesis is built around the idea that "the costs of air war accumulate, but its successes do not." The data are used to show that the American aerial campaign was never able to stop the North Vietnamese from supplying sufficient men and materiel for large offensive operations while, at the same time, the cost in terms of life, injury, destruction, and disruption for the Indochinese was enormous.

The work, definitely not a combat narrative, is divided into 14 chapters, five appendices and a "Statistical Summary." With the help of statistics, tables, and graphs, the coverage is extremely thorough, even though the volume went to press ahead of the final air offensive, "Linebacker II." Following a valuable introduction to the concepts of air war operations and equipment, topics discussed include the characteristics of the air war in North and South Vietnam, along the Ho Chi Minh Trail, in Laos and Cambodia, the monetary costs of the campaign, legal aspects both constitutional and international, the ecological impact, and the development of electronic measures and counter-measures for aerial operations.

Probably not the final word on the air war, the Air War Study Group's product is still, by far, the most complete and detailed report on the subject to appear to date. Indeed, it can be classed along with The Pentagon Papers as one of the most valuable resources students of our subject will have to draw on for many years yet to come.

1492 Little, John A. "They Need Us Down There." U.S. Army Aviation Digest, XVII (March 1971), 10-13. A look at U.S. Army organic aviation in South Vietnam.

1493 Littlewood, Arthur R. "'Surprise! No Parachute.'" Infantry, LIII (Nov.-Dec. 1963), 15-17. Helicopter vertical assault.

1494 "Living Inside a Bull's Eye: The Bombing of Hanoi." Time, C (Oct. 23, 1972), 42-47. Reports on the bombing from both the American and North Vietnamese sides.

1495 "Living on Air: How Khe Sanh Survived." Time, XCI (March 1, 1968), 19. Aerial resupply of the U.S. Marine Corps defenders.

1496 Lobelson, Robert M. "The Chopper: Key to Army Mobility." Journal of the Armed Forces, CIII (Dec. 25, 1965), 8-11. Troop delivery by vertical assault ala 1st Air Cav.

1497 ______. "The Other Side of the Coin." Journal of the Armed Forces, CIII (Nov. 20, 1965), 8-11. The development and deployment of such counterinsurgency aircraft as the Cessna A-37.

1498 "Locations of USAF Operations in Southeast Asia." Air Force Times, XXVII (Feb. 15, 1967), 4. A captioned map.

1499 "The Lockheed C-141 Starlifter." Air Pictorial, XXIX (April 1967), 107-111. An illustrated look at the U.S. Air Force transport, including its Vietnam use.

1500 "The Lockheed C-141 Starlifter." Air Progress, XXV (July 1969), 27+.

1501 "The Lockheed C-130 Hercules." Air Progress, XXI (April 1965), 12-17+; XXIV (Feb. 1968), 33-36+; XXV (Sept. 1969), 48-51+. Details on the U.S. Air Force transport and its operations.

1502 "The Lockheed C-130 Hercules." Naval Aviation News, (Nov. 1971), 20-21. As employed by the U.S. Navy and U.S. Marine Corps.

1503 "The Lockheed C-130 Hercules: The First Twenty Years."

Air Pictorial, XXXVI (Aug.-Sept. 1974), 302-305, 350-353. A pictorial review with some attention to Vietnam.

1504 Lockwood, Bill G. "The Evolution of the Armed Helicopter." U.S. Army Aviation Digest, XIV (Nov. 1968), 32-35. With suitable attention to the airwar in SEA.

1505 Lockwood, Lee. "North Vietnam Under Siege." Life, LXII (April 7, 1967), 33-44D. An illustrated look at the U.S. bombing campaign.

1506 Lomax, Louis E. Thailand: The War that Is, the War that Will Be. New York: Random House, 1967. 175p. An eyewitness report concerning, among other things, the use of that country's air bases by the U.S. for prosecution of the air war over North and South Vietnam.

1507 "Long, Long Trail Unwinding." Newsweek, LXXXII (July 9, 1973), 26-27. The coming end to air operations over Laos and Cambodia.

1508 Lonie, F. R. "Interdiction in a South-East Asian Limited War." Royal Air Forces Quarterly, IX (Winter 1969), 293-296. A British-Australian view of the success of such American operations.

1509 "Look Down that Long Road." Time, LXXXV (Feb. 19, 1965), 16-21. A report on the Vietnam conflict, including air.

1510 Loomis, William. "Military Strategists in Vietnam Are Still Wedded to the Graduated Response Concept." Data, XIII (Dec. 1968), 19-21. The political tail (or head) wagging the air war dog.

1511 Looney, Joe. "Aces Speak Out." Air Force Times, XXXIII (Oct. 11, 1 972), 63. Interviews with Capts. Richard "Steve" Ritchie and Chuck DeBellevue.

1512 _____. "B-52 Crews Get Two MIG's in the Final Days." Air Force Times, XXXIII (Feb. 14, 1973), 4. Downed in December 1972 during "Linebacker II."

1513 _____. "Ritchie First Ace." Air Force Times, XXXIII (Sept. 13, 1972), 1+. Capt. "Steve" Ritchie's combats over North Vietnam.

1514 Loory, Stuart H. "Story Behind the Raid on Son Tay Prison." Congressional Record, CXVII (Feb. 11, 1971), S1333-S1335. Reprints a Los Angeles Times report on the unsuccessful effort.

1515 Loosbrock, John F. "North of the Border." Air Force and

Space Digest, XLIX (March 1966), 8-9. Thoughts on the U.S. bombing campaign against North Vietnam.

1516 Lopes, Francis I. "Army Aircraft Vulnerability and Survivability." U.S. Army Aviation Digest, XVII (Nov. 1977), 2-5+. Based on the Vietnam experience.

1517 Lord, Charles, Jr. "Crusader." Air Classics, VIII (Dec. 1971), 52-56. A profile of the F8U-1P, including its U.S. Navy use over Vietnam.

1518 Lorenzo, Peter, Jr. "The Canberra Goes to Southeast Asia." Navigator, XV (Spring 1968), 44-45. The light bomber's use over Vietnam.

1519 Lovy, Andrew. Vietnam Diary, October 1967-July 1968. New York: Exposition Press, 1970. 129p. Reminiscences of the fighting with some comments on the air aspects.

1520 Lowe, George E. "Vietnams and Munichs." U.S. Naval Institute Proceedings, XCII (Oct. 1966), 62-71. The bombing of Hanoi's petroleum storage facilities in June 1966 viewed as an example of what needed to be done to halt Communist aggression.

1521 Lowe, Thomas E. "The 481st Tactical Fighter Squadron in Vietnam: A Personal Account." American Aviation Historical Society Journal, XX (Summer 1975), 78-88. Reminiscences of the fighter-bomber war.

1522 Lowenstein, James G., and Richard M. Morse. Vietnam: December 1969, a Staff Report Prepared for Use of the Committee on Foreign Relations, United States Senate. Washington: U.S. Government Printing Office, 1970. 18p.

1523 ______. Vietnam: May 1972, a Staff Report Prepared for Use of the Committee on Foreign Relations, United States Senate. Washington: U.S. Government Printing Office, 1972. 32p. Both of the above reports contain some material relative to the subject.

1524 Lubenow, Larry R. "'Do You Read Me?'" Army, XVIII (May 1968), 51-53. Military/air jargon of the Vietnamese conflict.

1525 Lucas, Jim G. Dateline: Vietnam. New York: Award House (dist. by Crown), 1966. 334p. Dispatches covering two years of war, including air, by the noted U.S. Marine Corps correspondent of World War II. A revised edition of 350 pages was issued two years later by the same firm.

1526 _____. "Linkup: Heliborne Infantry and Armor." Armor, LXXVIII (Nov.-Dec. 1969), 14-17. A report on operations in South Vietnam.

1527 Ludvigsen, Eric C. "Vietnam--In 21 Volumes." Army, XXVII (Aug. 1977), 30-32. A preview of the as-yet unavailable official history, The United States Army in Vietnam, now being prepared.

1528 Luehrs, R. E. "Marine Medical Evacuation." Marine Corps Gazette, LIII (May 1969), 56-57. Includes a few of the helicopter aspects.

1529 Lukens, Howard I. "The Heli-Tactic Gap." Army, XXI (Aug. 1971), 43-46. The need for better tactics in the deployment of Army helicopters in Southeast Asia.

1530 Lumsden, Malvern. Incendiary Weapons. (A Sirri monograph.) Cambridge, Mass.: Published for the Stockholm International Peace Research Institute by MIT Press, 1976. 255p. Includes a look at the American air use of napalm in Southeast Asia.

1531 Luttwak, Edward. A Dictionary of Modern War. New York: Harper & Row, 1971. Some information relative to our topic is contained.

1532 Lynch, Mike. "The Air Force's Civilian Airmen." Airman, XII (Oct. 1968), 38-42. Rapid Area Maintenance in South Vietnam.

1533 "MAC Breaks Airlift Marks." Air Force Times, XXVII (Feb. 1, 1967), 43. The shipment of materiel and personnel to Vietnam by air.

1534 "MAC: The Command with Airlift for Its Middle Name." National Defense Transportation Journal, XXII (May-June 1966), 28+. A look at the Vietnam role of the Military Airlift Command.

1535 "MAC the FAC's Last Mission." Time, LXXXV (April 30, 1965), 31. The adventures of one forward air controller over South Vietnam.

1536 McArdle, Frank H. "The KC-135 in Southeast Asia." Air University Review, XIX (Jan.-Feb. 1968), 20-33. One of the most useful accounts of the Stratotanker's role.

1537 McCain, John S., Jr. "How the POW's Fought Back." U.S. News and World Report, LXXIV (May 14, 1973), 46-52+. American survival and resistance in North Vietnamese camps.

1538 ______. "In Vietnam, the Enemy Is Beaten: An Interview." Reader's Digest, XCIV (Feb. 1969), 75-79. Thoughts on the war by a U.S. Navy admiral.

1539 McCarthy, Richard D. The Ultimate Folly: War by Pestilence, Asphyxiation, and Defoliation. New York: Knopf, 1969. 176p. A stinging review of U.S. activities in South Vietnam, including the spraying of herbicides and use of napalm by the air services.

1540 McCaslin, Fred C., Jr. "ABCCC." Signal, XXXI (Nov.-Dec. 1976), 26-29. A capsule view of the man and machines of the U.S. 7th Airborne Command and Control Squadron.

1541 McCauley, Brian. "Operation End Sweep." U.S. Naval Institute Proceedings, C (March 1974), 18-25. Helicopter mine clearing of North Vietnam's harbors.

1542 McChristian, Joseph A. The Role of Military Intelligence, 1965-1967. (Vietnam Studies series.) Washington: U.S. Army, Center of Military History, 1974. 182p. Its uses in planning the ground-air operations.

1543 MacCloskey, Monro. Alert the Fifth Force: Counterinsurgency, Unconventional Warfare, and Psychological Operations of the United States Air Force. (Military Research series.) New York: Rosen, 1969. 190p. With considerable attention paid to South Vietnam.

1544 ______. The United States Air Force. New York: Praeger, 1967. 244p. A history with some attention to the SEA war.

1545 McConnell, Arthur F. "Mission: 'Ranch Hand.'" Air University Review, XXI (Jan.-Feb. 1970), 89-94. An examination of the U.S. Air Force role in spraying defoliants over Southeast Asia.

1546 McConnell, John P. "Airlift." Air Force Policy Letter for Commanders, no. 4 (April 1967), 16-20. Testimony by the Air Force Chief of Staff before Congressional defense posture hearings that year.

1547 ______. "Airpower in Limited Conflicts." Air Force Policy Letter for Commanders, no. 5 (May 1966), 2-7. Remarks on Vietnam made at the Citadel on April 16, 1966.

1548 ______. "As the Air War Heats Up in Vietnam: An Interview." U.S. News and World Report, LX (May 9, 1966), 27-29. Thoughts on prosecuting the air campaign.

1549 ______. "Controlling the Scope and Pace of Conflict." Air

Force Policy Letter for Commanders, no. 10 (October 1967), 2-7. A speech on the aerial strategy of Vietnam made before the Past Commanders Dinner at the Golden Anniversary of Kelly Air Force Base on September 6, 1967.

1550 ______. "The Lesson of Vietnam: Airpower." Vital Speeches, XXXII (Jan. 1, 1966), 182-184. A December 6, 1965, address before the Detroit Economics Club; also printed in Air Force Policy Letter for Commanders, no. 1 (Jan. 1966), 1-6.

1551 ______. "The Role of Airpower in Vietnam: Strategic Persuasion." Vital Speeches, XXXII (Oct. 15, 1965), 12-15. A September 16, 1965, address on the use of airpower in obtaining political ends.

1552 ______. "Some Reflections on a Tour of Duty." Air University Review, XX (Sept.-Oct. 1969), 2-11. Thoughts of the retiring Chief of Staff on the air war in Southeast Asia.

1553 ______. "Strategic Offensive." Air Force Policy Letter for Commanders, no. 4 (April 1968), 4-8. The air campaign against North Vietnam.

1554 ______. "The U.S. Air Force's Score in a Limited War: Impressive." Air Force and Space Digest, XLIX (Sept. 1966), 52.

1555 ______. "What the Air Force Is Learning in Vietnam." Air Force and Space Digest, L (July 1967), 44-47. The application of new tactics and firepower.

______, jt. author see Brown, Harold

1556 McConnell, Lewis. "'Copters Carry the Cargo of Men, Materiel, Munitions." Army Digest, XXVI (Feb. 1971), 26-30. Helicopter logistics in Southeast Asia.

McCoy, Alfred W., jt. editor see Adams, Nina

1557 McCoy, Fred. "An Aerial Blocking Force." Armor, LXXXVII (March-April 1972), 29-34. Armed helicopters.

1558 McCullen, Don. "Helicopters Lead the War Against the Guerrillas in the Mekong Delta." Illustrated London News, CCXLVI (March 6, 1965), 2-7. A pictorial review of the campaign south of Saigon.

1559 McCutcheon, Keith B. "Air Support for III MAF." Marine Corps Gazette, LI (Aug. 1967), 19-23. Work of the 1st Marine Aircraft Wing.

1560 ______. "Getting There, Any Way, Any Time." Journal of the Armed Forces, CVI (July 26, 1969), 21-22+. U.S. Marine Corps aviation in Vietnam.

1561 ______. "Marine Aviation in Vietnam, 1962-1970." U.S. Naval Institute Proceedings, XCVII (May 1971), 122-155. This, the most useful account of the subject yet available, was reprinted in Frank Uhlig, Jr., ed., The Naval Review 1971 (Annapolis, Md.: United States Naval Institute, 1971), p122-155.

1562 ______. "Marine Corps Aviation: An Overview." Marine Corps Gazette, LII (May 1968), 22-27. With some attention paid to the SEA war.

1563 McDaniel, Eugene B., and J. L. Johnson. Before Honor. Philadelphia: Holman, 1975. 192p. POW experiences in North Vietnam.

1564 MacDonald, Charles B. "The Vietnam War: Part II, Military Aspects of the War." In Encyclopedia Americana, 1978 ed., 30 vols. (Danbury, Conn.: Americana Corp., 1978), vol. 28, p112c-112g.

1565 "The McDonnell F-4 Phantom." Aerospace International, II (Nov. 1966), 16-25. A profile of the fighter.

1566 "The McDonnell F-4 Phantom." Air Progress, XVIII (Fall 1962), 8-9; XXIII (May 1967), 30-33; XXIV (March 1968), 44-45+; XXV (Aug. 1969), 23-26+.

1567 "The McDonnell F-4 Phantom." Flight, XCII (March 27, 1965), 832-835; XCIII (June 30, July 14, 1966), 1091-1101; XCIV (Sept. 21, Oct. 12, 1967), 483-487, 629-630; XCV (Aug. 15, 1968), 253-258; XCVI (Nov. 20, 1969), 768-771.

1568 "The McDonnell F-4 Phantom." Interavia, XVIII (Nov. 1963), 1698-1701; XX (Feb. 1965), 259-263; XXI (May 1966), 737-741.

1569 "The McDonnell F-4 Phantom." Naval Aviation News (March 1961), 24-26; (Jan. 1962), 20-22; (March 1963), 12-13; (Sept. 1968), 15-19; (March 1971), 20-21. Its use by the U.S. Navy and Marine Corps.

1570 McDougal, Winn. "Aerial Field Artillery for the Corps." Field Artillery Journal, XLII (March-April 1974), 54-58. Employment of armed helicopters by the U.S. Marine Corps.

McDowell, Ernest R., jt. author see Ward, Richard

1571 McDowell, James I. "A Day in the Tuy Hoa Valley with

Gunships and Slicks." Army, XVII (Feb. 1967), 60-62. U.S. Army airmobile and gunship operations.

1572 McFall, A. Dodge. "Farewell to the 'SPADs.'" U.S. Naval Institute Proceedings, XCI (April 1965), 54-59. A look at the use and retirement of the Douglas Skyraider. See also the comments by Lt. Col. Ralph E. Poore and Lt. Douglas M. Horne in the August 1965 issue, 110-111, and by Cmdr. L. E. Brumbach in the December 1965 issue, 115-117.

1573 McGarvey, Patrick J., comp. Visions of Victory: Selected Vietnamese Communist Military Writings, 1964-1968. (Hoover Institute on War, Revolution, and Peace, no. 81.) Stanford, Calif.: Stanford University Press, 1969. 276p. Twelve key speeches or published statements on war aims, strategy, and tactics useful for background information to those studying our topic.

1574 McGlasson, W. D. "'Beautiful! Beautiful!'" National Guardsman, XXII (Nov. 1968), 2-9. Air Guardsmen in action over South Vietnam.

1575 ______. "Those Gung Ho Guardsmen in Vietnam." Air Force and Space Digest, LI (Nov. 1968), 47-51. Exploits of Air Guard flyers.

1576 McGrath, Edward G. "The Story of the Oriskany Fire." Navy, IX (Dec. 1966), 32-35. Aboard the carrier in Tonkin Gulf on October 26, 1966.

1577 McGrath, John M. Prisoner-of-War: Six Years in Hanoi. Annapolis, Md.: United States Naval Institute, 1975. 114p. Memoirs of a U.S. Navy pilot downed over North Vietnam in 1967.

1578 McGrath, Joseph A., Jr. "Evasion and Escape: Still a Stepchild." Air University Review, XXVII (Sept.-Oct. 1976), 47-56. With considerable attention to the subject vis-à-vis Vietnam.

1579 McGrory, Mary. "Illicit Bombs Away: The Case of [Gen. John] Lavelle." America, CXXVII (Oct. 7, 1972), 249. Comments on the U.S. Air Force general's exceeding of orders.

1580 Mack, Jerold R., and Richard M. Williams. "The 552nd Airborne Early Warning and Control Wing in Southeast Asia: A Case Study in Airborne Command and Control." Air University Review, XXV (Nov.-Dec. 1973), 70-78. A review of deployment, objectives, and achievements.

1581 Mackay, Ian. Australians in Vietnam. Adelaide, South

Australia: Rigby, 1968. 201p. Including air and helicopter forces.

1582 McKee, Seth J. "The Role of the U.S. Air Force in Counterinsurgency." Air Force Policy Letter for Commanders, no. 2 (Feb. 1965), 15-20. With attention to South Vietnam.

1583 McKenna, James L. "The Air Force Chopper Comes of Age." Review, XLVII (March-April 1968), 39-40. Airlift and rescue operations in Vietnam.

1584 Mackey, William A. "Flying the Phantom." Flying Review International, XIX (July 1964), 26-28. A pilot's comments on the McDonnell F-4B fighter.

1585 Macknight, Nigel. "F-105's Over Southeast Asia." Air Pictorial, XXXIX (April 1977), 140-143. Nice views of Thunderchief fighter bomber raids and aircraft.

1586 McLaughlin, Burl W. "Khe Sanh: Keeping an Outpost Alive." Air University Review, XX (Nov.-Dec. 1968), 57-77. The commander of the U.S. Air Force 834th Air Division describes the successful aerial resupply operation in detail.

1587 ______. "TAC Airlift Revamped in Vietnam." Armed Forces Management, XV (Aug. 1969), 72-73. U.S. Air Force tactical airlift operations.

1588 McLaughlin, George W. "The Air War in South Vietnam." Air Force Policy Letter for Commanders, no. 11 (Nov. 1969), 21-25. A talk before the ROA of Pennsylvania given on September 27, 1969.

1589 McLaughlin, John. "The War in Vietnam: The Myths and the Realities." Air Force Magazine, LV (Nov. 1972), 62-66. A September 19, 1972 address before the Air Force Association Convention.

1590 McLaughlin, William A. "Air Resupply Activity at Plei Me." Air Force Policy Letter for Commanders, no. 1 (Jan. 1966), 6. Tactical airlift in support of ground activities in late 1965.

1591 McLean, Donald, ed. Guide to Combat Weapons of Southeast Asia. Forest Grove, Ore.: Normount Technical Publications, 1971. 348p. A look at over 170 weapons, including aircraft, manufactured in Europe, the Soviet Union, China, North Vietnam, and the United States for use in the conflict.

1592 McNamara, E. G. "Australian Military Operations in Vietnam." Journal of the Royal United Service Institution,

CXIII (Nov. 1968), 310-316. A review of their participation in the air and ground campaigns.

1593 McNamara, Robert S. "The Continuing Use of B-52's in Vietnam." Air Force Policy Letter for Commanders, no. 9 (Sept. 1, 1965), 4. A statement by the Defense Secretary made in August 1965 before the Senate Appropriations Committee on "Arc Light" operations.

1594 ______. "Report on Air Strikes in Vietnam." Air Force Policy Letter for Commanders, no. 5 (May 15, 1965), 2. Text of remarks made at an April 26, 1965 news conference.

1595 "McNamara and the [Joint] Chiefs [of Staff] 'Fight' the Air War." Air Force Policy Letter for Commanders, no. 10 (Oct. 1967), 8-24. Reprinted from the September 9, 1967, issue of the Journal of the Armed Forces.

1596 MacSorley, Frank R., Jr. "F-4 Shoot-Out." American Aviation Historical Society Journal, XIV (Fall 1969), 196-198. A review of Phantom activities over North Vietnam.

1597 MacWhinney, Al. "Vietnam [Forward Air] Controllers Stay Clear." Air Force Times, XXVI (Sept. 22, 1965), 15. FAC's and close air support of ground troops.

1598 McWilliams, Harry H., 3d. "Arc Light: The Tactical Sledge Hammer." Armor, LXXVIII (Sept.-Oct. 1969), 35-37. B-52 strikes on "enemy" positions in South Vietnam.

1599 Maddox, Bobby J. "Close Air Support." Armor, LXXIII (Jan.-Feb. 1964), 59-62. Its role in aid of ground forces.

1600 Maddox, W. J. "Air Mobility in Vietnam." Astronautics and Aeronautics, IV (Oct. 1966), 68-73. U.S. Army and ARVN use of helicopters for vertical assault.

1601 "The Magnificent Dozen." Aerospace Safety, XXIV (March 1968), 1-4. The story of Capt. Robert Cooley, an F-105 pilot whose Thunderchief was crippled during an air strike over North Vietnam but was successfully navigated back to base.

1602 "Major Fuel Storage Areas Struck." Naval Aviation News, (Sept. 1966), 10. U.S. Navy carrier planes in the June 1966 raids.

1603 "Major Sings Out the Praises of 'Puff, the Magic Dragon.'" Air Force Times, XXVII (March 29, 1967), 16. The AC-47 gunship in action over South Vietnam.

1604 "Major U.S. [Air] Bastion Springs Up in Thailand." Business

Week, (May 13, 1967), 38-39. On the development of air bases there.

1605 "Major U.S. Tactical Bases in Vietnam." Air Force and Space Digest, L (March 1967), 82. A captioned chart.

1606 Malley, Robert J. "Forward Airfield Construction in Vietnam." Military Engineer, LIX (Sept.-Oct. 1967), 318-322. Building airfields, sometimes under fire.

1607 Malone, Henry O. "Close Air Support for Mobile Air Warfare." Armor, LXXIII (Jan.-Feb. 1964), 28-29. Help for armored and vertical assault forces.

1608 Malone, Paul B., 3d. "Jitterbugging: [Mekong] Delta Dance of Death." Army, XIX (July 1969), 49-53. Infantry, helicopter, artillery, airplane combination tactics of the 1st Reconnaissance-Commando Brigade of the U.S. 9th Infantry Division.

1609 Mandeville, Robert C. "What U.S. Bombs in North Vietnam: A Navy Pilot's Account--Excerpt from a Statement, December 23, 1966." U.S. News and World Report, LXII (Jan. 9, 1967), 13. Objectives of American attacks to be military in nature.

1610 Manning, Paul A. "VMCJ." Marine Corps Gazette, LVI (Oct. 1972), 40-43. A brief history of Marine Composite Reconnaissance Squadrons, especially VMCJ-1, in Vietnam from August 1964 to May 1971.

1611 Manning, Stephen O., 3d. "Something Big Coming." Airman, XVII (Sept. 1973), 24-32. A look at "Operation Linebacker II."

1612 ______, and Len Brady. "Twenty Years on the Line." Airman, XX (Jan. 1976), 2-7. A history of the B-52 Stratofortress.

1613 "Many Air Operations Tallied in Cambodia." Air Force Times, XXX (June 10, 1970), 18. A month of air raids following the great "incursion."

1614 "Many Puffs, Many Dragons." Flight International, LXXXIX (Jan. 6, 1966), 41. The AC-47 gunship.

1615 "Marine Aviation in Vietnam." Naval Aviation News, (Jan. April, Nov., Dec. 1966), 14, 18, 20, 16. A review of its accomplishments in the I Corps area.

1616 "Marine [Aviators] in Vietnam." Naval Aviation News, (Oct. 1967), 20-21. A look at their activities.

1617 "Marine Colonel Praises Air Force for Its Duc Co Operation." Air Force Policy Letter for Commanders, no. 12 (Dec. 1965), 29. U.S. Air Force close air support in aid of the leathernecks.

1618 "Marines Get New Mission in Vietnam: 30,000 Combat Troops Guard the Big U.S. Air Base at Da Nang." Navy, VIII (April 1965), 45-49. Base security was the original reason for sending the Marines into Vietnam, other operations escalating out of that purpose.

1619 "'Market Time' Air Surveillance." Naval Aviation News, (April 1968), 35. The U.S. Navy use of patrol planes to check Communist seaborne infiltration of South Vietnam.

1620 Marks, W. R., Jr. "Mission: Helicopters." Marine Corps Gazette, LVI (May 1972), 30-35. Marine Helicopter Squadron 1 in South Vietnam.

1621 Marlar, Ron. "Attacking the North: The Air Force Begins a Second Year of Strikes Against the Reds." Air Force Times, XXVI (Feb. 23, 1966), 14. 1965 statistics.

1622 Marquez, Toby. "The Navy's New [C-2A] Greyhound Cargo Plane Lands on the [USS] Kitty Hawk Off Vietnam." Navy X (Feb. 1967), 36-37. Details on a new way of aerial replenishment.

1623 Marshall, Samuel L. A. Ambush: The Battle of Dau Tieng, Also Called the Battle of Dong Minh Chau, War Zone C, "Operation Attleboro," and Other Deadfalls in South Vietnam. New York: Cowles Book Co., 1969. 242p. In the fall of 1966, a sweep into a big rubber plantation by the heliborne 196th Infantry Brigade provoked a counterthrust by a Vietcong division, which brought the commitment of additional U.S. forces and close air and "Arc Light" support. Fighting, here reconstructed by interviews, was often at the squad and platoon level.

1624 _____. Battles in the Monsoon: Campaigning in the Central Highlands of Vietnam, Summer 1966. New York: William Morrow, 1967. 408p. Examines a number of sweeps made north of Saigon with some attention to helicopter and other air activities in support of the Allied operations.

1625 _____. "Fight at Monkey." Harper's Magazine, CCXXXIII (Nov. 1966), 111-114+. An excerpt from item 1624.

1626 _____. "Observations from a Vietnamese Notebook." Army, XVI (Dec. 1966), 16-28. Thoughts on the conduct of the war in South Vietnam.

1627 _____. West to Cambodia. New York: Cowles Book Company,

1968. 253p. Units of the 4th and 25th Infantry Divisions and Special Forces, with air support, campaign along the Vietnamese-Cambodian border from August to November 1966 to guard against infiltration.

1628 ______, and David H. Hackworth. Bird, the Christmas Tide Battle. New York: Cowles Book Co., 1968. 206p. What happened when 800 Vietcong attacked 150 GI's guarding Landing Zone Bird.

1629 Martin, Edward. "Antiseptic War: Bombing by Navy Attack Planes." Newsweek, LXIX (May 29, 1967), 48-49. Raids by U.S. Navy carrier planes on North Vietnamese targets.

1630 ______. "City in Waiting: The Viet Cong Campaign to Isolate Quang Tri." Newsweek, LXIX (April 24, 1967), 40-41. Includes comments on the U.S. aerial response.

1631 Martin, Robert P. "Eyewitness in South Vietnam where Americans Are Fighting: A Close-Up of the Shadow War." U.S. News and World Report, LVI (June 1, 1964), 36-39. An early report on U.S. ground-air operations.

1632 ______. "The Strange War the U.S. Is Not Winning: An Eyewitness Report from the Front in Vietnam." U.S. News and World Report, LV (Sept. 30, 1963), 48-50. The role of U.S. air and ground advisors in South Vietnam.

1633 Martin, Tom. "Ability, Nerve of C-123 Crews the Key to the Vietnam Combat Airlift." Air Force Times, XXIII (Jan. 19, 1963), 5. U.S. Air Force Providers in support of South Vietnamese ground forces.

1634 Marvellino, Mike. "Spotlight on the Enemy." Army Digest, XXIV (Jan. 1969), 30-32. U.S. Army and Air Force night searchlight and flare dropping operations.

1635 Mason, Francis K. Air Facts and Feats: A Record of Aerospace Achievement. Garden City, N.Y.: Doubleday, 1970. 223p. Includes a few "facts and feats" applicable to our topic.

1636 Mason, Herbert M., Jr. The New Tigers. New York: David McKay, 1967. 241p. U.S. fighter pilots, especially those flying over Vietnam.

1637 ______. The United States Air Force: A Turbulent History. New York: Mason-Charter, 1976. 284p. Includes much attention to the SEA conflict in later chapters.

1638 Matheson, Bruce J. "Airframes vs. Boatspaces." Marine Corps Gazette, LIII (Oct. 1969), 46-47. Discusses U.S.

Marine Corps air-ground officers' debate over the employment of helicopters in Vietnam.

1639 Matloff, Maurice, ed. American Military History. Army Historical Series. Washington: U.S. Government Printing Office, 1969. 701p. Chpt. 28, "The U.S. Army in Vietnam," was revised as a special supplement by Charles B. McDonald and Charles V. P. von Luttichau and issued by the GPO in 1972.

1640 "Matter of Opinion?: Harrison Salisbury's Reports of U.S. Bombings of Namdinh." Reporter, XXXVI (Jan. 12, 1967), 20+. Critical of a report put forth in the New York Times reporter's account, which is cited below.

1641 "Matter of Probability: U.S. Target Errors." Newsweek, LXVIII (Aug. 22, 1966), 64. Comments on accidental bombings of non-military targets.

1642 Mauldin, Bill. "Attack: Pleiku, South Vietnam." New Republic, CLII (Feb. 20, 1965), 8-9. Five U.S. helicopters were destroyed in the February 7, 1965, Vietcong mortar attack on the U.S. advisory compound and airstrip there, with eight GI's killed.

1643 ______. "Our New Commitment in Vietnam." Life, LVIII (Feb. 19, 1965), 30-35. An illustrated follow-up to item 1642.

1644 Mauldin, Bruce P. "Double-Header Airmobile Operations in Vietnam." U.S. Army Aviation Digest, XI (Aug. 1965), 27-29. Preparations for the involvement of the U.S. 1st Air Cavalry Division.

1645 Maurer, Maurer. USAF Victory Credits, Southeast Asia: A Preliminary List. Washington: Office of Air Force History, Department of the Air Force, 1972. 21p. Covers the period from July 10, 1965, to February 14, 1968; the full and final list of "kills" by fighter pilots is still in preparation.

1646 Maxwell, Jess E. "'Eagle One' Hits the Spot." Air Force Times, XXVI (Nov. 10, 1965), 14.

1647 ______. "Skyraiders Evoke World War I Memories." Air Force Times, XXVI (Dec. 8, 1965), 15. U.S. Air Force and Navy A-1 "SPAD" operations over South Vietnam.

1648 ______. "They Jump to Save Lives." Today's Health, XLIII (March 1965), 42-45+. The U.S. Air Force air-sea rescue service.

1649 Mayer, Charles B. "Boeing B-52F's on Guam." American

Aviation Historical Society Journal, XI (Fall 1966), 186-187. Their participation in "Arc Light" missions over South Vietnam.

1650 Mayer, W. E. "Why American POW's Held Up So Well Under Pressure: An Interview." U.S. News and World Report, LXXIV (April 16, 1973), 39-40. Discipline, faith, and inter-cell communication.

1651 Mazur, Stephen A. Vietnamese Air Force Rotary Wing Undergraduate Pilot Training Program. (Air Command and Staff College Research Study.) Maxwell Air Force Base, Ala.: Air University, 1971. 57p. An analysis.

1652 Mead, P. W. "Battlefield Aircraft." Journal of the Royal United Service Institution, CX (May 1965), 141-143. Such COIN planes as the Cessna A-37.

1653 "Medal of Honor Winner Finally Gets His Due." Air Force Times, XXIX (July 30, 1969), 3. Presentation of the award to U.S. Air Force Lt. Jack W. Mathis.

1654 "Medics' New Strides in Vietnam." Newsweek, LXVI (Dec. 13, 1965), 98+. Helicopter medevac operations.

1655 Meissner, Joseph P. "The Battle of Duc Lap." Army, XIX (May 1969), 50-56. The North Vietnamese attack on the Special Forces camp, three miles from the Cambodian border, launched on August 23, 1968; Col. Rex R. Sage, senior U.S. Army advisor on the scene, later credited U.S. Air Force tactical air and AC-47 gunships with having saved the camp from being overrun.

1656 "Men and Dogs on Sentry Duty." Airman, X (July 1966), 29-31. Air base security in South Vietnam.

1657 Menaul, S. W. B. "The Use of Air Power in Vietnam." Journal of the Royal United Service Institution, CXVI (June 1971), 5-15. A review by an RAF Air Vice Marshal.

1658 Merdinger, Charles J. "Civil Engineers, Seabees, and Bases in Vietnam." In Frank Uhlig, Jr., ed., The Naval Review, 1970 (Annapolis, Md.: U.S. Naval Institute, 1970), p254-275. Base and airfield development and construction.

1659 Merick, W. S. "Report from the Scene: The Fight for Survival in Cambodia." U.S. News and World Report, LXXIV (April 30, 1973), 32+. With some comment on bombing and air operations.

1660 Merrell, Jack G. "The Air Force Logistics Command." Air University Review, XX (July-Aug. 1969), 2-13. With some information on its Vietnam role.

1661 ______. "Effective Logistic Support: The Key to Air Force Operational Readiness." Defense Industries Bulletin, V (June 1969), 1-8. A shorter version of item 1659.

1662 Merryman, James H. "Thoughts in Retrospect and Tribute." U.S. Army Aviation Digest, XX (May 1974), 2-5. U.S. Army aviation in Vietnam.

1663 Mertel, Kenneth D. "The Agility of Air Mobility." Army, XVII (May 1967), 26-30. An initial vertical assault saves marching the soldiers in.

1664 ______. "Combat Night Air Assault." U.S. Army Aviation Digest, XV (June 1969), 2-6. A review of the first major actions of the 1st Air Cavalry Division against North Vietnamese Army divisions in 1965-1966.

1665 ______. "Direct Fire Support: Helicopter Style." U.S. Army Aviation Digest, XIV (Aug. 1968), 2-8. Helicopter gunships in support of the 1st Air Cav.

1666 ______. "Find the Enemy: Airmobile Style." U.S. Army Aviation Digest, XIII (Aug. 1967), 2-7. Vertical assault in South Vietnam.

1667 ______. "Highway Mission: Airmobile Style." U.S. Army Aviation Digest, XIV (Nov. 1968), 2-7. Vertical support of supply traffic moving north of Saigon.

1668 ______. Year of the Horse--Vietnam: The 1st Air Cavalry in the Highlands. New York: Exposition Press, 1968. 380p. A review of 1st Air Cav activities, 1965-1968, from which many of Mertel's citations above are drawn or for which they were originally penned.

1669 "Message: Strikes Against North Vietnam." Nation, CC (Feb. 22, 1965), 181. Attempts at aerial coercion against Hanoi.

1670 Messex, Curtis L. "Air Drop Mission to Katum." Air Force Magazine, LIV (Sept. 1971), 46-51. Dropping the 173rd Airborne Brigade during "Operation Junction City" in February 1967.

1671 ______. "Night on the Ho Chi Minh Trail." Air Force Magazine, LV (Jan. 1972), 56-60. U.S. Air Force night interdiction missions.

1672 Meyer, John C. "The Eleven Day Air Campaign." Air Force Policy Letter for Commanders, no. 6 (June 1973), 22-25. Stratofortresses vs. North Vietnam in "Operation Linebacker II."

1673 _____. "The Situation in Vietnam." Air Force Policy Letter for Commanders, no. 4 (April 1969), 5-11. Text of an address by the general to the Salesman's Association of the Paper Industry on February 18, 1969.

1674 Meyers, Gilbert L. "Why Not More Targets in the North?" Air Force and Space Digest, L (May 1967), 74, 77-78. Questions the political vs. the military aspects of the bombing campaign.

1675 Meyerson, Harvey. "Choppers and the New Kind of War." Look, XXXII (April 30, 1968), 92+. The use of helicopters in airmobile operations in South Vietnam.

1676 _____. Vinh Long. Boston: Houghton, Mifflin, 1970. 256p. A look at the war in the Mekong Delta area between 1967-1969 by a Chicago Daily News reporter long on the scene; some attention to helicopter and aerial aspects.

1677 Middleton, W. D. "The Seabees in Vietnam." U.S. Naval Institute Proceedings, XCIII (Aug. 1967), 54-64. Their role in base and airfield construction and development; illustrated.

1678 "MIG and Phantom: How They Compare." U.S. News and World Report, LX (May 9, 1966), 6. Details on both planes and notes on combat over North Vietnam.

1679 "MIG Kill Scoreboard." Air Force Times, XXVII (Jan. 18-25, March 29, 1967), 4, 19, 16. Summaries of U.S. Air Force victories.

1680 Mildren, Frank T. "From Mekong to the Delta: A Fighting Year for the U.S. Army's Best." Army, XVIII (Nov. 1968), 82-95. With some attention to Army aviation's role.

1681 Milheev, IUri. On the Side of a Just Cause: Soviet Assistance to the Heroic Vietnamese People, translated from the Russian. Moscow: Progress Publishers [1970?] 127p. An English-language Russian publication with some information on SAM's and MIG's.

1682 "The Military Airlift Command." In Frank Uhlig, Jr., ed., The Naval Review, 1967 (Annapolis, Md.: United States Naval Institute, 1967), p270-276. A review of its responsibilities, including Vietnam.

1683 "Milk Run." Naval Aviation News, (March 1968), 15. U.S. Navy carrier plane raids over North Vietnam.

1684 Millar, T. B. "Australia and the War in Vietnam." In J. L.

Moulton, ed., Brassey's Annual: The Armed Forces Yearbook, 1969 (New York: Praeger, 1969) p226-233. A useful review.

1685 Miller, B. L. "Electronic Warfare." Aviation Week and Space Technology, XCI (Aug. 25-Sept. 8, 1969), 71+, 52-53+, 67+. A review of its Vietnam application.

1686 ______. "F-105 Modified for Blind Bombing Role." Aviation Week and Space Technology, XC (Jan. 20, 1969), 64-65+. Equipping the Thunderchief for electronic warfare operations over North Vietnam.

1687 ______. "Major Role in Electronic Air Warfare Won by Radar Chaff." Aviation Week and Space Technology, LXXXVIII (March 11, 1968), 54-55+. New applications of an idea introduced by the British during World War II; the metallic chaff is also known as "Window."

1688 Miller, Maurice G. "The Crusade for Airmobility." U.S. Army Aviation Digest, XIII (July 1967), 13-16. The idea that helicopters could be used to land troops in vertical assault.

1689 Miller, Robert H. "The Airlifters." Aerospace Safety, XXIII (Sept. 1967), 20-22. U.S. Air Force tactical airlift operations in South Vietnam.

1690 Miller, Roger J., and James A. Cochran. "Counterinsurgency in Perspective." Air University Review, XIV (Sept.-Oct. 1963), 64-74. Cautions against many of the claims made by COIN advocates, including those suggesting an aerial role.

1691 Miller, Ronnie M. "Hornets and Horseshoes." Infantry, LIX (May-June 1967), 39-40. A look at the 116th Assault Helicopter Company in action near the "Iron Triangle," northwest of Saigon.

1692 Millett, Stephen M. "The Air Force, the Courts, and the Controversial Bombing of Cambodia." Air University Review, XXVII (July-Aug. 1976), 80-88. A review of the legal maneuvering surrounding the aerial campaign.

1693 Milton, T. R. "Air Power: The Equalizer in Southeast Asia." Air University Review, XV (Nov.-Dec. 1963), 2-8. Suggests a big role for aircraft in COIN operations in Vietnam.

1694 Miner, James G. "Chinook Recovery Mission in Vietnam." U.S. Army Aviation Digest, XIV (Oct. 1968), 34-35+ Salvaging a downed helicopter for repair and reuse.

1695 Mingus, Ron. "Bin Thuy School Indoctrinates FAC's." Air Force Times, XXIV (May 24, 1967), 18. Incountry preparation of forward air controllers fresh from the U.S.

1696 ______. "New Idea for F-4C's: MIG Killers Use Pod-Slung Guns." Air Force Times, XXVII (June 14, 1967), 16. Hard as it may be to believe, air-war thinking in many nations had concluded sometime prior to the writing of this article that cannon were obsolete for dogfighting with the advent and development of the air-to-air missile. In Vietnam, it was found, as this citation shows, that combat often took place at ranges too close to allow the missiles to do their work. Therefore, it was necessary to return to guns. For Phantom pilots and American air leaders alike, this discovery must be classed as one of the key lessons of the Vietnam war.

1697 "Mini-Barrier: Actions Over North Vietnam." Newsweek, LXIX (May 1, 1967), 44. Air campaigning with political restrictions as to zones of attack and targets to be struck.

1698 "Minipads." U.S. Army Aviation Digest, XIII (Feb. 1967), 10. The development of small landing pads for helicopters in Vietnam.

1699 Miska, Kurt H. Grumman A-6A/E Intruder; EA-6A; EA-6B Prowler. Aircraft in Profile, no. 252. Windsor, Eng.: Profile Publications, 1973. 25p. Details on construction and operation of the U.S. Navy attack plane, the Intruder, and electronic warfare aircraft, the Prowler.

1700 ______. "An Introduction to the Intruder." American Aviation Historical Society Journal, XIV (Summer 1969), 112-114. Details on the Grumman A-6A U.S. Navy attack plane.

1701 ______. "USN and USMC Intruder Markings." American Aviation Historical Society Journal, XVI (Summer 1971), 79-85. Including identification employed over Southeast Asia.

1702 "Mr. Nixon Strikes Back: The Haiphong Raid." Newsweek, LXXXIX (April 24, 1972), 21-22. American aerial reaction to the North Vietnamese Easter invasion.

1703 Mitchell, James R. "Down on the Ninety-Ninth." Air Force Magazine, LVI (Sept. 1973), 112-116. A fighter pilot is rescued after being downed over North Vietnam.

1704 Mitchelmore, Garry E. "The Air Force Medal of Honor." Airman, XIV (June 1970), 4-7. A look at those who earned it.

1705 "A Modern Dragon Fights the VC." Air Force Times, XXVI (July 6, 1966), 14. The AC-47 gunship.

1706 Moeser, Robert D. U.S. Navy: Vietnam. Annapolis, Md.: United States Naval Institute, 1969. 247p. A book of photographs, many concerned with Navy/Marine Corps aerial activities.

1707 ______. "Yankee Station." U.S. Naval Institute Proceedings, XCIII (July 1967), 90-105. An illustrated look at U.S. Navy carrier operations off Vietnam.

1708 "The Mohawk Surveillance System." Interavia, XXI (March 1966), 338-339. A review of the U.S. Army OV-1 observation plane's capacities.

1709 Mohr, Donald A. "Guns a Go-Go." U.S. Army Aviation Digest, XXII (June 1976), 8-13. The development of the ACH-47 helicopter gunship.

1710 Momyer, William W. Air Power in Three Wars: World War II, Korea, Vietnam. Washington: Office of Air Force History, Department of the Air Force, 1978. 358p. A valuable analysis with emphasis on the Vietnam conflict; makes extensive use of "Corona Harvest" documents.

1711 ______. "Close Air Support." National Defense, LVIII (Nov.-Dec. 1973), 210-213. Lessons of the Indochina War as noted by the general who led the U.S. 7th Air Force in Vietnam from July 1, 1966, to July 31, 1968.

1712 ______. "Close Air Support in the U.S. Air Force." International Defense Review, VII (Feb. 1974), 77-79. A review of its role.

1713 ______. "The Evolution of Fighter Tactics in Southeast Asia." Air Force Magazine, LVI (July 1973), 58-62. An important analysis of the subject.

1714 ______. "Our Top Airman in Vietnam: An Interview." Airman, XI (May 1967), 4-7. His thoughts on the prosecution of the air war.

1715 ______. "TAC Air's Responsiveness." Air Force Magazine, LV (Dec. 1972), 32-37. An interview with examples drawn from Southeast Asia.

1716 ______. "TAC: Vietnam and Beyond." TAC Attack, XIII (Sept. 1973), 4-7. Lessons learned by the U.S. Air Force Tactical Air Command and their future application.

1717 ______. "Tactical Air Forces." Air Force Policy Letter for

Commanders, no. 5 (May 1970), 27-32. Their Indochina role as reported to the 51st Preparedness Meeting of the American Ordnance Association on October 1, 1969.

1718 ______. "Tactical Lessons of Vietnam." Aviation Week and Space Technology, XCVIII (May 21, June 4, 1973), 7+, 59+. An important analysis.

1719 ______. "The Vietnamese Air Force, 1951-1975: An Analysis of Its Role in Combat." In A. J. C. Lavalle, ed., USAF Southeast Asia Monograph Series, Vol. III (Washington: U.S. Government Printing Office, 1977), p1-82. Monograph #4; undocumented, but still the most important study on the topic yet available.

1720 Mondey, David C., ed. The International Encyclopedia of Aviation. New York: Crown Publishers, 1977. 480p. Highly illustrated with material relative to our topic.

______, jt. author see Taylor, John W. R.

1721 "Monsoons Fail to Stop Vietnam Air Support." Aviation Week and Space Technology, LXXXIV (March 14, 1966), 80-81. U.S. Air Force close air support to ground forces in heavy weather.

1722 Moore, Joseph B., Jr. "Accent on Mobility: Helicopters Add Speed and Power to the Lightning's Punch." Army Digest, XXIV (Feb. 1969), 10-12. The use of helicopters by the U.S. 25th Infantry Division in South Vietnam.

1723 Moore, Robert L., Jr. "I Fought in Vietnam." U.S. News and World Report, LVI (June 3, 1964), 40-47.

1724 ______. "True Story of the War in Vietnam." U.S. News and World Report, LVI (May 18, 1964), 38-41. Both of Moore's citations apply to the American advisory period, with some attention to helicopter and air operations.

1725 Moore, W. C. "Why Hanoi's Offensive Failed." U.S. News and World Report, LXXIII (Aug. 7, 1972), 37. Reasons included the massive application of Allied air power.

1726 "More Bombs Than Ever." Time, CI (Jan. 1, 1973), 10-12. "Operation Linebacker II" and attacks in Laos and Cambodia.

1727 "More Escalation, Why?: Bombing MIG Airfields." Nation, CCIV (May 8, 1967), 679-680. Comments on the necessity of taking out North Vietnamese interceptor bases.

1728 "More of the Same: Air Force Chief [Gen. John P.]

McConnell Supports Bombing." Time, XC (Oct. 13, 1967) 27. The Chief-of-Staff's testimony before Congress.

1729 "More on Lavelle." Newsweek, LXXX (Sept. 18, 1972), 50. The U.S. Air Force general relieved for exceeding his orders.

1730 "More RAAF Men to Vietnam." Flight International, LXXXIX (May 26, 1966), 904-905. For aerial operations in the conflict.

1731 "More Revelations on Bombings: [U.S. Senate Armed Services Committee] Hearings on Military Operations in Cambodia." Time, CII (Aug. 20, 1973), 28. The so-called "secret bombings."

1732 Moorer, Thomas H. "The Decisiveness of Air Power in Vietnam." Air Force Magazine, LVI (Nov. 1973), 24-25. Thoughts on the subject by the former Chief of Naval Operations.

1733 _____. "North Vietnam Bombing Held Critical." Aviation Week and Space Technology, XCVIII (March 5, 1973), 12-13. As a tool for progressing the stalled Paris peace talks.

1734 Moreau, James W. "The Coast Guard in the Central and Western Pacific." In Frank Uhlig, Jr., ed., The Naval Review, 1973 (Annapolis, Md.: United States Naval Institute, 1973), p270-295. See especially the subsection "Coast Guard Aviators in Vietnam," p.292-294.

1735 Morgan, Garry L. "B-52 Bailout." Combat Crew, no. 9 (Sept. 1974), 4-5. Over North Vietnam during "Operation Linebacker II."

1736 Morgan, Terry L. Bomber Aircraft of the United States. New York: Arco Publishers, 1967. 96p. An illustrated account with examples of aircraft employed in Southeast Asia.

1737 _____. Fighter Aircraft of the United States. New York: Arco Publishers, 1966. 96p. An illustrated account with examples of aircraft employed in Southeast Asia.

Morison, Samuel L., jt. compiler see Rowe, John S.

1738 Morrison, Joseph C. "A Different Kind of War." Combat Crew, XVII (June 1966), 4-9. The crew of a U.S. Air Force E-11 of the 28th Bomb Wing flies bombing missions over Vietnam.

1739 Morrissey, John C. "Attack: Thunderstick Style." Fighter

Weapons Newsletter, IV (Dec. 1967), 1-7. U.S. Air Force F-105 attacks on North Vietnam.

Morse, Richard M., jt. author see Lowenstein, James G.

1740 Moser, Don. "U.S. Paratroopers in a Stepped-Up War: The Battle Jump, 'Operation Junction City.'" Life, LXII (March 10, 1967), 72-77. Useful illustrations and accounts.

1741 Moses, George W. "Helicopter Low-Level Night Operations." U.S. Army Aviation Digest, XIX (May 1973), 2-5. Tactical gunship operations.

1742 Moskin, J. Robert. "Two Nights of War: A B-52 Returns, a Boy Is Wounded." Look, XXXI (May 30, 1967), 54. A look at one "Arc Light" mission.

1743 _____. "Enemy Land at War: North Vietnam." Look, XXXI (July 25, 1967), 45-51. Nicely illustrated with information on bomb damages.

1744 _____. The U.S. Marine Corps Story. New York: McGraw-Hill, 1977. 1,039p. Includes a good amount relative to the air war in SEA, including Khe Sanh.

1745 Moss, Donald W. "[Helicopter] Gunship Tactics." Infantry, LIX (Jan.-Feb. 1969), 26-29. Operations in support of ground troops.

1746 Moulton, J. L., ed. Brassey's Annual: The Armed Forces Yearbook. New York: Praeger, 1961-1973. Includes much information relative to our topic, some of it for various years cited under the authors' names herein.

1747 "Mouth of the Dragon: Attempts to Knock Down the Bridge at Thanh Hoa." Newsweek, LXIX (Jan. 2, 1967), 24. U.S. air attacks on the target.

1748 Mrozek, Donald J. "Surrogate Intervention: Alliances and Air Power in the Vietnam War." In Robin D. Higham, ed., Intervention or Abstention: The Dilemma of American Foreign Policy (Lexington: University Press of Kentucky, 1975), p184-201. On U.S. and Australian air involvement in Vietnam under the SEATO covenant.

1749 Mulkey, Jesse G. "Marine Air Observer." Marine Corps Gazette, LIII (May 1969), 35-37. Thoughts by a U.S. Marine Corps flyer in action over the I Corps area of South Vietnam.

1750 Mullen, Warren E. "Aerial Rocket Artillery." U.S. Army Aviation Digest, XIV (Dec. 1968), 18-24. Rockets fired from U.S. Army helicopter gunships over South Vietnam.

1751 Mulligan, Hugh A. No Place to Die: The Agony of Vietnam. New York: William Morrow, 1967. 362p. An AP correspondent recalls two six-month tours in Vietnam in 1965-1966, including vivid descriptions of helicopter warfare and naval aviation.

1752 ______. "Stand by to Launch Aircraft: Operations on the USS Independence." Reader's Digest, XC (Jan. 1967), 84-88. An excerpt from item 1751.

1753 Mulquin, James J. "The Corsair II in Combat." Ordnance, LIV (March-April 1970), 506-509. The Vought A-7 over Southeast Asia.

1754 Munson, Kenneth G. Bombers in Service: Patrol and Transport Aircraft Since 1960. (The Pocket Encyclopedia of Aircraft in Colour series.) London: Blandford, 1972. 155p. Subsequently published in America by the New York firm of Macmillan; includes aircraft relative to our topic.

1755 ______. The English Electric Canberra, Mk. I & IV. (Aircraft in Profile, no. 54.) Windsor, Eng.: Profile Publications, 1971. 12p. Details and operations of the light bomber employed over Vietnam by the RAAF.

1756 ______. Fighters in Service: Attack and Training Aircraft Since 1960, rev. ed. (The Pocket Encyclopedia of Aircraft in Colour series.) New York: Macmillan, 1975. 155p. Originally published by the London firm of Blandford; includes aircraft relative to the SEA subject.

1757 ______. Helicopters and Other Rotorcraft Since 1907. (The Pocket Encyclopedia of Aircraft in Colour series.) New York: Macmillan, 1969. 178p. Originally published by Blandford, London; includes whirlybirds relative to our topic.

______, jt. author see Taylor, John W. R.

______, jt. author see Taylor, Michael J. H.

1758 Murata, Stephen K. "When the Thunderbirds Roar." Aerospace Historian, XV (Spring 1968), 16-27. U.S. Air Force F-100 Supersabres in actio

1759 Murphy, Charles J. V. "New Multi-Purpose U.S. Army in Vietnam." Fortune, LXXIII (May 1966), 122-129+. With attention to the airmobile role.

1760 Murphy, Dennis J. "Let's Practice What We Preach About Helicopter Operations." Marine Corps Gazette, LIII (Aug. 1969), 18-24. Safe operation of U.S. Marine Corps helicopters in Vietnam and elsewhere.

Murray, Everett, jt. author see Hilbert, Marquis D.

1761 Nalty, Bernard C. "Air Power and the Fight for Khe Sanh." Air Force History, (1973), 3-126.

1762 ______. ______. Washington: Office of Air Force History, 1973. 134p. The most extensive study of the subject yet available.

1763 "Name of the Game: Operations Code Names." Newsweek, LXVII (March 21, 1966), 26. As employed in Vietnam; e.g., "Operation Junction-City."

1764 "Naval Air Chronology, 1964-1973." Naval Aviation News, (Feb. 1965-Feb. 1974), 6-7. An annual publication, always on the same pages of the February issue, with details on aerial operations over Southeast Asia and elsewhere.

1765 Naval and Maritime Chronology, 1961-1971. Annapolis, Md.: United States Naval Institute, 1973. 321p. With information relative to the SEA war; compiled from the pages of the first ten issues of the annual, The Naval Review. Users will still want to consult the 1972-1974 volumes of that yearbook for U.S. Navy and U.S. Marine Corps aerial activities over Southeast Asia, 1971-1973.

1766 "Naval Aviators in Vietnam." Naval Aviation News, (June 1966), 6-7. A review of their activities.

1767 "Navy Air-Sea Patrols Guard the Vietnam Coast." Aviation Week and Space Technology, LXXXIV (March 21, 1966), 70-71. To keep out infiltrated supplies from North Vietnam.

1768 "Navy F-4 Downs North Vietnamese MIG-21." Aviation Week and Space Technology, XCVI (Jan. 24, 1972), 20-21. In combat over North Vietnam in early January 1972.

1769 Neel, Spurgeon. "'Dust Off'--When I Have Your Wounded." U.S. Army Aviation Digest, XX (May 1974), 6-9. U.S. Army helicopter rescue and medevac operations over Southeast Asia.

1770 ______. Medical Support of the U.S. Army in Vietnam, 1965-1970. (Vietnam Studies series.) Washington: U.S. Army, Center of Military History, 1973. 196p. As the above citation indicates, includes the work of medevac helicopters.

1771 Neilands, J. B., et al. Harvest of Death: Chemical Warfare in Vietnam and Cambodia. New York: Free Press, 1971. 304p. See especially Chapter IV, "Herbicides in Vietnam."

1772 Nelson, Barry J. "The 17th Combat Aviation Group." U.S.

Army Aviation Digest, XIII (Dec. 1967), 14-17. Helicopter operations over South Vietnam.

1773 Nelson, David C., and Robin Garr, 3d. "History of the 67th Tactical Reconnaissance Wing." Tactical Air Reconnaissance Digest, II (Feb., May, Aug. 1968), 22-26, 6-11, 29-33. Including operations over Vietnam.

1774 Neumeier, Richard L. "The American Bombing of North Vietnam." Unpublished master's thesis, University of Chicago, 1968. Based on secondary sources; a review of political and military operations and applications into 1967.

1775 New, H. L. "Flying the A-7E Corsair." Marine Corps Gazette, LVI (Nov. 1972), 68-70. A Marine pilot's assessment of the Corsair II in action.

1776 New, Noah C. "Perspectives on Close Air Support." Marine Corps Gazette, LVII (May 1973), 14-19. With examples drawn from the Indochina fighting by the U.S. Marine Corps.

1777 "The New Air War in Vietnam." U.S. News and World Report, LXXII (April 24, 1972), 15-17. The opening of "Operation Linebacker" in response to the North Vietnamese Easter invasion.

1778 "New Arms, More Bombs." Time, XCIX (June 5, 1972), 28. Aerial combat over Southeast Asia and the introduction of new weapons systems.

1779 "New Ball Game?" Newsweek, LXV (May 3, 1965), 53-54. The air war.

1780 "New Bombing Clout: Smart Bombs." Newsweek, LXXIX (June 5, 1972), 53. Brief details on tv directed missiles in use against North Vietnamese targets.

1781 "New Bombing Policy." Newsweek, LXXVI (Dec. 21, 1970), 21-22. Additional target areas.

1782 "New Bombing Strategy: A Reduced Number of Untouched Targets." Time, XC (Sept. 22, 1967), 29. U.S. raids over North Vietnam.

1783 "New Bombings." Commonweal, LXXXIII (Feb. 11, 1966), 548-549. Comments on U.S. raids over North Vietnam.

1784 "New Breed Flying in Vietnam." Air Force Times, XXVI (Feb. 23, 1966), 15. Thoughts on U.S. Air Force flyers.

1785 "New Cargo Test Held in Vietnam." Air Force Times, XXIV (April 22, 1964), 11. U.S. Air Force C-123's and "Operation Speedload."

1786 "New Communist Blows Hit U.S. Air Power." Aviation Week and Space Technology, LXXXVIII (Feb. 12, 1968), 18-19. Vietcong attacks on American air installations in South Vietnam.

1787 "New Fangs for the Cobra." Journal of the Armed Forces, CVII (March 14, 1970), 13-14. Rockets for the Bell AH-1G Hueycobra.

1788 "New Fury in Vietnam: The Dong Xoai Battle." Life, LIX (July 2, 1965), 30-40A. Nicely illustrated with some photos and comments relative to air.

1789 "New 'Kill' Policy Set for Pilots." Air Force Times, XXVII (Nov. 30, 1966), 15. All victory claims had to be for aircraft shot down in the air; destroying planes on the ground did not count for credit.

1790 "New Metal Birds: The Bell Company's HU-1A, the World's First Offensive Helicopter." Newsweek, LX (Oct. 29, 1962), 37-38. A look at the Huey.

1791 "New Phase in the Air War Against North Vietnam." U.S. News and World Report, LXIII (Sept. 25, 1967), 22. Attacking North Vietnamese MIG bases.

1792 "New Route Speeds Vietnam Air Evacuation." Air Force Times, XXVI (Aug. 10, 1966), 7. Via the Philippines.

1793 "New Tempo in the Air War in Vietnam." U.S. News and World Report, LX (May 2, 1966), 8. U.S. raids on North Vietnam.

1794 "New Totals on Plane Losses in Vietnam." U.S. News and World Report, LXII (Feb. 20, 1967), 16. A chart.

1795 "New Turn in the Bombing War, but Will Hanoi Quit?" U.S. News and World Report, LXIII (Sept. 4, 1967), 6. Attacks on new targets inland of the Chinese border.

1796 "New Vietnam Strikes Approach Chinese Border." Aviation Week and Space Technology, LXXXVII (Aug. 21, 1967), 19-20. A report.

1797 "A Newsman's View of Vietnam." Air Force Policy Letter for Commanders, no. 9 (Sept. 1966), 24-31. A reprinting of a Chicago Tribune correspondent's published letters of July 17-20, 1966.

1798 "Next: Bomb Vietnam Where It Hurts?" U.S. News and World Report, LIX (Dec. 6, 1965), 35-37. An analysis of the campaign on North Vietnam with thoughts on additional target areas thus far untouched.

1799 "Next War: Massed Helicopters?" U.S. News and World Report, LVI (April 20, 1964), 62-63. A forecast which would come true in about a year and a half with the arrival in South Vietnam of the U.S. 1st Air Cavalry Division.

1800 Ngo-Vinh-Long. "American POW's: Their Glory Is All Moonshine." Ramparts Magazine, XI (May 1973), 11-14. If they hadn't been bombing North Vietnam, they wouldn't have been shot down, and thus there would be no glory in "Operation Homecoming," or for that matter, no homecoming to worry over.

1801 ______. "Leaf Abscission?" Bulletin of the Concerned Asian Scholars, II (Oct. 1969), 54+. On the aerial destruction of South Vietnamese crops by herbicides.

1802 Nguyen-Cao-Ky. Twenty Years and Twenty Days. New York: Stein and Day, 1976. Memoirs of the former South Vietnamese premier, including his days as head of the VNAF.

1803 Nguyen-K-Vien. Vietnam, Test by Fire. Washington: Joint Publications Research Service, 1965. 5p. Reprinted from La Voix du Peuple, no. 17 (April 6, 1965), on the American raids over North Vietnam.

1804 Nguyen-Nghe. Facing the Skyhawks. Hanoi: Foreign Languages Publishing House, 1964. 60p. North Vietnamese comments on the early days of the air war.

1805 "Nha Trang." Air Force Times, XXVIII (June 5, 1968), 16. A look at the American air installation there.

1806 Nielson, Dennis E. "An Old Breed of Cat." Navigator, XV (Summer 1968) 27-28. U.S. Air Force B-57's over Vietnam.

1807 "Night Assault: The Quang Tin Battle." Time, LXXXIX (June 9, 1967), 45. Including role of AC-47 gunships.

1808 "Night Warfare A-6's." Journal of the Armed Forces, CVI (Feb. 8, 1969), 14-15. The electronic warfare version of the Grumman A-6 U.S. Navy intruder.

1809 Nihart, Brooke. "Army Reports Helicopter Success in Laos, Air Force Skeptical." Journal of the Armed Forces, CVIII (April 5, 1971), 24+. In fact, many were indeed lost in that operation.

1810 _____. "The MIG Killers: After Seven Years of War--Aces." Journal of the Armed Forces, CIX (July 1972), 32-35. On a rash of American victories early in that year.

1811 "Nine Flying Roles in Vietnam Told by Nine Air Force Pilots." Air Force Policy Letter for Commanders, no. 5 (May 1966), 12-25. These include (1) "The Forward Air Controller," by Capt. J. R. Gilchrist; (2) "Tactical Fighter Operations Controller," by Capt. B. J. Vinson; (3) "F-105 Missions," by Lt. Col. H. E. Galyon; (4) "Tactical Airlift," by Capt. E. D. McHalek; (5) "Reconnaissance Missions," by Capt. S. R. Matthews, Jr.; (6) "KC-135 Refueling," by Capt. S. L. Tucker; (7) "Strategic Airlift," by Major H. G. Tinsley, Jr.; (8) "B-52 Missions," by Major H. C. Braly; and (9) "Aerospace Rescue and Recovery," by Capt. B. C. Hepp. See also "Air: The Essential Element in Vietnam," item 103.

1812 Nixon, Richard M. "Airpower in Cambodia." Air Force Policy Letter for Commanders, no. 10 (October 1973), 2-6. Text of an August 20, 1973, speech before the VFW 74th National Convention.

1813 _____. Public Papers of the Presidents: Richard M. Nixon, 1969-1973. 4 vols. Washington: U.S. Government Printing Office, 1971-1975. Includes all of RN's public statements, while in office and prior to the war's conclusion, relative to the air war and bombing raids over North Vietnam, Cambodia, and Laos.

1814 _____. RN: The Memoirs of Richard Nixon. New York: Grosset & Dunlap, 1978. 1100p. The former President discusses the Vietnam War, 1969-1973, including such air operations as "Linebacker II."

1815 "Nixon's Blitz Leads Back to the Table." Time, C (Jan. 8, 1973), 9-14. B-52's in "Operation Linebacker II."

1816 "Nixon's Secret Bombing Survey." Newsweek, LXXIX (May 1, 1972), 50-51. A look into the politics behind the air operations.

1817 "No Credit Given 'Kills' on the Ground." Air Force Times, XXVII (Jan. 4, 1967), 11. Towards becoming an ace.

1818 Noel, Martin A., Jr. "The Heavyweight Champ." TAC Attack, XII (Oct. 1972), 16-19. F-105 Thunderchief raids on North Vietnam.

1819 Norman, Lloyd. "Cambodia: The Inside Story of the Bombing Cover-Up." Newsweek, LXXXII (Aug. 6, 1973), 32-33. Politics vs. military expediency.

1820 ______. "Debating the Future of 'Flying Tanks.'" Army, XXII (Feb. 1972), 18-21. Armed helicopters.

1821 ______. "Strategic Airpower in Vietnam." National Guardsman, XXI (Oct. 1967), 2-7. On the use of B-52 Stratofortresses.

1822 "North Vietnam: The Dike Bombing Issue." Department of State Bulletin, LXVII (Aug. 21, 1972), 207-209. A reply to North Vietnam claims of "foul play."

1823 "North Vietnamese Quickly Return Phuc Yen to Full Operation." Aviation Week and Space Technology, LXXXVII (Nov. 6, 1967), 22-23. Despite U.S. air raids on that MIG base.

1824 "The Northrop F-5 in Vietnam." Flying Review International, XXI (April 1966), 475-476. Testing the Freedomfighter in combat.

1825 Norton, Jay. "The A-26 Invader." TAC Attack, XV (June 1975), 16-17. Its use over South Vietnam in the early days of the war.

1826 "Notice to the North: Concerning Air Opposition." Time, LXXXVIII (Dec. 30, 1966), 17. U.S. fighter victories.

1827 "Now, Heavier Bombing of North Vietnam." U.S. News and World Report, LX (June 13, 1966), 6.

1828 "Now It's Reds [Who Are] Forcing the Air War." U.S. News and World Report, LXXII (April 3, 1972), 16. U.S. response to the North Vietnamese Easter invasion.

1829 "Now Picture This: Images of the Vietnam War Captured in the Combat Artists Program." Army Digest, XXII (June 1967), 8-14. With some examples relative to our topic.

1830 "Now, the Make-or-Break Test in Vietnam." U.S. News and World Report, LXXII (April 17, 1972), 17-18. The Allied air-ground response to the Easter Invasion.

1831 "O-1 Modified: FAC's Get Machine Guns." Air Force Times, XXVI (June 15, 1966), 15. Protection for the FAC "Bird Dogs."

1832 "O-2's Fly to North of the DMZ." Air Force Times, XXVIII (Nov. 1, 1967), 16. Spotting fire for close air support.

1833 "The OV-10 Bronco." Naval Aviation News, (Oct. 1972), 20-21. The ultimate COIN aircraft of the Vietnam War.

1834 "OV-10A Description." Naval Aviation News, (Sept. 1968), 24. Preliminary Bronco details.

1835 "The OV-10A in Vietnam." Naval Aviation News, (Sept. 1969), 30. As flown by U.S. Navy squadron VS-41.

1836 O'Ballance, Edgar O. "The Air Defense of North Vietnam." Marine Corps Gazette, L (Nov. 1966), 78-79. A quick look at North Vietnamese interceptor and antiaircraft capacity.

1837 ______. "The Ho Chi Minh Trail." Army Quarterly, XCIV (April 1967), 105-110. Development and attacks on the chief North Vietnamese supply route into South Vietnam.

1838 ______. The Wars in Vietnam, 1954-1973. New York: Hippocrene Books, 1975. 204p. The first concise chronological and operational account.

1839 Oberdorfer, Donald. Tet! Garden City, N.Y.: Doubleday, 1971. 385p. A full account of the North Vietnamese and Vietcong uprising of 1968, including the air phase.

1840 O'Brien, George E., Jr. "C-130's Lift Troops from Ving Tau." Air Force Times, XXVI (Nov. 10, 1965), 15. A U.S. Air Force tactical airlift feat.

1841 ______. "Captain's Treetop Sorties Destroy Viet Cong Cover." Air Force Times, XXV (Aug. 11, 1965), 4. The exploits of U.S. Air Force Capt. Jerry L. Henry.

1842 ______. "Jets Gulp Fuel Fast in Vietnam." Air Force Times, XXVI (Sept. 8, 1965), 20. Aerial refueling.

1843 ______. "Long Day Begins Early for the FAC Pilots at My Tho." Air Force Times, XXVI (Sept. 22, 1965), 15. "A day in the life of an FAC."

1844 ______. "'Recce-Tech' Pilots Like Their Dangerous Job." Air Force Times, XXVI (Aug. 18, 1965), M9. Reconnaissance operations over Vietnam.

1845 O'Brien, Robert J. "Propaganda Flights Paying Big Dividends in Vietnam." Air Force Times, XXIII (July 31, 1963), 8. Suggested defection of Vietcong caused by air-dropped pamphlets.

1846 Oden, Delk. "'Airmobility' a Key Word in the Modern Army." Data, XII (Aug. 1967), 9-10. Helicopters and troops in vertical assault operations.

1847 ______. "The Army and Airmobility." Military Review, XLII (Oct. 1962), 57-63. The development of mission, equipment, and personnel.

1848 ______. "Days of Decisions: Years of Challenge." U.S.

Army Aviation Digest, XIII (June 1967), 6-9. Army airmobility in Vietnam.

1849 Odgers, George. The Royal Australian Air Force: An Illustrated History. Sydney, Australia: Ure Smith, 1965. 191p. Ends with Vietnam.

1850 Odneal, Billy L. "Raid Type Operations Via Helicopter Airmobile Forces." U.S. Army Aviation Digest, VIII (Sept. 1962), 3-8. Helicopters and Special Forces in Vietnam.

1851 O'Doherty, John K. "Battleground Vietnam." Airman, VII (June 1963), 4-9. Air-ground conflict during the American advisory period.

1852 "Off at the Elbow: A U.S. Aerial Ambush." Time, LXXXIX (Jan. 13, 1967), 24. U.S. fighters vs. North Vietnamese MIG's, "Operation Bolo."

1853 "Off Limits to Bombers: The President's Restrictions of the U.S. Bomber Fleet." Newsweek, LXVII (Feb. 28, 1966), 34.

"An Officer: His Life and His Squadron" see "[A U.S. Navy Air] Officer..."

1854 O'Gorman, John P. "Battles Are Bloody Maneuvers: A View from the Cockpit." Air University Review, XVIII (Sept.-Oct. 1967), 20-28. Thoughts on close air support.

1855 "Old Man and the MIG's: America's Top MIG Killer." Time, LXXXIX (June 2, 1967), 16. U.S. 8th Tactical Fighter Wing boss Col. Robin Olds who led "Operation Bolo" cited above.

1856 Olds, Robin. "Forty-Six Years a Fighter Pilot." American Aviation Historical Society Journal, XIII (Winter 1968), 235-239. Reminiscences before the Second Annual Western Aerospace Historical Symposium on October 4, 1968.

1857 ______. "How I Got My First MIG." Air Force and Space Digest, L (July 1967), 38-40+. More reminiscences.

1858/9 ______. "The Lessons of Clobber College." Flight International, XCV (June 26, 1969), 1053-1056. Experiences as a fighter pilot in Vietnam and elsewhere.

1860 Oliphant, Tom. 'War in the Back Pages: Secret Statistics of the Number of Bombs Dropped." Ramparts Magazine, XI (Nov. 1972), 43-44+. Critical of American bombing raids in Indochina.

1861 Oliver, Luis G. "Tactical Electronic Warfare: ECM Are

Good When You Know How to Use Them." Tactical Air Warfare Center Quarterly Report, II (Spring 1971), 4-9+. Pitfalls in electronic counter-measures to avoid.

1862 Oliver, Robert L. "The Assault Helicopter Company and Night Tactical Operations." U.S. Army Aviation Digest, XII (April 1966), 2-5. With emphasis on counterinsurgency fighting.

1863 Olmstead, Merle. Aircraft Armament. (Modern Aircraft series.) New York: Sports Car Press (dist. by Crown), 1970. 112p. Nicely illustrated; see especially chapters V and VII for material relative to the subject.

1864 O'Lone, R. G. "USAF Chief Defends Vietnam Effectiveness." Aviation Week and Space Technology, LXXXVI (March 27, 1967), 89-90. Gen. John P. McConnell's August 1967 Congressional testimony is cited in item 2574.

1865 Olson, Robert A. "Air Mobility for the Army: A Case Study of Policy Evolution in Relation to Changing Strategy." Military Affairs, XXVIII (Winter 1964/65), 163-172. An important contemporary analysis of the blending of troops and helicopters.

1866 "One Bridge, One Buffalo: The Bombing of the Long Bein Bridge Near Hanoi." Time, XC (Aug. 18, 1967), 27. An American air raid designed to knock it out.

1867 "The 125th Attack Squadron, U.S. Navy." United Aircraft Quarterly Bee Hive, XLII (Spring 1967), 22-25. Portrait of a U.S. Navy attack squadron flying A-4's off carriers in the Gulf of Tonkin.

1868 "One Kind of Routine: Ap Nha Mat Area and 'Operation Harvest Moon' at Tam Ky." Newsweek, LXVI (Dec. 20, 1965), 34. Some 20 miles south of Da Nang, U.S. Marines and ARVN troops fought to repel an advancing enemy force; SAC B-52's dropped tons of explosive on the "enemy" on December 12-14.

1869 "One More Rung: The Bombing of Oil Storage Depots Near Hanoi and Haiphong." National Review, XVIII (July 12, 1966), 659-660. U.S. Navy and Air Force fighter bomber attacks of late June-early July.

1870 "One Thousandth Sortie Logged by Unit in Vietnam Combat." Air Force Times, XXVI (Sept. 15, 1965), 35. The U.S. Air Force 307th Tactical Fighter Squadron.

1871 O'Neill, Robert J. The Strategy of General Giap Since 1964. (Canberra Papers on Strategy and Defence, no. 6.) Canberra: Australian National University Press, 1969. 20p. Some brief comments on aerial defense.

1872 "Operation 'Cedar Falls': A Pilot's View of the Results of Close Air Support." Air Force Times, XXVII (Feb. 8, 1967), 15. U.S. Air Force B-52 and fighter bomber strikes on Vietcong positions in the "Iron Triangle," January 8-26, 1967.

1873 "'Operation Dewey Canyon.'" Marine Corps Gazette, LIII (May 1969), 4. A brief review.

1874 "'Operation Junction City': History Made a Jump Zone." Air Force Times, XXVII (April 12, 1967), 16. A report on the only U.S. assault parachute drop of the conflict.

1875 "'Operation Rescue': The Fifth Air Rescue Detachment in South Vietnam." Time, LXXXV (March 12, 1965), 21A. A look at its operations.

1876 "'Operation Starlight.'" Naval Aviation News, (July 1966), 12-13. Emphasis on the role of the 3rd Marine Aircraft Wing in shutting off the Vietcong escape during the August 1965 fight between the 3d Marine Division and the 2d Vietcong Regiment near Chu Lai.

1877 "'Operation Steel Tiger': U.S. Sorties Over the Ho Chi Minh Trail." Newsweek, LXXVII (Jan. 18, 1972), 25. The aerial attempt to interdict Communist troops and supplies.

1878 "Operation Successful, Results Nil: Commandos Attempt to Rescue U.S. POW's." Newsweek, LXXVI (Dec. 7, 1970), 26-28. The Son Tay prison camp raid.

1879 "Operations in Vietnam Focus on Tan Son Nhut." Air Force Times, XXIII (April 3, 1963), 2. Fighting near Saigon's airport.

1880 Oppenheimer, Harold L. "Military Lessons of the Vietnam War: Rockets and Helicopters Bring Fundamental Changes to the Art of Land Warfare." Navy, XI (Oct. 1968), 14-20. A review.

1881 O'Rourke, Gerald G. "Flying the Fabulous Phantom." Reader's Digest, XCII (Feb. 1968), 132-135. Combat over North Vietnam.

1882 Osborne, Arthur M. "Air Defense for the Mining of Haiphong." U.S. Naval Institute Proceedings, C (Sept. 1974), 113-115. Aerial support for the aerial mining operation.

1883 Osborne, John. "Bombs Away." New Republic, CLXVIII (Jan. 6, 1973), 14-15. "Operation Linebacker II."

1884 Ostick, Charles T. "Armed Helicopter Operations." Infantry, LIV (July-Aug. 1964), 19-22. In support of ARVN ground troops and U.S. advisors in South Vietnam.

1885 Otto, Wayne R. "Lifesavers Unlimited." Army Digest, XXI (Sept. 1966), 20-22. The U.S. Army's 57th Medical Detachment (Helicopter, Ambulance).

1886 Overly, Norris M. "Held Captive in Hanoi: An Ex-POW Tells How It Was." Air Force and Space Digest, LIII (Nov. 1970), 86-90. Grim memories of an Air Force flyer.

1887 "The P-3 in Vietnam." Naval Aviation News, (March 1968), 29. Patrol operations of the Orions of VP-5.

1888 "POW." Naval Aviation News, (Dec. 1973), 8. North Vietnamese Thoughts of Commander Jack Fellowes on his days in a prison camp.

1889 "POW's: The Price of Survival." Time, LXXXI (April 16, 1973), 26+. A review of some of the experiences survived by men returned to the U.S. in "Operation Homecoming."

1890 "'Pack Rats' Call the Shots in the Vietnam Air War." Air Force Times, XXVI (April 27, 1966), 14. Air controllers.

1891 Palmer, Dave Richard. Summons of the Trumpet: U.S.-Vietnam in Perspective. San Rafael, Calif.: Presidio Press, 1977. 304p. A history of the American military involvement in SEA with much information relative to the air war.

1892 "Pandora's Box." Newsweek, LXV (June 28, 1965), 32-33. Thoughts on the rather uncoordinated bombing of targets in North Vietnam.

1893 Pandzieri, Aldo. "Vietnam Boneyard." Air Classics, VIII (Feb. 1972), 37-41. An illustrated look at the aircraft disposal site at Tan Son Nhut airdrome.

1894 Paquette, Dean R. "The Helicopter Is the Key." Data, XIV (Aug. 1969), 22-23+. To American ground operations in South Vietnam.

1895 Parker, Michael. "Marines Blunt the Invasion from the North: Action in the DMZ." Life, LXI (Oct. 28, 1966), 30-39.

1896 ______. "There to Stay: The U.S. Build-Up in Thailand." Newsweek, LXXX (July 3, 1972), 36+. Airfield and base construction and development.

1897 Parmly, O. Wolcott. "Weapon Pods for Aerial Combat." Ordnance, XLVIII (Nov.-Dec. 1963), 312-315. For use in supplementing the air-to-air missiles of fighter planes.

1898 Parrish, John A. 12, 20, and 5: A Doctor's Year in Vietnam. New York: E. P. Dutton, 1972. 348p. A U.S. doctor spent most of his time sorting out medevac helicopter loads of recently killed and wounded men from the field in the I Corps area; the title reflects the corpsman's litany, "12 litter-borne wounded, 20 ambulatory wounded, and 5 dead."

1899 Parsons, Iain, ed. The Encyclopedia of Air Warfare. New York: Crowell, 1975. 256p. A large British-oriented illustrated history with a surprising amount of data relative to the SEA subject.

1900 Patchin, Kenneth L. "Strategic Airlift." In Carl Berger, ed., The United States Air Force in Southeast Asia, 1961-1973 (Washington: U.S. Government Printing Office, 1977), p187-200. The role of the MAC in speeding men and materiel to Vietnam and, later, back to the U.S.

1901 Pearman, Robert. "A Hill Called Ta Ko." United Aircraft Quarterly Bee Hive, XL (Winter 1965), 2-7. The role of close air support in the operation.

______, jt. author see Pickerell, James

1902 Pearson, Neville A. "Increased Mobility for Logistical Support." Armor, LXXIV (Sept.-Oct. 1965), 65-67. The role of Army transport helicopters.

1903 Pearson, Willard. "Day-and-Night Battle in Relief of an Outpost." Army, XVII (March 1967), 54-58. "Operation Hawthrone," June 3-15, 1966, with mention of the role of aircraft and helicopters therein.

1904 ______. The War in the Northern Provinces, 1966-1968. Vietnam Studies Series. Washington: U.S. Army, Center of Military History, 1975. 115p. Fighting in Quang Tri and Thau Thien provinces, with attention to the airmobile and close air support aspects given.

1905 Peatross, O. F. "Application of Doctrine: Victory at Van Tuong Village." In Frank Uhlig, Jr., ed., The Naval Review, 1967 (Annapolis, Md.: United States Naval Institute, 1967), p2-13. U.S. Marine Corps leathernecks vs. the Vietcong in I Corps with some attention to air support.

1906 Pedder, I. M. "The Role of Air Power in Guerrilla Warfare." Royal Air Forces Quarterly, V (Winter 1965), 269-275. Theory based on present and past activities;

Commonwealth orientation. Reprinted in Military Review, XLVI (June 1966), 82-88.

1907 Pendergrass, B. P. "'Swift Strike III': Assault Airfield Construction." Military Engineer, LVI (May-June 1964), 196-199. How to build air facilities under fire.

1908 The Pentagon Papers: The Defense Department History of United States Decision-Making on Vietnam. (The Senator [Mike] Gravel Edition.) 5 vols. Boston: Beacon Press, 1971. The final volume in this set includes commentaries and an index.

Toward the middle of 1967, Defense Secretary Robert S. McNamara ordered preparation of a top secret study of the U.S. role in Southeast Asia. When finished, the product consisted of 15 copies of a 47-volume set which was, in turn, made up of 3000 pages of narrative history by 36 anonymous civilian and government scholars and over 4000 pages of appended documents.

In June 1971, the New York Times, which had obtained most of the set from RAND Corp. author Daniel Ellsberg, began publishing a series of articles based on the study, a practice which the government was forced to accept by the U.S. Supreme Court.

Each of the collections leaves out sections of the 43 volumes declassified and none contains full details, as the original writers did not have access to personal papers of the Presidents, or Vietcong, or North Vietnamese records, etc. Additionally, such participants as Gen. Westmoreland have suggested inaccuracies as to events or decisions. Thus users should understand that the Pentagon Papers do not completely reflect historical reality and that it is necessary to switch back and forth between the commercially published and government sets.

Despite the above problems, this study offers students of the air war as well as of the conflict in general the opportunity to obtain a close-up look at how the Executive branch tended to operate with regard to the military options and gives the student of air conflict the best opportunity to examine aerial decision-making for any war since World War II.

"The Pentagon Papers," official U.S. government set see United States. Defense Dept. (item 2599)

"The Pentagon Papers," New York Times edition see Sheehan, Neil

1909 Pentland, Geoffrey G. Aircraft of the Royal Australian Air Force, 1921-1971. Dandenong, Australia: Kookaburra Technical Publications, 1971. 147p. Including Canberra light bombers such as those flown by No. 2 Squadron over Vietnam.

1910 Perry, M. D. "The Dusty Agony of Khe Sanh." Newsweek, LXXI (March 18, 1968), 28-37. A detailed look at the great siege, including air aspects.

1911 ______. "Evil Eye Complex: 'Operation Texas.'" Newsweek, LXVII (April 4, 1966), 56+. Combat in and over the A Shau Valley.

1912 ______. "Vietnam, a Black Week's Omen: The Battle of Quang Ngai." Newsweek, LXVI (June 14, 1965), 53-54. Vietcong attacks on villages in the I Corps area.

1913 Peterson, Iver. "Bomber Pilots Like Their Work (the Enlisted Men Are Not so Gung-Ho)." New York Times Magazine, (March 19, 1972), 4+. Ground and air operations in response to the Easter invasion.

1914 Peterson, L. C. "Vindication of the SAM." Ordnance, LI (May-June 1967), 583-586. Use of the Russian-made surface-to-air missile by the North Vietnamese against American aircraft.

1915 Pew, T. W. "Yankee Station: Inviting Retaliation in the Gulf of Tonkin." Nation, CCV (Aug. 28, 1967), 141-142. Some suggested earlier in the fighting that North Vietnamese patrol boats or MIG's might attempt to attack American carriers.

1916 "Phan Rang." Air Force Times, XXIX (Sept. 11, 1968), 14. A quick look at the big American air installation there.

1917 "Phan Rang Squadron Marks Its 52nd Birthday." Air Force Times, XXIX (July 2, 1969), E1. The U.S. Air Force 8th Tactical Bombardment Squadron.

1918 "Phantom--Fighter Fantastic." Flying Review International, XIX (July 1964), 21-25. Details on the McDonnell-Douglas F-4.

1919 "Phantoms vs. MIG's: The Growing Air Battle." U.S. News and World Report, LXII (Jan. 16, 1967), 11-12. Combat over North Vietnam.

1920 "Photo Reconnaissance." Naval Aviation News, (May 1972), 17. As conducted by the U.S. Navy over North Vietnam.

1921 "Photo View [of] Operation Linebacker." Combat Crew, XXIII (April 1973), 28-31. American air raids in response to the Communist Easter 1972 invasion of the south and the Christmas 1972 raids designed to revitalize the Paris peace talks.

1922 "Photos Detail Heavy Damage to North Vietnamese Targets by

USAF Bombings." Aviation Week and Space Technology, XCVIII (April 23, 1973), 9, 14-23. One of the best sources easily available for such illustrations.

1923 "Phu Cat." Air Force Times, XXVIII (April 24, 1968), 18. A quick look at the air facility there.

1924 Piccirello, Albert C. "The Assam Dragons." American Aviation Historical Society Journal, XVI (Summer 1971), 131-138. U.S. Air Force F-4's of the 25th Tactical Fighter Squadron in action.

1925 ______. "Southeast Asia Air Operations: Part I, U.S. Army and U.S. Marine Corps Tactical Air in Thailand." American Aviation Historical Society Journal, XV (Fall 1970), 198-199. A look at planes and bases.

1926 ______. "Southeast Asia Air Operations: Part II, Commando Sabre." American Aviation Historical Society Journal, XV (Winter 1970), 268-269. "Misty FAC."

1927 ______. "Southeast Asia Air Operations: Part III, Combat Air Refueling." American Aviation Historical Society Journal, XVI (Spring 1971), 61-62. Photographs.

1928 ______. "Southeast Asia Air Operations: Part IV, Special Air Warfare." American Aviation Historical Society Journal, XVI (Fall 1971), 213-214. Electronic warfare.

1929 ______. "Southeast Asia Air Operations: Part V, 'Wolfpack' Markings." American Aviation Historical Society Journal, XVII (Spring 1972), 53-54. Camouflage on the F-4's of the U.S. Air Force 8th Tactical Fighter Wing.

1930 Pickerell, James H. Vietnam in the Mud. Indianapolis: Bobbs-Merrill, 1967. 129p. Highly illustrated with stinging criticism of U.S. air power.

1931 ______, and Robert Pearman. "The Marines' War in Vietnam." Marine Corps Gazette, XLVIII (Dec. 1964), 42-47. A photo essay on a U.S. Marine Corps helicopter assault in the I Corps area during 1964.

1932 Pickett, George B., Jr. "The Army's Tactical Mobility Concept." U.S. Army Aviation Digest, X (Nov. 1964), 1-5. Flying troops about and supporting them with helicopters.

1933 Picou, Lloyd J. "Artillery Support for the Airmobile Division." Military Review, XLVIII (Oct. 1968), 3-12. A scholarly version of the next citation.

1934 ______. "'Call Falcon' for Prompt Aerial Fire Support."

Army, XVII (June 1967), 46-48+. Examines the U.S. 2d Battalion, 20th Artillery in South Vietnam.

1935 Pike, Douglas. "North Vietnam in the Year 1972." Asian Survey, XIII (Jan. 1973), 46-59. A review of political, military, and bombing activities.

1936 "Pilot Report from Vietnam: A Letter." Aviation Week and Space Technology, LXXXV (Sept. 19, 1966), 21+. Thoughts on the value and success of the air campaign against North Vietnam; discussed in the issues for October 3 and 24 and November 14 and 21, 1966, and January 9, 1967.

1937 "Pilot Wins Medal of Honor." Air Force Times, XXVIII (Feb. 3, 1968), 3. U.S. Air Force Major Merlyn H. Dethlefsen.

1938 "Plane Converted in Four Months for Vietnam Duty." Air Force Times, XXVII (July 19, 1967), W10. The U.S. Air Force O-2B for use in psychological warfare operations.

1939 "Plane for All Seasons: The U.S. Navy's A-6 Intruder." Time, LXXXVIII (Nov. 25, 1966), 38. Details for the general newsmagazine reader.

1940 Plattner, C. W. "The Airmobile Concept Proves Effectiveness in Guerrilla Fight: Vietnam War Operations." Aviation Week and Space Technology, LXXXIV (Jan. 10, 1966), 26-32. A review of the heliborne 1st Air Cavalry in the Ia Drang Valley.

1941 ______. "Carrier Pilots Show Little Stress in North Vietnam Raids." Aviation Week and Space Technology, LXXXVI (April 24, 1967), 80-81+. A report on the reactions of U.S. Navy flyers.

1942 ______. "F-5 Combat Trials." Aviation Week and Space Technology, LXXXIV (Jan. 17, 1966), 28-32. Testing the Freedom Fighter over Vietnam.

1943 ______. "Marine Control of the Air Tested in Combat." Aviation Week and Space Technology, LXXXIV (Feb. 14, 1966), 90-91+. Activities of the U.S. Marine Corps 3d Marine Aircraft Wing.

1944 ______. "SAM's Spur Changes in Combat Tactics, New Equipment." Aviation Week and Space Technology, LXXXIV (Jan. 24, 1966), 26-31. One of the earliest commercial examinations of electronic counter-measures.

1945 ______. "Tactical Raids by B-52's Stun the Viet Cong." Aviation Week and Space Technology, LXXXIII (Nov. 29,

1965), 16-21. A report on SAC "Arc Light" operations over South Vietnam.

1946 ______. "VNAF Emphasizing Training and Experience." Aviation Week and Space Technology, LXXXIV (April 4, 1966), 74-75+. Under the wing of the U.S. Air Force.

1947 ______. "The War in Vietnam." Aviation Week and Space Technology, LXXXIV (Jan. 3-17, 1966), 11, 16-21, 26-32, 28-32. Details about the air war.

1948 ______. "War in Vietnam: Combat Dictates Shift in Navy Air Tactics." Aviation Week and Space Technology, LXXXIV (Feb. 7, 1966), 64-72. U.S. Navy fighters needed to offer more escort against enemy MIG's.

1949 ______. "War in Vietnam: FAC's Provide the Key to Faster Air Support." Aviation Week and Space Technology, LXXXIV (March 21, 1966), 58-60+. Rediscovery of a concept forgotten after the Korean War.

1950 ______. "War in Vietnam: Mohawk Helps Confirm Army Air Concept." Aviation Week and Space Technology, LXXXIV (Feb. 28, 1966), 70-72+. A report on the small plane's success over South Vietnam.

1951 ______. "War in Vietnam: North Vietnamese Sortie Rate Pressed as Political Purpose Fails." Aviation Week and Space Technology, LXXXIV (Feb. 21, 1966), 76-81+. Contends that the North Vietnamese needed air victories over American bombers to "keep face."

1952 ______. "War in Vietnam: U.S. Air Build-Up Spurs Base Construction." Aviation Week and Space Technology, LXXXIV (March 14, 1966), 72-73+. Building airfields in South Vietnam, need and purpose.

1953 "Pleiku on Guard Atop Plateau." Air Force Times, XXVIII (July 3, 1968), 14. A quick look at the U.S. Air Force facility.

1954 Pletcher, Kenneth E. "Aeromedical Evacuation in Southeast Asia." Air University Review, XIX (March-April 1968), 16-29. Getting out wounded men by helicopter and transport.

1955 Plumb, Charlie, as told to Glen de Werff. I'm No Hero. Independence, Mo.: Independence Press, 1973. 288p. Reminiscences of a U.S. Navy F-4 pilot downed on May 19, 1967, and held prisoner until 1973.

Pollinger, G. J., jt. author see Green, William

1956 Polmar, Norman. Aircraft Carriers. Garden City, N.Y.: Doubleday, 1969. 788p. A history which ends with Vietnam and Yankee Station.

1957 ______. "Corsairs for the Air Force." Air Force and Space Digest, LI (Feb. 1968), 32-39. Development of the A-7 attack plane; also printed in Aerospace International, IV (March-April 1968), 21-22+.

1958 ______. "How Sea-Based Airpower Meets Today's Challenge." Aerospace International, II (Nov. 1966), 8-10+. A report on U.S. Navy air operations over North Vietnam.

1959 ______. "Support by Sea for the War in the Air." Aerospace International, III (July-Aug. 1967), 29-31+. U.S. Navy carrier planes in action over North Vietnam.

1960 ______. "Target: Downed Pilot." Aerospace International, II (Nov. 1966), 37-40. Rescue of a U.S. Navy carrier pilot who ditched at sea after a North Vietnam mission.

1961 ______, ed. World Combat Aircraft Directory. London: MacDonald and Janes, 1975. 373p. Includes some information relative to the SEA topic; published in the U.S. the following year by Doubleday.

1962 Polson, Sam E. "Nobody Else Can Do It." Airman, XIII (March 1969), 48-51. The work of the U.S. Air Force 22nd Military Airlift Squadron.

1963 Poole, Gordon L. "Air Strike." Airman, VII (Oct. 1963), 6-9. A-1E's vs. the Vietcong.

1964 ______. "The Dirty Thirty." Airman, VII (Oct. 1963), 10-15. U.S. Air Force advisors to the VNAF during the American advisory period.

1965 ______. "'Load 'em, Move 'em." Airman, VII (Sept. 1963), 10-13. The U.S. Air Force 8th Aerial Port Squadron at Saigon.

1966 "A Poor Guide to Action." Armed Forces Management, XIV (Oct. 1967), 44-45. Thus reported the Senate Armed Services Preparedness Investigating Subcommittee on the air war in Vietnam; the report is cited in full in item 2574.

1967 Porter, D. G. "Bombing the Dikes." New Republic, CLXVI (June 3, 1972), 19-20. Additional fuel for the controversy.

1968 Porter, Gareth. "Bombing and Negotiating: The 1973 Paris Peace Agreement." Unpublished paper presented before the 71st Annual Meeting, Organization of American Historians, New York City, April 14, 1978. An examination of the American diplomatic strategy of relying on the threat and use of bombing to influence the political outcome in Vietnam. Argues that the December 1972 bombing failed in its objectives because of internal North Vietnamese, internal U.S., and international factors.

1969 ______. A Peace Denied: The United States, Vietnam, and the Paris Agreement. Bloomington: Indiana University Press, 1976. 416p. While mostly a political discussion, the work does contain some information on "Linebacker" air operations, especially "Linebacker II" at Christmas 1972.

1970 Porter, W. C., and W. G. Von Platen. "Reconnaissance in COIN." Air University Review, XV (March-April 1974), 64-68. Observer operations in counterinsurgency warfare, à la Vietnam.

1971 Portisch, Hugo. Eyewitness in Vietnam, translated from the German by Michael Glenny. Chester Springs, Pa.: Dufour, 1967. 126p. A German journalist remembers his visits with U.S. forces; some comments on airmobile operations.

1972 Powell, Craig. "Air Power in Vietnam Does Support [U.S.] National Aims." Armed Forces Management, XIII (Feb. 1967), 69+. Suggests that bombing might convince the Communists to quit.

1973 ______. "Speed and Flexibility in Logistics Keep the Air Force at 'Go' in Vietnam." Armed Forces Management, XII (May 1966), 42-45+. The logistical situation in 1966 was much better than in 1965.

1974 Powell, Edwin L., Jr. "Increased Use of Airmobility Looms on the Army's Vertical Horizon." Armed Forces Management, XIV (May 1968), 56-57+. Following its Vietnam success.

1975 Powers, Robert C. "Linebacker Strike." U.S. Naval Institute Proceedings, C (Aug. 1974), 46-51. U.S. Navy air operations in response to the Communist Easter invasion of 1972.

1976 "A Prayer, a Take-Off, and the B-52 Strike Is On." Life, LIX (Nov. 12, 1965), 36-41. Illustrated look at a typical "Arc Light" mission over South Vietnam.

1977 "Pressure Goes Up: More Bombing Raids into North Vietnam." Business Week, (July 9, 1966), 37-38, 168. U.S. attacks on petroleum storage facilities.

1978 "Pressure on North Vietnam: Enough to Bring Peace?" U.S. News and World Report, LXXII (Jan. 26, 1972), 29-30. Comments on the air war written just weeks before the Easter invasion.

1979 Price, David H. "Skyraider Support." U.S. Army Aviation Digest, XII (Jan. 1966), 8-11. "SPAD" escort and close air support for Army helicopters.

1980 ______. "Your Closest Air Support." Infantry, LVI (Jan.-Feb. 1966), 569-573. In Vietnam, from armed helicopters, COIN aircraft, and "SPAD's."

1981 Price, Robert D. "Communications in an Airmobile Division." U.S. Army Aviation Digest, XI (Dec. 1965), 8-9. Keeping in touch between troops and helicopters.

1982 Priest, Robert D. "Down in the North." Airman, XVI (Sept. 1972), 18-23. Illustrated look at the rescue of a downed U.S. Air Force pilot.

1983 Prina, L. Edgar. "Defense Panel Criticizes War Effort." Navy, XIII (Dec. 1970), 34-36. Work of the U.S. Joint Logistics Review Board, with attention to bomb shortages; the report of that body is cited below.

1984 ______. "Smart Bombs and Menacing Mines: Sea-Air Power Takes the Spotlight as 'Gradualism' Ends." Sea Power, XV (June 1972), 9-12. Thoughts on the U.S. response to the Communist Easter invasion.

1985 Pritchard, Gilbert L. "The Air Force and Counterinsurgency." Air Force Policy Letter for Commanders, no. 11 (Nov. 1966), 14-23. Text of remarks made before the Los Angeles World Affairs Council on September 7, 1966.

1986 "The Private War of General Lavelle." Newsweek, LXXIX (June 26, 1972), 17-18. The U.S. Air Force commander relieved for exceeding his orders.

1987 Pro-Communist Eyewitness Reports of U.S. Bombings of Civilians in North Vietnam. (TT:67-30117.) Washington: Joint Publications Research Service, 1967. 15p. Translations.

1988 Profitt, N. C. "In Furious Battle." Newsweek, LXXIX (April 24, 1972), 31-33. The Communist Easter invasion and the Allied response, including air.

1989 "Project Corona Harvest: A New Study to Evaluate the Effectiveness of Air Power in Southeast Asia." Journal of the Armed Forces, CV (June 22, 1968), 121-124+. For additional details, see item 2512.

1990 "Prop-Driven Skyraiders Were No Phantoms to Downed MIG's." All Hands, no. 584 (Sept. 1965), 25. SPAD success early in the aerial conflict.

1991 "Protective Reaction Missions: Timetable, Comments on Recent Air Strikes." Commander's Digest, IX (Nov. 28, 1970), 1-2. Thoughts on close air support missions.

1992 Prow, John W. "Airlift for a Muddy War." Ordnance, LII (March-April 1968), 490-494. U.S. Air Force delivery of men and especially ammunition to South Vietnam.

1993 Pruden, Wesley, Jr. Vietnam: The War. (A National Observer Newsbook.) New York: Dow Jones, 1965. 159p. Includes some information relative to the early phase of our topic.

1994 "'Puff, the Magic Dragon': The AC-47 Gunship in Vietnam." Air Classics, VII (Dec. 1970), 62-65. Nicely illustrated piece.

1995 Pustay, John S. Counterinsurgency Warfare. New York: Free Press, 1965. 236p. An analysis of methods, including the roles of helicopters and air commandos.

1996 Putz, Victor B. "The Last B-52 Mission from Guam." Air Force Magazine, LVII (June 1974), 49-54. Most Stratofortresses were moved to Thailand where they would be closer to the war zone, but some continued to hit Cambodian targets from that island base almost to the end.

1997 Pytko, A. R. "An Epoch in Need." Marine Corps Gazette, LVII (May 1973), 42-48. U.S. Marine Corps aviation in Southeast Asia in 1972.

1998 Quattlebaum, Charles W. "The Headhunters." Infantry, LIX (March-April 1969), 39-40. A look at the U.S. Army's 219th Aviation Company (Airplane-Surveillance, Light) in South Vietnam.

1999 Quick, John. Dictionary of Weapons and Military Terms. New York: McGraw-Hill, 1973. 515p. Illustrated with references to many items relative to our topic.

2000 "Quiet Escalation: U.S. Air Strikes in Laos." Time, LXXXV (Jan. 22, 1965), 22. It was so quiet that this is one of the few articles on the subject to appear in the popular newsmagazines before 1970.

2001 "Quiet No More: Bombing Off the Demilitarized Buffer Zone." Time, LXXXVIII (Aug. 12, 1966), 20.

2002 "Quotes from Commanders on the Effectiveness of Air Power in Vietnam." Air Force Policy Letter for Commanders, no. 2 (Feb. 1967), 32. All the American leaders quoted found it invaluable.

2003 "RAAF Canberras Moving to Vietnam." Flight International, XCI (Jan. 5, 1967), 35-36. The light bombers of No. 2 Squadron.

2004 "RAAF Caribous--First In and Last Out of Vietnam." Royal Air Forces Quarterly, XII (Summer 1972), 133-136. The Australian C-7's played an important tactical role in support of the Australian brigade and were the last RAAF planes to leave.

2005 "RAAF Expansion Continues." Royal Air Forces Quarterly, VII (Spring 1967), 59-60. Into South Vietnam.

2006 "The RAAF in Vietnam." Flight International, XCIV (Oct. 24, 1968), 680-681. A report on its activities.

2007 Race, Jeffrey. War Comes to Long An: Revolutionary Conflict in a Vietnamese Province. Berkeley: University of California Press, 1972. 306p. After reviewing reasons for Vietcong success in that province of the Delta closest to Saigon, the author demonstrates in the second half the hows and wherefores of the U.S. attempt to restore the authority of the Saigon government by effecting a counter-revolution through firepower, including air strikes, air-mobile attacks, SEAL operations, and riverine forces.

2008 "Race Against Disaster: Invasion from the North." Life, LXXII (April 21, 1972), 42-46+. A photo essay on the Easter invasion and the Allied response.

2009 "Racing the Monsoon: Increased Bombing near China's Border." Time, XC (Sept. 1, 1967), 18. By U.S. fighter bombers.

2010 "Radar-Equipped EC-121's Guide Pilots to Targets." Air Force Times, XXVI (April 6, 1966), 14. The U.S. Air Force use of blind-bombing over North Vietnam.

2011 "Raids by B-52's on Viet Cong Held Effective." Air Force Times, XXVI (Sept. 29, 1965), 3. "Arc Light" operations.

2012 Ramme, Ernest L. "Supply for the Air Force: Life-Line to Vietnam." Review, XLV (March-April 1966), 26-28+. The aerial "Red Ball Express."

2013 Ramsey, Douglas K. "Bamboo Cages, Boils, and Six Years of Solitary." Newsweek, LXXXI (March 12, 1973), 33.

2014 _____. "Life Under the Viet Cong: A Crude Bamboo Cage."

U.S. News and World Report, LXXIV (March 26, 1973), 61. Reminiscences of an American POW.

2015 Ranch, Robert. "A Record of Sheer Endurance: The Siege of An Loc." Time, XCIX (June 26, 1972), 25-26. With mention of American aerial support for the defenders.

2016 Rankin, Alexander. "The Heavy Lift Helicopter in Counterinsurgency and Limited Warfare." Data, XIV (Dec. 1969), 12-13. Using the Chinook from South Vietnam as an example.

2017 Rathburn, Frank F. "Air Assault Division." Infantry, LIII (Sept.-Oct. 1963), 4-9. Building the Air Cavalry Division.

2018 Ravenstein, Charles A. "Air War Tally: 205 Men Down 137 MIG's." Air Force Times, XXXIV (June 5, 1974), 22. U.S. Air Force victories over North Vietnam during the conflict.

2019 Rawlings, Morris G. "Armed CH-47A Helicopter Employment." U.S. Army Aviation Digest, XII (Aug. 1966), 26-28. Employment of the Chinook gunship in South Vietnam.

2020 Ray, Marion C. "Vietnam Shuttle Run." Airman, XI (May 1967), 28-30. U.S. Air Force C-130 tactical airlift operations in South Vietnam.

2021 Rayman, Russell B. "Cambodian Airlift." Aviation, Space, and Environmental Medicine, XLVIII (May 1977), 460-464. Taking out the wounded.

2022 Raymond, Jack. "The Pilots of Da Nang Aren't Flyboys." New York Times Magazine, (Aug. 15, 1965), 16-17+. Aerial observers.

2023 Reader's Digest Almanac. Pleasantville, N.Y.: The Reader's Digest Association. An annual whose 1966-1973 volumes contain information relative to the SEA conflict.

2024 "Reconnaissance: Never Drop Your Guard." Data, XII (April 1967), 17-18. The hazards of gathering information.

2025 "The 'Red Ball Express' Sprouts Wings." United Aircraft Quarterly Bee Hive, XLI (Spring 1966), 2-7. MAC's movement of supplies to Vietnam modeled on the famous U.S. Army truck convoys in Europe during World War II.

2026 "Red Ball, 1966." National Defense Transportation Journal, XXII (July-August 1966), 28-30+. A review of operations.

2027 Redmond, DeLyle G. "Aviation Support to a Counterinsurgency War." U.S. Army Aviation Digest, XVIII (June

1972), 8-11+. A review of U.S. Army aerial operations in Southeast Asia.

2028 _____. "The Role of Helicopters in Conventional Warfare." U.S. Army Aviation Digest, XVIII (Jan. 1972), 6-9. With a nod towards the roles demonstrated over Southeast Asia.

2029 Reed, David. "Mission: Mine Haiphong." Reader's Digest, CII (Feb. 1973), 76-81. A look at the aerial mining operation.

2030 _____. "Our Limited War in the South China Sea." Reader's Digest, XC (April 1967), 88-92. The air-sea blockade known as "Operation Market Time."

2031 _____. "Up Front in Vietnam." Reader's Digest, XCI (Sept. 1967), 189-194+. Ground and airmobile operations are reviewed; an excerpt from the following item.

2032 _____. Up Front in Vietnam. New York: Funk & Wagnalls, 1967. 217p. A collection of anecdotes, including experiences flying with Phantoms, aboard helicopters, and with medevac crews; names are named and units designated.

2033 Reichert, H. E. "Lamps in the Gulf of Tonkin." U.S. Naval Institute Proceedings, XCIX (March 1973), 115-118. Examines the Light Airborne Multi-Purpose System of the U.S. Navy SH-2D helicopter in naval gunfire support missions for the USS Sterrett.

2034 Reinburg, J. H. "Low Altitude Close Air Support." Army, XIV (March 1964), 29-31. The sort provided by A-1E's and helicopter gunships.

2035 _____. "Tactics for Lara." Ordnance, L (Nov.-Dec. 1965), 300-302. The use of Light Armed Reconnaissance Aircraft in Vietnam.

2036 _____. "Trials of Close Support Aircraft." Army, XVI (March 1966), 67-68. Exploits of Skyraider pilots over South Vietnam.

2037 Reithmaier, L. W. "The Phantom II, Record-Breaking Fighter." Flying, LXX (May 1962), 62-63+. Details on the McDonnell F-4.

2038 "The Relief of An Loc." Newsweek, LXXIX (June 26, 1972), 34. How the ARVN, with the aid of U.S. aircraft, held on in the face of the North Vietnamese Easter invasion.

2039 Renshaw, Clarence. "Vietnam's Angels of Mercy." Infantry, LVI (Nov.-Dec. 1966), 42-44+. Helicopter ambulance companies of the U.S. Army's 1st Logistical Command.

2040 "Report on B-52 Operations from U-Tapao." Combat Crew, XX (Aug. 1969), 25-27+. A useful look at "Arc Light" activities from a base in Thailand.

2041 "Report on the War." Time, LXXXII (Sept. 20, 1963), 32-33. South Vietnam during the American advisory period.

2042 "Report Reveals Bomb Shortage." Air Force Times, XXXI (Nov. 11, 1970), 10. The word from the Joint Logistics Review Board.

2043 "Rescue Crews Flying Helicopters and Amphibious Aircraft Made More than 560 'Saves' Before the End of 1966." Airman, XI (April 1967), 36-38. A review with highlights.

2044 "Rescuemen Saved 945 Lives in 1967." Air Force Times, XXVIII (Jan. 31, 1968), 33. A brief review.

2045 "Rescuers Rack Up 1000 Combat Saves." Air Force Times, XXVIII (March 14, 1968), 28. A summary of aerial rescues to date.

2046 "Resupply in the Pickle Barrel." Air University Review, XV (Nov.-Dec. 1963), 74-76. C-7 and C-47 operations over South Vietnam.

2047 Rhodes, Nolan C. "'Operation Duke.'" Military Engineer, LXI (Sept.-Oct. 1969), 330-333. How the 937th Engineer Group provided support for the 1st Air Cavalry Division in Binh Dinh Province.

2048 Richardson, David C. "Bombing: An Admiral's Report." Newsweek, LXIX (May 29, 1967), 49. An interview.

2049 Rider, J. W. "The Helicopter in Vietnam: Use and Misuse." Marine Corps Gazette, LI (Oct. 1967), 30-32. Thoughts on the whirlybird in airmobile operations.

2050 ______, and W. L. Buchanan. "Cobra or Bronco: An Assessment of a Mission." Marine Corps Gazette, LII (May 1968), 36-39. Which was the better COIN warbird, the AH-1G helicopter gunship or the OV-10 aircraft.

2051 Rigg, Robert B. How to Stay Alive in Vietnam: Combat Survival in the War of Many Fronts. Harrisburg, Pa.: Stackpole Books, 1966. 95p. Tips, with some comment on close air support and helicopters.

2052 ______. "Kinesthetic Warfare: Mode of the Future." Military Review, XLV (Sept. 1965), 13-19. The use of helicopters.

2053 "Ripping the Sanctuary: Bombing Raids on the Hanoi-Haiphong Complex." Time, LXXXVIII (July 8, 1966), 11-17. This account of U.S. raids on North Vietnamese oil facilities was abridged in Reader's Digest, LXXXIX (Sept. 1966), 87-91, under the title, "Turning Point in Vietnam."

2054 Risner, J. L. "Down in Thanh Hoa: Jet Ace." Time, LXXXVI (Sept. 24, 1965), 28. On the loss of U.S. Air Force flyer Robinson Risner.

2055 Risner, Robinson. "Day After the Night." Airman, XX (Sept. 1976), 30-34. An interview whereby a former POW reflects on his experiences.

2056 _____. The Passing of the Night: My Seven Years as a Prisoner of the North Vietnamese. New York: Random House, 1974. 264p. The title from which the preceding item was excerpted.

2057 Roberts, Adam. "Two Years of Bombing." New Society, no. 224 (Jan. 12, 1967), 61-62. Thoughts on the value of same.

2058 Roberts, Donald A. "About the Mohawk in Vietnam." U.S. Army Aviation Digest, XIV (Oct. 1968), 28-31. A review of its role and success.

2059 Roberts, Mike. "They Kept Trying." Airman, XVIII (June 1974), 38-41. How a pair of U.S. Air Force pararescue specialists saved five B-52 crewmen.

2060 Roberts, T. D., et al. Area Handbook for Laos. Washington: U.S. Government Printing Office, 1968. 349p. Prepared by the Foreign Area Studies Office at American University, this guide contains important background information relative to our topic.

2061 Robertson, Bruce. Aircraft Markings of the World, 1912-1967. Letchworth, Eng.: Harleyford Publications, 1967. 232p. Ends with markings for Allied aircraft of the Vietnam conflict.

2062 Robertson, John. "Spiraling Air Loses a New Vietnam Poser." Electronic News, XII (Aug. 28, 1967), 1+. Concerns the loss of fighter-bombers over North Vietnam.

2063 Robinson, Charles A., Jr. "Vietnam Mine Clearing Keyed to Helicopters." Aviation Week and Space Technology, XCVIII (Feb. 12, 1973), 14-17. The U.S. Navy sweeping of North Vietnamese ports.

2064 Robinson, Donald B. The Dirty Wars: Guerrilla Actions and

Other Forms of Unconventional Warfare. New York: Delacorte, 1968. 356p. Includes useful background information relative to our topic.

2065 Rodwell, Robert R. "Bringing Them Back." *Flight International*, XCI (Feb. 2, 1967), 169-171. The 3d Aerospace Rescue and Recovery Group's control of SAR forces in Southeast Asia.

2066 ______. "The Mobility Machine." *Flight International*, XCI (Feb. 16, 1967), 241-245+. U.S. Army use of helicopters in South Vietnam.

2067 ______. "A Night with 'Spooky.'" *Flight International*, XCI (Jan. 26, 1967), 124-128. AC-47 gunship operations over South Vietnam.

2068 ______. "Vignettes on Vietnam." *Flight International*, XCI (Jan. 12-Feb. 16, 1972), 59-63, 124-128, 169-171, 241-245+. Incidents from the air war, some cited above.

2069 Roesler, David E. "It Works, All We Must Do Is Sell It." *Armor*, LXXVIII (Nov.-Dec. 1969), 18-20. Tank-helicopter cooperation with examples from Vietnam.

2070 Rogers, Bernard W. *Cedar Falls-Junction City: A Turning Point*. (Vietnam Studies series.) Washington: U.S. Army, Center of Military History, 1974. 172p. The best account yet available on U.S. Army ground-air operations in South Vietnam during the first five months of 1967.

2071 Rogers, R. Joe. "Army Aviation in Vietnam." *U.S. Naval Institute Proceedings*, XCV (March 1969), 137-141. A review aimed at a naval readership.

2072 "Rolling the Thunder: [Gen.] William W. Momyer, the Man Who Is Running the Air War." *Time*, XC (April 10, 1967), 23. The efficient general succeeded Lt. Gen. Joseph H. Moore in command of the U.S. 7th Air Force on July 1, 1966.

2073 "Rolling Thunder." *Time*, LXXXVI (April 15, 1966), 29. A review of U.S. air strikes over North Vietnam, made under this code name.

2074 Ronchetti, R. J. "Reconnaissance Patrol." *U.S. Army Aviation Digest*, XV (May 1969), 6-7. Experiences of seeking information in an Army light plane.

2075 Ronen, Ron. "Leadership and the Dogfight." *Marine Corps Gazette*, LVI (May 1972), 57-58. Tactics in air-to-air combat.

2076 Roos, Frederick W. "USAF Tail Codes." American Aviation Historical Society Journal, XVI (Spring 1971), 72-76; XVII (Summer 1972), 137-139; XVIII (Winter 1973), 245-247. Including some on aircraft which fought over Indochina.

2077 Roscoe, Theodore. On the Seas and in the Skies: A History of the U.S. Navy's Air Power. New York: Hawthorn Books, 1970. 690p. Includes information relative to SEA.

2078 Rose, Jerry A. "Communiqué from Hill 327 at Da Nang." New York Times Magazine, (April 25, 1965), 10-11+.

Rose, Stanley E., jt. author see Zraket, Charles A.

2079 Rose, Steven, ed. CBW: Chemical and Biological Warfare. Boston: Beacon Press, 1969. 209p. A collection of papers from the 1968 London Conference on Chemical and Biological Warfare which scores the U.S. for air-dropping napalm and herbicides in South Vietnam.

2080 Roth, H. F. "'Bird Dogs' and Guerrillas." Ordnance, LI (March-April 1967), 483-484. O-1 aircraft over South Vietnam.

2081 Roth, Michael J. C. "'Nimrod': King of the Ho Chi Minh Trail." Air Force Magazine, LIV (Oct. 1971), 30-34. Operations of the Allies' A-26 Invader.

2082 "Rough Time for the Choppers: Service in the Laos Operation." Time, XCVII (Feb. 22, 1971), 25. Many were lost in the offensive.

2083 Rowan, Stephen A. They Wouldn't Let Us Die: The Prisoners-of-War Tell Their Story. Middle Village, N.Y.: Jonathan David Publications, 1973. 252p. Based on interviews with returned pilots.

2084 Rowe, John S., and Samuel L. Morison, comps. The Ships and Aircraft of the U.S. Fleet, 9th ed. Annapolis, Md.: United States Naval Institute, 1972. 283p. Revised several times, this guide provides useful information on U.S. Navy/Marine Corps aircraft and Navy carriers.

2085 Rowley, Ralph A. "The In-Country Air War, 1965-1972." In Carl Berger, ed., The United States Air Force in Southeast Asia, 1961-1973 (Washington: U.S. Government Printing Office, 1977), p37-68. The best available summary of U.S. Air Force combat activities over South Vietnam.

2086 Rowny, E. L. "An Army View on Air Mobility." Air Force Policy Letter for Commanders, no. 1 (Jan. 1965), 9-14.

A November 17, 1964, talk before the annual meeting of the Association of the U.S. Army at a time when the Army and Air Force were still squabbling over who would play which air role.

2087 Roy, Jeffery. "Recovery Mission SOP." U.S. Army Aviation Digest, XVII (Nov. 1971), 31-33. A rescue mission over Southeast Asia.

2088 "A Rugged Rescue." Approach, XIV (April 1969), 30-33. Lt. Clyde E. Lassen's June 19, 1968, exploit.

2089 Ruhl, Robert K. "All Day's Tomorrow." Airman, XX (Nov. 1976), 24-26+. U.S. Air Force Major George E. Day won the Medal of Honor by escaping from North Vietnam in 1967; he was subsequently recaptured and held POW until 1973.

2090 _____. "Raid on Son Tay." Airman, XIX (Aug. 1975), 24-31. The U.S. Air Force-Special Forces raid of November 21, 1970, was designed to free POW's, but found the camp, some 23 miles west of Hanoi, deserted.

2091 _____. "Rendezvous with the Rattlesnake." Airman, XVIII (Dec. 1974), 30-38. Following an attack on North Vietnamese SAM sites on April 19, 1967, U.S. Air Force Major Leo K. Thorsness, an F-105 pilot of the 357th Tactical Fighter Squadron, downed a MIG-17 attacking the parachutes of his wing-plane's bailed-out crew and single-handedly took on four more MIG's attempting to interfere with the crew's heliborne rescue, frustrating their effort. Low on fuel, he sought a KC-135 only to give up his turn to a Thunderchief more in need than he; flying on, Thorsness landed at a forward base in South Vietnam with only 10 minutes fuel left in his tanks. Eleven days later, the gallant pilot was shot down and held prisoner for nearly six years. He received the Congressional Medal of Honor from President Nixon in a White House ceremony on October 15, 1973.

2092 Russell, Bertrand. "Vietnam and the Restraints on Aerial Warfare." Bulletin of the Atomic Scientists, XXVI (Jan. 1970), 9-12. Lord Russell was completely opposed to American operations; for a reply by A. E. Berthoff, see the October issue, p49-50.

2093 Russo, A. J. A Statistical Analysis of the U.S. Crop Spraying Program in South Vietnam. (RM-5450-1-ISA/ARPA.) Santa Monica, Calif.: RAND Corp., 1967. 49p. This memo suggests that chemical operations against rice fields caused more losses to civilians than to the Vietcong and recommended that the program be reviewed.

2094 Rutherford, Billy E. "Assignment: Vietnam." U.S. Army Aviation Digest, XVI (April 1970), 26-29. Army aviation over the south.

2095 Rutledge, Howard E. In the Presence of Mine Enemies, 1965-1973: A Prisoner-of-War. Old Tappen, N.J.: Revell Co., 1973. 124p. Memories of a U.S. flyer downed over North Vietnam in the early days of the air campaign, with thoughts, abstracted in the following item, of "Linebacker II."

2096 ______. "A POW View of Linebacker II." Armed Forces Journal International, CXV (Sept. 1977), 20. Praises it for bringing about the Paris accords and release of the POW's.

2097 Ryan, John D. "The U.S. Air Force Support Team: Tonkin to Linebacker." Air Force Magazine, LVI (May 1973), 52-54+. A review of U.S. Air Force operations in Southeast Asia by the Chief of Staff.

2098 Ryan, Thomas G. "The A-7D Corsair II: That Super-Accurate SLUF." Air Force Magazine, LV (March 1972), 27-32. Praise for the attack abilities of the "Short, Little, Ugly Fellow" over Southeast Asia.

2099 Rynott, Keith J. "Aerial Artillery." U.S. Army Aviation Digest, XII (July 1966), 7-9. Armed helicopters over South Vietnam.

2100 "SAM the Sham: Antiaircraft Weapons." Time, LXXXVI (Dec. 17, 1965), 29. A report dismissing the North Vietnamese intent to use the Russian-made surface-to-air missiles against American warplanes.

2101 "S.A.T.S.--The Short Airfield for Tactical Support." Interavia, XX (Nov. 1965), 1703-1705. A description of a portable airstrip and auxiliary equipment developed for the U.S. Marine Corps and first employed at Da Nang.

2102 "S.T.A.R. Over Vietnam." Airman, IX (Nov. 1965), 26-27. U.S. Air Force transport "Speed Through Air Resupply" operations.

2103 Saar, John. "Air Carrier War." Life, LXXII (Feb. 4, 1972), 26-31. U.S. Navy carrier planes over North Vietnam.

2104 ______. "Nervous Air Mission to An Loc and Back." Life, LXXII (May 12, 1972), 36-37. Account of a newsman joining U.S. close air support aircraft helping the ARVN to hold An Loc against North Vietnamese soldiers during the Easter invasion.

2105 _____. "Report from the Inferno." Life, LXXII (April 28, 1972), 30-36. An Loc.

2106 _____. "The Shock of War: The Battle for An Loc." Life, LXXII (May 12, 1972), 34B-40. Illustrated sequel to the above citation.

2107 Sabia, Robert V. "The AO and the Field Commander." Marine Corps Gazette, LII (May 1968), 45-49. The aerial observer, U.S. Marine Corps.

2108 Sabiston, Thomas J. "Army Aviation Operations in Vietnam." U.S. Army Aviation Digest, IX (Jan. 1963), 14-20. U.S. Army CH-21 Shawnee helicopters in 1962.

2109 St. John Turner, Paul. Lockheed C-130 Hercules. (Aircraft in Profile, no. 223). Windsor, Eng.: Profile Publications, 1970. 15p. Development, characteristics, and combat operations of the U.S. Air Force transport.

2110 "The Saintly and the Sadists: Returned POW's Description of Treatment." Time, CI (March 12, 1973), 16-17. Interviews with returned pilots as to their lives in North Vietnamese camps.

2111 Salisbury, Harrison E. Behind the Lines: Hanoi, December 23, 1966-January 7, 1967. New York: Harper & Row, 1967. 243p. The noted New York Times correspondent visited the North Vietnamese capital and saw much of the effects of American air raids.

2112 _____. "Flak from Hanoi: U.S. Bombing Raids." Time, LXXXIX (Jan. 6, 1967), 13-14. A report filed during the above visit.

2113 Salmon, Malcolm. North Vietnam: A First-Hand Account of the Blitz. Sydney Australia: Sydney Tribune [1969?] 16p. A report on American bombing raids by an Australian journalist.

2114 "Same War with a Big Difference: The Siege of Plei Me." Newsweek, LXVI (Nov. 8, 1965), 31-32. An "enemy" encirclement of the Special Forces camp southwest of Pleiku which was held by the Allies with the support of massive air strikes.

2115 Sample, Jim. "Cambodia Operations Involve Many in the Air Force." Air Force Times, XXX (May 27, 1970), 8. A brief look at U.S. Air Force involvement in the incursion.

2116 _____. "Leader Tells of POW Camp Raid." Air Force Times, XXXI (Dec. 16, 1970), 4. An interview with Brig. Gen. Leroy J. Manor concerning the unsuccessful Son Tay effort.

2117 Sams, Kenneth. "Air Power in Vietnam." Airman, X (April 1966), 8-11. An illustrated look.

2118 _____. "Air Power: The Decisive Weapon." Air Force and Space Digest, LXIX (March 1966), 69-83. A report on U.S. air operations in Indochina.

2119 _____. "The Air War in Vietnam: Countering Escalation." Air Force and Space Digest, XLVIII (Dec. 1965), 72-80. Tit-for-tat aerial response in U.S. raids on North Vietnam.

2120 _____. "The Battle of Long My: Air Support in Action." Air Force and Space Digest, XLVIII (March 1965), 34-37. How U.S. and VNAF A-1 Skyraiders "saved" a regional force surrounded near that point in December 1964 after their truck convoy was ambushed.

2121 _____. "The Fall of A Shau." Air Force and Space Digest, XLIX (June 1966), 70-74. The loss of the Special Forces camp in that valley despite limited air help.

2122 _____. "How the South Vietnamese Are Taking Over Their Own Air War." Air Force Magazine, LIV (April 1971), 24-30. VNAF "Vietnamization."

2123 _____. "Rescue from Kon Glun." Aerospace Historian, XIII (Spring 1966), 12-14.

2124 _____. "Tactical Air Support: Balancing the Scales in Vietnam." Air Force and Space Digest, XLVIII (Aug. 1965), 37-40. The aerial support for the ARVN and U.S. Special Forces in the June 9-11, 1965, battle of Dong Xoai in Phuoc Long province.

Samuels, Seymour, 3d., jt. author see Leider, Robert

2125 Sanders, Sol W. "After the Show of Force: Still a Losing War in Vietnam." U.S. News and World Report, LVII (Aug. 24, 1964), 31-33. Aerial reaction to the Gulf of Tonkin incident relative to the air-ground fighting in South Vietnam.

2126 _____. "Bombing the Reds' Lifeline in Laos: An Eyewitness Report, Ho Chi Minh Trail." U.S. News and World Report, LX (Jan. 24, 1966), 37-39. The interdiction campaign designed to halt Red infiltration.

2127 _____. "Flying with GI's in Vietnam." U.S. News and World Report, LIV (Jan. 14, 1963), 42-44. U.S. Army and Air Force advisors in "action."

2128 _____. "Opening a New Front in Vietnam." U.S. News and World Report, LVII (Aug. 17, 1964), 26-28. Beginning the air war.

2129 "Sanitizing the Sanctuaries." Time, XCV (May 11, 1970), 16-18. The Allied air-ground incursion into Cambodia.

2130 Savage, L. H. "Air Transportable Bridges in Vietnam." Military Engineer, LX (March 4, 1968), 97-98. Their dispatch and assembly in the field.

2131 Savers, A. R. "The 'Shadow' Proves Its Versatility." Air Force Times, XXX (July 22, 1970), 16. The U.S. Air Force AC-119 gunship.

2132 Scalise, Tom. "Portrait of a Fighting Airman." Airman, XI (Jan. 1967), 28-29. U.S. Air Force 1st Lt. Kemp "Buddy" Roedema.

2133 "Scenario for Attack: Step-Up Expected." Newsweek, LXVIII (July 4, 1966), 16. Air-ground combat in South Vietnam.

2134 Schandler, Herbert Y. The Unmaking of a President: Lyndon Johnson and Vietnam. Princeton, N.J.: Princeton University Press, 1977. 419p. Includes discussion of the air war in American political and military strategy.

2135 Schell, Jonathan. The Military Half: An Account of Destruction in Quang Ngai and Quang Tin. New York: Knopf, 1968. 212p. A New Yorker correspondent followed the path of U.S. Army Task Force "Oregon" through these two provinces in central Vietnam and herein suggests that American firepower was used indiscriminately to destroy entire regions. Visiting the FAC's in Quang Ngai province, he was shocked to read the gallows humor in the ready room of the airmen who sprayed defoliants: "Only You Can Prevent Forests."

Schell's other reports and this book caused Gen. Westmoreland to order a special investigation and Saigon embassy official James D. Hataway, Jr., having made it, concluded that the newsman's account was much exaggerated.

2136 ______. The Village of Ben Suc. New York: Knopf, 1967. 132p. The author looks at a town some 30 miles from Saigon which was destroyed by American bombs and bulldozers in January 1967 as part of "Operation Cedar Falls," its inhabitants being evacuated to a refugee camp.

2137 Schell, Orvill, Jr. "Silent Vietnam: How We Invented Ecocide and Killed a Country." Look, XXXV (April 6, 1971), 55+. A critical look at "Operation Ranch Hand."

2138 ______. "Vietnam, Another Day's Work: Activities of the Forward Air Control." New Republic, CLVIII (March 2, 1968), 21-22. Calling down raids on suspected Vietcong hideouts and positions.

2139 Schemmer, Benjamin F. "Bien Hoa Air Base: Short on Toilet Paper, but Long on Teamwork." Journal of the Armed Forces, CIX (June 1972), 15-17. A report on the author's visit to the American air facility.

2140 _____. The Raid. New York: Harper & Row, 1976. 326p. The most complete account available on the 1970 Son Tay POW camp raid.

2141 _____. "Vietnam Casualty Rates Dropped 37 Per Cent After the Cambodia Raid, but for American Pilots, It's Still a Very Deadly War." Journal of the Armed Forces, CVIII (Jan. 18, 1971), 28-30. Combat on the ground vs. air raids over North Vietnam.

2142 Schlitz, William P. "The Siege of Ben Het." Air Force and Space Digest, LII (Aug. 1969), 48-49. How U.S. Air Force pilots aided in the defense of the Special Forces camp in Kontum province near the Laotian border under attack by North Vietnamese soldiers and two tanks, which were knocked out.

2143 _____. "Specialists in Air Base Defense: The U.S. Air Force's Combat Security Police." Air Force and Space Digest, LII (July 1969), 38-42. A look at their activities at the various airdromes in South Vietnam.

2144 Schneebeck, Gene A. "Airmobile Engineer Support for Combat." Military Engineer, LIX (Nov.-Dec. 1967), 397-399. Heliborne-engineers in South Vietnam, from the 8th Airmobile Engineer Battalion.

2145 _____. "Airmobile Engineers." U.S. Army Aviation Digest, XIII (Dec. 1967), 18-21. Another look at the 8th Airmobile Engineer Battalion.

2146 _____. "Bangalore Torpedos for Expedient LZ Clearing." Military Engineer, LX (May-June 1968), 176-177. Engineer use of those charges to clear helicopter landing zones in the South Vietnamese jungle.

2147 Scholin, Allan R. "Air Build-Up in Vietnam." Air Force and Space Digest International, I (October 1965), 40-41. The arrival of additional U.S. Air Force planes in South Vietnam.

2148 _____. "An Air Power Lesson for Giap." Air Force and Space Digest, LI (June 1968), 90-94. U.S. air activity in support of the Khe Sanh defenders.

2149 _____. "Cargo and Transport Aircraft." Aerospace International, II (Dec. 1966), 32-37. Including those employed in Vietnam.

2150 _____. "Close Air Support: How It Works Today." National Guardsman, XXI (March 1967), 2-9. With examples from the war in South Vietnam.

2151 _____. "Expanded Tactics by U.S. Aircraft in Operations Over North Vietnam." Air Force and Space Digest International, II (June 1966), 43-44. A report on U.S. air raids for an international readership.

2152 _____. "A Gallery of U.S. Tactical Aircraft." Aerospace International, I (Dec. 1965), 46-49+. U.S. Navy, Marine Corps, and Air Force, including those in use over Vietnam.

2153 _____. "Logistics Lifeline to Southeast Asia." Air Force and Space Digest, (Dec. 1965), 42-48. This look at the MAC was reprinted in Air Force and Space Digest International, II (June 1966), 4-8.

2154 _____. "Mission: Recce North." Air Force and Space Digest, LI (May 1968), 42-46. A report on U.S. Air Force aerial reconnaissance missions over North Vietnam.

2155 _____. "Momyer and TAC: A Perfect Fit." Air Force and Space Digest, LI (July 1968), 29-33. The background and views of U.S. 7th Air Force boss William W. Momyer.

2156 _____. "New Strategy for Air Strikes Against the Viet Cong in Southeast Asia." Air Force and Space Digest, XLVIII (April 1965), 21. "Arc Light" missions for the B-52's.

2157 _____. "1966 Scope of Operations and Types of Targets." Aerospace International, III (March 1967), 39. A statistical summary.

2158 _____. "No Beginning, No End--No Typical Day." Air Force and Space Digest, LI (April 1968), 46-51. Examples of the various kinds of missions which air power might be and was called on to perform in the Indochina conflict.

2159 _____. "U.S. Tactical Aircraft in Southeast Asia." Air Force and Space Digest, XLIX (March 1966), 103-104+; L (March 1967), 118-119+. Types and mission.

2160 Schreadley, R. L. "The Naval War in Vietnam, 1950-1970." U.S. Naval Institute Proceedings, XCVII (May 1971), 180-209. A review, including air; reprinted in Frank Uhlig, Jr., ed., The Naval Review, 1971 (Annapolis, Md.: United States Naval Institute, 1971), p180-209.

2161 Schreck, Paul V., Jr. "The Command and the Control Helicopter." U.S. Army Aviation Digest, XIV (Aug. 1968), 29-31. Its role in airmobile operations.

2162 Schurmann, Franz. The Logic of World Power: An Inquiry Into the Origins, Currents, and Contradictions of World Politics. New York: Pantheon, 1974. 593p. Includes a look at the Vietnam conflict; very critical towards the U.S. Air Force and Army, and claims (p501), "what failed so miserably and drastically was the helicopter...."

2163 Scott, Peter D. The War Conspiracy: The Secret Road to the Second Indochina War. Indianapolis: Bobbs-Merrill, 1972. 240p. Beginning with the Civil Air Transport/Air America role, the author links their activities with the eventual invasion and bombing of Cambodia and Laos.

2164 Scott, Thomas H., Jr. "The 'Red Ball' Flies and Rolls Again." Army Digest, XXII (Feb. 1967), 8-12. U.S. Air Force and Army transport in Vietnam modeled on the famous truck convoys in Europe during World War II.

2165 Scotti, Michael J., Jr. "Out of the Valley of Death." U.S. Army Aviation Digest, XVI (May 1970), 12-14. U.S. Army helicopter rescue missions in Southeast Asia.

2166 Scroggin, O. O. "Countering the Counterinsurgency Imbalance." Tactical Air Warfare Center Quarterly Report, II (June 1970), 24-27. By adding massive close air support.

2167 Seamans, Robert C., Jr. "The Absolutely Essential Bombing." Air Force Policy Letter for Commanders, no. 4 (April 1972), 31-32. Text of a talk on the aerial interdiction campaign reprinted from the January 28, 1972, issue of the New York Times.

2168 ______. "Progress in Air Armament." Ordnance, LVII (Jan.-Feb. 1972), 282-284. Growing out of the Indochina conflict with examples of new hardware.

2169 "Seawolves in the Delta." Naval Aviation News, (March 1970), 16-17. U.S. Navy helicopters in the river war in the Mekong Delta, especially those from HC-1.

2170 "'Seawolves' on Patrol." Naval Aviation News, (March 1968), 20-21. U.S. Navy UH-2C's of HC-1 over the Mekong Delta.

2171 Secord, M. D. "The Viet Nam Air Force." Air University Review, XV (Nov.-Dec. 1963), 60-67. The most useful contemporary look at the VNAF during the American advisory period.

2172 "Secret Agony of the POW's." Newsweek, LXXI (April 9, 1973), 30+.

2173 "The Secret Bombing of Cambodia: The ABC's of a Growing

Dispute." U.S. News and World Report, LXXV (Aug. 13, 1973), 64-65. The dispute continued after operations ended.

2174 "Senate Investigators Urge TAC Review." Aviation Week and Space Technology, LXXXV (Aug. 22, 1965), 85-89+. The hearings are cited below.

2175 "Senate Probers Rap Policy [and] Urge Bigger Bombing Effort." Air Force Times, XXVIII (Sept. 13, 1967), 4. These hearings are also cited below.

2176 Seneff, George P., Jr. "Army Air Mobility: Proving the Thesis." Air Force and Space Digest International, I (Dec. 1965), 30-31. A brief review of U.S. 1st Air Cavalry Division operations in the Ia Drang Valley.

2177 ______. "Jungle Warfare: The Helicopter's Role." Sperryscope, XVII (Spring 1966), 1-5. A report based on the Vietnam experience.

2178 Serletic, Matthew M. "Aero Scout: What's It All About." U.S. Army Aviation Digest, XVII (March 1971), 30-31. A look at aerial observation.

2179 Service, Brian. "Aboard the U.S. Carrier Forrestal." Air Pictorial, XXXI (March 1969), 72-77. An illustrated look at operations from "Yankee Station."

2180 "Seven Days of Zap: The Siege of Plei Me." Time, LXXXVI (Nov. 5, 1965), 31A-35. B-52's were used here for the first time in Vietnam in direct tactical support of U.S. ground troops.

2181 "Seven More: MIG-17's Downed." Time, LXXXIX (May 19, 1967), 32. In combat over North Vietnam.

2182 "7th [Bomb] Wing Wins Praise for Vietnam Job." Air Force Times, XXVI (Dec. 29, 1965), 9.

2183 "Seventh Fleet Air Power." Naval Aviation News, (June 1965), 20. Aboard carriers in Tonkin Gulf.

2184 "The Seventh Fleet Is There: From the South China Sea Her Carriers Influence the Land Battle in Vietnam." Navy, VIII (May 1965), 40-41. A pictorial.

2185 "75th TC Wing Operations." Tactical Air Reconnaissance Digest, II (Nov. 1968), 4-7. A review of the wing's operations over Southeast Asia.

2186 Sexton, Martin J., and J. E. Hopkins. "The Assault on

Mutter's Ridge." Marine Corps Gazette, LIV (March 1970), 20-25. With some attention to the air phase.

2187 "Shackling the True Potential of Air Power: The Stennis Subcommittee Summary Report on the 'Air War Against North Vietnam.'" Air Force and Space Digest, L (Oct. 1967), 47-50+. A review of the report which is cited below.

2188 Shadbolt, Stuart W. "A Fighter Pilot Looks Back." Airman, XI (May 1967), 3. A eulogy to U.S. Air Force Capt. Charles Tofferi.

2189 "The 'Shadow' Comes to Tuy Hoa." Air Force Times, XXX (Oct. 8, 1969), 16. Basing the AC-119 gunship.

2190 "Shambles: More American Air Power Replacing the Deteriorating Vietnamization Program." Nation, CCXIV May 8, 1972), 579-580. Actually, the ARVN with air help was not doing bad, as events of the Easter invasion would show.

2191 Shaplen, Robert. "Letter from Indochina." New Yorker, XLIX (June 2, 1973), 40-46+. A report on the war in Cambodia and Laos, including air.

2192 _____. "Letter from Thailand." New Yorker, XLIX (Jan. 14, 1974), 67-83. Concerning American air facilities.

2193 _____. "Our Involvement in Laos." Foreign Affairs, XLVIII (April 1970), 478-493. A review with some attention to aerial matters.

2194 _____. The Road from War: Vietnam, 1965-1970. New York: Harper & Row, 1970. 368p. With ample attention to our topic.

2195 Shapley, D. "Weather Warfare: Pentagon Concedes Seven Year Vietnam Effort." Science, CLXXXIV (June 7, 1974), 1059-1061. U.S. Air Force attempts brought little success.

2196 Sharp, U. S. Grant. "Admiral Sharp Comments on the Vietnam Air War." Seapower, XIV (Sept. 1971), 36-37. Remarks made to the San Diego Council of the U.S. Navy League on July 21, 1971.

2197 _____. "The Air Campaign Against North Vietnam." Air Force Policy Letter for Commanders, no. 10 (Oct. 1967), 8-11. Statement before the Senate Armed Services Committee, August 9, 1967.

2198 _____. "Air Power Could Have Won in Vietnam." Air Force Magazine, LIV (Sept. 1971), 82-83. The former

C-in-C Pacific favored an extensive bombing campaign against North Vietnam with no "pauses."

2198a _____. Strategy for Defeat: Vietnam in Retrospect. San Rafael, Calif.: Presidio Press, 1978. 324p. The admiral's memories of the air war.

2199 _____. "We Could Have Won in Vietnam Long Ago." Reader's Digest, XCIV (May 1969), 118-123. By a concerted bombing campaign.

2200 Sharpe, Gerald. "Nighthawk." Army Digest, XXV (March 1970), 61.

2201 Shaughnessy, Thomas J. "Rotars for the Rangers." Army, XXII (May 1972), 38-42. Equipping the Rangers with helicopters.

2202 Sheehan, Brian. "Can Strike Command Really Strike?" Airman, IX (Jan. 1965), 6-9. An interview with Gen. Paul D. Adams which was reprinted in Air Force and Space Digest International, I (March 1965), 22-24+.

2203 _____. "Mission to Quang Tin." Airman, X (April 1966), 16-20. A B-52 "Arc Light" mission.

2204 Sheehan, Donald J. "The Battle of Bunker Hill." Airman, XII (June 1968), 10-11. The Tet assault by the "enemy" on Bien Hoa airdrome.

2205 Sheehan, Neil, et al. The Pentagon Papers, the Secret History of the Vietnam War: The Complete and Unabridged Series as Published by the New York Times. New York: Quadrangle Books, 1971. 677p. Published in paperback by Bantam Books in the same year.

2206 Shepard, Elaine. The Doom Pussy. New York: Trident Books, 1967. 300p. A narrative of men in action, especially aerial, by a reporter for the Mutual Broadcasting System and North American Newspaper Alliance.

2207 Shepard, William C. "Riding Shotgun in Vietnam." Army Information Digest, XX (Sept. 1965), 6-10. A look at U.S. Army armed helicopters.

2208 Sherrill, Clay A. "A Routine Strike Mission." Airman, XII (Feb. 1968), 4-9. Details from briefing to post-mission landing and debriefing.

2209 Shershun, Carroll S. "'If You're Down, Call Crown.'" Air Force Times, XXIX (July 9, 1969), 14. Work of the U.S. Air Force HC-130P's of the 39th Aerospace Rescue and Recovery Squadron base at Tuy Hoa airbase.

2210 _____. "The Lifesavers: Southeast Asia's Rescuemen." Air Force and Space Digest, LII (June 1969), 39-44. An expanded version of the above citation.

2211 _____. "'Never Fear, Pedro's Here!'" Airman, XIII (Aug. 1969), 10-13. More on the 39th.

2212 _____. "Rescue Men Break All Records in '68." Air Force Times, XXIX (Jan. 29, 1969), 16. A summary.

2213 _____. "Where Heroes Are Made." Airman, XIV (April 1970), 32-36. U.S. Air Force aerospace rescue and recovery.

2214 Shore, Moyers, 2nd. The Battle for Khe Sanh. Washington: Historical Branch, G-3 Division, Headquarters, U.S. Marine Corps, 1969. 203p. The most complete official Marine Corps version we are likely to have, until the publication of the official Marine Vietnam history by the History and Museums Branch.

2215 Showalter, N. D., Jr. "B-52 Bombers Over Vietnam." Navigator, XIII (Summer 1966), 24-25. A brief look at the "Arc Light" duty.

2216 "Showdown at Khe Sanh." Time, XCI (Feb. 2, 1968), 25-26. With mention of the air phase.

2217 Shrader, Cecil L. "The New Blitzkrieg." Armor, LXXXI (Sept.-Oct. 1972), 12-16. Armor and air cavalry.

2218 Shuffer, George M., Jr. "Finish Them with Firepower." Military Review, XLVII (Dec. 1967), 11-15. Close air support, helicopter gunships, and artillery fire in the December 5, 1965, battle of Nha Mat, north of Saigon.

2219 Shultis, Donald C. "Air Base Security in a Limited-War Area." Air University Review, XVIII (July-Aug. 1967), 58-64. How it was done in Southeast Asia in "Operation Safe-Side."

Siddall, Abigail T., jt. editor see Higham, Robin

2220 Sidey, Hugh. "Decision of Mind and Experiences, Not of Heart and Hope: The Oil Dump Bombings at Hanoi and Haiphong." Life, LXI (July 8, 1966), 28B. How the American leadership came to escalate the air war.

2221 _____. "How the Raid Was Planned: The Attempt to Rescue the POW's." Life, LXIX (Dec. 4, 1970), 36. The unsuccessful Son Tay attempt.

2222 _____. "Question of When Not to Obey: The Case of General

John Lavelle." Life, LXXII (June 30, 1972), 12. The U.S. 7th Air Force boss fired for exceeding his authority.

2223 Sigholtz, Robert H. "Jump into War Zone C." Infantry, LVII (Sept.-Oct. 1967), 38-40. The U.S. 173d Airborne in "Operation Junction City."

2224 Sights, Albert P., Jr. "Air Transport As an Element of Military Power." In Frank Uhlig, Jr., ed., The Naval Review, 1967 (Annapolis, Md.: United States Naval Institute, 1967), p84-105. With some attention to its Vietnam use.

2225 ______. "Graduated Pressure in Theory and Practice." U.S. Naval Institute Proceedings, XCVI (July 1970), 40-45. The failure of "Operation Rolling Thunder" was caused by the bombing pauses which gave the North Vietnamese the time to recoup.

2226 ______. "Strategic Bombing and Changing Times." Air University Review, XXIII (Jan-Feb. 1972), 14-26. The use of B-52's over South Vietnam and fighter-bombers against the industrial and communications base of North Vietnam was a complete reversal of the practice in World War II.

2227 ______. "Tactical Bombing: The Unproved Element." Air Force and Space Digest, LII (July 1969), 55-59. Its use as a political tool.

2228 "The Sikorsky CH-54A Skycrane." United Aircraft Quarterly Bee Hive, XL (Summer 1965), 28-32. The power helicopter which saw some U.S. Army service in Southeast Asia.

2229 "Sikorskys in Vietnam." United Aircraft Quarterly Bee Hive, XLI (Summer 1966), 8-11. Their success with the American armed services.

2230 Simler, George B. "Air Power in Southeast Asia." Air Force Policy Letter for Commanders, no. 6 (June 1968), 10-15. Text of an address to the AFA Convention on April 5, 1968.

2231 ______. "North Vietnam's Air Defense System." Air Force and Space Digest, L (May 1967), 81-82. A report and analysis.

2232 Simmonds, E. H. S. "Laos and the War in Vietnam." World Today, XXII (May 1966), 199-206. The supply connection.

2233 Simmons, Edwin H. "Marine Corps Operations in Vietnam, 1965-1966." In Frank Uhlig, Jr., ed., The Naval Review,

1968 (Annapolis, Md.: United States Institute, 1968), p2-35.

2234 ______. "Marine Corps Operations in Vietnam, 1967." In Frank Uhlig, Jr., ed., The Naval Review, 1969 (Annapolis, Md.: United States Naval Institute, 1969), p112-141.

2235 ______. "Marine Corps Operations in Vietnam, 1968." U.S. Naval Institute Proceedings, XCVI (May 1970), 290-320.

2236 ______. "Marine Corps Operations in Vietnam, 1969-1972." In Frank Uhlig, Jr., ed., The Naval Review, 1973 (Annapolis, Md.: United States Naval Institute, 1973), p196-223. All of the above include air and helicopter attention; taken together, Simmons' articles come the closest to being a full U.S. Marine Corps history that we presently have.

2237 ______. The United States Marines, the First Two Hundred Years, 1775-1975. New York: Viking Press, 1976. 342p. The last chapters deal with Southeast Asia; the author is presently director of the History and Museums Division, Headquarters, U.S. Marine Corps.

2238 Simons, W. E. Coercion in Vietnam? (RM-6016-PR.) Santa Monica, Calif.: RAND Corp., 1969. 120p. An examination of the public record for the first half of 1965 designed to determine whether U.S. air raids on North Vietnam represented an attempt at military coercion. The surprising answer here is that only briefly were the bombers a prominent feature of U.S. policy.

2239 Simpson, John D. "Operation Cedar Falls." Military Engineer, LX (July-Aug. 1968), 257-258. Operations in the Iron Triangle in 1967.

2240 Sims, Edward H. Fighter Tactics and Strategy, 1914-1970. New York: Harper & Row, 1972. 266p. Ends with Vietnam.

2241 "A Singular Aircraft: The A-37 in Vietnam." Air Force and Space Digest, LII (June 1969), 49-51. A pictorial.

2242 "Sitting Ducks of Aerial War." Ebony, XXII (Nov. 1966), 58-60+. FAC's over South Vietnam.

2243 Skarich, Anton J. "The Triple Nickel Winks at the World." U.S. Army Aviation Digest, XVI (Jan. 1970), 2-5. Airlift operations.

2244 Sklarewitz, Norman. Counterinsurgency: Marines at Work in Vietnam." Marine Corps Gazette, XLVII (Jan. 1963),

56-57. A pictorial on the U.S. Marine Corps helicopter squadron at Da Nang.

2245 ______. "Dateline Da Nang: The Choppers Move North." Marine Corps Gazette, XLVII (Jan. 1963), 3. In support of the ARVN.

2246 ______. "Dateline: Soc Trang." Marine Corps Gazette, XLVI (Dec. 1962), 54-56. A pictorial on the U.S. Marine Corps helicopters based at Soc Trang.

2247 "'Skoshi Tiger.'" Air Force and Space Digest, XLIX (March 1966), 66. Combat testing of the Northrop F-5 Freedom Fighters in Vietnam.

2248 "'Skoshi Tiger': Evaluating the F-5 in Combat." Air Force and Space Digest, XLIX (Aug. 1966), 45-48.

2249 "Smart Bombs for Cheap Bombing." Journal of the Armed Forces, CVIII (May 3, 1971), 18-19. Television-guided bombs were not inexpensive, but were less expensive than the aircraft delivering them!

2250 Smith, Allan L. "All but Four." U.S. Army Aviation Digest, XV (Oct. 1969), 10-16. A U.S. Army helicopter rescue mission.

2251 Smith, Desmond. "Vietnam by Helicopter: Operations of the 1st Air Cavalry Division." Nation, CCIV (June 12, 1967), 745-750. A review.

2252 Smith, Gene. "Son Tay." Air Progress, XXVIII (March 1971), 50-54+. The unsuccessful 1970 POW camp raid.

2253 Smith, J. P. "Death in the Ia Drang Valley." Saturday Evening Post, CCXL (Jan. 28, 1967), 80-85. A report on the 1965 operations of the 1st Air Cavalry Division.

Smith, K. Wayne, jt. author see Enthoven, Alain C.

2254 Smith, Melden E., Jr. "The Strategic Bombing Debate: The Second World War and Vietnam." Journal of Contemporary History, XII (Jan. 1977), 175-191. Points out the differences.

2255 Smith, Philip R., Jr. "Army Airmobility--Concept to Reality." Army Digest, XXIV (Sept. 1969), 12-19. With emphasis on the 1st Air Cavalry Division.

2256 Smith, R. B. "Leatherneck Square." Marine Corps Gazette, LIII (Aug. 1969), 34-42. U.S. Marine Corps air-ground operations in the area of the DMZ.

2257 Smith, Russell H. Gradualism and the Air War Against North Vietnam. (Air War College Professional Study.) Maxwell Air Force Base, Ala.: Air University, 1971. 17p. A look at politics and bombing strategy.

2258 ______. "The Presidential Decision on the Cambodian Operation." Air University Review, XXII (Sept.-October 1971), 45-53. Includes a look at the military-air considerations.

Smith, Warren R., jt. author see Haggerty, James J.

2259 Smith, William H. "Countering a Viet Cong Ambush." U.S. Army Aviation Digest, XI (Aug. 1965), 30-32. By shooting up Vietcong positions from armed helicopters.

2260 ______. "Mission: Eliminate." U.S. Army Aviation Digest, XII (March 1966), 2-6. How an ARVN Ranger battalion with U.S. Army helicopter support defeated an attacking Vietcong unit in 1965.

2261 ______. "Mission: Rescue." U.S. Army Aviation Digest, XII (Jan. 1966), 12-14. A helicopter rescue mission in South Vietnam.

2262 ______. "Operation Knockout." U.S. Army Aviation Digest, XI (Nov. 1965), 13-18. U.S. helicopter operations in South Vietnam.

2263 Smither, W. "RAAF Helicopters in Vietnam Battle." Royal Air Forces Quarterly, VI (Winter 1966), 312-313. The only journal article on the subject located.

2264 ______. "The RAAF in Vietnam." Royal Air Forces Quarterly, VI (Autumn 1966), 237-239. A review of operations to that time.

2265 Sobel, Lester A., ed. South Vietnam: U.S.-Communist Confrontation in Southeast Asia, 1961-1965. (Interim History Series.) New York: Facts on File, Inc., 1966. With some information relative to the air war.

2266 Sochurek, Howard. "Air Rescue Behind Enemy Lines." National Geographic Magazine, CXXXIV (Sept. 1968), 346-349. A nicely illustrated account.

2267 ______. "American Special Forces in Action in Vietnam." National Geographic Magazine, CXXVII (Jan. 1965), 38-65. A nicely illustrated account with some mention of helicopters.

2268 Solntsev, N. "Sentinels of Vietnam's Skies." New Times, no. 20 (May 17, 1967), 24-26. North Vietnamese air defenses and air warning network.

2269 "Something for Real: The Men Who Fly Vital Military Cargo into Vietnam." Newsweek, LXVIII (July 4, 1966), 18-19. Air National Guard C-141 crews.

2270 "Something New in the Sky: The Air War over Laos." Newsweek, LXXIX (Jan. 13, 1972), 19. Actually, the interdiction campaign there had been going on for years.

2271 "Sortie and Loss Rates Over South Vietnam, 1965-1970." Journal of the Armed Forces, CVIII (Jan. 18, 1971), 30. A table.

2272 "Southeast Asia: Safety's Contribution to Combat Strength." Aerospace Safety, XXIII (Sept. 1967), 6-17. Viewed as vital.

2273 "Special Air Warfare Tactics." TIG Brief, XVIII (March 18, 1966), 13. Comments on the Air Force Field Manual 3-5 cited below.

2274 "Special Group Defends Bases." Air Force Times, XXIX (Sept. 18, 1968), 14. The 821st Combat Security Police Squadron (TAC).

2275 "Special Mission Flights by MAC Increased by North Vietnamese Invasion." Aviation Week and Space Technology, XCVI (May 15, 1972), 18. Airlift operations to South Vietnam in light of the Easter invasion.

2276 "Special Report on Vietnam: The New Interdiction Campaign." Aviation Week and Space Technology, XCVI (May 15, 1972), 14-20. The aerial attempt to cut down on infiltration with attacks on trails in Laos, Cambodia, and the Vietnams.

2277 Spector, Ronald. "Getting Down to 'the Nitty-Gritty': Military History, Official History, and the American Experience in Vietnam." Military Affairs, XXXVIII (Feb. 1974), 11-12. On the preparation of the armed forces' official histories in light of the monumental tomes offered after World War II.

2278 Spore, John B. "Battle Mobility in Vietnam." Air Force and Space Digest, XLIX (July 1966), 46-50, 53. Occasioned through the use of helicopters.

2279 Sprinkle, James D. "The Hueycobra in Vietnam." American Aviation Historical Society Journal, XX (Fall 1975), 162-170. An operational account.

2280 ______. "The Hueycobra: Its Origins." American Aviation Historical Society Journal, XX (Spring 1975), 30-36. The need for and development of the AH-1G gunship helicopter.

2281 "Squadron Scores High in Fourth War: The Oldest Flying Unit in the Air Force." Air Force Times, XXIX (Nov. 27, 1968), 14. The 8th Tactical Bombardment Squadron.

2282 Stapleton, Homer L. "Trung Luong: Set Piece in Vietnam." Military Review, XLVII (May 1967), 36-44. With appropriate attention to the air and airmobile aspects.

2283 Starey, Donn A. Mounted Combat in Vietnam. (Vietnam Studies Series.) Washington: U.S. Army, Center of Military History, 1978. A look at U.S. tank and air cavalry operations.

2284 Starnes, W. L. "Cam Ranh Army Airfield." Military Engineer, LIX (Sept.-Oct. 1967), 358-359. Its construction and development.

2285 Steinkraus, Robert F. "Air-Ground Co-Ordination." Marine Corps Gazette, L (May 1966), 29-31. Including close air support.

2286 "Step-Up in the [Air] War and Its Risks." Newsweek, LXVIII (May 9, 1966), 25-26. Thoughts at a time when concern was still to be found in certain circles as to the Chinese response.

2287 Stern, Kurt, and Jeanne Stern. Ricefield--Battlefield: A Visit to North Vietnam, translated from the German. Berlin: Seven Seas Publishers, 1969. 163p. Contains eyewitness accounts of American air attacks.

2288 Stevens, Loretto C., ed. Seven Firefights in Vietnam. Washington: Office of the Chief of Military History, Department of the Army, 1970. 157p. Each of the following stories make some larger or smaller mention of the use by the Army of armed and/or troop-carrying helicopters: (1) "Fight at Ia Drang, 14-16 November 1965" by John A. Cash; (2) "Convoy Ambush on Highway 1, 21 November 1966" by John Albright; (3) "Ambush at Phuoc An, 18 June 1967" by John A. Cash; (4) "Fight Along the Rach Ba Rai, 15 September 1967" by John Albright; (5) "Three Companies at Dak To, 6 November 1967" by Allan W. Sandstrum; (6) "Battle of Lang Vei, 7 February 1968" by John A. Cash; and (7) "Gunship Mission, 5 May 1968" by John A. Cash.

2289 Stevens, Paul D. "RF-101's in Southeast Asia." American Aviation Historical Society Journal, XIV (Winter 1969), 282-288. The reconnaissance version of the U.S. Air Force F-101 fighter.

2290 Stevenson, Charles A. The End of Nowhere: American Policy Toward Laos Since 1954. Boston: Beacon Press, 1972. Has much to say about air operations and policy. For additional information on this subject as well as the spill-over throughout SEA, readers might wish to see the recently-published memoirs of America's former top spy William Colby, entitled Honorable Men: My Life in the CIA (New York: Simon & Schuster, 1978), the Indochina chapter of which is printed in Book Digest, V (June 1978), 34-69.

2291 Stiles, Dennis W. "Air Power: A New Look from an Old Rooftop." Air University Review, XXVII (Nov.-Dec. 1975), 49-59. A review with attention paid to Southeast Asia.

2292 Stillie, Edward O. "Tactical Air Employment: Current Status and Future Objectives." Air University Review, XIX (Nov.-Dec. 1967), 50-61. With examples drawn from the Indochina fighting.

2293 Stilwell, Richard G. "An Evolution in Tactics: The Vietnam Experience." Army, XX (Feb. 1970), 15-23. The lieutenant general looks at insurgency as a boulder, which had to be broken into various size pieces until it is reduced to powder, in an effort to explain the American concept in Southeast Asia.

2294 Stockstill, Louis R. "Army, Marines Differ over Vietnam Helicopter Role." Army-Navy-Air Force Journal and Register, C (March 23, 1963), 22-23. The U.S. Marine Corps long resisted the idea of the helicopter gunship.

2295 ______. "The Forgotten Americans of the Vietnam War." Air Force and Space Digest, LII (October 1969), 38-49. The POW's.

2296 Stokes, R. "Dark Clouds: Marines at Khe Sanh Owe Their Security to Forward Air Controllers." Newsweek, LXXI (March 4, 1968), 29-30. Who kept track of enemy movements and called down artillery fire and close air support strikes.

2297 Stoner, John R. "The Closer the Better." Air University Review, XVIII (Sept.-Oct. 1967), 29-41. The U.S. Air Force Request Network and Tactical Air Control System in Vietnam.

2298 "The Story of 883." Airman, XVI (Jan. 1972), 35-36. An AC-119K "Shadow" crew in Southeast Asia.

2299 "Story of the Marines at Khe Sanh: A Battlefront Report." U.S. News and World Report, LXIV (Feb. 19, 1968), 40-41. With some attention to the air aspects of the siege.

2300 Stovall, Dale. "The Rescue of Bengal 505 Alpha." Air Force Magazine, LVII (Sept. 1974), 129-134. The U.S. Air Force rescue of a downed U.S. Navy A-6A Intruder crew.

2301 Strausz-Hupé, Robert. "On the Southeast Asian Confrontation." Air Force and Space Digest, LI (May 1968), 38-41. An analysis with examples from the air war.

2302 Strickland, Donald A. The March Upcountry: Deciding to Bomb Hanoi. Wilmette, Ill.: Medina University Press International, 1973. 51p. "Operations Linebacker and Linebacker II."

2303 Stricklin, Charles R. "The End and the Beginning." Airman, XVII (June 1973), 10-15. POW's.

2304 "Strike [Aircraft in Service, 1966]." Flight International, XC (Aug. 18, 1966), 258-259+. Includes 24'-to-1" drawings of many aircraft flown over Indochina.

2305 "Strike Motion Pictures." Naval Aviation News, (May 1967), 10. Taken by U.S. Navy planes during raids over North Vietnam.

2306 "Strike Sortie Record." Journal of the Armed Forces, CIII (Jan. 22, 1966), 15. Over North Vietnam in 1965.

2307 "Striking in the Air." Time, LXXXVII (April 22, 1966), 30. U.S. raids on North Vietnam.

2308 "String Runs Out, U.S. Pause to End: Congress Reacts." Time, LXXXVII (Feb. 4, 1966), 21-26. Renewing the American air campaign against North Vietnam.

2309 Stroop, Paul D. "The Naval Air Force, Pacific." Navy, VIII (July 1965), 17-20. At the time of the Tonkin Gulf incident and later.

2310 Strum, Ted R. "An Act of Valor." Airman, XIV (Aug. 1970), 32-36. U.S. Air Force Sgt. Thomas A. Newman earns the Air Force Cross and the Cheney Award for activities in Southeast Asia.

2311 _____. "Battle of the Bridge." Airman, XIII (Dec. 1969), 31-35. Attacks on the Doumer span in North Vietnam.

2312 _____. "Countdown to Eternity." Airman, XIV (May 1970), 58-64. How Col. Howard M. Dallman won the Air Force Cross at Khe Sanh.

2313 _____. "Flight Check to Glory." Airman, XIII (Sept. 1969), 50-54. Lt. Col. Joe M. Jackson's Medal of Honor winning C-123 flight to Kham Duc on May 12, 1968.

2314 _____. "Khe Sanh's Deadly Deluge." Airman, XII (July 1968), 22-27. The difficulties of supply by air during the siege.

2315 ______. "The Lucky Duc." Airman, XIV (Oct. 1970), 24-29. The Southeast Asian exploits of U.S. Air Force Lt. Col. William Boyd, Jr.

2316 ______. "Miracle at the River." Airman, XIV (June 1970), 32-37. How Capt. James P. Fleming won the Medal of Honor by saving a trapped Special Forces reconnaissance team with his UH-1F helicopter on November 26, 1968.

2317 ______. "Miracle Mission." Airman, XVII (Aug. 1973), 42-47. Lt. Joe M. Jackson's exploit examined in detail.

2318 ______. "They Call It LATAF." Airman, X (April 1966), 44-47. The U.S. Air Force Logistics Activities Task Force in South Vietnam.

2319 "Suddenly, a Hot War in Indochina Skies: Cambodia and Laos, New Targets." U.S. News and World Report, LXXII (Jan. 3, 1972), 21-22. The interdiction campaign.

2320 Sullivan, William H. "The Treatment of American Prisoners-of-War in North Vietnam." Department of State Bulletin, LXI (Oct. 13, 1969), 316-317. Suggests that it is unpleasant.

2321 Sully, Francoise. "Hunting Skunks." Newsweek, LXVI (Sept. 6, 1965), 25. Work of the FAC's.

2322 ______. "'I Smell Charlies All Around': Operation Junction City." Newsweek, LXIX (March 6, 1967), 23-25. An on-the-scene report with some attention to aerial aspects.

2323 ______. "Let There Be Light: A Flare-Dropping Mission." Newsweek, LXIV (July 13, 1964), 41. An eye-witness report on a night illumination mission over South Vietnam.

2324 ______. "Thai Ally: Major U.S. Installations in Thailand." Newsweek, LXIX (March 27, 1967), 51. The big U.S. airbases such as U-Tapao.

2325 ______. "Thai Ally: Missions over North Vietnam." Newsweek, LXIX (March 27, 1967), 51. A second report on the same page describing U.S. fighter-bomber strikes launched from Thai bases.

2326 Summers, Laura. "Cambodia: Model of the Nixon Doctrine." Current History, LXV (Dec. 1973), 252-256+. Giving them the tools to do the job without American aid except for training.

2327 ______. "The Cambodian Civil War." Current History, LXIII (Dec. 1972), 259-262+. Events in that nation since March 1970, including air.

2328 Sunderman, James F. "Air Escort: A COIN Air Concept." Air University Review, XV (Nov.-Dec. 1963), 68-73. Skyraider escort of helicopters or helicopter gunship escort of transports as shown by U.S. Air Force, Army, and VNAF units over South Vietnam.

2329 ______. "Night Flare Strike." Air University Review, XV (Sept.-Oct. 1964), 82-91. Example from the war in South Vietnam.

2330 ______. "Tactical Air Control in the Vietnamese Air Force." Air University Review, XIV (Sept.-Oct. 1963), 75-81. As learned from and overseen by American advisors.

2331 "Support by FAC's Found Vital to Success in Laos." Air Force Times, XXXI (May 26, 1971), 21. The role of the Forward Air Controllers in the invasion.

2332 "Sure Wins One and Two." Army, XIII (June 1963), 43-47. ARVN use of helicopters in a pair of operations against the Vietcong.

2333 "Surviving in Southeast Asia: Our Life Support Systems in Combat." Aerospace Safety, XXV (Sept., 1969), 2-4. A review.

2334 Swanborough, F. Gordon. Military Transports and Training Aircraft of the World. London: Temple Press, 1965. 128p. An illustrated examination, which includes aircraft employed in South Vietnam.

2335 ______. United States Navy Aircraft Since 1911, 2d ed. Annapolis, Md.: United States Naval Institute, 1977. 545p. Revision of an edition first offered in 1968 by firm of Funk & Wagnalls; includes aircraft in use over SEA.

2336 ______. Vertical Flight Aircraft of the World. Fallbrook, Calif.: Aero Publishers, 1964. 120p. Includes several models of helicopters in use over South Vietnam.

2337 ______, and Peter M. Bowers. United States Military Aircraft Since 1909, rev. ed. (Putnam Aeronautical Books.) London and New York: Putnam, 1972. 675p. Includes many aircraft employed over Southeast Asia.

______, jt. comp. see Green, William

______, jt. author see Taylor, John W. R.

2338 Swanson, Jon E. "Aeroscouts in Action." Infantry, LX (Sept.-Oct. 1970), 46-49. Army air observers over Southeast Asia.

2339 Swartzrauber, S. A. "River Patrol Relearned." In Frank Uhlig, Jr., ed., The Naval Review, 1970 (Annapolis, Md.: United States Naval Institute, 1970), p120-157. With some mention of helicopter gunships.

2340 Swearengen, Mark A. "Siege: Forty Days at Khe Sanh." Marine Corps Gazette, LVII (April 1973), 23-28. Thoughts on the 1968 defense, including aerial aspects.

2341/2 Sweeney, Ken. "When Rockets Put Pleiku in Jeopardy." Air Force Times, XXX (Oct. 21, 1970), 19. Vietcong attacks on the U.S. air facility there.

2343 "Sweep and Countersweep: Operation Junction City." Newsweek, LXIX (March 13, 1967), 50. With mention of the paratroop landing and helicopter activities.

2344 Swenson, J. Elmore. "The Army Concept Team in Vietnam (ACTIV)." U.S. Army Aviation Digest, XIV (July 1968), 16-18. Tactical planning and airmobile needs assessment.

2345 _____. "The 11th Aviation Group in Concept and Combat." U.S. Army Aviation Digest, XVI (May 1970), 16-22. Outgrowth of the above citation.

2346 Swenson, Mark E. "Vietnam: Limited War Strategy at a Dead End?" Air Force and Space Digest, LI (April 1968), 60-62. Comments on the lack of success to date.

2347 Swift, Jack. "A Fly by Night Operation." Airman, XIII (Sept. 1969), 31-33. Activities of the U.S. Air Force 3d Special Operations Squadron over South Vietnam.

2348 _____. "The World's Littlest Fighter." Airman, XIII (Aug. 1969), 40-44. The Northrop F-5 Freedom Fighter over Vietnam.

2349 Swift, William D., and Curtiss J. Herrick, Jr. "'Anybody See the Ground Troops?'" U.S. Army Aviation Digest, XIII (Oct. 1967), 32-35. Helicopter gunship close air support operations in the Phuoc Thanh area in October 1964.

2350 Sykes, Charles S., Jr. Interim Report of Operations of the 1st Cavalry Division (Airmobile), July 1, 1965 to December 31, 1966. Albuquerque, N.M.: 1st Cavalry Division Association, 1967. 90p. The outfit's vertical assault activities in South Vietnam.

2351 Sylva, David. "A Letter from Vietnam." Airman, XII (June 1968), 32-33. Thoughts on the air war.

2352 "TAC Unit Performs Unique Support Role." Journal of the

Armed Forces, CIII (Jan. 1, 1966), 3. The 4440th Aircraft Delivery Group took U.S. Air Force aircraft to South Vietnam.

2353 "Tactical Air Action Blunts Armored Drive." Aviation Week and Space Technology, XCVI (May 15, 1972), 17-18. Attacks on enemy tanks approaching An Loc.

2354 "Tactical Air Power." Ordnance, LII (March-April 1968), 463-466. An assessment with comments on South Vietnam.

2355 "Tactical Elements of the VNAF Find Training Tested in Combat." Air Force Times, XXV (Sept. 30, 1964), 19. VNAF operations in support of ground troops in 1964.

2356 "Tactical Mobility." Ryan Reporter, XXIII (May-June 1963), 9-12. A look at the helicopter as a means of delivering troops to a battlefield.

2357 "Tale of Two Broken Cities: Quang Tri and An Loc." Time, CI (Jan. 15, 1973), 25-26. Casualties of stiff air-ground fighting.

2358 "Tan Son Nhut." Air Force Times, XXIV (Sept. 25, 1968), 14. A look at the U.S. airbase there.

2359 "Target: Hanoi--Attacks on the Hanoi-Haiphong Oil Tanks." Newsweek, LXVIII (July 11, 1966), 21-22. Operational and political analysis.

2360 "Target: SAM." Time, LXXXVI (Sept. 3, 1965), 28. Attacking North Vietnamese missile sites.

2361 Tarrow, Arthur B. "USAF Hospital Clark and the Vietnam Casualties." Air University Review, XVIII (Nov.-Dec. 1966), 85-89. Wounded were taken to the Clark Airbase Hospital near Manila.

2362 "Task Group 'Ivory Coast': The Attempt to Rescue POW's." Newsweek, LXXVI (Dec. 7, 1970), 28. The unsuccessful Son Tay raid.

2363 Tate, Grover C. "A Weekend Warrior's Vietnam Diary." Air Force and Space Digest, L (June 1967), 38-39+. Thoughts of an Air National Guard pilot's active duty in South Vietnam.

2364 Taylor, Edmond. "Battle in the Delta: The Co Cong Victory." Reporter, XXXIV (Jan. 13, 1966), 21-25. ARVN troops vs. the Vietcong, with helicopter support.

2365 ______. "Battle over Tan Hiep: With Lt. Gary Walters."

Reporter, XXXIII (Dec. 16, 1965), 26-29. ARVN troops and their American advisor in action.

2366 Taylor, Jim. "[Airlift] Into Bu Dop." Airman, XII (May 1968), 24-27. A tactical airlift operation.

2367 ______. "Combat Assault with the VNAF." Air Force Times, XXXI (Nov. 18, 1970), 16. The South Vietnamese Air Force in action.

2368 ______. "Fifteen-Year-Old Vietnamese Air Force Shows Big Build-Up." Air Force Times, XXX (July 29, 1970), 16. Vietnamization.

2369 ______. "Helping to Build the VNAF: USAF Advisers in Southeast Asia." Air Force and Space Digest, LIII (Dec. 1970), 47-49. A look at the Vietnamization program.

2370 ______. "Stalk the VC." Airman, XIV (Oct. 1970), 44-47. U.S. Air Force tactical reconnaissance and photography operations.

2371 ______. "VNAF: Vietnam's Growing Air Power." Airman, XV (April 1971), 42-47. A progress report on Vietnamization.

2372 ______. "Vietnam--1968." Airman, XIII (Jan. 1969), 25-33. The air war as captured by artists in the U.S. Air Force Art Program.

2373 Taylor, John B. "Milk Run." Airman, XIX (Feb. 1975), 42-47. Memories of how a routine supply flight over Vietnam almost became a disaster for one C-130 crew.

2374 Taylor, John W. R., ed. Aircraft Annual. 13 vols. London: Ian Allan, 1961-1973. A yearbook of aircraft with information during these years on aircraft which took part in the Indochina fighting; distributed in America by Sportshelf of New Rochelle, N.Y.

2375 ______, ed. Combat Aircraft of the World from 1909 to the Present. New York: Putnam, 1969. 647p. Includes those of the Vietnam conflict.

2376 ______. "Counterinsurgency Air Force." Royal Air Forces Quarterly, III (Summer 1963), 83-88. Requirements for same with thoughts on the American air role in South Vietnam.

2377 ______. Encyclopedia of World Aircraft. London: Odhams, 1966. 159p. Illustrated; includes many operating over Indochina.

2378 ______. Helicopters and VTOL Aircraft. Garden City, N.Y.: Doubleday, 1968. 96p. Illustrated; includes helicopters of the Indochina war.

2379 ______. Jane's All the World's Aircraft. 12 vols. New York: McGraw-Hill, 1961-1973. The most important aircraft yearbook cited in this bibliography, originally published by the London firm of Low. Contains information on the Allied and North Vietnamese aircraft of the Indochina conflict.

2380 ______. "The MIG-19 'Farmer.'" Air Pictorial, XXV (Aug. 1963), 244-245. The Russian fighter, models of which were given to the North Vietnamese Air Force.

2381 ______. Milestones of the Air: Jane's One Hundred Significant Aircraft. New York: McGraw-Hill, 1969. 158p. An illustrated aircraft history with several units chosen from among those which flew over Southeast Asia.

2382 ______. Military Aircraft of the World. New York: Scribner's, 1971. 230p. Includes many which flew over Indochina.

2383 ______. "The Push-Button Age." In his A History of Aerial Warfare (London: Hamlyn, 1974), p221-237. With limited information on the air war over Southeast Asia.

2384 ______. Warplanes of the World, new ed. New York: Arco Books, 1966. 203p. Includes many of the Vietnam war.

2385 ______, and David Mondey. Spies in the Sky. New York: Scribner's, 1972. 128p. See especially Chapters IX, "Vietnam and the Quiet Ones," and X, "ECM, AEW, and ASW."

2386 ______, and Kenneth G. Munson, eds. History of Aviation. New York: Crown, 1976. 511p. Extremely well-done illustrated history with excellent comments on the Indochina war; published in London in 1972 by New English Library.

2387 ______, and ______. History of Aviation: Aircraft Identification Guide. London: New English Library, 1973. 192p. A companion to item 2386 highlighting just the aircraft, including those of the Indochina conflict.

2388 ______, and F. Gordon Swanborough. Military Aircraft of the World, rev. ed. New York: Scribner's, 1973. 240p. Includes those aircraft of the Southeast Asian war; a third edition with the same pagination was published in London by Ian Allan in 1975.

2389 Taylor, Maxwell D. Swords and Plowshares. New York: W. W. Norton, 1972. 434p. Memoirs of the famous airborne general-turned-diplomat, with interesting information relative to the SEA air war.

2390 Taylor, Michael J. H., and John W. R. Taylor. Helicopters of the World. New York: Scribner's, 1976. 128p. Illustrated; includes those of the American armed services.

2391 ______, and Kenneth Munson, comps. Jane's Pocket Book of Light Aircraft, edited by John W. R. Taylor. New York: Collier Books, 1976. 260p. Includes helicopters.

2392 ______, and ______, comps. Jane's Pocket Book of Major Combat Aircraft, edited by John W. R. Taylor. New York: Macmillan, 1974. 263p. Includes those of the U.S. Navy, Marine Corps, and Air Force in Southeast Asia.

2393 Taylor, Milton C. "South Vietnam: Lavish Aid, Little Progress." Pacific Affairs, XXXIV (Fall 1961), 242-256. An early analysis with several aerial comments.

2394 "Teamwork Required in Tactical Air War." Air Force Times, XXV (Sept. 30, 1964), 16. Early comments on TAC in Southeast Asia.

2395 "Telephone Poles: The Bombing of Soviet SAM Missile Sites." Newsweek, LXVI (Aug. 9, 1965), 22. American raids on North Vietnamese air defense facilities.

2396 Teplinsky, Boris. "Air War in Vietnam." New Times, no. 51 (Dec. 22, 1965), 11-14. An earlier Russian comment.

2397 ______. "The Air War Over Indochina." International Affairs, no. 2 (Feb. 1967), 40-47. A Soviet view.

2398 Termena, Bernard J. "Logistics." In Carl Berger, ed., The United States Air Force in Southeast Asia, 1961-1973 (Washington: U.S. Government Printing Office, 1977), p245-256. Bases and supply delivery.

2399 Terry, Frederick G. "The Armed Helicopter." Infantry, LVII (July-Aug. 1967), 16-19. With examples drawn from the Vietnam fighting.

2400 "That Extra Edge." Army, XVIII (Nov. 1968), 105-106. Armed helicopters.

2401 "That Others May Live: The Aerospace Rescue and Recovery Service." Newsweek, LXVII (April 4, 1966), 58. Almost identical coverage of the 3d Group as in following item.

2402 "That Others May Live: The Third Aerospace Rescue and

Recovery Group." Time, LXXXVIII (July 22, 1966), 27. A brief look at this U.S. Air Force group's Indochina operations.

2403 "Thin Line of Distinction: The North Vietnamese Dikes." Time, C (Aug. 14, 1972), 32. Additional comment on the bombing controversy.

2404 "The Third Munitions Maintenance Squadron." Combat Crew, XVII (July 1966), 10. Quick profile of a U.S. Air Force unit in South Vietnam.

2405 "The 33rd Photographic Reconnaissance Wing." Aero Album, VIII (Summer 1969), 32-37. An illustrated look at that U.S. Air Force unit in Southeast Asia.

2406 "Thirty Tons from 30,000 Feet: B-52 Raids." Time, XCII (Aug. 2, 1968), 28+. Stratofortress "Arc Light" operations over South Vietnam.

2407 "Thirty Tons of Deadly Adaptability: The Phantom F-4." Life, LXIX (Sept. 25, 1970), 30-31. An illustrated look at the McDonnell-Douglas fighter.

2408 Thomas, Theodore K. "The Rotar Dimension." Marine Corps Gazette, LVII (May 1973), 25-32. The role of helicopters in the U.S. Marine Corps.

2409 Thomis, Wayne. "Whispering Death: The F-111 in Southeast Asia." Air Force Magazine, LVI (Feb. 1973), 22-27. After initial groundings for physical failures, the swept-wing fighter-bomber proved quite successful in the late stages of the conflict.

2410 Thompson, Fred N. "The Long Way Home." Airman, XV (Sept. 1971), 29-31. The adventures of a POW.

2411 Thompson, Paul Y. "Aircraft Shelters in Vietnam." Military Engineer, LXI (July-Aug. 1969), 273-274. The Hardened Shelter Program designed to protect aircraft from Vietcong rocket attacks.

2412 Thompson, Thomas E. "Know Your Army Helicopters." Army Information Digest, XVIII (March 1963), 47-51. Pictures and details on many Army whirlybirds which would see service in Southeast Asia.

2413 ______. "Winning the Obstacle Race: The Role of Air Cavalry in Vietnam." Interavia, XXI (May 1966), 569-573. The prime example being the 1st Air Cavalry Division adventure of 1965 in the Ia Drang Valley.

2414 "Those Who Must Die: The Battle at Dong Xoai." Time,

LXXXV (July 18, 1965), 28-30. The Vietcong attack on the Special Forces camp there and its success in preventing heliborne reinforcements from landing.

2415 "Three Carrier Strikes." Naval Aviation News, (May 1967), 12-13. By U.S. Navy warplanes from the carriers Kittyhawk, Coral Sea, and Ticonderoga on "Yankee Station" in the Gulf of Tonkin.

2416 "Three Point Program Speeds Airlift to Southeast Asia." Air Force Times, XXVI (April 27, 1966), 15. "Operations Quick Stop, Red Ball, and Fast Fly."

2417 "Three RAAF Squadrons in Vietnam." Flight International, XCI (May 11, 1967), 767. A report on their activities and composition.

2418 "Thunder Rolls On: American Warplanes Pound Oil Installations." Time, LXXXVIII (July 15, 1966), 28. The U.S. Navy-Air Force strikes on storage facilities near Hanoi and Haiphong.

2419 "Thunderchief: The Big Stick." Flying Review International, XIX (January 1964), 21-23. A look at the Republic F-105.

2420 "Tide Turning in the Vietnam War?" U.S. News and World Report, LIX (Sept. 27, 1965), 35-37. An early analysis.

2421 Tierney, Richard K. "Airmobile Pathfinders." U.S. Army Aviation Digest, (Feb. 1966), 2-5. The 1st Air Cavalry Division.

2422 _____. "The 11th (Aviation) Group." U.S. Army Aviation Digest, XI (Dec. 1965), 2-7. Its composition and activities.

2423 _____. "The Flying Crane." U.S. Army Aviation Digest, X (Nov. 1964), 12-15. The Ch-54A helicopter.

2424 "'Tigers' Guard Da Nang." Air Force Times, XXVIII (June 26, 1968), 14. The U.S. Air Force 366th Security Police Squadron.

2425 Tilford, Earl H. "When We'd Only Just Begun: An Early Rescue Attempt, 1963." American Aviation Historical Society Journal, XXII (Fall 1977), 188-192. In March 1963, two U.S. Marine Corps UH-3D helicopters attempted to insert a four-man American-Vietnamese rescue team at the crash site of an Army OV-1, but lost one whirlybird in the effort.

2426 Tillema, Herbert K. Appeal to Force: American Military Intervention in the Era of Containment. New York: Crowell, 1973. 260p. An analysis with some comments relative to the SEA air war.

2427 Tippin, Garold L. "Assault by Air." Infantry, LVII (Nov.-Dec. 1968), 12-17. Putting troops down in a vertical assault in South Vietnam.

2428 Tison, Joseph T. "Employment of an Airborne Command Post in a High-Threat Environment." U.S. Army Aviation Digest, XXI (June 1975), 12-13. With examples from the Southeast Asian conflict.

2429 "To a Darkling Target Aboard a B-52." Time, XCIX (May 1, 1972), 15. An "Arc Light" mission.

2430 "To Kill a MIG." TAC Attack, XIII (Jan. 1973), 16-19. Combat over North Vietnam.

2431 Tocci, Vincent R. "[North] Vietnam: They Still Fight, They Still Build." Air Force Policy Letter for Commanders, no. 11 (Nov. 1969), 16-20+. Despite American air raids.

2432 Toftoy, Charles. "Nhay Du--All the Way." Infantry, LVII (Jan.-Feb. 1967), 3-6. A look at the ARVN 1st Airborne Battalion.

2433 Tolson, John J., 3d. Airmobility, 1961-1971. (Vietnam Studies series.) Washington: U.S. Army, Center of Military History, 1974. 304p. The most useful official study on the subject presently available.

2434 ______. "Pegasus." Army, XXI (Dec. 1971), 10-19. The author, a former boss of the 1st Air Cavalry Division, herein describes the 1968 relief of Khe Sanh.

2435 Tomlinson, Frank J. "The Great Seven." Aerospace Safety, XXIV (June 1968), 2-6. A look at the A-7 Corsair II.

2436 "Tonnage of the USAF Operated Airlift System." Airman, XI (March 1967), 14-15. A brief review.

2437 Tooker, D. K., et al. "Armed Helicopters." Marine Corps Gazette, L (May 1966), 45-51. Thoughts on their use in Vietnam by the U.S. Marine Corps.

2438 Toor, Francis E. "The Air Force Civil Engineer's Role in Counterinsurgency." Air University Review, XV (July-Aug. 1964), 64-72. One of the few pieces on the subject.

2439 "Torture, Solitary, Starvation: POW's Tell the Inside Story." U.S. News and World Report, LXXIV (April 9, 1973), 33-34. Reports on life in Hanoi's POW compounds.

2440 "Touchy Times for American Advisors." Time, XCIX (May 29, 1972), 31. With the ARVN during the Easter invasion.

2441 Towle, Bob. "Spooky and Charlie: Language at War." Air Force Times, XXXIII (March 14, 1973), 33+. Vietnam war terminology.

2442 Trager, Frank N. "Vietnam: The Military Requirements for Victory." Orbis, VIII (Fall 1964), 563-583. An early analysis which does not neglect the air aspects.

2443 "Trap in the Sky: Phantoms Down Seven MIGs." Newsweek, LXXIX (Jan. 16, 1967), 36. The 8th TFS vs. MIG's over North Vietnam.

2444 Tregaskis, Richard W. Vietnam Diary. New York: Holt, 1963. 401p. An eyewitness account of the period from October 1962 to January 1963 rendered by the author in the style of his famous Guadalcanal Diary.

2445 Trevino, Benito A. "Don't Give Up the Ship." U.S. Army Aviation Digest, XVI (June 1970), 22-24. Keeping damaged helicopters flying, with examples from SEA.

2446 "Trigger Happy: Civilian Casualties." New Republic, CLV (Aug. 27, 1966), 6-7. Condemnation of American bomb "spillage" over South Vietnam.

2447 Trimble, Robert. "F-100 Super Sabre: Part III, the F-100 Sees Heavy Action over Vietnam." Air Classics, XI (Sept. 1975), 24-35. An illustrated account.

2448 ______. "Skyraider." Air Classics, XI (Feb. 1975), 32-37. A profile of the A-1E and its operations over Southeast Asia.

2449 Troelstrup, Glenn C. "In Vietnam, Suddenly It's a Stepped Up War: The Battle of Plei Me. U.S. News and World Report, LIX (Nov. 22, 1965), 50-52. In support of the defenders, U.S. Air Force pilots flew 696 close air support sorties.

2450 ______. "How the Navy Helps Fight a Jungle War." U.S. News and World Report, LXI (Sept. 12, 1966), 44-46. Riverine warfare and armed helicopters.

2451 ______. "Jet Seat View of an Air Strike: The Battle of Plei Me." U.S. News and World Report, LIX (Nov. 22, 1965), 52-53. A firsthand report.

2452 Trung-Sen. The Winter 1966-Spring 1967 Victory and Five Lessons Concerning the Conduct of Military Strategy. Hanoi: Foreign Languages Publishing House, 1967. 71p.

2453 Tulich, Eugene N. The U.S. Coast Guard in Southeast Asia During the Vietnam Conflict. Washington: Public Affairs,

Division, U.S. Coast Guard, 1975. 65p. With some attention to air-sea rescue operations.

2454 Tully, Robert B. "Mobility on the Battlefield." Military Review, XLVII (Dec. 1967), 72-77. A review from the horse to the helicopter.

2455 Tuohy, William. "'Big E' at Work: Aerial Missions off the USS Enterprise." Newsweek, LXVII (April 16, 1966), 42+. U.S. Navy air raids over North Vietnam from her deck.

2456 _____. "The Relief of Duc Co." Newsweek, LXVI (Aug. 23, 1965), 28-29. With some attention to the aerial phase.

2457 Turaids, Tavaris. "Medical Aspects of Survival in Southeast Asia." Approach, XIII (Jan. 1968), 27-32. With regard to downed pilots; reprinted in the U.S. Army Aviation Digest, XIV (Oct. 1968), 56-63.

2458 Turley, G. H., and M. R. Wells. "Easter Invasion, 1972." Marine Corps Gazette, LVII (March 1973), 18-29. A useful summary with attention to aerial matters provided.

2459 Turnbow, Woody W. "Attack Helicopter Survivability." Armor, LXXXII (Sept.-Oct. 1973), 22-24. With examples from Southeast Asia.

2460 Turner, John A. "VNAF Takes Gunship Role in the Delta." Air Force Times, XXX (June 3, 1970), 15. Vietnamization south of Saigon.

2461 Tuso, Joseph F. "Navigator's Log: Jack Armstrong to the Age of Aquarius and Beyond." Air Force and Space Digest, LIII (June 1970), 60-64.

2462 "Tuy Hoa." Air Force Times, XXVIII (June 19, 1968), 14. A quick look at the American air facility there.

2463 "Twelfth Air Commandos Receive Presidential Unit Citation." Air Force Policy Letter for Commanders, no. 12 (Dec. 1968), 31. For operations over South Vietnam.

2464 "Twelve Cardinal Rules." U.S. Army Aviation Digest, XVII (Dec. 1971), 6-7. For helicopter gunship tactics over Southeast Asia.

2465 "Twenty-Four-Hour Airlift to Vietnam." Fortune, LXXII (Aug. 1965), 135-137. MAC in action.

2466 "The 27th Communications Squadron." Combat Crew, XVII (July 1966), 11. The U.S. Air Force unit in South Vietnam.

2467 "200,000 Bombs Dropped on Viet Cong by B-52's." Air Force Times, XXVI (July 27, 1966), 15. Since the start of "Arc Light" operations in June 1965.

2468 "Two of the 'MIG Killers' Were B-52 Tail Gunners." Armed Forces Journal International, CXI (May 1974), 38. Victories during "Linebacker II" in December 1972.

2469 "UH-1B's Attack Viet Cong." Aviation Week and Space Technology, LXXXI (Aug. 31, 1964), 78-79. U.S. Army gunships vs. Communist guerrillas.

Listed here are title entries beginning with the abbreviations "U.S.," "USAF," and "USS."

2470 "U.S. Aircraft Losses in Southeast Asia, 1962-1970." Journal of the Armed Forces, CVIII (Jan. 18, 1971), 30. A table.

2471 "U.S. and Vietnam Initiate Combined Air Strikes." Department of State Bulletin, LII (March 15, 1965), 371-372. Little has been written about VNAF raids into North Vietnam.

2472 "U.S. Army Aviation: A Special Issue." Aerospace International, III (July-Aug. 1967), 1+. With emphasis on Vietnam activities.

2473 "U.S. Combat Air Operations in Cambodia Terminated: White House Statement, August 15, 1973." Department of State Bulletin, LXIX (Sept. 3, 1973), 326-327. Text of the document closing down years of aerial conflict over Southeast Asia.

2474 "U.S. Combat Aircraft." Flying Review International, XXIII (Feb. 1968), 67-72+. Includes a look at all then flying over Indochina.

2475 "U.S. Combat Airplanes: A Pictorial." Ordnance, LII (March-April 1968), 467-470. Including those flown over Indochina.

2476 "U.S. Combat in Vietnam: The First Year." Army, XVI (Oct. 1966), 111-124. A review with attention to the airmobile aspects.

2477 "U.S. Electronic Espionage: A Memoir." Ramparts Magazine, XI (Aug. 1972), 35-50. Includes air-dropped sensors in Vietnam.

2478 "U.S. Guided Bombs Alter Vietnam Air War." Aviation Week and Space Technology, XCVI (May 22, 1972), 16-17. The use of the so-called "smart bombs."

2479 "U.S. Helicopter Crews 'Fire First.'" In John Galloway, ed., The Kennedys and Vietnam: An Interim History (New York: Facts on File, 1971), p33-35. A brief recapitulation of U.S. Army and Marine Corps helicopter operations over South Vietnam, October-December 1962.

2480 "U.S. Leads 3-to-1 in Kills: MIG's Rated a Threat." Air Force Times, XXVII (April 19, 1967), 13. The results of aerial dogfighting over North Vietnam.

2481 "U.S. Naval Operations Against North Vietnam, August 1964-November 1968." In Frank Uhlig, Jr., ed., The Naval Review, 1969 (Annapolis, Md.: United States Naval Institute, 1969), p358-364. A chronology which includes the activities of carrier warbirds.

2482 "[A U.S. Navy Air] Officer: His Life and His Squadraon." Naval Aviation News (Aug. 1970), 8-10. An illustrated look at one man aboard his carrier off Vietnam.

2483 "U.S. Pilots: 'We Are Not Hot-Shot Charlies.'" Newsweek, LXV (April 19, 1965), 36-37. Interviews with pilots on the air war over Vietnam.

2484 "U.S. Presses Vietnam Air Interdiction." Aviation Week and Space Technology, (May 15, 1972), 9, 14-16. "Operation Linebacker I" in response to the Easter invasion.

2485 "U.S. Statement on Vietnam's Laos Operations: American Role Limited to Air and Artillery Support." SEATO Record, X (April 1971), 18-19. Both supporting elements were extremely heavy.

2486 "U.S. to Accelerate North Vietnam Air Attacks." Aviation Week and Space Technology, LXXXVIII (March 25, 1968), 17-18. And so it proved.

2487 "USAF Almanac: The USAF, Facts and Figures." Air Force Magazine, LVI (May 1973), 146-158. Includes statistics from the Southeast Asia conflict.

2488 "USAF and the Congressional Medal of Honor." Air Force and Space Digest, LIII (Sept. 1970), 22-23. Its awarding to Col. William A. Jones.

2489 "USAF Bombs Hit Hard at Rails and Trucks." Aviation Week and Space Technology, XCVIII (April 30, 1973), 14-20. In support of friendly troops in Cambodia.

2490 "USAF Closes the [Gen. John] Lavelle Case." Air Force Magazine, LV (Dec. 1972), 20. The 7th Air Force boss who exceeded his orders.

2491 "USAF Expands Vietnam Repair Capability." Aviation Week and Space Technology, LXXXVI (May 22, 1967), 74-78. By training and aiding more mechanics.

2492 "USAF F-4C Carries Varied Ordnance Loads: Photographs." Aviation Week and Space Technology, LXXXVI (April 24, 1967), 75-78. Bombs, rockets, and sundry bullets available to the Phantom.

2493 "USAF Medal of Honor Winners, 1918-1970." Air Force and Space Digest, LIII (July 1970), 59. A listing.

2494 "USAF, Navy Bombard MIG Installations at Hoa Lac, Kep Bases in North Vietnam: With Photographs." Aviation Week and Space Technology, LXXXVI (May 8, 1967), 18-23. This source is useful for the photographs alone.

2495 "USAF Operations in Vietnam." Journal of the Armed Forces, CIII (Feb. 26, 1966), 10. A quick look.

2496 "USAF Strike Sorties Show Big Increase During the Year." Air Force Times, XXVI (Dec. 22, 1965), 14. A chart.

2497 "USAF War Deaths Total 640." Air Force Times, XXIX (April 2, 1969), 2. Figures to March 31, 1969.

2498 "The [USS] Bon Homme Richard off Vietnam." Naval Aviation News (May 1967), 36.

2499 "The [USS] Constellation off Vietnam." Naval Aviation News (Feb. 1967), 12. These two citations deal with American aircraft carriers.

Regular "U" listings resume here

2500 Ulsamer, Edgar. "Air Rescue in Southeast Asia: Right from Hanoi's Own Backyard." Air Force Magazine, LV (Oct. 1972), 30-34. The June 1972 rescue of downed U.S. Air Force pilot Capt. Roger C. Locher by a task force including HH-53 helicopters, A-1 fighters, and a C-130 command ship with F-4's and F-105's flying anti-MIG cover.

2501 ______. "SRAM--The Last Word in Defense Suppression." Air Force Magazine, LV (Feb. 1972), 28-34. The Short Range Attack Missile employed by U.S. aircraft against North Vietnamese air defense objectives late in the conflict.

2502 Underwood, John W. "'Best' Bomb Strike Described by FAC." Air Force Times, XXVI (Feb. 8, 1967), 14. During "Operation Cedar Falls."

2503 ______, and G. B. Collinge. The Light Plane Since 1909.

Glendale, Calif.: Heritage Press, 1975. Highly illustrated; includes the types used by FAC's in Vietnam.

Listed here are all entries for which the "United States" is the author.

2504 United States. Air Force. Air Force Civil Engineer Handbook: Facility Design and Construction. (AFM 88-54.) Washington, 1962. 626p. On how to build airfields; employed in South Vietnam.

2505 ____. ____. Air Force Register. 13 vols. Washington: U.S. Government Printing Office, 1961-1973. An annual listing of officers.

2506 ____. ____. Civil Engineering, General: Maintenance and Repair of Expeditionary and Theater of Operation Airfield Facilities. (AFM 85-33.) Washington: U.S. Government Printing Office, 1967. 122p. An important guidebook for Air Force Civil Engineering personnel in South Vietnam.

2507 ____. ____. Emergency Rescue: Survival. (AFM 64-5.) Washington: U.S. Government Printing Office, 1961. 160p. What to do if shot down over hostile territory.

2508 ____. ____. Honors and Ceremonies: Decorations, Service Awards, Unit Awards, Special Badges, Favorable Communications, Certificates, and Special Devices. (AFM 900-3.) Washington: U.S. Government Printing Office, 1966. 116p. Of use in Southeast Asia.

2509 ____. ____. Mission Employment Tactics: Special Air Warfare Tactics. (AFM 3-5.) Washington: U.S. Government Printing Office, 1966. 120p. A "bible" for use over Southeast Asia.

2510 ____. ____. Survival: Search and Rescue. (AFM-64-5.) Washington: U.S. Government Printing Office, 1969. Unpaginated. Succeeds "Emergency Rescue: Survival" cited in item 2507.

2511 ____. ____. Tactical Air Operations: Counter Air, Close Air Support, and Air Interdiction. (AFM 2-1.) Washington: U.S. Government Printing Office, 1969. Basic information, based on the Vietnam experience.

2512 ____. ____. Air Command and Staff College. USAF Counterinsurgency Orientation Course. 2 vols. Maxwell Air Force Base, Ala.: Air University, 1962. Based on the best techniques then known; taught to officers who would have a role to play in Southeast Asia.

(____. Air Force. Air University--cont.)

2513 ____. ____. Air University. "Project Corona Harvest." Maxwell Air Force Base, Ala., 1971- . The U.S. Air Force data and studies on airpower in Southeast Asia are still, for the most part, classified and are thus unavailable to most users of this bibliography. The scholar should be aware of the existence of this project should it become available on a non-classified basis in the future.

2514 ____. ____. Judge Advocate General. International Law: The Conduct of Armed Conflict and Air Operations. (AFP 110-31.) Washington: U.S. Government Printing Office, 1976. Unpaginated. Contains several examples relative to our topic.

2515 ____. ____. Office of Air Force History. Aces and Aerial Victories: The United States Air Force in Southeast Asia, 1965-1973, edited by James N. Eastland, Jr., et al. Washington: U.S. Government Printing Office, 1976. 188p. A well-illustrated undocumented account of U.S. Air Force fighters vs. North Vietnamese MIG's during the years 1965-1973, with lists and victory totals.

2516 ____. ____. ____. "Air Force Medal of Honor Winners." In Carl Berger, ed., The United States Air Force in Southeast Asia, 1961-1973 (Washington: U.S. Government Printing Office, 1977), p353-364. Illustrations of each with details on their exploits.

2517 ____. ____. ____. "Air Operations over Northern Laos." In Carl Berger, ed., The United States Air Force in Southeast Asia, 1961-1973 (Washington: U.S. Government Printing Office, 1977), p121-136. An illustrated look at various interdiction efforts.

2518 ____. ____. ____. "Base Defense." In Carl Berger, ed., The United States Air Force in Southeast Asia, 1961-1973 (Washington: U.S. Government Printing Office, 1977), p257-270. An illustrated examination of the problems of guarding U.S. air facilities in South Vietnam.

2519 ____. ____. ____. "Vietnamization." In Carl Berger, ed., The United States Air Force in Southeast Asia, 1961-1973. (Washington: U.S. Government Printing Office, 1977), p309-320. The training of VNAF personnel and the eventual turning-over to them of control and aircraft for operations.

2520 ____. ____. Office of Information. Air Force Base Guide: Background Information. (USAF Publication 69-8.) Washington: U.S. Government Printing Office, 1969. Unpaginated. Contains some information relative to our topic.

2521 ____. ____. ____. The United States Air Force, 1965-66 ed. Washington: U.S. Government Printing Office, 1965. 23p. A brief illustrated overview.

2522 ____. ____. ____. Internal Information Division. USAF Historical Aircraft. (USAF Pamphlet 70-7.) Washington, 1970. 21p. Pictures and details; some planes from our period.

2523 ____. ____. School of Systems and Logistics. Logistics in Southeast Asia: A Symposium. Wright-Patterson Air Force Base, Ohio, 1967. 220p. An exchange of experiences for future use in Indochina.

2524 ____. ____. 2d Air Division. "Air Force Annual Summary of North Vietnam Strikes." Air Force Policy Letter for Commanders, no. 4 (April 1966), 19-22. The text of the February 5, 1966, release 66-014 from the 2d Air Division HQ in South Vietnam.

2525 ____. ____. 7th Air Force. "Air Force Annual Vietnam Summary, 1966." Air Force Policy Letter for Commanders, no. 2 (Feb. 1967), 5-9. U.S. 7th Air Force release 67-022 of January 1967.

2526 ____. ____. ____. "Air Force Vietnam News Summary, 1965." Air Force Policy Letter for Commanders, no. 2 (Feb. 1966), 23-26. Similar in style, content, and source to the above citation.

2527 ____. ____. ____. An Econometric Study of Aerial Interdiction in Southern Laos, 10 October 1970-30 June 1971. (USAF Academy Technical Report 77-4.) Boulder Colo.: United States Air Force Academy, 1977. "Operation Commando Hunt."

2528 ____. ____. ____. "Summary of Airpower in Vietnam: July 1965-July 1966." Air Force Policy Letter for Commanders, no. 8 (Aug. 1966), 12-17. Excerpts from materials furnished by the 7th Air Force HQ.

2529 ____. ____. ____. "Tactical Airpower Decisive at Khe Sanh." Air Force Policy Letter for Commanders, no. 6 (June 1968), 48. The text of 7th Air Force news release 4-68-138.

2530 ____. ____. ____. "Vietnam Communiqué." In each weekly issue of the Air Force Times from 1966-1973. Previous communiques were issued by HQ, 2nd Air Division.

2531 ____. Army. The Air-Ground Operations System. (FM 100-26.) Washington: U.S. Government Printing Office,

(____. Army--cont.)

1973. Unpaginated. To a large extent, based on the Southeast Asia experience.

2532 ____. ____. Air Movement of Troops and Equipment. (TM 57-210.) Washington: U.S. Government Printing Office, 1965. Unpaginated. Tactical and strategic airlift.

2533 ____. ____. Airmobile Operations. (FM 57-35.) Washington: U.S. Government Printing Office, 1963. 76p. Based on theory and experiment.

2534 ____. ____. ____, revised. (FM-57-35.) Washington: U.S. Government Printing Office, 1968. 150p. Succeeds the 1963 edition cited immediately above; the first field manual subject to benefit from the experiences of the 1st Air Cavalry Division in Vietnam. Yet another edition was published in 1971 reflecting additional experience gained in Southeast Asia.

2535 ____. ____. Army/Air Force Doctrine for Airborne Operations. (FM 57-1.) Washington: U.S. Government Printing Office, 1967. Unpaginated. Also issued by the Air Force as AFM 2-51.

2536 ____. ____. Army/Air Force Doctrine for Tactical Airlift Operations. (FM 100-27.) Washington: U.S. Government Printing Office, 1967. Unpaginated. Also issued by the Air Force as AFM 2-50.

2537 ____. ____. Army Air Transport Operations. (FM 55-46.) Washington: U.S. Government Printing Office, 1967. 90p. Succeeds the manual issued in 1965 (cited as item 2540), and reflects Vietnam experience.

2538 ____. ____. Army Airfield-Heliport Design. (TM 5-823-1.) Washington: U.S. Government Printing Office, 1965. 62p. Employed in base construction by Army Engineers in Vietnam.

2539 ____. ____. Army Aviation Organizational Aircraft Maintenance. (TM 1-10.) Washington: U.S. Government Printing Office, 1965. 83p.

2540 ____. ____. Army Aviation Transport Services and Units in the Field Army. (FM 55-46.) Washington: U.S. Government Printing Office, 1965. 69p. Succeeded by the 1967 Army Air Transport Operations (see item 2537).

2541 ____. ____. Army Aviation Utilization. (FM 1-100.) Washington: U.S. Government Printing Office, 1966. 68p.

Designed to acquaint commanders with details on Army Aviation.

2542 ____. ____. Aviation Battalion. (FM 1-15.) Washington: U.S. Government Printing Office, 1965. 75p. See next entry.

2543 ____. ____. Army Division Aviation Battalion and Group. (FM 1-15.) Washington: U.S. Government Printing Office, 1967. 131p. Succeeds item 2542.

2544 ____. ____. Counterguerrilla Operations. (FM 31-16.) Washington: U.S. Government Printing Office, 1967. 164p. Succeeds FM 31-16, first issued in 1963.

2545 ____. ____. Divisional Armored and Air Cavalry Units. (FM 17-36.) Washington: U.S. Government Printing Office, 1965. 276p.

2546 ____. ____. Evasion and Escape. (FM 21-77.) Washington: U.S. Government Printing Office, 1965. 121p. For all ranks, including aviation.

2547 ____. ____. Handbook on the North Vietnamese Armed Forces. Washington, 1966. Unpaginated. Contains useful background information relative to the air war topic.

2548 ____. ____. Report on [the] War in Vietnam (as of June 30, 1968). Washington: U.S. Government Printing Office, 1969. 347p. Pt. I: "Report on Air and Naval Campaigns Against North Vietnam and Pacific Command-wide Support of the War, June 1964-July 1968," by Adm. U.S. Grant Sharp; Pt. II: "Report on Operations in South Vietnam, January 1964-June 1968," by Gen. William C. Westmoreland. This study represents one of the most useful histories of the Southeast Asian conflict available to July 1968; Admiral Sharp's attention to the air war and General Westmoreland's accounts of heliborne operations are valuable.

2549 ____. ____. Special Forces Air and Amphibious Operations. (ASUBJSCD 31-20.) Washington: U.S. Government Printing Office, 1966. The section dealing with air and helicopter aspects is useful to our topic.

2550 ____. ____. U.S. Army Area Handbook for North Vietnam. (DA pam 550-57.) Washington: U.S. Government Printing Office, 1967. 494p. A study of the chief "enemy" nation with some attention to air bases and aerial capability. Prepared by the Foreign Area Studies Division at American University.

2551 ____. ____. U.S. Army Area Handbook for Vietnam. Wash-

(____. Army--cont.)

ington: U.S. Government Printing Office, 1954. 513p. Prepared by the Foreign Area Studies Division, Special Operations Research Office, American University as a revision to the edition published in 1962.

2552 ____. ____. 1st Air Cavalry Division. Combat Tactics and Air Assault Techniques. Division pamphlet 350-1. Japan: [PPC?] 1967. 102p. The hows of helicopter vertical assault.

2553 ____. ____. Office of the Chief of Information. Special Warfare, U.S. Army: An Army Specialty. Washington: U.S. Government Printing Office, 1962. 142p. Includes a look at the use of helicopters and light planes.

2554 ____. ____. ____. "Vietnam Reports from the Battlefields." Army, XVI (June-Sept., Dec. 1966), 26-32, 59-65, 55-59, 53-61, 16+; XVII (Jan.-Sept., Dec. 1967), 44-55, 56-62, 54-58, 64-65, 26-30, 42-48, 33-37, 57-64, 54-57. Includes many of the engagements fought during those two years with information on air support and helicopter activities.

2555 ____. ____. 25th Division. Tropic Lightning, Vietnam: 1 October 1967 to 1 October 1968. Doraville, Ga.: Love Enterprises [1968?] 208p. A highly-illustrated unit history with many helicopter assault photos.

2556 ____. Congress. House. Appropriations Committee. Briefings on the Bombings of North Vietnam. 93d Cong., 1st sess. Washington: U.S. Government Printing Office, 1973. 130p. A review.

2557 ____. ____. ____. Armed Services Committee. Military Airlift: Hearings. 89th Cong., 1st and 2d sess. Washington: U.S. Government Printing Office, 1966. 570p. An analysis, with sections appropriate to our topic, held between October 6, 1965, and January 27, 1966.

2558 ____. ____. ____. ____. Military Airlift: Report. 89th Cong., 2d sess. Washington: U.S. Government Printing Office, 1966. 42p. Findings and recommendations based on the above hearings.

2559 ____. ____. ____. ____. Military Posture Briefings. 12 vols. Washington: U.S. Government Printing Office, 1961-1973. Annual Department of Defense evaluations containing many comments on our topic.

2560 ____. ____. ____. ____. Armed Services Investigating Subcommittee. Unauthorized Bombing of Military Targets in

North Vietnam: Hearings. 92d Cong., 2d sess. Washington: U.S. Government Printing Office, 1972. 52p. A look into the case of Gen. John Lavelle held on June 12, 1972.

2561 ____. ____. ____. ____. Special Subcommittee on Tactical Air Support. "Air Force Documents Views on Close Air Support." Journal of the Armed Forces, CIII (Feb. 19, 1966), 15+. Text of documents furnished by U.S. Air Force Gen. Schriever to the Pike Subcommittee.

2562 ____. ____. ____. ____. Close Air Support: Hearings. 89th Cong., 1st sess. Washington: U.S. Government Printing Office, 1966. 18p. A look into problems of close air support in Vietnam.

2563 ____. ____. ____. ____. Close Air Support: Report. 89th Cong., 2d sess. Washington: U.S. Government Printing Office, 1966. 14p. Findings and recommendations based on the examination reported in the citation immediately above.

2564 ____. ____. ____. ____. Subcommittee on Military Airlift. Military Airlift: Hearings. 91st Cong., 2d sess. (HASC, no. 91-51.) Washington: U.S. Government Printing Office, 1970. 570p. Hearings held between January 22 and February 26, 1970, on the U.S. Air Force role as manager of all tactical and strategic airlift programs, which also looks at its Military Airlift Command and Tactical Air Command in the Southeast Asian conflict.

2565 ____. ____. ____. ____. Subcommittee on Research and Development. Vertical and Short Takeoff and Landing (V/STOL) Aircraft: Hearings. 88th Cong., 2d sess. Washington: U.S. Government Printing Office, 1964. 591p. Hearings held between May 13 and August 12, 1964.

2566 ____. ____. ____. ____. ____. Vertical and Short Takeoff and Landing (V/STOL) Aircraft: Report. 88th Cong., 2d sess. Washington: U.S. Government Printing Office, 1964. 14p. Findings and recommendations based on the above hearings.

2567 ____. ____. ____. ____. Foreign Affairs Committee. Subcommittee on National Security Policy and Scientific Developments. American Prisoners-of-War in Southeast Asia, 1970: Hearings. 91st Cong., 2d sess. Washington: U.S. Government Printing Office, 1970. 148p. Hearings held between April 29 and May 6, 1970.

2568 ____. ____. ____. ____. ____. American Prisoners-of-War in Southeast Asia, 1971-1972: Hearings. 92nd Cong.,

(____. Congress. House. Armed Services Committee. Foreign Affairs Committee--cont.)

1st-2d sess. 3pts. Washington: U.S. Government Printing Office, 1971-1972. Hearings held off and on between March 23, 1971 and March 16, 1972.

2569 ____. ____. ____. ____. ____. American Prisoners-of-War in Vietnam: Hearings. 91st Cong., 1st sess. Washington: U.S. Government Printing Office, 1969. 118p. Hearings held November 13-14, 1969.

2570 ____. ____. ____. ____. ____. Missing in Action in Southeast Asia, 1973: Hearings. 93d Cong., 1st sess. Washington: U.S. Government Printing Office, 1973. 77p. Hearings held on December 5, 1973. Taken together, these POW-MIA hearings constitute one of the largest bodies of literature available to students of the subject.

2571 ____. ____. ____. Science and Astronautics Committee. Subcommittee on Science, Research, and Development. A Technology Assessment of the Vietnam Defoliant Matter: A Case History. Committee Print. 91st Cong., 1st sess. Washington: U.S. Government Printing Office, 1969. 73p. A report prepared by the Library of Congress Legislative Reference Service, Science Policy Division.

2572 ____. ____. Senate. Armed Services Committee. Bombing in Cambodia: Hearings. 93d Cong., 1st sess. Washington: U.S. Government Printing Office, 1973. 512p. The Congressional examination of the so-called "secret bombings."

2573 ____. ____. ____. ____. Imprisonment and Escape of Lt (jg) Dieter Dengler, USNR: Hearings. 89th Cong., 2d sess. Washington: U.S. Government Printing Office, 1966. 28p. Lt. Dengler's September 16, 1966, testimony on his prison escape which followed the downing of his aircraft over North Vietnam.

2574 ____. ____. ____. ____. Preparedness Investigating Subcommittee. Air War Against North Vietnam: Hearings. 5 vols. 90th Cong., 1st sess. Washington: U.S. Government Printing Office, 1967. These volumes, totalling 515 pages, represent testimony given on August 9-10, 16, 22-23, 25, 28-29, 1967, and constitute an important source of information on the topic to that time.

Vol. I: Testimony of Adm. U. S. Grant Sharp, Navy Commander-in-Chief, Pacific; Vol. II: Testimony of Gen. Earle G. Wheeler, Army, Chairman; Joint Chiefs of Staff, and Lt. Gen. William A. Momyer, Air Force Commander, 7th Air Force; Vol. III: Testimony of Gen. John P. McConnell, Chief of Staff, Air Force, and Adm. Thomas

H. Moorer, Chief of Naval Operations; Vol. IV: Testimony of Robert S. McNamara, Secretary of Defense; and Vol. V: Testimony of Gen. Harold K. Johnson, Army, Chief of Staff; Major Gen. Wallace M. Greene, Commandant, Marine Corps, and Major Gen. Gilbert L. Meyers, U.S. Air Force (ret.).

2575 ____. ____. ____. ____. ____. Air War Against North Vietnam: Summary Report. (Committee print.) 90th Cong., 1st sess. Washington: U.S. Government Printing Office, 1967. 10p. Findings and recommendations based on the above hearings.

2576 ____. ____. ____. ____. ____. Investigation into Electronic Battlefield Program: Report. 92nd Cong., 1st sess. Washington: U.S. Government Printing Office, 1971. 20p. Includes a brief look at the dropping of sensors from the air.

2577 ____. ____. ____. ____. ____. Unauthorized Bombing of Military Targets in North Vietnam: Hearings. 92nd Cong., 2d sess. Washington: U.S. Government Printing Office, 1972. 52p. A look at the Lavelle case held on June 12, 1972.

2578 ____. ____. ____. ____. ____. U.S. Air Force Tactical Air Operations and Readiness. 89th Cong., 2d sess. Washington: U.S. Government Printing Office, 1966. 70p. Hearings held May 9-10, 1966, with some information relative to our topic.

2579 ____. ____. ____. ____. ____. U.S. Air Force Tactical Air Operations in Southeast Asia: Hearings. (Committee print.) 90th Cong., 1st sess. Washington: U.S. Government Printing Office, 1967. 12p. A brief look with some attention to matters of interest.

2580 ____. ____. ____. ____. ____. U.S. Tactical Air Power Program: Hearings. 90th Cong., 2d sess. Washington: U.S. Government Printing Office, 1968. 240p. Hearings held May 14-June 6, 1968, with much information relative to SEA.

2581 ____. ____. ____. Foreign Relations Committee. Bombing Operations and the Prison-of-War Rescue Mission in North Vietnam: Hearings. 91st Cong., 2d sess. Washington: U.S. Government Printing Office, 1971. 48p. Hearings on the Son Tay raid and U.S. interdiction operations held on November 24, 1970.

2582 ____. ____. ____. ____. The Effectiveness of Bombing as a Tool in Vietnam: A Staff Study Based on the Pentagon Papers. (Committee print, study no. 5.) 92nd Cong.,

(____. Congress. Senate. Foreign Relations Committee--cont.)

2d sess. Washington: U.S. Government Printing Office, 1972. 29p. Concludes that bombing as a political tool was not effective.

2583 ____. ____. ____. ____. The Gulf of Tonkin; The 1964 Incidents: Part I, Hearings. 90th Cong., 2d sess. Washington: U.S. Government Printing Office, 1968. 110p. Hearings held on February 20, 1968, detailing the North Vietnamese attack and U.S. aerial response of August 2-4, 1964.

2584 ____. ____. ____. ____. The Gulf of Tonkin; The 1964 Incidents: Part II, Supplementary Documents to February 20, 1968. 90th Cong., 2d sess. Washington: U.S. Government Printing Office, 1968. 14p.

2585 ____. ____. ____. ____. Moral and Military Aspects of the War in Southeast Asia: Hearings. 91st Cong., 2d sess. Washington: U.S. Government Printing Office, 1970. 108p. Testimony heard on May 7 and 12, 1970, with regard to the Cambodian intervention.

2586 ____. ____. ____. ____. U.S. POW's and MIA's in Southeast Asia: Hearings. 93rd Cong., 2d sess. Washington: U.S. Government Printing Office, 1974. 116p. Hearings held on January 28, 1974; should be used in conjunction with the House hearings cited in items 2567-2570.

2587 ____. ____. ____. ____. Vietnam Commitments, 1961: A Staff Study Based on the Pentagon Papers. (Committee print, study no. 1.) 92nd Cong., 2d sess. Washington: U.S. Government Printing Office, 1972. 38p. Includes understandings relating to the SEA air war.

2588 ____. ____. ____. ____. The Vietnam Hearings: With an Introduction by Senator J. William Fulbright. New York: Random House, 1966. 294p. The commercial version of the 1965 Senate hearings.

2589 ____. ____. ____. ____. Subcommittee on U.S. Security Agreements and Commitments Abroad. Laos: April 1971, a Staff Report. 92nd Cong., 2d sess. Washington: U.S. Government Printing Office, 1971. 11p. Includes much information on the aerial interdiction of the Ho Chi Minh Trail.

2590 ____. ____. ____. ____. ____. U.S. Air Operations in Cambodia: April 1973, a Staff Report. 93rd Cong., 1st sess. Washington: U.S. Government Printing Office, 1973. 10p. "Secret bombing."

2591 ____. ____. ____. Judiciary Committee. Subcommittee to Investigate Problems Connected with Refugees and Escapees. Problems of War Victims in Indochina: Hearings. 92nd Cong., 2d sess. 2 pts. Washington: U.S. Government Printing Office, 1972. Emphasis on U.S. bombing raids and the extent to which targets were military.

2592 ____. ____. ____. ____. Refugee and Civil War Casualty Problems in Laos and Cambodia: Hearings. 91st Cong., 2d sess. Washington: U.S. Government Printing Office, 1970. 107p. Additional interest in U.S. aerial operations.

2593 ____. ____. ____. ____. War-Related Civilian Problems in Indochina: Hearings. 92nd Cong., 1st sess. Washington: U.S. Government Printing Office, 1971. Still more attention to the role of U.S. air activities.

2594 ____. ____. ____. Labor and Public Welfare Committee. Medal of Honor Recipients, 1863-1968. 90th Cong., 2d sess. Washington: U.S. Government Printing Office, 1968. 1,087p. With information on Indochina winners to 1968; for further data, see the item immediately following.

2595 ____. ____. ____. Veterans' Affairs Committee. Vietnam Era Medal of Honor Recipients, 1964-1972. (Committee print.) 93rd Cong., 1st sess. Washington: U.S. Government Printing Office, 1973. 236p. With full information all recipients, including those connected with the air war.

2596 ____. Defense Department. Department of Defense Annual Report for the Fiscal Year Including Reports of the Secretary of Defense, Secretary of the Army, Secretary of the Navy, and Secretary of the Air Force. 12 vols. Washington: U.S. Government Printing Office, 1962-1964. Annual reports containing much information relative to the SEA air war.

2597 ____. ____. Dictionary of United States Military Terms for Joint Usage. Washington: U.S. Government Printing Office, 1968. 316p. Includes many terms employed for the Southeast Asian conflict.

2598 ____. ____. United States-Vietnam Relations, 1945-1967. 12 vols. Washington: U.S. Government Printing Office, 1971. The released official version of the famous "Pentagon Papers"; these 12 volumes contain 43 of the 47 original studies.

2599 ____. ____. Armed Forces Information and Education Office. Pocket Guide to Vietnam. (DOD PG-21A.) Washing-

(____. Defense Department--cont.)

ton: U.S. Government Printing Office, 1966. 94p. A handy guide for background information to the air war.

2600 ____. Joint Logistics Review Board. Logistic Support in the Vietnam Era: Monographs. 18 vols. Washington, 1970. Studies of various phases of supply and support in Southeast Asia.

2601 ____. ____. Logistic Support in the Vietnam Era: A Report. 3 vols. Washington, 1970. Vol. I, A Summary Assessment with Major Findings and Recommendations; Vol. II, A Review of Logistic Support in the Vietnam Era; Vol. III, Monograph Summaries and Recommendations.

2602 ____. Marine Corps. Air Movement of Fleet Marine Force Units. (FMFM 4-6.) Washington: U.S. Government Printing Office, 1966. 235p. Air movement of troops, supplies, and equipment by fixed-wing aircraft.

2603 ____. ____. Air Support. (FMFM 7-3.) Washington; U.S. Government Printing Office, 1966. 292p. U.S. Marine Corps doctrine on close air support.

2604 ____. ____. Counterinsurgency Operations. (FMFM 8-2.) Rev. ed. Washington: U.S. Government Printing Office, 1968. 201p. Based on lessons learned in Vietnam to that date; the earlier edition, "Operations Against Guerrilla Forces," is cited in item 2606.

2605 ____. ____. Helicopterborne Operations. (FMFM 3-3.) Washington: U.S. Government Printing Office, 1963. Unpaginated. With much information relative to the early years of our topic.

2606 ____. ____. Operations Against Guerrilla Forces. (FMFM 8-21.) Washington: U.S. Government Printing Office, 1962. 135p. Mostly theory.

2607 ____. ____. Fleet Marine Force, Pacific. "Operations of U.S. Marine Forces, Vietnam." 66 vols. N.p., 1965-1971. Unpublished monthly historical summaries which, except for minor portions, have now been declassified.

2608 ____. ____. Historical Branch. Marine Corps Aircraft, 1913-1965, rev. ed. Marine Corps Historical Reference Pamphlet. Washington: Headquarters, U.S. Marine Corps, 1967. 73p. Ends with U.S. Marine Corps aircraft involved in South Vietnam.

2609 ____. ____. History and Museums Division. The Marines in Vietnam, 1954-1973: An Anthology and Annotated Bibliography. Washington: U.S. Government Printing Office, 1974. 277p. The anthology includes the Simmons articles cited above.

2610 ____. Navy Department. Deputy Chief of Naval Operations (Air). United States Naval Aviation, 1910-1970, 2d ed. Washington: U.S. Government Printing Office, 1971. 440p. Quite useful for naval air operations in Southeast Asia through most of our period.

2611 ____. ____. Naval History Division. Riverine Warfare: Vietnam. Washington: U.S. Government Printing Office, 1972. Contains some helicopter-oriented material.

2612 ____. ____. Office of Information. The Navy in Vietnam. Washington: U.S. Government Printing Office, 1968. 33p. Some emphasis on naval air operations.

2613 ____. ____. 7th Fleet. "Two Year Summary." Naval Aviation News, (Oct. 1966), 6-7. Emphasis on carrier air operations.

2614 "United States War Losses in Vietnam." Metropolitan Life Statistical Bulletin, L (Dec. 1969), 9-12. Including those of airmen and helicopter pilots and their crews.

2615 "Unparalleled Airlift Carried Out in Southeast Asia." Air Force Times, XXVIII (May 1, 1968), 18. The transport of men, supplies, and equipment to Vietnam.

2616 "The Unsung Pilots of Vietnam." U.S. News and World Report, LXXIII (Sept. 4, 1972), 34. The (South) Vietnamese Air Force.

2617 "The Untold Story of the Ho Chi Minh Trail." U.S. News and World Report, LXX (Feb. 15, 1971), 23-24. A U.S. aerial interdiction against it.

2618 "Up One Notch: Escalating the [Air] War." Newsweek, LXVII (March 14, 1966), 42. Attacks on North Vietnam.

Uphoff, Norman, jt. ed. see Littauer, Raphael

2619 Urban, Henry J. Close Air Support. (Air War College Report, no. 3206.) Maxwell Air Force Base, Ala.: Air University, 1966. 57p. A look at its application over South Vietnam.

2620 "The Value of Bombing the North." Time, LXXXVIII (Dec. 16, 1966), 29. A military and economic analysis.

2621 Valverde, Horace H. "FAC Visual Reconnaissance." Tactical Air Reconnaissance Digest, V (June 1971), 20-27. A review of the state of the art in Southeast Asia.

2622 Vance, William. "How the Army Got Its Shooting Helicopters." National Guardsman, XVII (May 1963), 2-4+. An interesting contemporary analysis.

2623 Vanderpool, Jay D. "We Armed the Helicopter." U.S. Army Aviation Digest, XVII (June 1971), 2-6+. A look at armed helicopters in Indochina.

2624 Van Dyke, Jon M. North Vietnam's Strategy for Survival. Mountain View, Calif.: Pacific Press, 1972. 336p. An important examination of the North Vietnamese air defense system.

2625 Van Feffin, Theodore, Jr. Republic F-105 Thunderchief. (Aircraft in Profile, no. 226.) Windsor, Eng.: Profile Publications, 1972. 24p. A technical and operational look at the "Thud."

2626 Van Staaveren, Jacob. "The Air War Against North Vietnam." In Carl Berger, ed., The United States Air Force in Southeast Asia, 1961-1973 (Washington: U.S. Government Printing Office, 1977), p69-100. A valuable operational summary.

2627 ______. "Interdiction in the Laotian Panhandle." In Carl Berger, ed., The United States Air Force in Southeast Asia, 1961-1973 (Washington: U.S. Government Printing Office, 1977), p101-120. Perhaps the best operational summary currently available.

2628 ______. USAF Plans and Policies in South Vietnam, 1961-1963. Washington: Office of Air Force History, Department of the Air Force, 1965. Examines the Air Force role during the advisory period.

2629 ______. USAF Plans and Policies in South Vietnam, 1965. Washington: Office of Air Force History, Department of the Air Force, 1967. A look at the subject during the Air Force build-up there.

2630 ______. USAF Plans and Policies in South Vietnam and Laos, 1964. Washington: Office of Air Force History, Department of the Air Force, 1965. Details on the Air Force involvement during the final year of the American advisory period.

2631 ______, and Herman S. Wolk. "Southeast Asia Political-Military Chronology, 1948-1967." Air Force and Space Digest, L (March 1967), 137-138+. Includes aerial activities.

2632 Van Vleck, James E. "Armed Helicopter Escort." U.S. Army Aviation Digest, XVI (Feb. 1968), 24-27. A look at the Army idea of having helicopter gunships cover troop or supply choppers.

Va-Thanh-Nien, jt. author see Bo-Thong-Tin

2633 Vellines, Charles H. "The 4440th Aircraft Delivery Group." Navigator, XV (Summer 1968), 10-11. A brief profile of the U.S. Air Force unit charged with bringing new aircraft from the U.S. to Southeast Asia.

2634 Vencill, Carleton P. "Extraction Without a Landing Zone." U.S. Army Aviation Digest, XVIII (April 1972), 18-21+. Indochina examples of helicopter rescue.

2635 Verrier, Anthony. "Strategic Bombing: The Lessons of World War II and the American Experience in Vietnam." Journal of the Royal United Service Institution, CXII (May 1967), 157-161. Contends that bombing without ground action could not produce "victory."

2636 "The Versatile Skyraider." Air Force Times, XXVI (Aug. 10, 1966), 14. The A-1 in South Vietnam.

2637 Vest, Davis G. "Toward a Fighter Posture for the Seventies." Marine Corps Gazette, LIV (Dec. 1970), 18-25. Suggested the war in Indochina would have been quite different if the North Vietnamese had held air superiority.

2638 "Victory at Khe Sanh." Time, XCI (April 12, 1968), 29-30. Includes a look at the air and airmobile aspects.

2639 "Victory in the Valley: The Battle Around Dak To." Time, XC (Nov. 24, 1967), 34. Does not neglect to mention the aerial contribution.

2640 "Victory on a Shattered Ridge: The Fight for Dak To." Life, LXIII (Dec. 1, 1967), 32-33. With illustrations.

2641 Vietnam, Democratic Republic of. American Aircraft Systematically Attack Dams and Dikes in the Democratic Republic of Vietnam. Hanoi: Foreign Languages Publishing House, 1968. 31p. The charge would bring debate in the U.S. from time to time.

2642 ______. South Vietnam: A Great Victory (Winter 1966-Spring 1967). Hanoi: Foreign Languages Publishing House, 1967. 71p. An English-language analysis for foreign consumption.

2643 ______. South Vietnam: A Month of Unprecedented Offensive and Uprising. Hanoi: Giai Phong Publishing House, 1968.

87p. A North Vietnamese view of the Tet offensive released in English for foreign consumption.

2644 ______. South Vietnam: The Initial Failure of the U.S. "Limited War." Hanoi: Foreign Languages Publishing House, 1967. 78p. A North Vietnamese analysis of fighting in the south.

2645 ______. The U.S. Military Adventure in South Vietnam. Hanoi: Foreign Languages Publishing House, 1962. 72p. With some comments on aerial advisors and assistance.

2646 ______. Judicial Studies Section. Fascist Terror in South Vietnam. Hanoi: Foreign Languages Publishing House, 1961. 96p. U.S. and South Vietnamese air and ground activities as seen by the North Vietnamese.

2647 ______. Red Cross. American Aircraft Systematically Attack Hospitals and Sanitary Centers of the Democratic Republic of Vietnam. Hanoi: Foreign Languages Publishing House, 1965. 24p. An early and continuing North Vietnamese claim.

2648 "Vietnam: A View from the Cockpit." Life, LVIII (May 7, 1965), 42B-42D. Captions and photographs on American air raids.

2649 "Vietnam Aces." Naval Aviation News, (July 1972), 3. U.S. Navy fighter pilots Cunningham and Driscoll.

2650 "Vietnam Air War Summed Up: 50,000 Strike Sorties Flown by the Air Force in 1965." Air Force Times, XXVI (Jan. 19, 1966), 14. A brief review.

2651 "Vietnam Airfields 'World's Busiest.'" Air Force Times, XXVIII (March 20, 1968), 16. With combat take-offs and landings.

2652 "Vietnam Airlift Support." Naval Aviation News, (May 1966), 16. U.S. Navy reserve participation in.

2653 "Vietnam Bombings: Pro and Con." U.S. News and World Report, LXIV (Jan. 29, 1968), 36-37. Political thoughts on the military necessity.

2654 "Vietnam Conflict." Naval Aviation News, (May 1965), 18. Tonkin Gulf participation by the U.S. Navy carriers Coral Sea, Hancock, and Ranger.

2655 "Vietnam Decisions Questions: [Joint] Logistics [Review] Board's Report." Air Force Times, XXXI (Nov. 11, 1970), 10. The report is cited in item 2601.

2656 "Vietnam 'Dust Off.'" Royal Air Forces Quarterly, VII (Winter 1967), 324-325. Australian helicopter operations.

2657 "Vietnam Forces Developing Own Brand of Slang." Air Force Times, XXIII (May 22, 1963), 4. Popular military terminology is a feature of every conflict.

2658 "Vietnam Gives Impetus to COINOPS 'Tools of the Trade.'" Data, XII (Jan. 1967), 34-38. The search for counter-insurgency operations weapons, including aircraft and helicopter gunships.

2659 "Vietnam Has Reshaped TAC." Air Force Times, XXVII (March 1, 1967), 6. Changes in the USAF Tactical Air Command.

2660 "Vietnam: Impact of the War on Its Environment." Congressional Quarterly Weekly Report, XXX (July 29, 1972), 1878-1882. With emphasis on herbicides and napalm.

2661 "Vietnam MIG-Base Strikes Shun Key Targets." Aviation Week and Space Technology, LXXXVI (May 1, 1967), 17-18. Avoiding damage to industrial targets.

2662 "Vietnam Puts Stress on TAC." Air Force Times, XXVI (Nov. 17, 1965), 5. The need for new planes.

2663 "Vietnam, Same Game, New Rules: Bombings Near China." Newsweek, LXX (Aug. 28, 1967), 17-18. U.S. raids into furthest North Vietnam.

2664 "Vietnam: The Pause Comes to an End, Bombing North Vietnam, the Bombers' Mission." Newsweek, LXVIII (Feb. 7, 1966), 15-18. Raids on North Vietnam.

2665 "Vietnam War Proving the Helicopter's Value as a Weapon, the Army Contends." Aviation Week and Space Technology, LXXX (April 20, 1964), 104-105+. A report.

2666 "Vietnamese Train for Anti-Guerrilla Air War." Aviation Week and Space Technology, LXXVII (Nov. 12, 1962), 92-93. U.S. help to the VNAF during our advisory period there.

2667 "Vietnamization in the Air." Time, XCVI (Nov. 2, 1970), 33. Increased American help to the VNAF.

2668 "Vietnam's Air War Starts to Heat Up: U.S. Airpower Backed Up by Missile-Firing MIG Fighters." Business Week, (May 21, 1966), 42-43. Title misleading; deals with North Vietnamese interceptor and air defense capability.

2669 "The View from the Cockpit." Aviation Week and Space Technology, LXXXVIII (May 6, 1968), 17. Thoughts on the Vietnam air war.

2670 "Vital Statistics of U.S. Air Power in Vietnam for 1965." Air Force and Space Digest, XLIX (Feb. 1966), 40-42. Missions flown, bombs dropped, etc.

2671 Vito, A. H., Jr. "Carrier Air and Vietnam: An Assessment." U.S. Naval Institute Proceedings, XCIII (Oct. 1967), 66-75. The most pointed analysis of the subject available.

2672 Vo-Hguyen-Giap. Banner of the People's War: The Party's Military Line. Introduction by George Boudarel. New York: Praeger, 1970. 128p. A collection of seven articles from the Nhan Dan and Quan Dan of December 1969 summarizing the 1959-1969 experience of the North Vietnamese armed forces.

2673 ______. Big Victory, Great Task: North Vietnam Minister of Defense Assesses the Course of the War. New York: Praeger, 1968. 120p. Translated texts of the original Hanoi newspaper articles serialized in Nhan Dan and Quan Doi Nhan Dan, September 14-16, 1967.

2674 ______. How We Won the War. Philadelphia: Recon Publications, 1976. 64p.

2675 ______. The Military Art of People's War: Selected Writings. Edited by Russell Stetler. New York: Monthly Review Press, 1970. 332p.

2676 ______. "The Strategic Positions of the Local People's War and the Local Armed Forces." Vietnam Documents and Research Notes, no. 104 (March 1972), 19-55. All of the famous general's writings here have some bearing on the SEA air war, if only for background information.

Von Platen, W. G., jt. author see Porter, W. C.

2677 Wacker, Rudolph F. "The View from the Cockpit: Close Air Support." Army, XX (July 1970), 16-25. As supplied to Allied ground soldiers by the U.S. air services.

2678 Wagner, Ray. American Combat Planes, new rev. ed. Garden City, N.Y.: Doubleday, 1968. 448p. Includes many from the Southeast Asian war.

2679 Wagnon, Bobby D. "Communication: The Key Element to Prisoner-of-War Survival." Air University Review, XXVII (May-June 1976), 33-46. Activities by U.S. POW's in North Vietnamese camps.

2680 Wahl, William E. "Where's the First Team?" U.S. Army Aviation Digest, XVI (March 1970), 32-33. U.S. 1st Air Cavalry Division.

2681 "Waiting: Khe Sanh and Saigon." Newsweek, LXXI (March 11, 1968), 58. Tet and the Marine struggle.

2682 Wakefield, Donald S. "U.S. Military Helicopter Operations." Interavia, XXV (July 1970), 830-833. A review.

2683 Wallace, J. N. "One Day in Vietnam's War: An Eyewitness Report." U.S. News and World Report, LXXII (June 26, 1972), 31. The air-ground battle of An Loc.

2684 ______. "Why the Burst of Optimism on the Ground War in Vietnam." U.S. News and World Report, LXXII (June 12, 1972), 33-35. The success of ARVN units, with U.S. air support, during the North Vietnamese Easter invasion.

2685 Walt, Lewis W. "Behind the Battle for Khe Sanh." Reader's Digest, XCVI (May 1970), 105-111. Political and military considerations.

2686 ______. "Combat General Tells What the Vietnam War Is Like." U.S. News and World Report, LXII (May 22, 1967), 36-39. An interview with the ranking Marine officer in South Vietnam.

2687 ______. Strange War, Strange Strategy: A General's Report on Vietnam. New York: Funk and Wagnalls, 1970. 208p. The general does not neglect U.S. Marine Corps aviation.

2688 Waltz, Robert W. "Today's Thinking in Air Force Reconnaissance: An Interview." Data, XIII (May 1968), 15-19. The general's views include some mention of Southeast Asia.

2689 "The War According to The Pentagon Papers." Newsweek, LXXVII (June 28, 1971), 17-22. An analysis of the report with comments relative to our topic.

2690 "War and Conflict." Aerospace International, VI (May-June 1970), 18-24. A review of the aerial war in Indochina.

2691 "The War in Laos." Life, LXX (March 12, 1971), 20-29. Illustrated.

2692 "The War in the Air." Army, XVI (Jan. 1966), 26-27+. With emphasis on Army aviation.

2693 "The War that Won't Go Away." Newsweek, LXXIX (April 17, 1972), 16-17+. Yet another look at the Easter invasion.

2694 "War Underground: Operation Cedar Falls." Newsweek, LXIX (Jan. 30, 1967), 56-57.

2695 Ward, Richard, and Ernest R. McDowell. McDonnell-Douglas A-4 A/L Skyhawk. Arco-Aircam Aviation Series. New York: Arco Publishers, 1971. 46p. An illustrated look at the U.S. Navy attack plane.

2696 Warner, Denis. "Bearing the Brunt at Con Thien." Reporter, XXXVII (Oct. 19, 1967), 18-21. Action in the I Corps area and aerial support.

2697 ______. "The Defense of Saigon." Reporter, XXXVIII (April 4, 1968), 15-19. Tet.

2698 ______. "Gains and Losses in Saigon: Jet Offensive." Reporter, XXXVIII (March 7, 1968), 21-24. Tet and the use of American air power in response.

2699 ______. "Hanoi's Summer Offensive: A Bigger War in Prospect." Reporter, XXXVI (June 29, 1967), 31-34.

2700 ______. "Report from Khe Sanh." Reporter, XXXVIII (March 21, 1968), 22-26. With comments on air support.

2701 ______. "Vietnam: Hard Battles Still to Be Fought." Reporter, XXXVIII (May 2, 1968), 16-19. Sums up the Tet offensive.

2702 "Was Lavelle Alone?" Newsweek, LXXX (Sept. 25, 1972), 64. The General John Lavelle case.

2703 Waskow, Thomas. "'I Sure as Hell Don't Want to Be the Last One Shot Down.'" Life, LXXIII (Dec. 8, 1972), 54-58. An airman's thoughts on the "Linebacker" operations.

2704 Watanabe, Seiki. "The North Vietnam Bombings: The Balance Sheet." Japan Quarterly, XII (July-September 1965), 297-302. An early English-language Japanese view.

2705 Waterhouse, Charles H. Vietnam War Sketches from the Air, Land, and Sea. Rutland, Vt.: Charles E. Tuttle Co., 1970. 126p. A pictorial.

2706 Watkins, Theodore C. "Problems of Getting the 1st Cavalry Division (Airmobile) over the Beach." U.S. Army Aviation Digest, XII (April 1966), 18-19. Assembling the helicopter troops for combat in South Vietnam.

2707 Watson, Jac D. "Marine Helicopters: Stunted Growth." U.S. Naval Institute Proceedings, XCIX (July 1973),

34-41. Vietnam showed that "the aging bird had learned few new tricks" not developed in Korea years before.

2708 Watt, Anthony. "Australians at War in Vietnam." Round Table, LVI (Oct. 1966), 354-362. With some attention to our topic.

2709 Watt, D. C. "Lessons of the American Defeat in Vietnam." Journal of the Royal United Service Institution, CXVIII (June 1973), 35-38. A brief assessment from the British viewpoint.

2710 Watts, Claudius E. "Aerial Resupply for Khe Sanh." Military Review, LII (Dec. 1972), 79-88. Another look at U.S. Air Force and Marine Corps tactical airlift operations in 1968.

2711 "The Way to Survive." Time, LXXXVIII (Aug. 12, 1966), 20-21. Aerospace rescue and recovery operations.

2712 "Weak Link: The Unauthorized Bombing Raids on North Vietnam Ordered by [Gen. John D.] Lavelle." New Republic, CLXVII (July 1, 1972), 8-9. An analysis of the chain of command.

2713 Weaver, K. F. "Of Planes and Men: The U.S. Air Force Wages Cold War and Hot." National Geographic Magazine, CXXVIII (Sept. 1965), 298-349. The "hot" war refers to the Indochina campaign.

2714 Weber, Richard E. "Nonstandard Construction with MX-19." Military Engineer, LXI (Jan.-Feb. 1969), 18-19. MX-19 was a mat for expedient airfield surfacing.

2715 "Week of a Thousand Sorties." Newsweek, LXXIX (Jan. 10, 1973), 22-23. The Christmas "Linebacker" operations.

2716 Wei-Wei. "Even Planes Fear the Militia: Some Impressions of Vietnam." Chinese Literature (Peking), no. 8 (1966), 107-116. A Red Chinese reporter's visit to the Vietcong in South Vietnam, with some attention to guerrilla reactions to American air raids.

2717 Weigley, Russell F. The American Way of War: A History of United States Military Strategy and Policy. (Macmillan Wars of the United States series.) New York: Macmillan, 1973. 590p. See especially chapters 17 and 18.

2718 Weisburg, Barry. Ecocide in Indochina: The Ecology of War. New York: Harper & Row, 1970. 241p. Reprints various articles from Ramparts, Atlantic, New Republic, and Liberation which heavily score U.S. use of anti-personnel bombs, napalm, defoliation, and search-and-destroy tactics.

2719 Weiss, C. "Prisoners and Patriots: Adventures in the POW Trade." Ramparts Magazine, XI (June 1973), 12-15. Not sympathetic to U.S. POW's.

2720 Weiss, George. "AC-130 Gunships Destroy Trucks and Cargo." Journal of the Armed Forces, CIX (Sept. 1971), 18-19. Action along the Ho Chi Minh Trail in Laos.

2721 _____. "Battle for Control of the Ho Chi Minh Trail." Journal of the Armed Forces, CVIII (Feb. 1971), 18-22. More on aerial operations over Laos.

2722 _____. "CO 2/17 Air Cavalry: 'Gunships Took Tanks, Survived Flak' in Laos." Journal of the Armed Forces, CVIII (April 19, 1971), 22-23+. A report of one U.S. Army Huey Cobra unit in the Laos invasion.

2723 _____. "Laos Truck Kills Approach 20,000." Journal of the Armed Forces, CVIII (May 3, 1971), 15+. A report of aerial attacks along the Ho Chi Minh Trail.

2724 _____. "TAC Air: Present and Future Lessons, Problems, and Needs." Journal of the Armed Forces, CIX (Sept. 1971), 30-35. Reflections on Southeast Asia.

2725 Weiss, Peter, and Gunilla Weiss. "Limited Bombing" in Vietnam: A Report on the Attacks Against the Democratic Republic of Vietnam by the U.S. Air Force and Seventh Fleet, After the Declaration of "Limited Bombing" by President Lyndon B. Johnson on March 31, 1968, translated from the German. London: Bertrand Russell Peace Foundation, 1969. 39p. Based primarily on information supplied by the North Vietnamese.

2726 Welch, Ron. "All Learn to Defend Bien Hoa." Air Force Times, XXVIII (May 15, 1968), 15. Base defense at the American air facility.

2727 Weller, Jac. "American Handicaps in Vietnam." Army Quarterly, XCVII (Jan. 1969), 193-202. Including air.

2728 _____. "Fire and Movement": Bargain Basement Warfare in the Far East. New York: T. Y. Crowell, 1967. 268p. A report on the war in South Vietnam.

2729 _____. "Gunships Key to a New Kind of War." National Guardsman, XXII (Oct. 1968), 2-8. U.S. Army Hueys, Chinooks, and Huey Cobras in South Vietnam.

2730 _____. "Helicopters: The American Experience." Army

Quarterly, CIII (July 1973), 420-428. Their employment over Southeast Asia.

2731 ______. "Our Vietnamese Allies: An Appraisal of Their Fighting Worth." National Guardsman, XXII (April 1968), 2-10. Viewed as high, especially the ARVN airborne units.

2732 ______. "The U.S. Army in Vietnam: A Survey of Arms, Operations, and Weapons." Army Quarterly, XCV (Oct. 1967), 40-56. Includes helicopters.

2733 ______. "The Vital Element of Vietnamization: RVNAF Training." Military Review, LII (Oct. 1972), 35-49. Including aerial instruction, especially on helicopters.

2734 Wells, Norman E. "Air Superiority Comes First." Air University Review, XXIV (Nov.-Dec. 1972), 10-25. Three threats of air superiority are discussed: antiaircraft batteries, SAM's, and interceptors.

2735 Wells, W. C. "The Riverine Force in Action, 1966-1967." In Frank Uhlig, ed., The Naval Review, 1969 (Annapolis, Md.: United States Naval Institute, 1969), p46-83. With some attention to air and helicopter support.

2736 Weseleskey, A. E. "The 'Seawolf' Helicopter Pilots of Vietnam." U.S. Naval Institute Proceedings, XCIV (May 1968), 128-130. U.S. Navy helicopter operations over the Mekong Delta area.

2737 Westing, Arthur H. "The Cratering of Indochina." Scientific American, CCXXVI (May 1972), 20-29. For a reply to this attack on American bombing operations, see the comments by Gen. S. L. A. Marshall in the September issue, p. 8+.

2738 ______. "Ecocide in Indochina." Natural History, LXXX (March 1971), 56-61. Thoughts on the American use of herbicides, napalm, etc.

2739 Westmoreland, William C. "'A New Concept of Warfare.'" Aerospace International, III (July-Aug. 1967), 8. The strategic importance of U.S. airpower in Vietnam.

2740 ______. A Soldier Reports. Garden City, N.Y.: Doubleday, 1976. 446p. The author was the chief of the Military Assistance Command, Vietnam, during much of the conflict; he has a lot to say about the use of aircraft and helicopters.

2741 Weyland, F. C., et al. "Airpower Halts an Invasion." Air

Force Magazine, LV (Sept. 1972), 60-68+. The North Vietnamese Easter invasion.

2742 "What Are the Rules for American Captives?: The Code of Conduct." U.S. News and World Report, LXXIV (April 16, 1973), 40. A discussion of expected POW behavior.

2743 "What Hit Hanoi?: North Vietnamese Declare U.S. Bombed Hanoi." Newsweek, LXVIII (Dec. 26, 1966), 28.

2744 "What Is Giap Up To?" Time, XCIX (May 29, 1972), 28+. The Easter invasion.

2745 "What the Bombing Did." Newsweek, LXXXI (Jan. 7, 1972), 11-12. Success of American air operations.

2746 "What the Christmas Bombing Did to North Vietnam." U.S. News and World Report, LXXIV (Feb. 5, 1973), 18. Damage estimates for "Operation Linebacker II."

2747 "What Two and a Half Years of Bombing Has Done to North Vietnam." U.S. News and World Report, LXIII (Sept. 11, 1967), 34-35. Created great difficulties.

2748 "What Went Wrong in Vietnam?: The Fallacies in U.S. Policy, Intelligence, Bombing, and Vietnamization." Newsweek, LXXIX (May 15, 1972), 24-25. An assessment.

2749 "What's New at Southeast Asian Bases." Air Force Times, XXIX (Feb. 19, 1969), 15.

2750 Wheeler, Earle G. "A Perspective on Firepower and Mobility." U.S. Army Aviation Digest, X (March 1964), 2-6. The general's thoughts on helicopters.

2751 "When a U.S. Rescue Mission Fizzled: The Son Tay Venture." U.S. News and World Report, LXXXI (July 19, 1971), 32. Undertaken in November 1970.

2752 "Whirling Dervishes: The First Cavalry Division (Airmobile) in the Central Vietnam Highlands and the Ia Drang Valley." Newsweek, LXVI (Dec. 13, 1965), 28. A brief look at the success of the heliborne cavalrymen.

2753 "Whirlybirds Get Claws." Science News Letter, XC (July 30, 1966), 79. Introduction of the Bell AH-1G Huey Cobra.

2754 Whitaker, Donald P. Area Handbook for the Khmer Republic (Cambodia). (DA pam 550-50.) Washington: U.S. Government Printing Office, 1973. 389p. Prepared by the Foreign Area Studies Division at American University; includes useful background information relative to our topic.

2755 White, Jim. "Air War Directors." Airman, XIII (Dec. 1969), 38-39. A brief look at the U.S. 7th Air Force Tactical Air Control Center, Southeast Asia.

2756 White, M. S. "Medical Aspects of Air Evacuation of Casualties from Southeast Asia." Aerospace Medicine, XXXIX (Dec. 1968), 1338-1341. Technical medical details.

2757 ______, et al. "Results of Early Aero-Medical Evacuation of Vietnam Casualties." Aerospace Medicine, XLII (July 1971), 780-784. A paper read before the Aerospace Medical Association meeting in San Francisco on May 6, 1969, which, as in item 2756, finds many soldiers surviving solely because of the practice.

2758 White, William D. U.S. Tactical Air Power: Missions, Forces, and Costs. (Studies in Defense Policy.) Washington: Brookings Institution, 1974. 121p. With some material on the SEA air war.

2759 Whiteside, Thomas. "Defoliation." New Yorker, XLVI (Feb. 7, 1970), 32-38. The airborne practice and its results over Indochina.

2760 ______. Withering Rain: America's Herbicidal Folly. New York: E. P. Dutton, 1971. 224p. A full and scathing attack on this U.S. aerial practice.

2761 Whitfield, Danny Y. Vietnam. (Historical and Cultural Dictionaries of Asia series, no. 7.) Metuchen, N.J.: Scarecrow Press, 1976. 377p. Includes useful background information.

2762 Whitlow, Robert H. The Advisory and Combat Assistance Era, 1954-1964. Vol. I of U.S. Marines in Vietnam. 9 vols. Washington: U.S. Government Printing Office, 1977. 190p. The first volume of a well-illustrated series; especially valuable after chapter 3, particularly Part II, "Marine Helicopters Go to War."

2763 Whitmer, Dennis K. "Aviation Communications Security." U.S. Army Aviation Digest, XIV (May 1968), 10-13. As practiced over South Vietnam.

2764 Whitney, Craig R. "Catkillers." U.S. Army Aviation Digest, XV (May 1969), 2-4. A profile of the Army's 220th Reconnaissance Airplane Company.

2765 "Who's Signalling What?: United States Air Raids on North Vietnam." New Republic, CLII (Feb. 20, 1965), 5-6. An early look at the coercive effect of American air attacks.

2766 Who's Who in America. Chicago: Marquis Publications, 1962-1973. Very useful for biographical data on American political and military air leaders, e.g., U.S. Air Force General William Momyer.

2767 "Whose Army?: The Lavelle Episode." Nation, CCXV (Oct. 2. 1972), 259-260. More comment on the protective reaction strikes ordered by the U.S. Air Force general.

2768 "Why Helicopter Losses Are Up." U.S. News and World Report, LXVI (May 19, 1969), 17. North Vietnamese antiaircraft capability was a major factor.

2769 "Why Khe Sanh Is Being Evacuated." U.S. News and World Report, LXV (July 8, 1968), 11. It had outgrown its usefulness (but would be reopened in 1971 for the Laos invasion).

2770 "Why Not a Tally?: Helicopter Losses." Nation, CCXII (March 22, 1971), 354. A controversy growing out of the Laos invasion.

2771 "Why U.S. Bombing Is More Accurate Now: The Use of Smart Bombs." Time, XCIX (June 5, 1972), 29. A brief look at the television-guided missiles.

2772 Wiegand, Kenneth F. "A Lesson Well Learned." U.S. Army Aviation Digest, XV (Sept. 1969), 18-22. On bad-weather flying of Army aircraft in Vietnam.

2773 "Wild Weasel." Electronic Warfare, II (Feb.-March 1970), 15+ A review of one electronic counter-measures practice against North Vietnamese Air Force airfields.

2774 "'Will to Win': The Battle for Hill 875, Overlooking Dak To." Time, XC (Dec. 1, 1967), 24+. With some information on air strikes.

2775 Williams, Adriel N. "Vietnam: The Acid Test for Airlift." Review, XLVII (March-April 1968), 54-55+. A review, with some emphasis on Khe Sanh.

Williams, Richard M., jt. author see Mack, Jerold K.

2776 Williams, Robert. "Pacification in Vietnam: The Destruction of Con Thinh." Ramparts Magazine, VII (May 1968), 21-24. Suggests the village destroyed by U.S. air-ground firepower.

2777 Williamson, Ellis W. "Combat Notes: Ben Cat-Iron Triangle." Infantry, LVI (March-April 1966), 40-43. With some attention to heliborne operations.

2778 ______. "Combat Notes: The Story of the First Large-Scale U.S. Army Unit Action in Vietnam." Infantry, LV (Sept.-Oct. 1965), 68-72. Air-ground events surrounding activities on May 5, 1965.

2779 Willson, R. O. "Marine Airborne EW-VMCJ." Navigator, XVI (Winter 1968), 5-6. U.S. Marine Corps electronic warfare aerial operations.

2780 Willwerth, James K. "Nightingale." Airman, XIII (May 1969), 30-33. U.S. Air Force aeromedical evacuation operations.

2781 Willworth, James. Eye in the Last Storm: A Reporter's Journal of One Year in Southeast Asia. New York: Grossmann, 1973. 178p. Includes one vignette on a helicopter operation accompanied by the author.

2782 Wilms, Peter. "The Canberra's Fine Record in Vietnam." Royal Air Forces Quarterly, IX (Summer 1969), 139-141. The Work of RAAF No. 2 Squadron flying out of Phan Rang air base.

2783 ______. "The RAAF in Vietnam." Royal Air Forces Quarterly, VIII (Autumn 1968), 212-214. A brief examination of its activities.

2784 Wilson, D. R. "Here Is the Corsair II." Approach, XIV (Sept. 1968), 16-20. A profile of the A-7 attack plane.

2785 Wilson, George C. "Army Continues Push for More Helicopters." Aviation Week and Space Technology, LXXXI (Nov. 30, 1964), 16-17. For Vietnam operations.

2786 ______. "Army Seeks Greater Mobility in Added Air Capacity." Aviation Week and Space Technology, LXXVIII (March 11, 1963), 84-85+. The growth of fixed- and rotary-wing aircraft under Army control.

2787 ______. "Congress Debates Air War Restrictions." Aviation Week and Space Technology, LXXXIV (Feb. 14, 1966), 2-9. A report on the House Close Air Support Hearings cited above.

2788 ______. "The Lavelle Case." Atlantic Monthly, CCXXX (Dec. 1972), 6+. One of the most reasoned accounts.

2789 ______. "New Bomb Eyed for Vietnam Use." U.S. Naval Institute Proceedings, XCIII (Dec. 1967), 146. A quick look at the development of "smart bombs" as reprinted from a September 10, 1967, report in the Washington Post.

2790 Wilson, Leonard R. "The Chinook--A Personal View." U.S. Army Aviation Digest, X (April 1964), 18-20. A pilot's report on the CH-47A.

2791 Wilson, Norde. "Another Pilot's Report from Vietnam: A Letter." Aviation Week and Space Technology, LXXXV (Oct. 24, 1966), 21+. A personal account of the air war excerpted in U.S. News and World Report, LXI (Oct. 31, 1966), 64, under the title, "A Combat Pilot's Plea: 'Give Us Half a Chance to Win.'"

2792 Winchester, James H. "Cargo Planes in the Vietnam War." NATO's Fifteen Nations, XI (Aug.-Sept. 1966), 50-53. A review of the vital airlift operations.

2793 _____. "'Dust Off! Dust Off!': Lifeline Home from Vietnam." Reader's Digest, LXXXVIII (May 1966), 60-66. Helicopter medevac operations in South Vietnam.

2794 _____. "Forward Air Controllers in Vietnam." NATO's Fifteen Nations, XII (March-April 1967), 44-47. A review of FAC activities.

2795 _____. "Helicopters in South Vietnam." NATO's Fifteen Nations, XI (Aug.-Sept. 1966), 54-58. A look at the many roles of the whirlybird.

2796 _____. "Our Fabulous Choppers: An Eyewitness Report." Popular Science, CLXXXVIII (Feb. 1966), 80-83+. A report on U.S. Army helicopter operations in South Vietnam.

2797 Windchy, Eugene G. Tonkin Gulf. Garden City, N.Y.: Doubleday, 1971. 358p. A review of the events of August 1964, including aerial response.

2798 Windrow, Martin C., ed. Aircraft in Profile. 14 vols. Garden City, N.Y.: Doubleday, 1967-1974. A continuing series of British-produced aircraft evaluations/histories; most of the appropriate titles are cited individually in this bibliography.

2799 "Wings of Destruction." Time, LXXXVI (Nov. 26, 1965), 33-34. U.S. air attacks on North Vietnam.

2800 Winkler, John L., and Francis G. Kinkaid. "Armed Reconnaissance." Fighter Weapons Newsletter, IV (Dec. 1963), 3-7. Theory which would be transferred to operations over Southeast Asia within two years.

2801 Winston, D. C. "Tactical Air Power Curtailment Seen Causing Excessive Losses." Aviation Week and Space Technology, LXXXVII (Oct. 30, 1967), 11, 17-18. By allowing the North Vietnamese to better their air defenses.

2802 ______. "Tempo of the North Vietnam Air War Increases." Aviation Week and Space Technology, LXXXVII (Oct. 16, 1967), 28-29. Just before a slow-down.

2803 Witterman, Benn H. "Romance with a 'Weenie Wagon.'" MAC Flyer, XVIII (July 1971), 16-20. An airman's view of the C-130 Hercules cargo plane.

2804 Witze, Claude. "Air Power: Front and Center." Air Force Magazine, LV (Feb. 1972), 8-10. A Southeast Asian report.

2805 ______. "Are the Viet Cong Feeling the Bite of U.S. Air Power?" Air Force and Space Digest International, I (Sept. 1965), 5-7. The author suggests the answer is "yes."

2806 ______. "Are There Unauthorized Conclusions?" Air Force Magazine, LV (August 1972), 11-12. Reasoned comments on the Lavelle case.

2807 ______. "The August 15 Bombing Halt." Air Force Magazine, LVI (Aug. 1973), 12-14. The military, and political consequences to be expected as the result of the end of U.S. aerial operations over Cambodia.

2808 ______. "The Case for a Unified Command: CINCSEA." Air Force and Space Digest, L (Jan. 1967), 23-29. Proposed one-commander concept which did not come about.

2809 ______. "A Fine Dish of Crow." Air Force Magazine, LVI (April 1973), 8-10. Reflections on the U.S. withdrawal from the Indochina conflict.

2810 ______. "Flying Ambulances for Vietnam Casualties." Air Force and Space Digest, XLIX (March 1966), 91+. Helicopter medevac activities.

2811 ______. "How Not to Win." Air Force and Space Digest, LIII (Dec. 1970), 10-12. Comments on the findings in the Joint Logistics Review Board Report cited above.

2812 ______. "Interdiction: Limited but Effective." Air Force and Space Digest, L (May 1967), 72-74. U.S. aerial attempts to cut off "enemy" supplies.

2813 ______. "It'll Kill You." Air Force and Space Digest, XLVII (Dec. 1964), 15-16. On the security of equipment at Bien Hoa airdrome.

2814 ______. "The Lavelle Case, Again." Air Force Magazine, LVI (Feb. 1973), 12-13. Additional reflections.

2815 ______. "Reasons for a POW Raid." Air Force and Space Digest, LIV (Jan. 1971), 8-9. Thoughts on the Son Tay raid in the light of reports of North Vietnamese inhumanity.

2816 ______. "Report from Vietnam." Air Force and Space Digest, XLVII (Aug. 1964), 12+. An eyewitness account.

2817 ______. "Soldier or Strangelove." Air Force Magazine, LV (Nov. 1972), 20-22. U.S. Air Force Major Gen. John Lavelle.

2818 ______. "The USAF Polishes Its New COIN." Air Force and Space Digest, XLV (June 1962), 46-47+. Tactics and aircraft.

2819 ______. "The U.S. Army Flies to Fight and Win." Aerospace International, III (July-Aug. 1967), 13-17. Helicopters and aircraft in South Vietnam.

2820 ______. "What Kind of Air War in Vietnam?" Air Force and Space Digest, L (Oct. 1967), 42-46. Thoughts on the techniques to be employed.

2821 ______. "The Year Air Power Was Tested and Paid Off." Air Force and Space Digest, LI (June 1968), 110-112. U.S. air operations over Southeast Asia in 1967.

Wolk, Herman S., jt. author see Van Staaversen, Jacob

2822 Wolverton, James R. "Gunships and Guerrilla Warfare." Tactical Air Warfare Center Quarterly Report, II (Sept. 1970), 22-27. Operations of the U.S. Air Force AC-47 and AC-119.

2823 Wong, Johnson H. "An Evaluation of the Pacification Program in South Vietnam and the Bombing of Vietnam." (Unpublished student essay.) U.S. Army War College Library, Carlisle Barracks, Pa., 1974. 32p. Available through the Commerce Department's National Technical Information Service as Report no. AD-A009-917/66A.

2824 Wood, Horace E., Jr. "Airlift: A Balanced View." Air University Review, XXIII (May-June 1972), 62-71. With examples from our topic.

2825 "The 'Workhorse' at Da Nang." Naval Aviation News, (July 1968), 36. A look at U.S. Navy C-117's.

2826 World Almanac and Book of Facts. New York, 1961-1973. Includes information on the SEA air war; published by the World Telegram, 1961-1965, and by Doubleday, 1966-1973.

2827 The World Book Encyclopedia Yearbook. Chicago: Field Enterprises Educational Corp., 1961-1973. An annual with useful information relative to the SEA air war.

2828 Worley, Robert F. "The Challenge of the Tactical and Close Air Support Mission." Air Force Policy Letter for Commanders, no. 11 (Nov. 1966), 8-13. Thoughts on operations over South Vietnam; excerpted in Ordnance, LI (Jan.-Feb. 1967), 375.

2829 "Worse than Silence: The Destruction of Bach Mai Hospital." Nation, CCXVI (Jan. 15, 1973), 68-69. U.S. bombs a North Vietnamese hospital during "Linebacker II."

2830 Wragg, David W. The World's Air Forces. London: Osprey, 1971. 232p. Includes data on the air fleets of Australia, the Vietnams, and the U.S.; published in America the same year by Hippocrene Books.

2831 Wright, William. "Air Assault Development." Aviation Week and Space Technology, LXXX (Feb. 17, 1964), 54-55+ Helicopter vertical assault.

2832 _____. "Army Explores Air Mobility Potential." Aviation Week and Space Technology, LXXX (April 16, 1964), 90-91+. More on the birth of vertical assault.

2833 Wuriu, Tom. "'Spooky' Changes VC Tactics." Air Force Times, XXVIII (May 29, 1968), 16. Night operations of the U.S. Air Force AC-47 gunships.

2834 "The Year of the Snake: Highlights of a Year of Combat in Vietnam." Army Information Digest, XXI (April 1966), 38-47. Includes army aircraft and helicopter operations since April 1965, especially the exploits of the 1st Air Cavalry Division.

2835 Yefremov, Vasily. "Vietnam: From One Enormity to Another." Soviet Military Review, no. 10 (Oct. 1972), 59-61. A Soviet view of U.S. air operations.

2836 Yool, William. "The United States Air Force." In J. L. Moulton, ed., Brassey's Annual: The Armed Forces Year Book (New York: Praeger, 1966), p82-88. With thoughts on its Vietnam role.

2837 York, Robert H. "Air Mobility Throughout the Spectrum." Army Digest, XXII (Aug. 1967), 9-10. Helicopter vertical assault in South Vietnam.

2838 _____. "Army Aviation: The Newest Member of the Team." U.S. Army Aviation Digest, XIII (June, 1967), 14-15+ A report, with comments on its Vietnam role.

2839 Yoshinaga, Gene N. The Cambodian Intervention: An Analysis. Air Command and Staff College Research Study. Maxwell Air Force Base, Ala.: Air University, 1971. 80p. Primarily military-air in emphasis.

2840 Yudkin, Richard A. "Vietnam: Policy, Strategy, and Air Power." Air Force Magazine, LVI (Feb. 1973), 31-35. A review.

2841 Zaiman, Robert. "TAC's Air Commandos." United Aircraft Quarterly Bee Hive, XXXVIII (Spring 1963), 5-9. Reprinted in Flying Review International, XIX (Oct. 1963), 18-20+.

2842 Zraket, Charles A., and Stanley E. Rose. "The Impact of Command Control and Communications on Air Warfare." Air University Review, XXIX (Nov.-Dec. 1977), 82-96. With several examples from our period.

III

AIR UNIVERSITY STUDIES

The studies cited in this section were prepared primarily at the Air War College and Air Command and Staff College, two important segments of the U.S. Air Force Air University located at Maxwell Air Force Base, Alabama, and are obtainable by interlibrary loan. Most were developed by students in response to specific course requirements while a few were composed by faculty members. Almost all of these papers reflect projects undertaken partially as the university's response to its role in "Operation Corona Harvest." Most of the papers are numbered for easy access by the Air University Library; however, those completed of late are not.

2843 Adkinson, John L. "A History of the Use of the TA-4F Aircraft as a Tactical Air Coordinator (Airborne) in the War in Southeast Asia." (Unpublished research study.) Air War College, Air University, 1977. 78p. Concerns the use of jets in the Tactical Air Coordinator role.

2844 Adkisson, Robert B. "Counterair: The Tasks and Effectiveness of Accomplishing These Tasks by the United States Air Force in North Vietnam." (Unpublished research study, no. AUC-28-68, pt. 1.) Air Command and Staff College, Air University, 1969. 28p.
A consideration of the effectiveness of U.S. Air Force planes against North Vietnamese MIG's; part of a series.

2845 Agnew, Malcolm J. "A Study of the Systems Used for Requesting, Controlling, and Distributing Out-Country Reconnaissance Information in Southeast Asia." (Unpublished research report, no. 2561.) Air War College, Air University, 1968. 138p.
Examines the buildup of the U.S. air reconnaissance system for the gathering of data by U.S. Air Force and Navy aircraft over Laos and North Vietnam and the sharing of information between the two services.

2846 Aldren, Donald D. "Command Arrangements for the Use of

Airpower in Limited War: A USN View." (Unpublished research report, no. 3709.) Air War College, Air University, 1969. 47p. A description of U.S. Navy carrier participation, emphasizing the advantage of then-existing command relationships. Compare with the Nakis and Nickel studies, items 2960 and 2964.

2847 Amrhein, Robert L. "Harvest Reaper/Combat Lancer." (Unpublished research study, no. AUC-39-68.) Air Command and Staff College, Air University, 1969. 159p. A look at early F-111 operations in SEA.

2848 Armistead, Samuel E., Jr. "South Vietnam's Tactical Fighter Force: Can It Do the Job Alone?" (Unpublished research study, no. 0045-70.) Air Command and Staff College, Air University, 1970. 56p. Answer in a word: no.

2849 Bartlett, Russell H. "Out-Country Counterair: People." (Unpublished research study, no. AUC-28-68, pt. 3.) Air Command and Staff College, Air University, 1969. 75p. A view of the personnel involved in the air campaign against North Vietnam.

2850 Bartrand, Louis E. "The AC-130/AC-119K Impact on Close Air Support/Interdiction Mission of the USAF." (Unpublished research study, no. 0150-71.) Air Command and Staff College, Air University, 1971. 51p. The role and effect of gunships in the SEA conflict.

2851 Batson, Louis R., Jr. "Counterair: Operational Support Activities in Relation to Counterair Operations by the USAF in North Vietnam." (Unpublished research study, no. AUC-28-68, pt. 4.) Air Command and Staff College, Air University, 1969. 48p. A digest of all AWC student-gathered data on the subject.

2852 Beardsley, Ralph J. "An Analysis of Out-Country Interdiction, 1965-1967 ('Hardware')." (Unpublished research study, no. AUC-27-68, pt. 2.) Air Command and Staff College, Air University, 1969. 57p. Sequel to the Beckett study, item 2856; concerns aircraft and armament.

2853 Beasley, Horace B. "Logistics Support for Army Aviation in Limited War." (Unpublished thesis, no. 0115-67.) Air Command and Staff College, Air University, 1967. 44p. Suggests the need for improved supply procedures and maintenance organization.

2854 Beck, Douglass D., et al. "B-52 Operations in Southeast Asia." (Unpublished research study, no. AUC-31-68.) Air Command and Staff College, Air University, 1969. 182p. A compilation of information contained in selected documents concerning Stratofortress activities over Southeast Asia.

2855 Beck, Jerry E. "Combat Skyspot: A Study of a Ground-Directed Radar Bombing System in a Limited War Environment." (Unpublished research study, no. 0085-70.) Air Command and Staff College, Air University, 1970. 69p. An analysis of U.S. Air Force blind bombing techniques in SEA.

2856 Beckett, Roderick G. "An Analysis of Out-Country Interdiction, 1965-1967 (Tasks)." (Unpublished research study, no. AUC-27-68, pt. 1.) Air Command and Staff College, Air University, 1969. 71p. A digest of 18 Air War College theses on the tasks involved.

2857 Bedhe, Ernest A. "U.S. Airpower and the Democratic Republic of Vietnam." (Unpublished thesis, no. 0120-67.) Air Command and Staff College, Air University, 1967. Concludes that American aerial objectives against North Vietnam were not being met due to a stagnant political-military doctrine and an unrealistic strategy.

2858 Bell, George W. "The Effect of North Vietnamese Defensive Capabilities on U.S. Counterair Operations." (Unpublished research report, no. 3565.) Air War College, Air University, 1968. 79p. Examines the systematic growth of North Vietnamese air defenses and the slow response of the U.S. in a constrained environment.

2859 Bennett, George F. "A Study of the Use of the RB-57 and U-2 Aircraft in Southeast Asia, 1965-1967." (Unpublished research report, no. 3566.) Air War College, Air University, 1968. 73p. The successes and failures in the use of those planes in aerial reconnaissance.

2860 Bianchi, Rocco D. "A Study of Helicopter Tactics Employed in South Vietnam." (Unpublished professional study, no. 2959.) Air War College, Air University, 1966. 29p. A brief overview of tactics and techniques of U.S. Army and Marine Corps helicopter units during 1964-1966.

2861 Bigelow, Robert B. "A Study of the Politically Specified Rules of Engagement for Air Operations in Southeast Asia, 1965-1967." (Unpublished research report, no. 3567.) Air War College, Air University, 1968. 78p. Traces the development of the rules of engagement.

2862 Blanton, Dwight W. "Airpower in the Defense of Khe Sanh, B-52 Operations (18 January-31 March 1968)." (Unpublished research report, no. 3718.) Air War College, Air University, 1969. 99p. An analysis of the success of

"Arc Light" operations in connection with the North Vietnamese siege of the U.S. Marine Corps base.

2863 Bond, Robert M. "Tactical Fighter Employment: A Requirement for Change." (Unpublished thesis, no. 0159-66.) Air Command and Staff College, Air University, 1966. 72p. Examines the causes of North Vietnamese antiaircraft gunfire damage to U.S. aircraft and suggests offensive countermeasures.

2864 Bourn, Daten O. "Analysis of C-141 Airdrop Capability in Southeast Asia." (Unpublished research study, no. 0155-70.) Air Command and Staff College, Air University, 1970. 45p. A look at the limitations involved with suggestions for overcoming them.

2865 Brant, Donald R. "The Evolution of Strategic Conventional Bombing Techniques in Southeast Asia and Their Future Application in Selected Areas of Conflict." (Unpublished research study.) Air War College, Air University, 1977. 57p. Reviews the lessons learned in operations "Arc Light" and "Linebacker."

2866 Brewster, Philip L. "Strategic Persuasion: Valid Role for Airpower?" (Unpublished thesis, no. 0255-67.) Air Command and Staff College, Air University, 1967. 69p. Examines the role of U.S. airpower in trying to persuade North Vietnam to quit and concludes the activity to be valid.

2867 Brodsky, Henry G. "Prepare the Wild Weasel." (Unpublished research study.) Air Command and Staff College, Air University, 1974. 62p. A look at the use of U.S. Air Force aircraft against "enemy" electronic countermeasures.

2868 Browne, Edward M. "The Aerial Scout--Man and Helicopter." (Unpublished professional study.) Air War College, Air University, 1972. 13p. Contrasts the role and mission of the U.S. Army helicopter scout with the old fashioned horse scout of Custer's day.

2869 Burkett, William M. "The Tactical Air Control Party: Crux of the Tactical Air Control System." (Unpublished professional study, no. 4200.) Air War College, Air University, 1971. 15p. The role and requirements of TACP on the ground in SEA.

2870 Buss, Robert H. "Target Selection System in Laos." (Unpublished research report, no. 3574.) Air War College, Air University, 1968. 49p. Examines facets of the Laos targeting system from 1965 through June 1967.

2871 Butera, James L. "Rescue Concepts and Doctrine." (Unpublished research study, no. AUC-26-68.) Air Command and Staff College, Air University, 1969. 68p. A view of Combat Aircrew Recovery operations in SEA.

2872 Butler, Robert K. "Analysis and Evaluation of Enemy Capabilities to Degrade Out-Country Interdiction Tactics." (Unpublished research report, no. 3575.) Air War College, Air University, 1968. 95p. A study of tactics, techniques, and equipment used by the North Vietnamese to counter U.S. Air Force and Navy air attacks in 1965-1967.

2873 Candelaria, Louis. "Psychological Considerations Affecting Target Selection in North Vietnam." (Unpublished research report, no. 3576.) Air War College, Air University, 1968. 135p. The role of U.S. air raids in strategic persuasion.

2874 Cecil, Charles P. "An Analysis of Offensive Out-Country Night Interdiction Tactics in Southeast Asia, 1965-1967." (Unpublished research report, no. 3580.) Air War College, Air University, 1968. 72p. Considers effectiveness and calls for additional changes.

2875 Chapman, Andrew J. "How to Increase the Effectiveness of Airpower in Counterguerrilla Warfare." (Unpublished professional study, no. 2979.) Air War College, Air University, 1966. 62p. Suggests the transfer of U.S. Army Aviation to tne U.S. Air Force.

2876 Chew, Robert S. "Principles of Aerial Interdiction." (Unpublished professional study, no. 3316.) Air War College, Air University, 1967. 82p. Examines the techniques of aerial interdiction in World War II and suggests how to apply the lessons learned then to the conflict in SEA.

2877 Clark, James C. "Strategic Airlift Doctrine and Concepts." (Unpublished research study, no. AUC-25-68.) Air Command and Staff College, Air University, 1969. 117p. Examines the development of strategic airlift in terms of capabilities and actual use with examples from SEA.

2878 Conley, Paul H. "KC-135 Air Refueling in Southeast Asia." (Unpublished research study, no. AUC-32-68, pt. 1.) Air Command and Staff College, Air University, 1969. 99p. A detailed overview of the operational support provided by the tanker forces to the tactical forces.

2879 Cox, Frank E. "The Effectiveness of USAF Counter-Air Targeting in North Vietnam." (Unpublished research report, no. 3587.) Air War College, Air University, 1968. 57p. A discussion of Joint Chiefs of Staff targeting concepts with a review of the development of the total strike program against North Vietnam; presents a résumé of operational limitations.

2880 Crabb, Cecil D., Jr. "Ordnance Constraints and Limitations in Out-Country Interdiction Operations, February 1965 to December 1967." (Unpublished research report, no. 3588.) Air War College, Air University, 1968. 50p. De-emphasis on ordnance development in the years after Korea led to the problems during the years herein examined.

2881 Crawford, Milton N. "Airlife in the Defense of Khe Sanh." (Unpublished research report, no. 3740.) Air War College, Air University, 1969. 88p. A review of aerial resupply for the Marines during the 1968 siege.

2882 Crawford, Thomas M., Jr. "Total Air Support and the Battle of Ben Het." (Unpublished professional study, no. 4029.) Air War College, Air University, 1970. 69p. A brief history of the May 6-July 2, 1969, South Vietnam battle and the role of tactical air support therein.

2883 Curtis, Edward H. "A Study of the RF-4C Weapon System in Out-Country Operations in Southeast Asia, 1965-1967." (Unpublished research report, no. 3591.) Air War College, Air University, 1968. 102p. Describes the RF-4C and its effectiveness in aerial reconnaissance work.

2884 Curtis, Oliver W. "Helicopter Employment in Guerrilla and Limited War." (Unpublished professional study, no. 2991.) Air War College, Air University, 1966. 80p. Reviews the history of helicopters in guerrilla warfare and studies helicopter employment in South Vietnam to determine the capabilities and limitations of the aircraft in the SEA environment.

2885 Davis, William J. "Da Nang Airbase: The Rocket Problem." (Unpublished research report, no. 3743.) Air War College, Air University, 1969. 38p. Concludes that a purely military solution to Vietcong rocket attacks was not possible.

2886 Dean, Orien G., Jr. "Measuring the Effectiveness of Airpower Employed Against North Vietnam, February-September 1965." (Unpublished professional study, no. 2995.) Air War College, Air University, 1966. 69p. Identification and description of the North Vietnam targeting system.

2887 Dilworth, Billy G., 3d. "The Problems of Measuring B-52 Effectiveness in Limited War." (Unpublished research study.) Air Command and Staff College, Air University, 1972. 54p. Stresses the lack of available quantitative assessment data.

2888 Doneen, Dennis D. "A Historical Analysis of the Vietnamese Air Force Supply System." (Unpublished research study.) Air War College, Air University, 1977. 92p. Problems of the VNAF especially after 1961.

2889 Donohue, Frederic M. "Mission of Mercy." (Unpublished professional study.) Air War College, Air University, 1972. 10p. A brief, first-hand review of the planning, training, and execution of the Son Tay POW camp raid.

2890 Donovan, James A. "The A-1 Aircraft in Southeast Asia." (Unpublished professional study, no. 4108.) Air War College, Air University, 1971. 19p. Tasks and missions history of the Skyraider over South Vietnam.

2891 Dougherty, Charles R. "History of the Forward Air Controller." (Unpublished professional study, no. 3902.) Air War College, Air University, 1970. 86p. From World War II through Vietnam.

2892 Dougherty, Joseph M. "The Use of Herbicides in Southeast Asia and the Criticism." (Unpublished professional study.) Air War College, Air University, 1972. 58p. A look at "Operation Ranch Hand," which claims criticism of it at the time was invalid.

2893 Eaton, Norman D. "Command Arrangements for Out-Country Air Operations." (Unpublished research report, no. 3597.) Air War College, Air University, 1968. 91p. In spite of enumerated deficiencies, the 1967-1968 system was found to be adequate.

2894 Eells, Gordon L. "Advanced Aircraft for the Forward Air Controller." (Unpublished thesis, no. 0640-67.) Air Command and Staff College Air University, 1967. 82p. Recommends a family of FAC aircraft, including a mix of O-2A and OV-10A warbirds.

2895 Ehmke, Charles A. "The Use of Non-Lethal Chemical Agents in Limited Warfare." (Unpublished thesis, no. 0420-66.) Air Command and Staff College, Air University, 1966. 58p. Investigates ways of obtaining favorable world opinion on the U.S. airborne use of chemicals over South Vietnam.

2896 Elwood, Niles T. "Big Eye/College Eye." (Unpublished research study, no. AUC-30-68.) Air Command and Staff College, Air University, 1969. 178p. This April 1965-December 1968 project is analyzed.

2897 Enos, James W. "A Study of Air Operations in North Vietnam." (Unpublished professional study, no. 3341.) Air University, 1967. 92p. Examines the ways in which U.S. air operations contributed to overall American goals in SEA.

2898 Fahrney, John W. "U.S. Air Force Offensive Counterair Tactics over North Vietnam, February 1965 to January 1968." (Unpublished research report, no. 3599.) Air War College, Air University, 1968. 133p. A consideration of North Vietnamese defenses during that period and the tactics of U.S. Air Force aircraft which allowed them to operate in the hostile antiaircraft-MIG-SAM environment.

2899 Farris, Robert H. "An Evaluation of USAF Concepts for the Employment of Helicopters in Counterinsurgency Operations." (Unpublished thesis, no. 0730-67.) Air Command and Staff College, Air University, 1967. 136p. Examines the role of the helicopter in COIN operations and concludes that U.S. Air Force concepts at the time of writing were not objective, dynamic, or flexible.

2900 Faurer, Theodore M. "The First and Last U.S. A-47 Squadron." (Unpublished professional study.) Air War College, Air University, 1975. 25p. Reminiscences of the U.S. Air Force 4th Commando Squadron over SEA from August 1965 to July 1966.

2901 Fidler, Joseph E. "Counterair Hardware: North Vietnam, 1965-1967." (Unpublished research study, no AUC-28-68, pt. 2.) Air Command and Staff College, Air University, 1969. 65p. Extracts from student-prepared studies on the topic delivered to the Air War College in 1968.

2902 Flint, Roy K. "Campaigning with the Infantry in Vietnam." (Unpublished professional study, no. 4049.) Air War College, Air University, 1970. 18p. A brief review of helicopter, ground, and air support operations by and for the 3d battalion of the 22nd Infantry prepared by an Army officer for the information of Air Force officers.

2903 Forbert, Samuel, Jr. "A Study of the Tactics Used to Secure Out-Country Reconnaissance Information in Southeast Asia." (Unpublished research report, no. 3604.) Air War College, Air University, 1968. 62p. A look at tactical reconnaissance and the use of tactical sensors.

2904 Fratt, Merlyn D., Jr. "KC-135 Air Refueling in Southeast Asia: Support Requests." (Unpublished research study, no. AUC-32-68, pt. 2.) Air Command and Staff College, Air University, 1969. 104p. Examines some of the different types of support requests made on the U.S. Air Force Tanker Task Forces in SEA.

2905 Funk, Dale R. "Study of the Use of B-52 Bombers in the War in Vietnam." (Unpublished professional study, no. 3350.) Air War College, Air University, 1967. 89p.

2906 Garrett, Clifford E. "A Preliminary Study of the Politically Specified Rules of Engagement for Air Operations in Southeast Asia." (Unpublished professional study, no. 3354.) Air War College, Air University, 1967. 63p. Traces U.S. Air Force rules of engagement in 1964-1965.

2907 Gibson, Charles V. "An Analysis and Evaluation of Defensive Interdiction Tactics in North Vietnam." (Unpublished research report, no. 3608.) Air War College, Air University, 1968. 69p. Judges tactics against aircraft losses.

2908 Ginsburg, Gordon A. "The Lavelle Case: Crisis in Integrity." (Unpublished professional study.) Air War College, Air University, 1974. 154p. A case study of the unauthorized raids approved by the General and the relative ease with which he avoided personal results.

2909 Goertz, Robert D. "An Analysis of Air-to-Air Missile Capability in Southeast Asia." (Unpublished thesis, no. 0450-68.) Air Command and Staff College, Air University, 1968. 86p. Examines the success of the Sparrow, Sidewinder, and Falcon armaments in combat with North Vietnamese MIG's.

2910 Good, Paul R. "Evaluation of Air-to-Air Missiles in Southeast Asia During 1972." (Unpublished professional study.) Air War College, Air University, 1974. 95p. Another look at the effectiveness of the Sparrow and Sidewinder.

2911 Goodrich, John R. "Evaluation of the Development of Armed Helicopters." (Unpublished research report, no. 3758.) Air War College, Air University, 1969. 53p. Historical and operational developments in South Vietnam.

2912 Grant, Harold E. "USAF MAAG Missions in Counterinsurgency War: Republic of South Vietnam, 1965-1968." (Unpublished research report, no. 3759.) Air War College, Air University, 1969. 180p. A history of the VNAF and the U.S. Air Force Advisory Group, 1964-1968.

2913 Gray, David L. "An Analysis of the F-4 Weapon System in Out-Country Counterair Operations, 1965 to the Present." (Unpublished research report, no. 3611.) Air War College, Air University, 1968. 125p. U.S. Phantoms vs North Vietnamese MIGS.

2914 Graybeal, Dodson B. "Air Force Reserve Participation in the Southeast Asia Conflict: AFRES Aircraft." (Unpublished research report, no. 3760.) Air War College, Air University, 1969. 63p. A review of reserve airlift operations and their overall contribution to the U.S. Air Force war effort.

2915 Hall, James H. "United States Target Selection Policy for Out-Country Operations in Southeast Asia, January 1964 Through June 1967." (Unpublished research report, no. 3612.) Air War College, Air University, 1968. 106p. A chronological summary.

2916 Hartman, William B. "Gunship Roles and Capabilities." (Unpublished professional study.) Air War College, Air University, 1974. 56p. A review of the development and operations of the fixed-wing gunship from the introduction of the AC-47 in 1965 through the advanced AC-130 employed at the war's end.

2917 Hegerle, Matthew J. "Analysis and Evaluation of Research and Development Support for Out-Country Air Operations." (Unpublished research report, no. 3614.) Air War College, Air University, 1968. 144p. Documents the activities in U.S. Air Force research and development in providing hardware solutions to SEA operational requirements.

2918 Hicks, Joseph W., Jr. "U.S. Assistance to Laos." (Unpublished research report, no. 3767.) Air War College, Air University, 1969. 118p. A review, with emphasis on aerial matters.

2919 Hopkins, James R. "The Impact of Bombing Restraints on Military Operations in Southeast Asia, 1968." (Unpublished research report, no. 3770.) Air War College, Air University, 1969. 67p. A look at the impact on aerial operations of President Johnson's 1968 bombing halt.

2920 Howard, Brown G., 3d. "USAF Airpower Against North Vietnam." (Unpublished thesis, no. 1147-67.) Air Command and Staff School, Air University, 1967. 44p. A review of the 1965-1966 campaign.

2921 Jamieson, James R. "Lessons Learned in Southeast Asia: TAC Air." (Unpublished professional study.) Air War College, Air University, 1976. 79p. With emphasis on activities in 1972-73.

2922 Johnson, James D. "Proposed Increased Helicopter Armament." (Unpublished study, class 62-C.) Squadron Officer School, Air University, 1966. 23p. Concludes that U.S. armed helicopters could handle additional firepower.

2923 Johnson, William N. "North Vietnamese Surface-to-Air Missiles vs. United States Air Force Aircraft: A Current Study." (Unpublished research study.) Air Command and Staff School, Air University, 1972. 63p. Suggests that, by 1972, the U.S. Air Force (and Navy) had overcome the advantages enjoyed by "enemy" SAM's.

2924 Jordan, James D. "Navy Aircraft and Tactics in Southeast Asia Out-Country Air Interdiction Operations." (Unpublished Research Report, no. 3623.) Air War College, Air University, 1968. 57p. An analysis of the capabilities of the A-4 and A-6 warbirds.

2925 Kasler, James H. "The Hanoi POL Strike." (Unpublished professional study.) Air War College, Air University, 1974. 20p. A review of the mission by the leader of the U.S. Air Force's 388th Tactical Fighter Wing.

2926 Kiernan, Philip D. "Out-Country Interdiction: People." (Unpublished research study, no. AUC-27-68, pt. 3.) Air Command and Staff College, Air University, 1969. 50p. Examines personnel problems involved in the 1965-1968 air campaign against North Vietnam and Laos.

2927 Kingston, Raymond F. "Rules of Engagement: Mission Accomplishment in Southeast Asia." (Unpublished professional study, no. 4379.) Air War College, Air University, 1971. 18p. First-hand description of one mission made impossible to achieve by the Rules of Engagement issued after President Johnson's 1968 bombing halt.

2928 Kinney, Philip R. "Airmobility: Concepts in Conflict." (Unpublished thesis, no. 1341-67.) Air Command and Staff College, Air University, 1967. 35p. Examines the differences between Army and Air Force procedures in airmobility and recommends changes to terminate the inter-service conflict.

2929 Kirk, William L. "'Gradualism' in the Air War over North Vietnam." (Unpublished professional study, no. 4167.) Air War College, Air University, 1971. 26p. A look at the effects of step-by-step political retaliation by air on the prosecution of the American war effort.

2930 Kirtley, Robert L. "Night Interdiction, the Key to Future Counterinsurgency." (Unpublished professional study.) Air War College, Air University, 1974. 71p. Lessons learned in the conduct of night raids along the Ho Chi Minh trail in Laos.

2931 Kosa, Milton E. "Objectives, Plan of Operations, and Command and Control for Out-Country Interdiction, 1965-1967." (Unpublished research report, no. 3624.) Air War College, Air University, 1968. 84p. Concludes that limited military objectives and gradualism prevented U.S. airpower from making a greater contribution toward ending the conflict.

2932 Krull, Larry D. "VNAF O-1 Operations, 1962-1968." (Unpublished research study, no. AUC-42-68, pt. 3.) Air

Command and Staff College, Air University, 1969. 56p. Examines the VNAF use of the birddog during those years.

2933 Kulla, Vernon M. "Interdiction Plans, Concepts, and Doctrine: North Vietnam, 1965-1967." (Unpublished research study, no. AUC-27-68, pt. 5.) Air Command and Staff College, Air University, 1969. 83p. A digest of 19 AWC student reports presented in 1968.

2934 LaRe, John. "A Study of Special Air Missions in Support of Southeast Asia (Out-Country) Operations." (Unpublished research report, no. 3627.) Air War College, Air University, 1968. 65p. The role of defoliation and psychological SAM's in support of the aerial interdiction campaign against North Vietnam.

2935 Lidie, Kenneth F. "An Analysis of the Materiel Support for Out-Country Interdiction from February 1965 to December 1967." (Unpublished research report, no. 3631.) Air War College, Air University, 1968. 62p. Maintenance and supply functions in support of U.S. air raids into North Vietnam and Laos.

2936 Little, Richard E. "An Analysis of the Present Tactical Fighter Weapons Systems Capabilities in Southeast Asia Out-Country Interdiction Operations." (Unpublished research report, no. 3632.) Air War College, Air University, 1968. 133p. Examines the ability of U.S. Air Force fighter-bombers to successfully raid North Vietnamese targets.

2937 Locke, Jesse C., Jr. "Special Air Warfare: Southeast Asia." (Unpublished professional study, no. 4307.) Air War College, Air University, 1971. 15p. A look at the build-up of the VNAF and the introduction of U.S. Air Force units into the Vietnamese War.

2938 Long, Francis J. "Do Strategic Bombers Have a Role in Conflicts Short of General War?" (Unpublished professional study, no. 3082.) Air War College, Air University, 1966. 72p. A general review with comments on the use of Stratofortresses in SEA.

2939 Lonie, Frank R. "Air Interdiction: Vietnam in Perspective." (Unpublished professional study.) Air War College, Air University, 1975. 20p. Focuses on lessons learned during the 1964-1968 period.

2940 Lukens, Leland K. "Old Airplanes in New Wars." (Unpublished research study, no. AUC-38-68.) Air Command and Staff College, Air University, 1969. 236p. An important analysis of the roles played by the AC-47,

A-1E, A-26, and T-28 in the early years of the Vietnamese conflict.

2941 Maberry, Fred W. "Counterair Defensive Operations, United States Airpower, North Vietnam." (Unpublished research report, no. 3637.) Air War College, Air University, 1968. 106p. Addresses SAM tactics, MIG activities, and the development of U.S. "Wild Weasel" operations.

2942 McCleskey, James L. "Truck Killers in Southeast Asia." (Unpublished research study, no. 0925-70.) Air Command and Staff College, Air University, 1970. 72p. Examines "enemy" road networks and the effectiveness of various kinds of U.S. aircraft against them.

2943 McKinney, Ewing J. W. "A Study of Military Operations in the Vietnamese War, from October 1960 to 20 November 1963." (Unpublished professional study, no. 3441.) Air War College, Air University, 1967. 153p. A general review of ground-air-and sea events.

2944 McKinzie, John W. "Night Owl." (Unpublished research study, no. AUC-40-68.) Air Command and Staff College, Air University, 1969. 159p. A look at the results of tactical fighter night operations in SEA.

2945 Magee, Lawton W. "A Study of Counterair Operations Conducted by the United States Navy in North Vietnam and Laos, 1965-67." (Unpublished research report, no. 3639.) Air War College, Air University, 1968. 61p. The offensive and defensive counterair operations by U.S. Navy carrier planes and Marine Corps air elements in relation to the primary strike effort.

2946 Mamlock, Stanley M. "Use of Jet Fighter Aircraft as a Forward Air Control Vehicle in a Non-Permissive Environment." (Unpublished professional study, no. 3955.) Air War College, Air University, 1970. 93p. The FAC role of the F-100 over South Vietnam.

2947 Mariconda, Albert J. "Facilities Support for Out-Country Interdiction Operations." (Unpublished research report, no. 3640.) Air War College, Air University, 1968. 91p. Suggests that facilities were adequate for the mission in hand.

2948 Mason, Thomas M. "A Study of USAF/USN Information Mission Crossfeed for Interdiction in North Vietnam." (Unpublished research report.) Air War College, Air University, 1968. 86p. The coordination of data between the two services relating to "Operation Rolling Thunder."

2949 Mathews, Bruce A., et al. "Out-Country Reconnaissance,

1965-67." (Unpublished research study, no. AUC-29-68.) Air Command and Staff College, Air University, 1969. 261p. A look at concepts, doctrines, and operations.

2950 Maxson, William B. "Factors Influencing the Effectiveness of Airpower in Night Visual Interdiction." (Unpublished professional study, no. 4188.) Air War College, Air University, 1971. 21p. A record of interviews with the members of one U.S. Air Force night attack squadron in SEA.

2951 Mihura, Max L. "The Non-Nuclear Role of the B-52 in Southeast Asia." (Unpublished thesis, no. 1680-67.) Air Command and Staff College, Air University, 1967. 45p. Examines the Stratofortress role in "Arc Light" operations and concludes it to be quite effective.

2952 Miller, Donald E. "The USAF Advisory Mission in Counter-insurgency War: South Vietnam, 1954-1964, a Historical Narrative." (Unpublished research report, no. 3804.) Air War College, Air University, 1969. 89p. A review of the growth of the U.S. Air Force advisory effort in those years and its contribution to the development of the VNAF.

2953 Miller, Edward L. "Analysis of Logistic Support for Out-Country Reconnaissance in Southeast Asia, 1965-1967." (Unpublished research report, no. 3650.) Air War College, Air University, 1968. 103p. The U.S. Air Force organization for logistic support and supply procedures are evaluated.

2954 Miller, John T. "An Analysis of Aircrew Personnel Flying Out-Country Interdiction Missions." (Unpublished research report, no. 3651.) Air War College, Air University, 1968. 164p. A look at the problems involved in keeping U.S. Air Force units in SEA manned with qualified air crews.

2955 Minter, Billy M. "Command and Control of Counterair Operations Over North Vietnam, February 1965 to December 1967." (Unpublished research report, no. 3652.) Air War College, Air University, 1968. 77p. Examines North Vietnamese defenses and U.S. countermeasures against them.

2956 Minter, Rondel E. "A Review of the Requirements for Airborne Forward Air Controllers in Close Air Support Operations." (Unpublished thesis, no. 1158-66.) Air Command and Staff School, Air University, 1966. 46p. Recommends the formation of airborne FAC units and the location of same at Army division levels.

2957 Mitchell, James R. "Down on the 99th." (Unpublished professional study.) Air War College, Air University, 1973. 16p. Shot down in 1966 while on his 99th F-105 mission, the author recalls his helicopter rescue.

2958 Moore, Courtland C. "EB-66 Out-Country Electronic Reconnaissance, 1965-1967." (Unpublished research report, no. 3655.) Air War College, Air University, 1968. 79p. A chronology with an analysis of EB-66 tactics.

2959 Moser, Richard E. "561st Tactical Fighter Squadron: 'Wild Weasel' Rapid Deployment and Operations." (Unpublished professional study.) Air War College, Air University, 1974. 69p. The deployment of the 561st TFS in SEA during 1972 and a look at the lessons learned from its operations during the "Linebacker" campaign.

2960 Nakis, George M. "Command Arrangements for the Use of Airpower in Limited War: A USAF View." (Unpublished research report, no. 3808.) Air War College, Air University, 1969. 79p. Examines command arrangements for Army helicopters and USAF aircraft in Vietnam from the U.S. Air Force point of view; contrast with the Aldren study above and the Nickel study below.

2961 Nedbal, Charles F. "A Study of Aerial Target Selection in Vietnam." (Unpublished professional study, no. 2461.) Air War College, Air University, 1967. 43p. A look at the principles, procedures, and problems involved.

2962 Nelson, Allen S. "A Study of Military Operations in the Vietnamese War: From 7 February 1965 to 31 December 1966." (Unpublished professional study, no. 3462.) Air War College, Air University, 1967. 144p. Covers ground-air-sea operations.

2963 Nichols, David L. "The Day I Met SAM." (Unpublished professional study.) Air War College, Air University, 1973. 13p. Reminiscences of a U.S. Air Force fighter pilot concerning his attempted evasion of and damage to his plane by a North Vietnamese SAM.

2964 Nickel, Wallace E. "Command Arrangements for the Use of Airpower in Limited War: A U.S. Army View." (Unpublished research report, no. 3810.) Air War College, Air University, 1969. 62p. A look at command arrangements for U.S. Air Force aircraft and Army helicopters in Vietnam from the Army's point of view; contrast with the Aldren and Nakis studies, items 2846 and 2960.

2965 Norris, William C. "The 'Brute Force' Mission." (Unpublished professional study, no. 4424.) Air War College,

Air University, 1971. 21p. A review of the role of the F-105 Thunderchief in the SEA bombing war.

2966 Nowland, Benoni, 4th. "Night Interdiction: Past, Present, and Future USAF Capabilities." (Unpublished thesis, no. 1855-67.) Air Command and Staff College, Air University, 1967. 74p. Addresses problems and tactics, techniques, and equipment used in past conflicts as well as in the war in SEA.

2967 Osborne, Arthur M. "MIG's and Missiles Don't Mix." (Unpublished professional study.) Air War College, Air University, 1974. 10p. The initial mining of Haiphong harbor and the support given U.S. Navy aircraft by TALO's-equipped guided-missile cruisers.

2968 Palmer, Samuel S. "A Study of the Influence of Political and Military Considerations on Target Selection in North Vietnam, February 1965 through February 1968." (Unpublished research report, no. 3664.) Air War College, Air University, 1968. 78p. Suggests the success of the U.S. interdiction campaign should have been judged against these factors.

2969 Patterson, James H. "Provisional Corps Vietnam: Khe Sanh, January-June 1968." (Unpublished research report, no. 3816.) Air War College, Air University, 1969. 184p. A look at the significance of the change in the U.S. command structure in the I Corps of South Vietnam in March 1968 and the role of the Provisional Corps Vietnam as an implementing agency and customer for tactical airpower during the siege of the Marine bastion.

2970 Patterson, Jock P. "The F-111 in Combat." (Unpublished research study.) Air War College, Air University, 1977. 38p. Examines the combat operations of the swept-wing fighter bomber in 1972-1973. See also item 2989.

2971 Peter, Robert A. "Concepts and Doctrine of Tactical Electronic Countermeasures/Electronic Warfare, 1954 through 1968." (Unpublished research study, no. AUC-22-68.) Air Command and Staff College, Air University, 1969. 66p. A review of developments and operations during those years, with information relative to our topic.

2972 Peters, Charles R. "Night Close Air Support with Tactical Fighters." (Unpublished research study, no. 1070-70.) Air Command and Staff College, Air University, 1970. 116p. The TAC night training program and combat operations over South Vietnam.

2973 Pittman, Donald D. "Tactical Air Support (Strike) in the Defense of Khe Sanh." (Unpublished research report, no.

3820.) Air War College, Air University, 1969. 196p. A review of "Operation Niagara" in the defense of the Marine base, the roles of U.S. Air Force, Navy, and Marine Corps planes, and a look at the overall task assigned to tactical airpower. Should be used with the Nalty titles cited in items 1761 and 1762.

2974 Prevost, Herbert L. "A Study of Air Liaison Officer (ALO) Activities in Vietnam." (Unpublished research report, no. 3480.) Air War College, Air University, 1968. 88p. The role of U.S. Air Force ALO's in South Vietnam. (Someone should prepare a study of the Australian Special Air Service men as well.)

2975 Romanek, Henry. "Forward Assault Airlift Operations." (Unpublished professional study, no. 3152.) Air War College, Air University, 1966. 72p. Examines the differences between Army and Air Force concepts with some examples from Vietnam.

2976 Rosenbaum, Samuel F. "The Dilemma of United States Prisoners in Vietnam." (Unpublished research study, no. 1155-70.) Air Command and Staff College, Air University, 1970. 54p. Resistance vs. brainwashing and torture.

2977 Rosher, Galen D. "Airmobility, a 'State of Mind.'" (Unpublished research study.) Air Command and Staff College, Air University, 1976. 16p. A brief historical look at the concept.

2978 Sanders, James D. "Utilization of the B-52 in Vietnam: A Case Study for B-52 Operations in Limited War." (Unpublished thesis, no. 1452-66.) Air Command and Staff College, Air University, 1966. 60p. Examines and contrasts the roles of heavy- and fighter-bombers in SEA, recounts the use of the Stratofortress, and suggests applicable targets and tactics.

2979 Schneider, Franklin E. "Analysis and Evaluation of Search and Rescue in Out-Country Operations." (Unpublished research report, no. 3675.) Air War College, Air University, 1968. 192p. A summary of command, control, force structure, and tactics.

2980 Seaver, Maurice E., Jr. "Tactical Air: The Vietnam Verification." (Unpublished professional study, no. 4445.) Air War College, Air University, 1971. 24p. Suggests the Vietnam War confirmed the role of the U.S. Air Force TAC.

2981 Sharp, Wayne E. "Employment of Tactical Fighters in Hostile Surface-to-Air Missile Environments." (Unpublished thesis, no. 1518-66.) Air Command and Staff College, Air University, 1966. 74p. Recommendations on ways to neutralize the North Vietnamese SAM threat.

2982 Shook, Howard W. "Defoliation Operations in Southeast Asia." (Unpublished research study, no. AUC-44-68.) Air Command and Staff College, Air University, 1969. 108p. A review which concludes that these activities were effective.

2983 Smith, Russell H. "'Gradualism' and the Air War Against North Vietnam." (Unpublished professional study, no. 4452.) Air War College, Air University, 1971. 17p. A brief definition and criticism of gradualism as an aerial strategy.

2984 Sorlie, Donald M. "An Analysis of the F-105 Weapons System in Out-Country Counterair Operations, 1965-1967." (Unpublished research report, no. 3684.) Air War College, Air University, 1968. 127p. Examines revisions in tactics, techniques, and technology forced by the growing sophistication of North Vietnamese air defenses.

2985 Spillers, Jack C. "The Use of Helicopters for Tactical Bombing in Guerrilla Warfare." (Unpublished thesis, no. 1590-66.) Air Command and Staff College, Air University, 1966. 87p. Recommends the use of the whirlybird as a short-range tactical bomber in South Vietnam.

2986 Stalk, George E. "An Analysis of the Objectives of Out-Country Aerial Reconnaissance in Southeast Asia, 1965-1967." (Unpublished research report, no. 3686.) Air War College, Air University, 1968. 90p. Limitations and restraints vs. the need for hard information.

2987 Stavast, John E. "Problems of Command in a Prisoner-of-War Situation; Or, 'Lancer to Charlie, Charlie.'" (Unpublished professional study.) Air War College, Air University, 1974. 15p. The author concludes that the older rules of leadership proved valid in the North Vietnamese POW situation.

2988 Strait, Ernest D. "Engineer Support of the Air Force in South Vietnam." (Unpublished research study, no. AUC-45-68.) Air Command and Staff College, Air University, 1969. 120p. An examination of military construction policies and procedures.

2989 Taylor, Harris J. "The F-111 in Southeast Asia." (Unpublished Professional Study, no. 4248.) Air War College, Air University, 1971. 17p. A review of F-111 employment prior to 1972; use in conjunction with the Jock P. Patterson study cited in item 2970.

2990 Underwood, Roberts L. "Air Interdiction in Southeast Asia: An Overview." (Unpublished research report, no. 3840.) Air War College, Air University, 1969. 302p. A review of the 1965-1968 U.S. aerial campaign against targets in North Vietnam and Laos, with emphasis on lessons learned.

2991 United States. Air Force. Air University, Aerospace Studies Institute. "Corona Harvest: Able Mable." (Special report, no. 70-11.) Maxwell Air Force Base, Ala., 1970. 26p. A brief history of the first U.S. Air Force operation in SEA, 1962 photo-reconnaissance flights.

2992 ____. ____. ____. "Corona Harvest: An Analysis of the North Vietnamese Offensive Air Threat." (Special report no. 71-26.) Maxwell Air Force Base, Ala., 1971. 48p. A look at North Vietnam Air Force capabilities.

2993 ____. ____. ____. "Corona Harvest: Development of All-Weather and Night Truck Kill Capability." (Special report, no. 70-14.) Maxwell Air Force Base, Ala., 1970. 22p. A brief history of night interdiction and an analysis of the success of U.S. night raids on North Vietnamese lines of communication.

2994 ____. ____. ____. "Corona Harvest: Iron Hand/Wild Weasel." (Special report, no. 70-12.) Maxwell Air Force Base, Ala., 1970. 23p. An assessment of U.S. air attacks on North Vietnamese air defenses.

2995 ____. ____. ____. "Corona Harvest: Operation Junction City." (Special report, no. 70-20.) Maxwell Air Force Base, Ala., 1970. 17p. A brief review of the 1967 airborne campaign.

2996 Von Haven, Ellis J. "Logistic Support of Army Operations by Aerial Delivery Extraction Technique." (Unpublished research report, no. 3699.) Air War College, Air University, 1968. 54p. A detailed explanation of procedures and an analysis of the advantages; the idea was proved during the 1968 siege of Khe Sanh.

2997 Waller, Larry D. "Wild Weasel." (Unpublished research study, no. AUC-41-68.) Air Command and Staff College, Air University, 1969. 83p. History of and lessons learned from U.S. fighter-bomber attacks on North Vietnamese aerial defenses.

2998 Walters, John R. "VNAF A-1: Operations, Hardware, People, Support." (Unpublished research study, no. AUC-42-68, pt. 1.) Air Command and Staff College, Air University, 1969. 69p. A look at VNAF Skyraider operations, South Vietnamese pilots, and U.S. advisory and support activities.

2999 Ward, Donald T. "VNAF A-1 Operations, 1962-1968." (Unpublished research study, no. AUC-42-68, pt. 2.) Air Command and Staff College, Air University, 1969. 61p. A review of VNAF "SPAD" operations during those years.

3000 Wells, Obel H. "A Conventional Fight--With Helicopters." (Unpublished professional study.) Air War College, Air University, 1972. 18p. A quick look at the use of helicopters in the 1971 Laos invasion.

3001 Whatley, Douglas E. "The Effectiveness of U.S. Airpower in the Campaign Over North Vietnam." (Unpublished professional study, no. 4017.) Air War College, Air University, 1970. 46p. A review and analysis of operations in light of stated U.S. political goals, 1965-1968.

3002 Wheeler, Terrence G. "Special Air Warfare Concept and Doctrine." (Unpublished research study, no. AUC-21-68.) Air Command and Staff College, Air University, 1969. 124p. A review of then-available information on special air warfare activity.

3003 Whitehouse, Wendell H. "Air Force Forward Air Control and Visual Reconnaissance." (Unpublished research report, no. 3849.) Air War College, Air University, 1969. 136p. Examines the activities of FAC's over South Vietnam and makes suggestions for improvements.

3004 Wilkins, George I. "The FAC Factor in South Vietnam." (Unpublished professional study, no. 4265.) Air War College, Air University, 1971. 17p. The airborne role of the FAC in prosecuting the war effort.

3005 Wittekind, Robert L. "The Forward Air Controller." (Unpublished study, class 66-A.) Squadron Officer School, Air University, 1967. 19p. Compares training of fighter pilot FAC's with the SEA need.

3006 Wolf, Donald K. "Counterair in North Vietnam, 1965-1967." (Unpublished research study, no. AUC-28-68, pt. 5.) Air Command and Staff College, Air University, 1969. 38p. Extracts from Air War College discussions held in 1968.

3007 Wood, J. Ralph. "Air National Guard Participation in the Southeast Asia Conflict: Air National Guard Airlift." (Unpublished research report, no. 3851.) Air War College, Air University, 1969. 66p. A review of the Air National Guard airlift support for American forces and its coordination with Military Assistance Command operations.

3008 Yarrish, Joseph. "Out-Country Interdiction Support, North Vietnam, 1965-1967." (Unpublished research study, no. AUC-27-68, pt. 4.) Air Command and Staff College, Air University, 1969. 131p. Addresses logistics, facilities, intelligence, communications, research and development, and defoliation problems.

IV

GUIDE TO 16mm FILMS

Considering the scope of the conflict, the Southeast Asian war is considered by many to have been the most photographed in history. Millions of Americans, and others around the world, nightly saw scenes of battle, the preparations for battle, or the aftermath of battle on their television screens. Private filmmakers, television newsmen, and official government agencies shot literally millions of feet of film.

The purpose of this film guide is to provide users with citations to and borrowing information about 16mm productions concerning aerial aspects of the Indochina epic. While most references are to officially-made U.S. Army, Navy, Marine Corps, and Air Force films, some concern the efforts of private firms in this country. Citations are arranged alphabetically, by title. Additional information provided includes producing or sponsoring agency, serial number, designation as to color or black and white, sound, and running time.

3009 Air Force Logistics in Southeast Asia. USAF, 1968. (SFP-1586.) 16mm, color, sound, 21 min. Examines how the U.S. Air Force Logistics Command, employing modern technology, automation, and airlift, provided supplies, materiel, and services to American fighting men in Indochina.

3010 Air Force News Review, no. 042. USAF, 1967. (AFNR-142.) 16mm, black and white, sound, 24 min. A brief history of the U.S. Air Force, including its Vietnam role through 1966.

3011 Air Force News Review, no. 159. USAF, 1969. (AFNR-159.) 16mm, color, sound, 14 min. Includes a view of U.S. Air Force pilots instructing VNAF airmen in the operation of cargo aircraft.

3012 The Air Force Now, no. 7. USAF, 1970. (AFN-7.) 16mm, color, sound, 16 min. A brief look at U.S. Air Force

Medal of Honor recipients and a progress report on the Vietnam air war.

3013 The Air Force Now, no. 27. USAF, 1971. (AFN-27.) 16mm, color, sound, 15 min. Includes a discussion on POW's and takes a look at the duties of a tactical airlift squadron crew chief.

3014 The Air Force Now, no. 28. USAF, 1972. (AFN-28.) 16mm, color, sound, 15 min. Devoted to the tactical airlift team.

3015 The Air Force Now, no. 50. USAF, 1973. (AFN-50.) 16mm, color, sound, 18 min. Presents an interview with the crew of a lead B-52 taking part in "Operation Linebacker II."

3016 Air Force Veterinary Support for the Military Dog Program in Southeast Asia. USAF, 1968. (TF-6105.) 16mm, color, sound, 24 min. A review of the U.S. Air Force sentry dog program in South Vietnam air base security with emphasis on the veterinarian's responsibilities and duties.

3017 Air Rescue in Southeast Asia. USAF, 1973. (FR-839.) 16mm, color, sound, 16 min. Recreates the rescue of Capt. Gerald Laurence as typical of other combat saves in Indochina and shows the main components in the combat rescue service.

3018 Aircraft Fire and Rescue Procedures. USAF, 1968. (TF-6167.) 16mm, color, sound, 38½ min. Outlines the procedures for controlling aircraft fires and saving crewmen; demonstrates various techniques for warplanes, tankers, and cargo planes.

3019 Airlift from America. USAF, 1966. (SFP-1293.) 16mm, color, sound, 24 min. Examines the global mission of the U.S. Air Force Military Airlift Command, including medevac and assault airlift.

3020 The Airmobile Division. USArmy, 1966. 16mm, black and white, sound, 29 min. Describes the history, organization, and capabilities of the 1st Cavalry Division (Airmobile).

3021 The American Navy in Vietnam. USN, 1967. (MN-10276.) 16mm, color, sound, 28 min. Illustrates the U.S. Navy commitment, including naval air.

3022 Another Day of War: The United States Air Force in Vietnam. USAF, 1967. (SFP-1639.) 16mm, color, sound,

14 min. Portrays a "typical" day in the Indochina air war, including close air support, maintenance, civic action, air rescue, etc.

3023 The Army Air Mobility Team. USArmy, 1968. (TV-752.) 16mm, color, sound, 28 min. A look at Army aviation in Southeast Asia as part of the Big Picture series; demonstrates the use by soldiers of vertical and short-takeoff aircraft for support in combat operations.

3024 Assurance of Quality from McDonnell-Douglas. McDonnell-Douglas, 1968. 16mm, color, sound, 20½ min. Employing the F-4 Phantom as the model, this film examines how the firm's products are checked, tested, and inspected "from design to delivery."

3025 The Attack Carrier. USN, 1969. (MH-10164.) 16mm, color, sound, 28 min. A look at aerial operations from the USS Enterprise on "Yankee Station."

3026 The Ballad of John Greene. USN, 1971. (MC-11053.) 16mm, color, sound, 28 min. Examines the training and operations of U.S. Navy A-7 Corsair II pilots.

3027 The Battle. USN, 1965. (MH-10278C.) 16mm, color, sound, 14 min. Combat footage of a U.S. Marine Corps attack ("Operation Piranha") on a Vietcong stronghold; shows close air support and vertical assault via helicopters.

3028 The Battle of Khe Sanh. USAF, 1969. (AFIF-176.) 16mm, color, sound, 30 min. Recounts the siege of the Marine camp in 1968 and the American victory with emphasis on the role of air power.

3029 Beans, Bullets, and Black Oil. USN, 1968. (MN-10490.) 16mm, color, sound, 29 min. Resupply at sea in the Gulf of Tonkin, including vertical replenishment by helicopter.

3030 The Birth of a Helicopter. Sikorsky, 197? 16mm, color, sound, 23 min. The development and deployment of the Sikorsky/U.S. Marine Corps CH-53A assault chopper.

3031 But How Does It Fly? USAF, 1969. (SFP-1652.) 16mm, color, sound, 25 min. A look at the Cessna A-37 COIN aircraft.

3032 The Challenge. McDonnell-Douglas, 1969. 16mm, color, sound, 19 min. A review of U.S. Air Force air superiority operations in wartime, including footage from Southeast Asia.

3033 Chopper Pilot. USArmy, 1966. (TV-694.) 16mm, color, sound, 28 min. The training of Warrant Officer helicopter pilots for Vietnam with emphasis on the kinds of missions they could expect to fly there.

3034 Cleared for Take-Off. USN, 1969. 16mm, color, sound, 14 min. Examines how a U.S. Navy reserve squadron on two weeks' active duty performs an important logistical task in support of U.S. Naval efforts in Vietnam.

3035 Combat and Support Activities, Southeast Asia, May 1968: Khe Sanh, Victory for Air Power. USAF, 1968. (FR-1009.) 16mm, color, sound, 18 min. Details the overwhelming tactical and strategic air power which supported the Marine defenders at Khe Sanh from January to April, 1968.

3036 Counterinsurgency. USN, 1969. (AFIF-182.) 16mm, color, sound, 30 min. A look at the difficulties and techniques of COIN operations.

3037 A Day in Vietnam. USN, 1967. (MH-10382B.) 16mm, color, sound, 28 min. Operations of U.S. Marine Corps and Navy forces in and off Vietnam, including air.

3038 Eagle Eye Bravo. USN, 1970. (MH-10278H.) 16mm, color, sound, 14 min. Portrays the role and mission of the U.S. Marine Corps aerial observer in locating the "enemy" over South Vietnam.

3039 Excellence ... By Design. McDonnell-Douglas, 1966. 16mm, color, sound, 15 min. A look at the role of the aircraft designer, using the F-4 Phantom as model.

3040 The F-4. McDonnell-Douglas, 1966. 16mm, color, sound, 14½ min. Demonstrates the Phantom II in typical missions for the U.S. Navy, Marine Corps, and Air Force.

3041 F-4 ... Complete Air Force. McDonnell-Douglas, 1970. 16mm, color, sound, 15 min. A music-only view of the Phantom fighter, relying on color and mood to sway the viewer.

3042 Face of a Nation. USN, 1967. (MN-10228.) 16mm, color, sound, 28 min. Examines the role of U.S. Navy carriers, including those off Vietnam.

3043 Faces of Rescue. USAF, 1971. (SFP-1956.) 16mm, color, sound, 24 min. The work of the U.S. Air Force aerospace search and recovery helicopters in Indochina with dramatic footage of the saving of a downed F-105 pilot.

3044 The Fight for Life. USArmy, 1968. (TV-735.) 16mm, color, sound, 28 min. Demonstrates the work of the Army medical services in South Vietnam, including the use of "dust off" helicopters and paramedics.

3045 The First Infantry Division in Vietnam, 1965-1970. USArmy, 1970. (TV-807.) 16mm, color, sound, 28½ min. Footage of combat and civic action, close air support, and the use of helicopters.

3046 First on Target. USAF, 1965. (SFP-1165.) 16mm, color, sound, 25 min. The work of the U.S. Air Force Tactical Air Command.

3047 Friends and Neighbors and People We Know. USAF, 1970. (SFP-1875.) 16mm, color, sound, 28 min. Provides an overview of the U.S. Air National Guard in Vietnam, focusing on tactical fighter squadrons and their operations.

3048 Ground Support on High. USAF, 1963. (SFP-1194.) 16mm, color, sound, 28 min. A look at the F-105 Thunderchief and its capabilities.

3049 Hook Down, Wheel Down. USN, 1971. (MN-10731.) 16mm, color, sound, 57 min. A history of U.S. Navy aircraft carriers; Part II (reel 2) includes Vietnam footage.

3050 Hook, Line, and Helo. USN, 1969. (MC-10964.) 16mm, color, sound, 27½ min. Examines the various uses of the helicopter by the U.S. Navy and its unique capabilities in fleet and support operations.

3051 HUEY ... In a Helicopter War. Bell Helicopter, 1966. 16mm, color, sound, 26 min. Describes how the use of helicopters, especially the UH-1B, changed the logistics and tactics of the U.S. Army in Vietnam.

3052 The Indispensables: KC-135 Refueling. USAF, 1970. (SFP-1797.) 16mm, color, sound, 24 min. Deals with the role of the tanker aircraft over Southeast Asia with fighter and bomber pilots telling stories of combat refueling.

3053 Land the Landing Force. USN, 1967. (MN-10496.) 16mm, color, sound, 29 min. Operations of the U.S. Navy amphibious force, including Vietnam.

3054 Medal of Honor: Capt. Hilliard A. Willbanks. USAF, 1968. (SFP-1544Q.) 16mm, color, sound, 10min. Cites this hero, an FAC who employed his O-1 "Bird Dog" to direct fire from "friendly" troops until he was shot down.

3055 Medal of Honor: One for All. USAF, 1967. (SFP-1544P.) 16mm, color, sound, 5 min. Cites Major Bernard Fisher, the first U.S. Air Force pilot to win the Medal of Honor in the Vietnam conflict, for a rescue mission during the Battle of A Shau.

3056 Men of Maintenance: Southeast Asia. USAF, 1968. (SFP-1571.) 16mm, color, sound, 15 min. Highlights aircraft maintenance operations in Vietnam and Thailand.

3057 Men with Green Faces. USN, 1969. (MH-10585.) 16mm, color, sound, 29 min. Examines the role of U.S. Navy "Seal" teams in South Vietnam.

3058 Mission Dustoff: Helicopter Evacuation. USArmy, 1969. 16mm, color, sound, 12 min. Depicts the role of the helicopter ambulance and its crew in evacuating battlefield casualties in South Vietnam.

3059 Multi-Mission H-53. Sikorsky, 1973. 16mm, color, sound, 16 min. Examines the U.S. Navy, Marine Corps, and Air Force use of the H-53 helicopter.

3060 The Phantom Two. McDonnell-Douglas, 1965. 16mm, color, sound, 12 min. Examines the F-4's versatility in terms of specific mission capabilities.

3061 A Point in Time. USN, 1968. (MH-10847.) 16mm, color, sound, 15 min. Combat artist L. V. Zabel documents his visit to Southeast Asia with illustrations of his work, including air.

3062 Ready on Arrival. USN, 1966. (MC-10376.) 16mm, color, sound, 29 min. The story of U.S. Navy attack carriers, including those on "Yankee Station," and the men who man them.

3063 Ready to Strike. USArmy, 1967. (TV-724.) 16mm, color, sound, 28 min. The story of the U.S. 25th ("Tropical Lightning") Infantry Division in South Vietnam, including its use of helicopters.

3064 Saga of the Skyraider. McDonnell-Douglas, 1967. 16mm, color, sound, 14 min. Reviews the history of the AD-1 "SPAD" propeller-driven fighter, including its highly successful use over South Vietnam. Available only to junior college level and above audiences. Order from McDonnell-Douglas's Santa Monica Library.

3065 Sand and Steel. USN, 1966. 16mm, color, sound, 16 min. Describes Seabee construction of an expeditionary airfield in South Vietnam and how the strip functioned in support of the U.S. Marine air-ground team.

3066 Screaming Eagles in Vietnam. USArmy, 1967. (TV-714.)

16mm, color, sound, 28 min. The operations of the U.S. 101st Airborne Division in South Vietnam.

3067 The Sky Soldiers. USArmy, 1967. (TV-720.) 16mm, color, sound, 28 min. The heliborne U.S. 173rd Airborne Brigade in South Vietnam.

3068 The Sparrow Hawks. USAF, 1968. (FR-906.) 16mm, color, sound, 9 min. Pays tribute to forward air controllers, showing how those pilots searched for and marked enemy positions in South Vietnam.

3069 Support from the Sky. USN, 1966. (MH-10321.) 16mm, color, sound, 16 min. Examines the role of U.S. Marine Corps close air support in South Vietnam.

3070 TAC in Action. USAF, 1964. 16mm, black and white, sound, 15 min. Reviews TAC's role in South Vietnam.

3071 Tactical Air Power. USAF, 1967. (SFP-1597.) 16mm, color, sound, 20 min. Discusses the role of the TAC in COIN operations and introduces the F-111.

3072 Task Force 77. USN, 1970. (MH-10543.) 16mm, color, sound, 28 min. The premier official film concerning carrier operations from "Yankee Station."

3073 The Theory of Helicopter Flight. USN, 1969. (MH-10650.) 16mm, color, sound, 22 min. Includes a look at the uses of the craft in Indochina.

3074 There Is a Way. USAF, 1967. (SFP-1756.) 16mm, color, sound, 27 min. Portrays the lives of F-105 pilots who daily fought the air war over North Vietnam; shows footage of hazardous missions while pilots and crews discuss their jobs.

3075 They Clear the Way. USArmy, 1967. (TV-732.) 16mm, black and white, sound, 29 min. Examines the role of Army Engineers in Vietnam, including airfield construction and improvement; part of the Big Picture series.

3076 Thunderchief. USAF, 1963. (SFP-1183.) 16mm, black and white, sound, 5 min. Reviews the characteristics, capabilities, and navigation features of the Republic F-105.

3077 Twenty Five Hour Day: A Story of the Air Force F-105's. USAF, 1967. 16mm, color, sound, 27 min. Another examination of "Thud" operations over North Vietnam.

3078 USAF Air Commandos. USAF, 1965. (SFP-1268.) 16mm, color, sound, 13 min. Describes the duties and roles of the U.S. Air Force special forces flyers in South Vietnam.

3079 The Unique War. USAF, 1966. (AFIF-153.) 16mm, color, sound, 25 min. Explores the basic concepts of the Vietnam war as perceived at the time of the film's production.

3080 United States Air Force Combat Photography: Southeast Asia. USAF, 1968. (FR-885.) 16mm, color, sound, 27 min. Highlights the work of the Saigon-based 600th Photo Squadron.

3081 United States Air Force in Southeast Asia, 1967. USAF, 1968. (FR-1002.) 16mm, color, sound, 28 min. A review of U.S. Air Force activities and operations in the year before Tet.

3082 Vietnam: An Historical Document. CBS, 1975. 16mm, color, sound, 56 min. An overview and year-by-year summary of U.S. involvement, compiled by and featuring CBS News correspondents who covered the conflict. Available as film #9345 for rental from the University of California Extension Media Center, Berkeley, CA 94720, or for purchase from Carousel Films, Inc., 1501 Broadway, New York, NY 10036.

3083 Vietnam Crucible. USArmy, 1968. (TV-7?.) 16mm, color, sound, 29 min. A review of Army operations, including air, in Vietnam; from the Big Picture series.

3084 Wings of Eagles, Wings of Gold. USN, 1974. (MH-11587.) 16mm, color, sound, 27½ min. The history and heritage of U.S. Navy aviators, including their role in Southeast Asia.

3085 Wings of Freedom: The Vietnamese Air Force Today. USAF, 1969. (SFP-1687.) 16mm, color, sound, 29 min. Reviews the role and operations of the VNAF and American assistance to it.

BORROWING INFORMATION

With the exception of Vietnam: An Historical Document, all of the films listed above are available for free loan to schools, libraries, and organizations. Government films currently have postage paid both ways. There are some differences in ordering procedures between U.S. government and private firms.

AIR FORCE

All U.S. Air Force films should be requested on Air Force Form

2018, which is available from any U.S. air base or from the Central AV Library. Requests should be sent in at least three (3) weeks in advance of need. Address all requests to

Air Force Central Audio-Visual Library
Aerospace Audiovisual Service
Norton Air Force Base, CA 92409

If you require help in determining the location of your nearest air base, visit your local library or Air Force recruiter.

ARMY

All U.S. Army films should be requested on DA (Department of the Army) Form 11-44 available from the nearest large Army facility. If you require help in determining the location of your nearest Army facility, visit your local library, Army recruiter, or National Guard armory. All films may be borrowed from large Army installations, but be sure to book well in advance.

NAVY AND MARINE CORPS

U.S. Navy and Marine Corps films may be booked without a special form. Again, they should be ordered early. If you live in states east of the Mississippi River, address your request to:

Commanding Officer
Naval Education and Training
Support Center
Atlantic Naval Station
Bldg. Z-86
Norfolk, VA 23511

If you reside west of the Mississippi, requests should go to:

Commanding Officer
Naval Education and Training Support Center
Pacific Fleet Station
Post Office Building
San Diego, CA 92132

In the event any of these films are not available at the above sources, it is still possible to obtain them, although there may be a small borrowing fee involved. For details on borrowing (or purchase), consult the GSA's Reference List of Audiovisual Materials, available at many libraries. If it is not available, write directly to:

National Audiovisual Center
General Services Administration
Washington, D.C. 20409

AIRCRAFT MANUFACTURING FIRMS

The following three firms will loan the films they have produced as cited above. Address your requests in a timely manner to:

Public Relations Department
Bell Helicopter Company
Box 483
Fort Worth, TX 76101

McDonnell-Douglas Corporation
St. Louis Library
Dept. 091, Box 516
St. Louis, MO 63166

McDonnell-Douglas Corporation
Santa Monica Library
Film and Television Communications
3000 Ocean Park Blvd.
Santa Monica, CA 90406

Sikorsky Aircraft Company
Public Relations Department
Stratford, CT 06602

V

SOURCES FOR PHOTOGRAPHS

In addition to the photoduplication services of the Library of Congress and National Archives, it is often possible to obtain a limited number of official U.S. military aircraft photographs directly from the armed services. One should address an inquiry to the director of the following activities, provide some indication of the reason why photos are desired, be as specific as possible to aircraft type or unit desired, and seek a quotation of cost, if any.

ARMY

U.S. Army Audio-Visual Activity, Attn: ANAV-ALL, Room 5A570, The Pentagon, Washington, DC 20310

AIR FORCE

1361st Photo Squadron (AAVS) (MAC), 221 South Fern St., Alexandria, Va. 22202

NAVY and MARINE CORPS

Still Photo Branch, Office of Information, U.S. Department of the Navy, Washington, DC 20360

Aside from these sources, newspapers, private collectors, aircraft firms, and others maintain photographic files. Private collectors often advertise in such periodicals as Air Classics or Military Journal, while the addresses of aircraft firms (write to their Public Relations Departments) can be found in such books as Moody's Industrials in your local library reference department. Addresses for newspapers can also be found at a library, especially in the Ayer Directory.

ADDENDA

The citations in this section were produced or uncovered too late for inclusion in the main body of the text. All are, however, included in the index.

3086 Air War--Vietnam. With an Introduction by Drew Middleton. Indianapolis: Bobbs-Merrill, 1979. 362p.

3087 Collins, John M. "Vietnam Postmortem: A Senseless Strategy." Parameters, VIII (March 1978), 8-14.

3088 DeWeerd, Harvey A. "Strategic Decision-Making: Vietnam, 1965-1968." Yale Review, LXVII (Summer 1978), 481-492.

3088a Fails, William R. Marines and Helicopters, 1962-1973. Washington, D.C.: History and Museums Division, Headquarters, U.S. Marine Corps, 1969. 262p.

3089 Galston, A. W. "Warfare with Herbicides in Vietnam." In John Harte and R. H. Socolow, eds., Patient Earth (New York: Holt, 1971), p136-150.

3090 Gunston, William. F-111 General Dynamics. London: Ian Allan, 1978. 112p.

3091 Heselton, Leslie R., Jr. The Effectiveness of A-1 Bombing Attacks on Bridges. Arlington, Va.: Center for Naval Analysis, 1965. 30p.

3092 Jones, Brett A. A History of Marine Attack Squadron 223. Washington, D.C.: History and Museums Division, Headquarters, U.S. Marine Corps, 1978. 39p.

3093 Lewy, Guenther. American in Vietnam. New York and London: Oxford University Press, 1978. 576p.

3094 Lindley, John M. "History of Air-Sea Aviation: Wings over the Ocean, Part Sixteen." Naval Aviation News, (Nov. 1978), 34-39.

3095 McCarthy, James R., and George B. Allison. Linebacker II: A View from the Rock [Guam]. U.S. Air Force Southeast

Asia Monograph Series, v. 6, no. 8. Washington, D.C.: U.S. Government Printing Office, 1979. 208p.

3096 Milton, T. R. "From the Airlift to Vietnam and Beyond." Air Force Magazine, LXII (Feb. 1979), 38-43.

3097 Mitchell, William A. "Air Power and the Protection of Mekong River Convoys." American Aviation Historical Society Journal, XXIII (Summer 1978), 90-98.

3098 Nerenstone, M. A., and D. D. Cutbertson. Market Time: Countering Sea-Borne Infiltration in South Vietnam. Arlington, Va.: Center for Naval Analysis, 1966. 100p.

3099 Parker, Gary W. A History of Marine Medium Helicopter Squadron 161. Washington, D.C.: History and Museums Division, Headquarters, U.S. Marine Corps, 1978. 47p.

3100/1 Pittman, Benjamin C. "Gunship." Navigator, XXV (Winter 1978), 25-27.

3102 Quester, George H. "The Impact of Strategic Air Warfare." Armed Forces and Society, IV (Winter 1978), 179-206.

3103 Ruhl, Robert K. "Code of Conduct [for POW's]." Airman, XXII (May 1978), 20-27.

3104 Russett, Bruce M. "Vietnam and the Restraints of Aerial Warfare." Ventures, IX (Jan. 1969), 55-61.

3105 Sambito, William J. A History of Marine Fighter-Attack Squadron 232. Washington, D.C.: History and Museums Division, Headquarters, U.S. Marine Corps, 1978. 23p.

3106 ________. A History of Marine Fighter-Attack Squadron 312. Washington, D.C.: History and Museums Division, Headquarters, U.S. Marine Corps, 1978. 25p.

3107 Shawcross, William. The Sideshow: Nixon, Kissinger, and the Destruction of Cambodia. New York: Simon and Schuster, 1979.

3108 Shulimson, Jack, and Charles M. Johnson. The Landings and the Buildup, 1965. Vol. II of U.S. Marines in Vietnam. 9 vols. Washington, D.C.: History and Museums Division, Headquarters, U.S. Marine Corps, 1978. 261p.

3109 Stockdale, James B., and O. J. Marquez. "Breaking Locks and Finding Answers." All Hands, no. 746 (March 1979), 12-18.

3110 Stratton, Alice. "The Stress of Separation." U.S. Naval Institute Proceedings, CIV (July 1978), 52-59.

3111 Trueman, H. P. "The Helicopter and Land Warfare: Applying the Vietnam Experience." In James L. Moulton, ed., _Brassey's Annual: The Defence Yearbook_ (New York: Praeger, 1971), p190-204.

3112 Warner, Denis. _Certain Victory: How Hanoi Won the War._ Kansas City, Mo.: Sheed Andrews & McMeel, 1978. 295p.

3113 Watson, Ted M. "Twenty Years with the Same Lady [B-57]." _Interceptor_, XX (June 1978), 5-6.

SUBJECT INDEX